IRELAND AND EMPIRE

IRELAND AND EMPIRE

COLONIAL LEGACIES IN IRISH
HISTORY AND CULTURE

STEPHEN HOWE

OXFORD

UNIVERSITY PRESS

OXFORD
UNIVERSITY PRESS

Great Clarendon Street, Oxford OX2 6DP
Oxford University Press is a department of the University of Oxford.
It furthers the University's objective of excellence in research, scholarship,
and education by publishing worldwide in

Oxford New York

Athens Auckland Bangkok Bogotá Buenos Aires Calcutta
Cape Town Chennai Dar es Salaam Delhi Florence Hong Kong Istanbul
Karachi Kuala Lumpur Madrid Melbourne Mexico City Mumbai
Nairobi Paris São Paulo Singapore Taipei Tokyo Toronto Warsaw

and associated companies in Berlin Ibadan

Oxford is a registered trade mark of Oxford University Press
in the UK and certain other countries

Published in the United States
by Oxford University Press Inc., New York

British Library Cataloguing in Publication Data

Data available

Library of Congress Cataloging in Publication Data

Howe, Stephen, 1958–
Ireland and empire : colonial legacies in Irish history and culture / Stephen Howe.
Includes bibliographical references.
1. Ireland—History—20th century. 2. Great Britain—Foreign public opinion, Irish.
3. Postcolonialism—Northern Ireland—History. 4. Public opinion—Northern
Ireland—History. 5. Imperialism—Public opinion—History. 6.
Postcolonialism—Ireland—History. 7. Public opinion—Ireland—History. I. Title.
DA963 .H69 2000 941.5082 21—dc21 99–045413

ISBN 0–19–820825–1

1 3 5 7 9 10 8 6 4 2

Typeset by Jayvee, Trivandrum, India
Printed in Great Britain
on acid-free paper by
T. J. International Ltd.,
Padstow, Cornwall

For Daphna, with love

ACKNOWLEDGEMENTS

I am grateful to Neil Belton, Terry Eagleton, Richard English, Luke Gibbons, Adrian Guelke, Fred Halliday, Tom Hartley, Eamonn Hughes, Donal Lowry, Roisín MacDonough, Tom Paulin, Norman Porter, Steve Regan, Kevin Whelan, and Robin Wilson for varied kinds of intellectual and practical help. Students and seminar participants in Belfast, Dublin, Oxford, London, Novy Sad, Skopje and Warsaw on whom I have tried out some of the arguments here, and participants in the (sadly deceased) annual Lipman Seminar and the 1995 and 1999 Galway 'Colonialism' conferences, also helped me rethink my inchoate early ideas on the issues addressed here.

Thanks are due also to staff at the Bodleian, Nuffield College and Ruskin College libraries in Oxford, the New York Public Library, and the Linen Hall Library in Belfast.

I am indebted to Robin Wilson, Felice Kiel, Roisín MacDonough and Adrian Guelke for generous hospitality, as well as for their ideas.

At earlier stages Thomas Charles-Edwards, Niamh Hardiman, Brian Harrison, Alvin Jackson, Conor Cruise O'Brien, Cornelius O'Leary, Billy Roche and the late Raphael Samuel stimulated and fed an interest in Irish history and politics. On the 'comparative colonial history' side of the divide this work tries to straddle, similarly appreciated if sometimes indirect roles were played by Peter Burroughs, Michael Cowen, John Darwin, David Fieldhouse, Victor Kiernan, Peter Marshall, Terence Ranger and Edward Said.

Comparative historical awareness of 'postcolonial conditions' has been helped also at various stages by many of my students at Ruskin College: perhaps especially the South Africans, including Bandile Ketelo, Dumi Mbanjwa, Godfrey Mokate, Joyce Mokhesi, and Neo Ntjana. Also at Ruskin, Bob Purdie has been a selflessly supportive colleague, a constant source of ideas and inspiration on Irish affairs, and a dear friend; while Jackie Cameron's blend of efficiency and kindness has helped me out of more holes than I care to remember.

Thinking about Britishness and the history of the United Kingdom's multinationality has owed a lot to colleagues on the Council of Charter88, at the UK Democratic Audit and other parts of the constitutional reform 'family', including Anthony Barnett, Andrew Puddephatt, and Stuart Weir. My intellectual debts to the late Frank Wright will be evident in what follows: I only wish I had taken more opportunities to learn from him during his tragically short life.

Two debts outweigh all others: to John and Sylvia Howe, who (among other, more important things) first introduced me to Ireland on family holidays as a child; and to Daphna Vardi Howe, who did nearly everything to enable the pages that follow, except write them for me.

CONTENTS

1

Introduction

Ireland was for centuries the victim of English, or British, imperialist oppression. Ireland, north and south, is still the victim of imperialism. The Irish Republic is a neocolonial state. The Irish Republic is (also, or alternatively) a *post*colonial state. The 'Black and Tan war' of 1919–21 was the first great modern anticolonial struggle. The violence in Northern Ireland[1] after 1969 has been an anticolonial war of liberation. Ireland must recover its cultural identity from centuries of colonialist impositions. Northern Ireland is a British colony. The Unionist (or Loyalist, or Protestant) community in Northern Ireland is a colonial settler enclave.

To employ, or to contest, any or all of these statements is to take sides in a long and bitter intellectual conflict, which has accompanied, derived from and also itself shaped the recurrent political violence of modern Irish history.[2] Such claims have had a long-established, though always a minority, place in the political discourses of both the Irish Republic and Northern Ireland. They are of course especially, but not solely, associated with the Republican ideology of Sinn Fein and its allies. As M. L. R. Smith says in his analysis of Republican strategy: 'The notion of colonial subjugation is the strongest theme in Irish republican nationalism . . . (it) forms the central hypothesis of republican political analysis.' (1995:7)

These, however, are by no means the only ways in which ideas about colonialism are vigorously present in thinking in and about Ireland. Shifting intellectual register, we encounter a set of propositions less obviously political, more historical or cultural in focus and sometimes heavily academic in form. Taking their cue from postwar Afro-Asian theorists of colonial liberation, from the work of Edward Said and the school of 'colonial discourse analysis' which has followed his 1978 book *Orientalism*, and often from poststructuralist and postmodernist thought, a growing band of historians, political commentators, and especially literary and cultural theorists has sought to bring a battery of concepts drawn from those sources—postcoloniality, colonial discourse, cultural and linguistic imperialism—to bear on Ireland's past and present.[3] Alongside this—indeed operating, to a still disappointing degree, in parallel rather than interconnection with it—another body of historical writing has pursued links and comparisons across a broad historical timescale between English, and later

British, actions in Ireland and wider British Empire frameworks. The most sustained efforts in this vein have been those placing Ireland in an Atlantic framework, situating Irish experience in relation to early English/British colonial expansion in the New World. A third strand of intellectual work, again too often debilitatingly isolated from the others, has focused on the history and contemporary politics of Northern Ireland, asking such questions as whether the political culture of Unionism and Loyalism can adequately be analysed as 'settler colonial' in content, whether the continuing Union with Britain owes its existence to 'imperialism' in some sense of that much contested word, and whether Northern Irish Republicanism has been waging an 'anticolonial' struggle.

The revival of colonial models and images for understanding Ireland has, then, multiple roots and operates in several different modalities. Some stem from long-lasting traditions of historical enquiry, some from what has been called the 'new cultural nationalism' in modern Irish thought (O'Mahony and Delanty 1998), some from militant Republicanism, and some from new international forms of discourse about empires and their legacies. Not only has this European country become the focus for many of the most intense international debates about colonialism, culture and anticolonial/postcolonial nationalisms, but the particular mixture of postmodernism, poststructuralism and postcoloniality which has made its mark on North American, Indian, African and Middle Eastern cultural-political disputes has found a profound recent resonance in Ireland. As Terry Eagleton rather mockingly notes, Ireland has had powerful appeals for various, seemingly contrary, currents in contemporary international cultural studies:

[T]he ideological category of Irishness signifies on the one hand roots, belonging, tradition, *Gemeinschaft*, and on the other hand, again with marvellous convenience, exile, diffusion, globality, diaspora ... With wonderful   economy, it signifies a communitarianism nostalgically seductive in a disorientatingly cosmopolitan world, while offering itself at the same time as a very icon of that world in its resonance of political defeat, hybridity, marginality, fragmentation. (1997:11–12; see also his 1998b)

Indeed it might be argued (albeit at the risk of reinforcing beliefs about Irish primordialism or exceptionalism which are all too common in these spheres) that some at least of these debates *started* in Ireland, in all their manifestations from the politics of identity and difference, through the ethics of nationalism, to questions of historical method.

At worst, this revived colonial model involves the kind of inflated rhetoric that makes a British publisher's copywriter highlight the manichean question 'IRELAND: NEO-COLONY OR MODERN EUROPEAN STATE?', on the cover of a book which in fact sensibly omits to address this falsely posed antithesis (Hutton and Stewart 1991: back cover). Similarly though yet more capaciously, a popular overview of Irish life since the sixties, by a leading Dublin journalist and editor, is prefaced with the claim that:

The truth is that contemporary Irish society is an outcrop of two forms of colonialism. One, which can be seen quite obviously working its bloody way through Northern Ireland, is British colonialism . . . The other, less obvious but all-pervasive nevertheless, is the colonialism of religion: to a degree that of the Protestant churches, especially in the North, but more potently that of the Roman Catholic Church. (Coogan 1987b:Preface (unpaginated))

Tim Pat Coogan never returns to explain what he means by the 'colonialism' of the churches—leading one to suspect that he intends the term merely as a vague metaphor for 'great influence'. Nor does he even elaborate or substantiate the claim that Britain's role in Northern Ireland in the late 1980s remained 'colonialist'. Meanwhile an Irish Supreme Court Justice, Niall McCarthy, could see the continued use of wigs and gowns in law courts as evidence of 'post-colonial servility' (quoted Hussey 1995:125); while a former TD (that is, MP) and senior journalist believed that Ireland's primary education system possessed a 'central colonial characteristic (which) involves the transfer of large amounts of public money into the hands of local tribal leaders' (John Horgan, quoted ibid: 403). A prominent Irish-language activist, Prionnsias Mac Aonghusa, in 1992, thought that widespread support for the Maastricht Treaty indicated how 'The mind of the slave, of the hireling, and the vagabond is still fairly dominant in Ireland.' Such slavishness dictated a false assumption that 'it does not matter if Irish people or foreigners are running the state' (quoted ibid: 497). All this suggests how, in important spheres of discourse in and about Ireland (as elsewhere), the concept of colonialism has been so inflated and inflected as virtually to be emptied of specific meaning.

Conversely, a historian of Ireland's seventeenth century, Toby Barnard, is scornful of the very use of the colonial label for Ireland's past:

The term can obviously be used in various ways: as a metaphor, as a prescription, as an aspiration, in a strictly classical sense, as well as in making a more technical statement about constitutional and political dependence or about economic, racial and cultural subjection. In so far as 'colony' has entered general usage as something more than a loose descriptive metaphor, it owes most to a bizarre fusion of Catholic nationalist teleology and the observations of Marx and Engels on mid-nineteenth-century Ireland, and is pejorative. (Barnard 1990:40)

Barnard is undoubtedly too dismissive, as well as being himself terminologically vague (a fairly close acquaintance with the literature leaves me quite unclear what might be meant by a 'strictly classical sense' of the term colony[4]), and in his reference to Marx and Engels inaccurate, for they neither produced a theory of colonialism, nor defined an Irish 'colonialism' at all. Mistakenly dismissive in a different way is another distinguished historian of early modern

Ireland, Steven Ellis, who suggests at one point that whether the British-Irish relationship was a colonial one is merely 'a matter of opinion, since colonialism as a concept was developed by its modern opponents and constitutes a value-judgement which cannot be challenged on its own grounds.' (1996a:9) While it is undoubtedly true that 'colonialism' began life as a pejorative term, the subsequent scale, variety and richness of the historical and analytical literature organised around the concept has ensured that it has long since escaped that origin (just as has happened with many other terms whose original uses were polemical, but which have since become key reference points for historico-political debate, from 'Puritanism' to 'feminism').[5] What remains true, and very relevant to Irish history, is the more restricted point that in circumstances where the applicability or otherwise of the 'colonial' label is contested, there is a tendency (though far from a universal one) for the term to be employed more by those whose judgements on the phenomena discussed are most sharply negative. Despite these difficulties, Barnard, Ellis and others are pointing towards a real, deep-rooted and pervasive problem which is far more than terminological: a problem this book seeks at least to diagnose, if not to solve.

I attempt here to trace the ways in which the languages of imperialism, colonialism, postcoloniality and anticolonialism have been deployed historically in Irish contexts. First I offer a broad chronological sketch of how this question has evolved over the centuries, identifying some major patterns of historical change in Ireland in their relation to English, then British overseas expansion elsewhere. Next, uses of the tropes of colonialism, especially in their imbrication with languages of 'race', in relation to Irish nationalism before 1921, are analysed. I then survey the unusually vigorous and sometimes bitter political and methodological disputes over Irish historiography which have framed the issue, and in Chapter 7 the newer but equally heated cultural and literary debates where anticolonialism, postcoloniality, postmodernism and poststructuralism intersect in the Irish as in many other contexts. Chapter 8 looks at arguments over the Irish Republic as a 'neo-colony' or 'postcolonial' state; and Chapter 9 at the employment of colonial models in the Northern Ireland conflict since the 1920s and especially since severe violence re-erupted there in 1969. I then view in turn rival analyses of Ulster Unionism and the validity of claims that it is a settler colonial ideology; and several major recent attempts to set Irish events in comparative perspectives including specifically colonial ones. In conclusion I offer a typology and assessment of these various models and their degree of 'fit' with the historical evidence. I come to largely negative judgements about the empirical, theoretical and political adequacy of colonial and postcolonial frameworks for analysing contemporary Ireland and attempt instead to place such analysis in a more appropriate European context. I also, however, underline (and I hope, at least in broad historiographical outline, demonstrate) the appropriateness and importance of seeing *some* aspects of Irish history in a British Empire framework.

A word about focus and procedure may be in order here. I am mostly dealing, not with the historical or literary sources usually labelled 'primary', but with the latterday accounts and interpretations called 'secondary'—the work of historians, cultural critics, political scientists and other writers of the late twentieth century, many of whom hold academic posts but some of whom are political activists or journalists, most of whom are in some way politically engaged with the 'matter of Ireland'. A great deal of the discussion is thus historiographical and conceptual, as opposed to primary historical research or the construction of a historical narrative. This is a discourse about discourses: and as will become clear, I am not among those who think that, in any case, all historical writing is that and only that. It is transdisciplinary, ranging from arguments about Bronze Age history to ones about political change in the late 1990s, from the work of development economists to that of literary critics. Inevitably, a net cast so wide has bigger holes in some places than in others, reflecting the gaps in my own knowledge and reading.

On the other hand, it is perhaps more than usually necessary to emphasise that in my focus on colonial and postcolonial models in Irish studies, I am critically analysing neither a narrow academic 'school' nor a political faction, but a broad intellectual tradition or a discursive formation—indeed a series of them—of Irish 'anti-imperialism' and 'decolonisation'. This includes writers, publicists and academics of very diverse political allegiances. I am not seeking to imply that adherence to the 'colonial model'—or rather, to any of the various colonial models proposed for understanding Ireland— inherently endorses the Republican worldview, let alone that all or any of the individuals discussed support the policies or the actions of the IRA or any other group responsible for violence past or present. Such insistence is not as otiose in this context as it would be in most, for certain Irish critics, as for instance Conor Cruise O'Brien, appear frequently to assert such direct connections; while others, like Seamus Deane, make equally dramatic claims in the opposite direction, suggesting that Irish 'revisionist' historiography directly supports Loyalist violence. And since I mount some harsh criticisms of certain writers associated with the Field Day project, I should also emphasise how heavily I have relied on their work, including Field Day's massive *Anthology of Irish Writing*—as, I suspect, every student of Ireland will do for many years to come.

In other words, I am attempting both to organise a reliable map of selected parts of the terrain, which may be of use to those who share few or none of my views, and to chart a particular course across it. The first task is exegetical, the second in large part polemical. I have attempted to distinguish between these tasks, to give a fair account of claims which I then criticise, sometimes very strongly. Naturally, I hope too to have gone some little way beyond either

exegesis or negative polemic, and to have said something new. But I fully recognise—as I believe anyone not afflicted with extreme epistemological naivity
must do—that the tasks cannot be wholly separated. One of the major lessons
of modern Irish studies, notably exemplified in the work on the Irish Ordnance
Survey of historian J. H. Andrews, followed by playwright Brian Friel, is that
to make a map of a landscape is always not only to simplify it, but to impose
one's own meaning on it and even, at the extreme, to do violence to it and its
inhabitants.

This study is also, closely and unavoidably, shaped by political contexts.[6] On
22 May 1998, dual referenda in Northern Ireland and the Irish Republic produced decisive majorities for a new power-sharing Assembly in the former, and
for revision of the previous irredentist constitutional claims in the latter. A far
more hopeful political prognosis seemed available for Ireland than at any time
in recent decades. But during 1998, confrontation at Drumcree and then a
hideously destructive bomb in Omagh brought new violence and tension, with
still unforeseeable consequences. Even as I undertake final revisions to this text,
in mid-1999, the portents are wildly contradictory: one small paramilitary
group has become the first to 'decommission' some weapons, but others have
refused to do so. Low-intensity but pervasive violence persists, especially in the
form of so-called punishment shootings and beatings by paramilitaries on both
sides. The leaders of the Ulster Unionist Party and the Social Democratic and
Labour Party have jointly received the Nobel Peace Prize, but still struggle to
reach agreement on constitutional arrangements.

By the time of publication the situation will have undergone further shifts,
for better or worse. There appears a possibility, if the more hopeful trends pre-
vail, that those parts of my work dealing with Irish Republican views of nationality and colonialism, and with 'colonial' traditions among some Ulster
Unionists, may by the time this book appears be not so much the analysis of
living ideologies as among the early obituaries for newly deceased ones. I hope,
but doubt, that it may be so. But even if it is, it is near-inevitable that intellectual
habits sprung from those ideologies' extended—international—hold will long
survive the demise of their political parent. Minerva's owl flies at dusk, said
Hegel. By the same token, some birds of the night may keep flying, dazed by the
daylight, long after the dawn of a peaceful Ireland has lit the sky.

2

Contexts and Concepts

(i) Typologies

One can identify six views, or clusters of views, on the contemporary relevance of imperialism and colonialism as categories for understanding contemporary Ireland and its history.

The first argues that British imperialism has played an unbroken, direct and consistent role in modern Ireland, deliberately 'dividing and ruling' through Partition, which split Ireland between a dependent pseudo-sovereign neo-colony in the south and a classic colonial enclave in the north. The dominant Protestant/Unionist community in Northern Ireland, by origin and still by ideology a transplanted colonial settler imposition, is (when considered at all) viewed as the conscious agent of this continued colonial domination. Revolution to overthrow both colonial and neocolonial structures is needed.

This is, or was, the view of Sinn Fein, the IRA and of pro-Republican Marxists: though there are divisions over how far the unfinished national revolution must also necessarily be a radical social revolution, while today certain leading Sinn Fein strategists have evidently if in part covertly reassessed the whole analysis.

A second, closely related, cluster of attitudes sees Britain's role in Ireland as a colonial one, and Irish development as deliberately stymied under the Union. A successful nationalist revolution in most of the country largely if not completely broke the hold of imperialism; this still requires completion by ending colonial rule in the north and unifying the country. Completing the unfinished project of 1916–21 is in the best interests of all Ireland's people, though imperialist ideology and/or relative economic privileges have blinded most Ulster Protestants to the fact.

This is the analysis of 'traditional' nationalists and Republicans, especially in the south, reflecting and (anachronistically) perpetuating the view of pre-1922 Sinn Fein and most other nationalists under the Union.

A third view is that whatever may or may not be the continuing relevance of British imperialism to the political institutions or economic development of Ireland, the colonial legacy retains an enormous *cultural* and *psychological* force. Indeed colonialism—identified in this view often as a primarily cultural, ideological or discursive rather than economic or political phenomenon—

remains the central battleground in Ireland north and south, in spheres from lyric poetry through state educational and language policies to popular amusements.

This view, though having some resonance in Republican and nationalist political circles, is primarily the preserve of literary and cultural theorists: the major attempt to fashion from it a directly political intervention has come from the Field Day collective.

Fourth is the claim that British imperialism, having subjugated Ireland for centuries, has been progressively and decisively weakened there as elsewhere. In the north it is not fully in control of events, and its role there has been largely reactive. To some extent in Northern Ireland and almost wholly in the south, it is now a junior partner in a 'collective imperialism' of the European Union, the USA and NATO to which the Irish Republic's ruling class now also belongs. The British state now tends to favour Irish unification through partnership with the Republic and with bourgeoisies north and south, to free itself from the cost and embarrassment of direct rule in the north and enable more rational exploitation of the island as a whole.

This has been the stance of most 'social Republicanism' and of many Irish Marxists since the 1950s, and recently of the Workers' Party and of orthodox Communists.

Fifth: Ireland, a former British colony—though a unique one in that it was for long periods almost fully integrated into a unitary English-ruled state—achieved effective independence in 1921. At least independence was, or became by the 1930s, as full as was practically thinkable for a small, economically weak territory with a powerful close neighbour in a world of increasing economic and cultural interdependence. That only twenty-six of the thirty-two counties gained this status in 1921 was primarily the result not of deliberate British policy but of the demands of Ulster Unionists. They, not British imperialism, created both Partition and the subsequent sectarian policies of the Northern Ireland state. The later evolution of north and south alike, including civil war in the former, is to be explained essentially by their internal dynamics. British imperialism, colonialism or neocolonialism, in any analytically useful or politically relevant sense, is not a significant factor today in any aspect of Irish life. Nor indeed can such concepts be the main template for understanding Ireland's past, for although some parts of it display colonial features others—more important ones, especially for the more recent past—are better captured via recognition of Ireland as an integral component of the multinational and multiregional history of the North Atlantic island group; or indeed through comparative European perspectives.

This is the view (though one covering a multitude of internal disagreements) not only of much mainstream academic analysis, but of 'revisionist' historiography insofar as any shared views can be attributed to such a heterogenous and largely fictive entity—including revisionist Marxist writing—and of those political forces in the Republic who see themselves as 'modernising' and secular, and those in the north who are selfconsciously anti-sectarian. It is not in principle incompatible with seeing Ulster Unionists as a settler-colonial community, but one which has over time become substantially autonomous from and indeed often opposed to the strategic desires of the former 'mother country's' rulers; though few analysts have advanced that particular combination of views.

A sixth ensemble of views departs sharply from the others in seeing the British Empire and its legacies as in many respects a progressive or civilising force. Among the legacies are communities of predominantly British descent and culture around the world. But the Anglo-Scottish descended community in Northern Ireland, members of which may or may not describe themselves as in some sense Irish, is *not* a colonial settler enclave in this sense but is either an integral part of the United Kingdom or, in an alternative formulation, a distinct nation. Imperialism is not an issue in modern Ireland, north or south, except insofar as it is deployed as a slogan in the service of undemocratic Catholic-Republican demands to change the political status of this part of the UK: indeed such demands might themselves be described as colonialist.

This is the basic attitude of most Ulster Unionists, plus many 'two nations' theorists: those who believe Northern Irish Protestants to form a distinct national community with rights to self-determination.

Evidently enough, syntheses of parts of these different views are possible. And in fact, as will become apparent, although I think the fifth captures most of the complex truth, elements of the third and fourth also have some credibility; while the sixth retains not only a powerful emotional hold on many people but has stronger intellectual underpinnings than are often credited to it.

Equally, even this categorisation oversimplifies: each of the six attitudes includes substantial internal diversity. Nonetheless the first three and some elements of the fourth—what may be described as the nationalist constellation—all share significant and disabling common features. These are that such colonial models, at least in their older variants, derive from a fairly simplistic Irish nationalist view of history, which comprises several (usually interrelated) claims.[1] These include, in most versions, the belief in an ancient, unitary, predestined Irish nation, which in the more romantic variants is claimed to have been not only unified and culturally autochthonous but uniquely cultured and egalitarian.[2] This nation is seen as having waged an eight centuries' fight against British imperialism, which is believed to have systematically and continuously sought to destroy it (this includes, often, such claims as that the eighteenth-century Penal Laws were a concerted attempt to destroy Irish Catholicism, and Famine of the 1840s an act of deliberate genocide). The behaviour of British governments, and of 'Ascendancy' landlords in Ireland, is seen as uniquely vicious, and is to be explained mainly in terms of their national and/or religious character rather than their socio-economic interests. A nationalist consensus is presumed as the overwhelmingly dominant modern political tradition. Always the heart of the fight, in at least some versions of the narrative, has been the revolutionary or physical force nationalism of which Sinn Fein today claims to be the sole rightful inheritor. The struggle is for the predestined return of complete independence for that ancient nation: a completion to which Partition, Ulster Unionism, economic dependence on foreigners, cultural imperialism, the English language or all of these are seen as central obstacles. Partition itself is viewed as wholly a British creation: while today only a British occupying army prevents reunification of the national territory. In the meantime all major Irish problems are to be explained in terms of external rather than internal influences. In most but not all variants, Irish nationalism is believed to be heavily identified with the Catholic church and a range of specifically Catholic themes and symbols; whilst contradicting this belief, but often held in conjunction with it, is an assertion that the nationalist tradition has been one to which religious differences were irrelevant. As an ensemble, these beliefs amount to a myth: one closely parallel to those prevalent in many other societies whose histories have been dominated—and written—by nationalist ideologues. The main innovation of recent years has been the open avowal, in some circles and especially those propagating a postmodernist-nationalist mélange, that it is a myth: supposedly a psychologically or politically necessary one.

The contemporary political consequences of this worldview, here as elsewhere where ethnic-nationalist claims have been pressed on divided societies, have been largely damaging: especially, of course, in Northern Ireland. There has, even after almost thirty years of renewed conflict and despite the new agreements of 1998, been disturbingly little sign of effective reconciliation between the Irish Nationalist tradition and the worldviews of Ulster Unionists, of those within the island who identify themselves as British. The dominant, if perhaps often unintended, effect of analysing Irish history in purely colonial terms, and viewing the Northern Ireland conflict as a colonial one, has been to wish away the complex historical ambiguities of identity-formation on the island, and especially in the north. Less directly, the appropriation of colonial discourse analysis and related politico-cultural trends to the Irish context may have something of the same effect.

(ii) Terminologies

Terminology is a particularly tricky and contested matter in colonial and post-colonial studies concerned with Ireland, as it is in global contexts. Insofar as debates over Ireland's recent past and contemporary position have sometimes revolved around claims that it shares 'Third World' or 'neocolonial' character-istics, it is necessary to register serious doubts about the general usefulness of those terms. The former is both insufficiently defined—its usage has changed several times over the roughly forty years since it was coined—and obviously essentialist. Given the widely diverging fortunes of the numerous states to which the label was once collectively applied, including notably the contrast between the economic dynamism of some (especially in east Asia) and the dire economic straits of others (notably in much of Africa) it is arguable that what-ever the term's former utility, it has now largely lost it. 'Neocolonialism', mean-while, has been far more a term of political polemic, heavily influenced by Cold War pressures, than of analysis. The same is true, yet more obviously, of 'imperialism', which has also usually been a pejorative, and at its most general has been a concept used to refer to any and every type of relation between a more powerful state or society and a less powerful one.

'Colonialism', initially a more precise term, has also been put to ever wider and more problematic uses. Early usages of 'colony', 'colonist' and 'colonial' denoted settlements of farmers or cultivators: hence, by extension, agricultural settlers in a new place and, from that, places outside Europe to which European migrants moved in significant numbers. For over three hundred years, until some point in the nineteenth century, 'colony' in English meant as Moses Finley points out 'a plantation of men [sic], a place to which men emigrated' (1976:171). Its root was the Latin *colere*, to cultivate or farm (an etymology it shares with 'culture', which should delight the colonial discourse theorists). Sir Thomas More, in his *Utopia*, seems to have been the prime mover in reviving the term and using it in this sense, in English (Armitage 1998:108). As one might expect from this, most writers in early modern Europe, and many later, saw agriculture as the purpose of colonies. So in Finley's view 'land is the element round which to construct a typology of colonies.' (1976:178) The British Colo-nial Laws Validity Act of 1865 defined a colony as 'all of Her Majesty's Posses-sions abroad in which there shall exist a legislature' (quoted Finley 167)—and only territories of white settlement had such bodies.

Thus, as the term was ordinarily used before this century, only conquered ter-ritories of white settlement—Australia, the South African Cape, the mainland Americas—were 'colonies'. South and South-East Asia or European possessions in most of Africa were not. During the late nineteenth and early twentieth cen-turies, however, the term was extended to embrace all areas subject to formal political rule and control by other (usually European) states. This is still the most common usage; thus making 'colonialism' a subset of the term 'imperial-ism', which is used also to denote informal modes of domination or influence.[3] There are evident problems with this definition, of which I shall note just three which are especially relevant to Irish history. First, it leaves open the question of numerous borderline cases—sometimes literally as well as metaphorically so.

When is the expansion of a polity over directly neighbouring territories to be described as colonialist? Second, does there have to be a clear pre-existing claim to sovereignty, at least of a *de facto* kind, which the intruders have overridden, before an occupation can be called colonial? Thirdly, given the usual association of the colonial idea with European (or 'white') rule over non-Europeans, which if any circumstances where neither or both conquerors and conquered are European should be called colonial?

Despite such problems, defining colonialism in this way enables a degree of clarity greater than that afforded by most current usages, many of which—in Irish as in other contexts—confuse or collapse together several different ideas, ranging from exercise of political sovereignty over territories outside a state's original boundaries, through migrancy and settlement of European populations in non-European regions, to (at the extreme of loose rhetorical usage, but an extreme frequently to be encountered in contemporary writing) anyone's, or any group's, assertion of superiority or domination over any other person or group.

It is also important to distinguish, at the least, between *colonialism*, a set of political systems involving conquest and rule by a state over other, previously independent and usually distant territories, and *colonisation*, denoting population movements in which the migrants retain strong links with their or their ancestors' state of former residence, and by this gain significant privileges over other inhabitants of the new territory, either wholly dispossessing them or instituting legal and other structures that systematically disadvantage those earlier inhabitants. Again, this way of defining the terms by no means disposes of all difficulties. For instance, it is clear that by such definitions Australia, Canada, Israel, Northern Ireland and South Africa—among other places—were all in origin consequences of colonisation; and that Australia and Canada, at least, are direct consequences of colonialism: though it is also evident that other forces went into their making too, and that (ironically) the anticolonialism of the colonisers also significantly shaped their present political status. It is far less clear how far any or all of them may now still be called colonial societies. If—as will be argued in detail for Northern Ireland later in this work—a society that was originally the product (among other things) of colonisation has subsequently experienced the substantial erosion or dismantling of the formal structures which once separated 'settlers' from 'natives' and privileged the former, and if moreover there has been increasing dissociation and even conflict between the settlers' descendants and their erstwhile sponsor state, then that society can no longer meaningfully be called colonial.

We should, therefore, distinguish not only between colonialism and imperialism, but between colonialism and colonisation. The second may most usually be a consequence of the first, though not invariably so. Indeed the line of causation may run the other way around, with a state asserting sovereignty over a territory in order to protect, or in response to the demands of, those of its subjects who have previously settled there: this was in fact a common pattern of English/British expansion.

The word 'Empire' began to be used in relation to the English Crown in the 1530s, meaning simply a claim to absolute sovereignty, especially *vis-à-vis* Rome.[4] It had as yet no connotations of overseas expansion, and its application to Ireland, whose Crown of course Henry VIII also claimed, remained inexplicit. Already, though, assertions of the Crown's rightful sovereignty over a *British* Empire were being made by court ideologues like John Dee. They were based on various myths of origin, the sixteenth-century favourite being a story derived from Geoffrey of Monmouth, that the legendary King Arthur had included Ireland—as well as Scotland and Wales, and in some variants even much of Scandinavia and France—in his British Empire. The idea of a British Empire as meaning a composite monarchy embracing the three kingdoms of England, Scotland and Ireland, and the principality of Wales fully entered official discourse with the Union of the Crowns under James VI and I in 1603. As the seventeenth century progressed, the phrase came to be used also to include the surrounding seas—a happily vague idea which could be, and in the early eighteenth century increasingly was, extended almost without limit to support notions that Britain's ever-greater maritime commercial and naval power gave it a global 'empire of the seas'. Some contemporaries wrote of British Empires in the plural: that of the British-Irish islands themselves, that of trade and commerce, and sometimes that of Britain's overseas colonies in the Americas (John Oldmixton, in 1708, may have been the first to write unhesitatingly of 'the British Empire in America') and its scattered enclaves of control in the East Indies and West Africa. Not until the second half of the eighteenth century, though, did the idea of a singular Empire including all overseas territories subject to the Crown become widespread; the Seven Years War, which greatly extended those territories, was probably the main catalyst for this new usage.

Ireland, then, was according to English contemporaries' claims and language part of an English Empire from at least the sixteenth century, and of a British one from the early seventeenth. In both cases it was so because it was asserted to be an integral part of a United Kingdom, *not* because it was an external territory conquered by that kingdom. Only in the later eighteenth century, after the newer usage of 'Empire' to describe the kingdom's overseas possessions took hold, did it become even possible to think about Ireland as part of *that* 'Empire'. We shall be seeing in some detail later on how far, and in what ways, it came to be viewed by policy-makers and analysts (and subsequent historians and critics), both British and Irish, as a part of that overseas territorial Empire, and how this interacted with its status as part of the United Kingdom itself. As the terminological shifts and overlaps themselves suggest, ambivalence and ambiguity resonate throughout the story.

(iii) **Metahistories**

Explanations for the course of modern Irish history, including its recurrent incidence of violent conflict, are thus to be sought in patterns of state-building, of political, economic and religious change not only in Ireland and Britain but across Europe and later the Atlantic world: patterns dating in part from the eleventh century, but more decisively from the sixteenth and seventeenth. Thus far almost all contemporary historians would agree: beyond that lies terrain of bitter dispute.

Broadly, we can summarise the historians' controversy about medieval and early modern Ireland by dividing interpretations of the Irish past between 'colonial' models and 'archipelago' ones. The former thinks in terms of one national entity being conquered and oppressed by another; the latter sees premodern Ireland in a more complex way, as one (or given its internal diversity more than one) of Europe's many 'frontier regions' from the early Middle Ages onwards. And the colonial model may in its turn be subdivided between those who view Ireland within an Atlantic framework, linking its colonial experience with those of the Americas, and those who identify it more in terms of a 'Third World' experience, associating its fate with African and Asian parallels. The balance of historians' judgements as to the appropriateness of one or another interpretive framework has, as we might expect, varied greatly according to which period has been the main focus. Writing about the sixteenth, seventeenth and earlier eighteenth centuries has, on the whole, evinced more support for the colonial model—usually in its Atlanticist variant—than that dealing with either earlier or later periods. Each different era, however, has its specialists supporting every one of these interpretive strands. The divisions overlap with, but certainly do not neatly correspond to, the by now somewhat wearisome dispute between so-called 'revisionist' historians of Ireland and adherents of more traditional nationalist historical interpretations.[5]

The archipelagic model takes its cue from J. G. A. Pocock's influential redescription of the so-called British Isles as the North Atlantic Archipelago (Pocock 1982[6]). Irish history is seen as part of a story of ever-shifting patterns of culture, language, religion and rule across those islands. Although the dominant strand in this story became the expansion of control by what was originally the English Crown over other parts of the archipelago, the patterns shifted too constantly and variously to be subsumable into a narrative of conquest and colonisation by one kingdom over others—let alone one 'nation' over the rest. It was also, in Pocock's vision (soon to be taken up by many others) a story not only of heterogeneity but of hybridity:

There are normanized Irish and hibernicized Normans; there are bilingual Anglo-Welsh, as well as monoglot Welsh and English; there are Lowland Scots assimilated to the clan world of the Highlands ... there are Celts who enter a Norse world and Norse-men assimilated to the Celtic pattern. (1975:609)

Thus Steven G. Ellis—the historian who has espoused the archipelagic inter-pretation in perhaps its strongest programmatic form—argues that medieval Ireland is best seen as part of two wider, overlapping worlds, the Gaelic and the British Isles, rather than as a distinct or cohesive nation and culture. The rela-tions of the English Crown to its Irish vassals bore many resemblances to that with the feudal baronage in England itself, rather than following a wholly dis-tinct 'colonial' pattern. '[T]he adoption for late medieval Ireland of an ana-chronistic Hibernocentric perspective, with associated nationalist themes, is a conceptual trap.' (1986:18)[7]

Medieval and early-modern Irish history, then, is in Ellis's opinion a part of the 'internal expansion' of Anglo-Norman kingship; but this does not fit at all precisely the later patterns either of settler colonialism or of the 'colonies of exploitation'. Unlike the former, settlers remained a minority. They neither physically destroyed nor wholly marginalised the indigenes. But there was a longer, more profound colonial impact and a larger settler population than in any of the African or Asian non-settlement colonies. In a sense, this 'mixed' experience had its closest equivalent in South Africa, which Ellis believes might 'perhaps offer some interesting parallels—and timely warnings!—for Irish his-torians.' (S. Ellis 1991:293; the parallel is again invoked, though little further developed, in Ellis 1996a.) However, in Ireland there was never anywhere near such a clear 'racial' division between settlers and natives as in South Africa. Despite three centuries of colonial rule:

the indigenous population of South Africa remains immediately distinguishable from the settlers in appearance and culture, whereas the descendants of 'the wild Irish' are now practically indistinguishable. The reasons for this acculturation also demonstrate why, in the last analysis, colonial models for Irish history ... raise as many problems as they solve. The geographical proximity of Ireland and Britain and their long-standing economic interdependence encouraged continual migration between the two islands, and consequently strong cultural ties, which cannot be described as colonial. And unlike 'migrant labourers' in South Africa, 'natives' from Ireland have long enjoyed largely the same status in mainland Britain as the local population. (1991:294)

Other recent work, above all the widely-praised synthesis attempted by Robert Bartlett (1993) and the briefer but even wider-ranging argument of Stein Rokkan (1980, Rokkan and Urwin 1983), places such arguments in a more fully European perspective. From a view like this the fate of Celtic Europe at the hands of an aggrandising Latin-Frankish ruling and warrior class closely paral-leled that of Slavic Europe and of much of the Mediterranean world. The story of medieval Europe is above all one of the expansion of 'Latin Europe', and then of what Rokkan calls Europe's central 'city belt', their conquests and colonisation west, east and south. If in this sense Ireland's story was indeed a colonial one, it was as part of a picture in which, literally, all European history is colonial history. And, following the etymologically dubious but now entrenched historians' habit of distinguishing between 'borders' (clear lines demarcating different sovereignties) and 'frontiers' (more nebulous zones of contact and/or conflict, corresponding perhaps to 'fuzzy' rather than clearly demarcated notions of collective identity—see for instance Kaviraj 1993), we must certainly see the divisions of the early-medieval archipelago as marked by frontiers rather than borders. As Steven Ellis points out, using the vocabulary of 'colonisation' for medieval or early modern Ireland is little if any less problematic than use of 'colonialism':

Should a distinction be made, for instance, between the introduction of English colonists in Co. Clare by the Gaelic earl of Thomond in the later sixteenth century and their introduction in Ulster following the expropriation of Gaelic lords? And what of the displacement of Gaelic proprietors in Ulster by Gaelic MacDonalds from Scotland? Or the expropriation of 'Old English' proprietors by 'New English' in Munster? (S. Ellis 1996a:7–8)

Yet for all this, there might still have been something distinctive about the nature of English expansion from the twelfth century onwards, something marking it out from Latinate–Frankish expansion elsewhere. A number of recent historians have suggested that not only was there an unusually centralised and powerful monarchical state forged from southern England after the Norman Conquest, but that within two generations of that a precocious sense of English identity—and, rapidly, of superiority—coalesced. This identity counterposed itself to ideas about the highly distinctive and supposedly inferior characteristics of the various Celtic peoples; a form of expansion was instituted which was both more statist, more bureaucratic, and more heavily premised on claims of sharp cultural, even racial, difference, than those encountered elsewhere in pre-Renaissance Europe.[8] John Gillingham argues that this English sense of Irish, Welsh and Scottish inferiority and barbarism may have derived mainly from the fact that slavery, and the use of war as 'slave-hunt—a kind of total war' (1995:57) persisted longer among the latter than the former. Even as this distinction faded, it was replaced by perceptions of England's neighbours as uncultivated in manners, idle and unenterprising, prone to anarchic violence, pastoral and unfitted for urban life. William of Newburgh thought the Irish 'rough and barbarous in their ways . . . and lazy in agriculture . . . no public authority was constituted among them.' (quoted in Davies 1990:21) The mental division of the world between civilised and barbarians, the foundation-stone for all subsequent English imperialist ideology, was on this view already laid in the twelfth century; and the 'Celtic' peoples were its first victims.[9] For a later period, Jenny Wormald finds close similarities between the rhetoric of early-seventeenth-century English hostility to the Scots, 'with its recurrent theme of backwardness, lack of civility, parisitism' and that directed at African and Asian peoples in the nineteenth century (1992:188).

Davies sees attitudes hardening from about 1200 onwards, in relation to both Ireland and Wales, and concurrently with the crystallisation of a sense of English identity itself. Distinctions between natives and conquerors were ever more sharply drawn, and distinction increasingly meant discrimination, with relationships of superiority and inferiority. A 'cult of uniformity' took hold, pressing for the homogenisation of legal, administrative, religious and other codes: homogenisation based on what was emerging as the English model (Davies 1990: esp. 111–28; see also Ohlmeyer 1998). What had begun as diverse and informal concepts of domination 'had given way to an ideology of unity, uniformity and conquest.' (ibid: 128) Thus by the mid-thirteenth century much of Ireland formed, as Robin Frame says, 'a single zone with England, within which English Common Law and English government developed.' (1995:68) Dublin, Cork, Drogheda, Limerick, Athlone, and Wexford were all under English rule.

The arguments depend at least as much on ideas about English development as they do on ones about Ireland itself. If Ireland was conquered by entities called England and the English, when were they?[10] Historians have proposed a very wide range of originating points for the idea of Englishness: from as early as the 720s when Bede wrote (and thus at least helped to form) the idea of a national church, to the late nineteenth century when a new national education system with its emphasis on English literature and English history was introduced. In between there are claims for the decades after the Norman conquest of 1066, when a centralised monarchical state was forged; the late fourteenth century when the English language started to be used for literary and legal purposes; the early sixteenth century when the English Church broke away from Rome, new kinds of claims for an 'Imperial' national sovereignty were made, new myths of origin forged (substantially by Welsh writers propagandising for the upstart Tudor dynasty) and—so some historians, following Geoffrey Elton, assert—a recognisably modern state machine was built. Alternatively the end of the century may be preferred, with Shakespeare's history plays presenting a putatively novel vision of national destiny, with the focusing of effort around the conflict with Spain and especially the defeat of the Armada, with an aggressive and nationalistic Protestantism taking its iconography from *Foxe's Book of Martyrs*, and with the beginnings of overseas expansion and settlement.

Then there is the mid-seventeenth century, with what historians once called the Puritan Revolution, the economic nationalism and colonial projects of the Commonwealth, Oliver Cromwell as 'God's Englishman'. The 1740s (when the present British National Anthem was adopted) or the 1790s with the mobilisation of popular sentiment against threats of revolution or French invasion, might be proposed—and each of these decades saw an outpouring of selfconsciously patriotic literature. More recently still, as already suggested, we have the late nineteenth century as another candidate for the real origins of Englishness: this was the era when, one might say, national identity was nationalised—spread far outside the ruling and writing elites by an expansionary state machine.

For all the argument about when modern senses of national identity may be said to have formed, there is little dispute that state formation in England was unusually early. The English tradition of strong central power was very long: in a story dotted with false claims of unbroken continuity and rapidly fabricated 'ancient traditions', this was a real one. Crucially for Ireland's as well as Britain's future, the English medieval monarchy probably exerted more effective authority, earlier, over more of the territory it claimed to rule than any of its European counterparts. Wales, by contrast, never developed a single central royal authority before English conquest. Scotland had fewer and bigger political units, and during the eleventh and twelfth centuries the power of the new Scottish monarchy gradually extended. But even then, Scotland's was a significantly weaker monarchy than England's—its finances shakier, its aristocracy more fractiously independent, its writ running less surely in remoter regions of the country. Ireland was little if any more of a political unit than was Wales, and far less of one than England had already become by the eleventh century. It could nonetheless be claimed that it was at least as much of a cultural unit as was England or Scotland: it was developing a single language, albeit composed of numerous regional dialects, a flourishing literature—especially epic poetry both secular and religious—in that language, and a distinctive church organisation. Both England and Scotland, by contrast, were essentially conquest kingdoms, ruled by Norman-French dynasties and aristocracies.

Yet the steady growth in English state capacity, and accompanying (or consequent) economic and cultural homogenisation, were unmatched elsewhere in the islands. Strong central royal power made foreign wars and territorial expansion possible, in Wales, Ireland, France and Scotland; and success in these in its turn reinforced state capacities.[11] None of the upheavals of the succeeding centuries destroyed the essential continuity of the central ruling institutions, Crown and Parliament: not the dynastic Wars of the Roses in the fifteenth, nor the switchback ride of religious changes in the sixteenth, nor even the power-struggle between the institutions themselves in the seventeenth. Maybe more important than all these were the successive extensions and rationalisations of power which they undertook, usually, in tandem, creating a small but effective state bureaucracy, national systems of taxation and legal regulation, and bringing the Church under governmental control.

Between about 1500 and 1600 several important English political words both changed their meaning and started to be much more widely used than before. From the 1530s 'the state' started to be used for the first time in something like its modern sense, as an impersonal source of authority. The word 'country', which had previously meant county or locality, began to be used to mean nation: it has this sense consistently in Shakespeare. 'Nation' itself became much more widely employed. 'Empire', meaning royal authority as absolute sovereignty, was proclaimed as an attribute of the English Crown, first in the 1533 Preamble to the Act of Appeals which began: 'This realm of England is an Empire'. And the word 'Commonwealth', meaning both 'the public good', and 'a national society', was also introduced and rapidly spread. Perhaps most significantly, all these terms started to be used more or less as synonyms, describing England—rolling together the ideas of monarchy, sovereignty, state, nation, society, and the welfare of the people.[12] This association of ideas had not happened before, and it was not apparently yet happening anywhere else (the nearest parallel was in Italy, and especially Florence, in the thought of people like Machiavelli; but there the political preconditions for the emergence of a national identity were absent). It sums up a great deal of what today we mean by nationalism. It sharply differentiated itself from neighbours. And it both strengthened and was strengthened by the state's territorial expansion, not least in Ireland.

Can we, however, use such a picture and the criteria suggested by historians like Davies, Frame and Gillingham in order clearly to distinguish between 'state-building' and 'imperialism'—identifying what happened within England as the former, Irish developments as the latter? The answer surely is no. We can only make such a distinction *retrospectively*. As R. R. Davies emphasises: 'The Anglo-Normans did not set out self-consciously on a conquest of "Wales" or "Ireland" as such, or plot the take-over of the kingdom of Scotland; they were not informed by national ambitions or national animus . . . In short, their enterprises were not national conquests in intention, scale or character. That they eventually came to be seen as such is largely to be explained by changing ambitions and perceptions, especially from the early-thirteenth century onwards, and by the national orientation and inescapable hindsight of modern historiographical interpretation.' (1990:3)

If, some considerable time after a conquest, the conquered population comes to accept the state into which their ancestors had been forcibly inducted as legitimate, then what has been happening is state-building. If they do not, it is colonialism. Thus within England, and broadly in Wales and Scotland, such acceptance was achieved by the expansionist Anglo-Norman monarchy. Local elites were co-opted, and came to associate their economic and other interests with the larger state. The incorporation of English regions, of Wales and of Scotland therefore could retrospectively be judged to have been an exercise in state-building. (And, it naturally follows, if still later populations withdraw their acceptance, as seems to have happened with a majority in Scotland and at least a substantial minority in Wales, then the retrospective judgement is again altered and the initial incorporation process will be reassessed as a colonialist one). In Ireland, the acceptance of legitimacy was never fully achieved, and such acceptance as there had been was later withdrawn, much of it with astonishing rapidity in 1916–21. Nothing *preordained* this failure, though a variety of factors including cultural and religious difference may have predisposed towards it. Most decisive of all may well have been a lesser willingness by the conquerors in Ireland than in Wales or Scotland to work for such acceptance by conceding to the interests and making space for the participation in government and economic accumulation of the local elites.

We should not, however, overstate those differences. Sean Connolly points out that, before the formal Union between England and Scotland and even for two generations after it, 'it would have been difficult to regard the bond between England and any part of Scotland as inherently more stable or permanent than the bond between England and Ireland.' (1995:196) Scotland—especially but not only the Highlands, especially but not only around the rebellions of 1715 and 1745—sometimes witnessed more physical repression, greater bloodshed, far fiercer attempts to crush threatening manifestations of cultural difference than did Ireland (ibid: 194–6). Conrad Russell even asks provocatively whether we should regard English/British rule over Ireland as a failure at all. Compared with the other major European 'composite monarchies' of the early modern period, like the Unions of Poland and Lithuania, Spain and the Netherlands, Spain and Portugal, or the Habsburg Empire and Bohemia, that of England and Ireland displayed remarkable longevity. Part of it, after all, still exists in 1999 (Russell 1995:133–6).

3

The Past in the Present

(i) Rulers and Rationales

By the late medieval period, the English Crown had a long-established if uncertainly grounded claim to sovereignty over Ireland; and significant parts of Ireland including most of the existing major towns were effectively dominated by English conceptions of lordship, language and law. Between then and the early seventeenth century, that drive for domination and assimilation both intensified and faced new challenges. It became intertwined with religious conflict, as the Protestant Reformation succeeded in England and Scotland but largely failed in Ireland. It began to shift from being an 'English', to becoming a 'British' domination, with the Union of the Crowns in 1603 and the establishment of joint English-Scottish colonising ventures in Ireland. And it became entangled, too, with English attempts at expansion across the Atlantic and in the Americas. This last was, though, a paradoxical relationship.

England was a comparative latecomer to long-distance colonisation, with her merchants and private backers of settlement projects—and, considerably later still and rather grudgingly, her government—only slowly engaging themselves in ventures to which the Spanish and Portuguese had long devoted massive resources. There were numerous reasons for this, but one appears to have been the fact that England was so intensely involved in efforts at conquest and plantation close to home, especially in Ireland, that attention and resources were lacking for more distant ventures. Thus although various historians, perhaps most systematically Nicholas Canny, have stressed the interconnections between English/British colonising projects in Ireland and those in the Americas, Canny has also underlined how the effort expended on expansion within the archipelago 'served to blunt (long-distance) colonial endeavour and even set it on false trails ... [W]hat happened in Ulster, and more generally in Ireland, during the first half of the seventeenth century also served to distort, and even hinder, wider colonial developments. For example, Scottish involvement with Ulster meant that Scots could not, even if the opportunity had presented itself, become seriously engaged in colonization further afield because they lacked the resources to do so.' (1998b:9, 15) Plantations in Munster and Ulster also drained English pools of capital and, perhaps most importantly, skilled settler labour which might otherwise have gone to North America. This, though, was not so clearly or strongly the case for England as it was for Scotland: the English plantations in Ulster and elsewhere, despite state sponsorship, attracted proportionally far fewer settlers than did the less centrally organised Scottish ones. One ironic effect of the heavy Scottish involvement in Ulster plantation, therefore, may have been to make the early British Atlantic Empire in the Americas more predominantly English, less truly British, than it would otherwise have been.

As for the Irish themselves, one of the great counterfactual questions in the history of European expansion—a question which much exercised later Irish nationalists from Wolfe Tone to Arthur Griffith—is whether Ireland might have had a significant independent colonial presence if it had not been subject to England. As things were, Irish elites were unable to operate as major projectors of or investors in American settlements. The few significant Irish investments in early colonial enterprise centred on the Caribbean islands of St Christopher and later Montserrat, and on the initially grandiose Amazon basin venture of which the only eventual, and indirect, product was to be the British colony of Guiana (Canny 1998b:17; Cullen 1994).

Ciaran Brady and Raymond Gillespie, reviewing the literature on the Tudor period, note the continued coexistence of two distinct images of Ireland: as a sovereign and fairly homogeneous kingdom, and as an arena for colonial exploitation. But as they also note, it was not a matter of English attitudes simply shifting from the one to the other: 'From the beginning there was an element of colonial exploitation in the attempt to constitute Ireland as a kingdom, and even in periods of intense colonial activity Ireland's sovereign status never disappeared from the minds of either the monarchs or their various subjects in the island.' (Brady and Gillespie 1986:17) Karl Bottigheimer made a similar point; that the years when 'Ireland was brought into conformity with the concept of what a kingdom of the realm should be, were also the years of most palpable reduction to colonial status.' (1978:60)

Nor was either the Reformation or even O'Neill's defeat at Kinsale an absolute watershed, resolving this dualism one way or the other. Henry VIII had taken the title of King of Ireland in 1541; and this seems to have been seen, especially by the great Henrician architect of state institution-building, Thomas Cromwell, as a stage in Ireland's full incorporation under English rule and legal forms. Yet it could readily come to have the opposite effect, as Irish—and more especially 'Old English'—magnates claimed rights deriving from Ireland's being a separate and equal royal domain.[1] And for Ireland, as for Wales but unlike Scotland, there was no clear pre-existing single sovereignty which Tudor and Stuart monarchs could claim to inherit even by mere right of conquest. Irish High Kings had never been more than first among equals, political authority had always been parcellised. As Fred Halliday has suggested (1997/8:17), flippantly but shrewdly, insofar as claims to national unity are crucial in the nationalist tradition, Ireland's great national hero should be Henry VIII, the first monarch of all Ireland! It may be that here—as was probably the case in the very different circumstances of colonial conquest in Africa centuries later—absence of powerful centralising precolonial states made colonial occupation more, not less, difficult to establish.[2] And if state-sponsored Reformation 'failed' in Ireland during the sixteenth century, it is far from evident that it did so more completely or decisively than it did in Wales or Scotland. As for cultural assimilation, it seems likely that linguistic Anglicisation went much further, quicker in Ireland than it did in Wales.[3] By the late seventeenth century, as Thomas Bartlett says, Ireland 'resembled not so much a model colony . . . but rather an unruly palimpsest, on which, though much rewritten and scored out, could be discerned in an untidy jumble "kingdom", "colony", "dependency" and, faintly, "nation".' (1998:254)

Nicholas Canny has traced in numerous works (e.g. 1973, 1978, 1988, 1991) the growth of a powerful English Protestant ideology of colonisation in Ireland, closely paralleling that developed for the North American colonies.[4] As he says, almost all promoters of schemes for settlement in Ireland drew comparisons between their plans and those of their contemporaries who were projecting settlements among the North American Indians (1988:2). Steven Ellis, though, urges forcefully that the differences are rather more striking than the similarities:

In the case of north America, it was never seriously intended by the crown, as it was in Ireland, to incorporate the territory as a core region of the English state . . . The depiction of Ireland as an Atlantic colony obscures this central feature of English rule there . . . Thus Atlantic World theories appear to absolve the historian from the duty to compare and contrast the actual operation of English administrative structures in the two countries. (1996a:14)

Others have doubted the strength even of the ideology. David Armitage, for instance, has argued forcefully that the association of Elizabethan English literary renaissance and overseas expansion is a retrospectively constructed myth: 'only with the rise of linguistic nationalism in the nineteenth century were literature and Empire traced back to common roots in the late sixteenth century.' (1998:100) It was a myth first built by late-Victorian and Edwardian British enthusiasts for Empire, and now reproduced, with opposed ideological intentions but in essential identical form, by post-Saidian analysts of colonial discourse in English literature. Armitage believes that in reality the impact of Empire, and the presence of colonial themes, in early modern English literature were extremely marginal—and where such themes do appear, the writers are more often than not highly critical of the colonial enterprise.[5] Like so many historians, Armitage emphasises how enthralled Elizabethan English writers were to classical precursors, not only for their literary models, but for their ideas about Empire (ibid: 103–9). His argument for the insignificance of the colonial theme rests, however, on some slightly strained arguments and partial read-ings—as well as largely neglecting Ireland. He sees Spenser, the most cited and debated example of a major Elizabethan writer whose career and work also centrally embraced Irish colonisation, mainly as a symptomatic failure: 'the generic abortion of Spenser's epic appears prophetic of the repeated failure of any British author ever to produce a complete and unequivocal epic poem in the classical tradition, and hence to provide either England or Scotland with its expected literary monument to empire.' (ibid: 117) This, however, is a strange claim. If British literature, that of far the largest and most successful modern colonial Empire, supposedly failed to produce a successful epic poem, that might surely be thought more a reason to question whether the epic should be seen as the necessary form of the great national literary-imperial monument, rather than a justification for believing that no such monument ever existed. In any case, Armitage proceeds to admit so many at least partial exceptions—most obviously, *Paradise Lost*—as to qualify his assertion almost out of existence.

The mixture of justifications for conquest and expansion seen in Ireland—providentialist and other religious arguments, commercial considerations, early notions of a civilising mission, claims drawn from a mythicised ancient or early-medieval history and from Roman precedents—was essentially similar to that deployed for north American, Caribbean and other ventures.[6] Like all modern empire-builders, the English presumed from the start that expansion did indeed require some form of moral justification, as both classical and reli-gious authorities taught[7]—even though Anthony Pagden suggests that 'because of their view of themselves as a commercial and agricultural, rather than a con-quering people, few Europeans were so little given to moral scruples over their imperial exploits as the English.' (1998:37)

Perhaps the most strongly advanced, and certainly subsequently most dis-cussed, early English legitimisation for colonial enterprise was a characteris-tically post-Reformation (in origin, perhaps specifically Calvinist) doctrine of entitlement through industry. John Locke later gave this a new, systematic, and secularisable—though certainly not in Locke's own writings secularised—for-mulation. Labour both reflected divine grace and created value: only by mixing his labour with the soil could a man justly claim rights to ownership of that soil. This Lockean theory has been argued not only to have supported the claims of colonial expansionists, but to have been formulated with that aim very centrally in mind, for the Americas (where John Locke had considerable personal inter-ests) and perhaps for Ireland too (Arneil 1992, 1994, 1996, Tully 1993).

It would seem, though, that however widely such arguments were deployed in relation to British America, they were little used in Ireland. The reasons are fairly obvious. Although some propagandists for conquest and settlement in

Ireland argued that there was no true civil society there, because of features like comparatively little urbanisation, or the limited authority of early Irish kings, it could hardly be shown that Irish land was either uninhabited or uncultivated, nor that the pre-conquest Irish had lived without formally constituted political society and systems of law, as Locke had claimed (falsely) that aboriginal Americans did.

The dominant approach to governing Ireland was, almost throughout, thus one of asserting that rightful sovereignty there had previously been ceded to the English Crown—at some one among variously preferred, and more or less mythic, past times—rather than that there was no prior claim to sovereignty, as Lockeans asserted of America and as the *terra nullius* doctrine was later to proclaim for Australasia. And it was to incorporate, assimilate and Anglicise the natives, not as in the Americas and Australia to exclude if not exterminate them[8]—no serious historian would contend today that even the Cromwellian clearances, the Penal Laws or the 1840s Famine were intended physically to eliminate the native Irish. In this crucial regard, ideologies of colonisation as well as methods of governance in Ireland differed quite radically from those used elsewhere in the Atlantic world. Ellis suggests that 'the main defining characteristic of colonisation in Ireland was its purpose. The intention was to incorporate Ireland and its inhabitants into a wider English (or later, British) state, and to create there a permanent European society which was culturally English and governed in the same way as England itself' (1996a:8).

The ghost of Calvinist and Lockean rationales for colonial settlement can perhaps most readily be discerned, even up to the present, in Northern Ireland. There, the argument that Scots and English settlers legitimated their occupation of Irish land by their industriousness, by cultivating it more productively than earlier inhabitants, and later developing handicraft and then manufacturing industry on it, had great popular force. The notion that a tidy farmyard and efficiently run farm, a clean and well-kept house, or Belfast's former industrial prosperity, reflect peculiarly Protestant virtues can still be encountered in northern Irish social stereotyping.

It is also a long step from Canny's comparison of colonising *discourses* to showing that the English *practice* in Ireland was a fully, homogeneously or successfully colonialist one.[9] One might quite consistently note the widespread presence of English discourses or ideologies of Irish colonisation, as does Canny, but nonetheless see the actual Elizabethan conquest of Ireland as having quite different roots—as stemming primarily from the failure of the Reformation in Ireland, as Steven Ellis (1985) sees it as doing, or as deriving from events on the periphery, where the ambition and greed of English officials or adventurers provoked unrest which in turn forced ever more direct and extensive state intervention (e.g. Ranger 1965). Therefore occupation and colonisation could be argued to have taken place either despite the absence of any particularly powerful ideological drive towards it, or alongside but substantially detached from and only weakly influenced by such a drive. Parallels might again be drawn with the late-nineteenth-century partition of Africa, which many historians believe to have had rather little direct connection to the undoubted presence of aggressively colonialist discourses in the Europe of the time. In both cases, *post hoc* is not necessarily *propter hoc*.[10]

The contrary view, arguing for a coherent and consequential colonialist ideology as having driven the process of English expansion throughout, is perhaps most strongly argued by Brendan Bradshaw. For Bradshaw, it is not the Reformation's failure in Ireland but the transformation of its character in England which was decisive. As, from the reign of Edward VI onward, a narrow, bigoted and repressive Calvinism took hold in English state policy, the resulting anti-Catholic animus provided the stimulus to conquest in Ireland. It is arguable that this emphasis on religious determinants and specifically on a supposed Protestant 'crusade' against Irish Catholicism very much reflects Father Bradshaw's own ideological formation and predispositions.[11] Certainly historians have continued to disagree on the explanatory weight which should be placed on the Reformation in determining the course of Irish history. Jonathan Clark (1994:72–5, 86–9, 285–9) is the most recent exponent of the view that religion was all-determining for Irish as, in his view, for British and colonial American politics. In a powerful (if again deeply ideologically inflected, and conservative) argument stitching together emphases on British multinationality, Atlanticism and an insistence on the 'ancien regime' nature of all political debate until at least the 1830s, Clark sees the confessional nature of the state as explaining everything from the early Tudors to O'Connell—and beyond:

The Reformation thus ensured that the power-base of English rule in Ireland soon became religious, not baronial, as the rebellion of 1594–1603 and the Catholic massacre of English and Scots settlers in 1641 demonstrated and successive traumatic episodes confirmed: the Cromwellian conquest, the Restoration land settlement, the civil war of 1689–93, the Penal Laws, the rebellion of 1798. (1994:73)

Canny however, like Brady and Gillespie, emphasises the complex divisions between different early-modern perceptions of Ireland. The strongest opponents of mass colonisation were the 'Old English'. They, like the projectors of settlements, tended to see Gaelic Irish tradition as barbaric, but 'their preferred solution . . . lay in persuading the members of the ruling elite in Gaelic society to adopt English ways and to become agents of reform within their lordships.' (Canny 1988:2) Regret at the failure to adopt this course had a long historiographical afterlife, as we shall see in the example of David Hume. The Old English pressed the case of Ireland as a kingdom, not a colony; and thus of its inhabitants as having the same rights as all other subjects of the Crown. Despite his emphasis on the parallels, and mutual influences, between English colonisation endeavours in Ireland and in North America Canny still urges that 'what was happening in Ireland was in certain respects a unique event that can only be understood when considered in a European context.' (1988:34)

Others objected to colonisation on different grounds. Sir William Fitz-william, long-serving governor under Elizabeth, worried that private colon-isation would provoke violent opposition from the natives which he would be unable to control. Administrators and commentators like Sir John Davies and Sir Francis Bacon advocated 'liberal' policies aimed at winning allies among the Irish rather than crushing them.[12] And a few, like John Long, briefly Archbishop of Armagh in the 1580s, complained at the drive for profit overriding concern for social and religious wellbeing (ibid: 4–5). Such anxieties helped make it imperative for all concerned, including the proponents of mass colonisation, to emphasise their desire to 'promote the social and religious reform of the popu-lation' in Ireland (ibid: 5). The sixteenth-century discourse of colonisation was therefore radically different from the images of it projected back by modern assumptions:

where to the twentieth-century mind the term 'colonization' conjures up the image of primitive people being exploited by Europeans, this was not necessarily the association with the word in the sixteenth century, and English advocates of colonization were clearly concerned to convince their superiors in government that they fostered no exploitative intentions. (ibid: 14)

Again, modern historiography tends to emphasise both the incompleteness of English conquest and the shifting, ambivalent nature of political, religious and cultural allegiances among both Irish-Gaelic and 'Old English' elites.[13] Indeed through much of the sixteenth century, the fiercest resistance to extension of royal authority came from the Old English aristocracy of the Pale. Among them, there had taken place a substantial convergence at least of interests and perhaps also of culture and status with the elites of the 'Old Irish' population; the two groups were no longer so readily distinguishable as many observers, both con-temporary and subsequent, supposed them to be. There could be no better illustration of this than the transmutation of Hugh O'Neill, English (and Protestant) raised and educated, soldier in Elizabeth's army, holder of an English earldom, apostle of cultural Anglicisation, into The O'Neill, self-proclaimed prince of an independent, Catholic, Gaelic Ireland (Hiram Morgan 1993a, esp. 85–112).[14] Despite later mythologising, it is at least as anachronistic to think of O'Neill as a nationalist or an anticolonial leader as it is to do so for Robert Bruce or Owain Glyndwyr.[15]

On the other hand, the leading contemporary proponent of 'primordialist' or 'ethnicist' as opposed to 'modernist' interpretations of nationalism, Anthony D. Smith, argues in the course of a wide-ranging comparative survey that a dis-tinct Irish ethnicity, which he sees as having been kept alive above all by religious institutions, persisted throughout. '(A) deeply embedded Catholicism and a dominant Catholic clergy were left as the main support and symbolic definer of Irish identity; persecution and discrimination merely served to reinforce the religious, even messianic, content of Irish ethnicity.' (Smith 1986:111) Adrian Hastings, similarly, like Smith rejecting the view that one cannot meaningfully speak of nations before the later eighteenth century, suggests that 'If I contemplate Irish history across the "longue duree", I can see no even moderately plausible alternative to what one may fairly call a nationalist interpretation.' (1997:91) And he urges that after the impact of the Reformation and counter-Reformation, it was inevitable that Protestants would by and large identify themselves with Britishness: 'While individual "new English" like Parnell could jump the dividing line, yet remain Protestants, it seems almost impossible to imagine that as a group they could have done so' (ibid: 89–90). Conversely, a 'nationalist spirit' had come into existence early and powerfully enough to make it near-unimaginable that the Irish would accommodate themselves to Union as Welsh and Scots did (ibid: 90–1).

Historians have divided on this point, failing to agree on how far the literary evidence, for instance, supports perceptions of a strong and distinct national-ethnic identity (Canny 1982b, Dunne 1980, Leerssen 1988, O Riordan 1990). Even those who have most strongly and systematically propounded colonial models for understanding early-modern Irish history have emphasised that it by no means necessarily follows from this that Irish resistance to English/British rule should be thought of as nationalist or anticolonialist (see e.g. Canny 1994).

Ciaran Brady documents the extent to which conflicts between English governors and Irish lords were not the result of a deliberate Tudor royal strategy of confrontation. The English state aimed not at the destruction of the latter's power, but at reformist assimilation, such as had succeeded in its English and Welsh domains. But the very activism and centralism of the governors undermined their own aims by provoking the very hostility the reforms were supposed to remove (here, as in post-1945 'second occupation' policies in British Africa, colonial activism was its own gravedigger). The guiding ideology, in Brady's view, was neither specifically Protestant nor aggressively colonialist (*contra* Bradshaw and Canny); rather it was premised on hope that the tactics which had succeeded in pacifying England would work for Ireland too. This involved an 'implicit arrogance . . . unearned and wholly unquestioned claims to cultural superiority' (Brady 1994:xv[16]), but very little that could be called racist or colonialist in the nineteenth- and twentieth-century meanings of those ideas. The English governors, Brady suggests, were wrecked by their sheer naive well-meaningness; by the late 1580s their reform project had expired: 'a victim neither of ideological change nor political convulsion, but of exhaustion, disillusion and neglect.' (ibid: 300)

The identities and self-perceptions of the elites, first 'Old English' and then

Protestant-settler, have thus aroused much historiographical controversy. They have most often been seen, pursuing the lead of Aidan Clarke, as 'colonial' and as having strong similarities with those formed in other colonial societies and especially those of the Americas. (Clarke 1978) Clarke emphasises, as many historians have done, that national and religious identities did not coincide. The Catholicism of most of the 'Old English' differentiated them from the Irish (who, adhering to the traditions of the ancient Celtic church, were not yet predominantly Catholic in what was becoming the homogenised, orthodox continental European sense) as well as from the English. As for the Protestant settlers, Canny follows his tracing of the English ideology of colonisation with an argument for the formation of a characteristically colonial—and distinctively Atlantic—identity among the colonists (1982a, 1987). Indeed he believes that by the early eighteenth century they had developed a self-confidence and an ideology of constitutional radicalism more advanced than that found anywhere else under English rule, including North America (Canny 1988:122–4).

The framework proposed by Aidan Clarke and Canny has been followed by a majority of recent historians of the era. Toby Barnard, however, has mounted some sharp criticisms of it. Complaining that Canny fails to distinguish between ideology, mentality, and identity (Barnard 1990:40), he suggests that closer attention to the varieties of all three in seventeenth-century Ireland reveals how the disagreements and ambiguities among modern historians reflect those among their subjects. A complex dispute was fought out among Irish Protestants as to whether they should regard themselves as colonists or as 'loyal subjects of the sovereign king of Ireland, a kingdom ruled over as one of three by the king of England.' (ibid: 41) The latter became the dominant view, underpinned by constitutional theory: 'there persisted the comforting idea of Ireland as a sister kingdom to England', even if a younger sister (Barnard 1998:309). But theory and practice increasingly diverged, with the reality an ever more evidently colonial one to which, by the early eighteenth century, a 'querulous' colonial nationalism was the only remaining response.

To generalise the colonial model beyond its actually very specific and rather late applicability, Barnard believes, results in a mistakenly teleological view—substantially derived from outdated perceptions of American experience—whose story runs roughly: conquest—colonisation—formation of colonial identity—emergence of nationalism—struggle for independence. Such a teleology has been increasingly discredited in recent writing on the North American settlements (e.g. Greene and Pole 1984, Fischer 1989). Its applicability to Ireland is yet more questionable. Continental European parallels, for instance with Bohemia, 'the one territory brought to heel almost as comprehensively as England aspired to treat Ireland' (Barnard 1990:44) are in Barnard's view for many purposes more illuminating, and were indeed often made by seventeenth-century commentators in Ireland themselves.[17]

(ii) Settlement and Sovereignty

The decisive transformation should probably be placed in the early seventeenth century. It began with the settlement in Ireland of a substantial Anglo-Scottish population which unlike most of the 'Old English' was differentiated from the indigenous majority in religion as well as language and culture, and in some cases found itself in direct economic competition with it.[18] Yet political allegiances by no means fully corresponded to these distinctions, at least until well after the war of the 1640s. This too must be put into a wider context, for which neither religious antagonisms nor 'internal colonialism' provide an adequate account. The context is a series of wars waged across the archipelago from the Scots' anti-episcopal mobilisation in 1639 until St Ruth's defeat at Aughrim in 1691, or even the crushing of the clan regiments at Culloden in 1746—a Hundred Years' War of the British Isles in which dynastic ambitions, religious principles, the aspirations of social classes, political factions, regions and nations-in-the-making all featured, and for which the crucial precipitating crises came first in Ulster ('the crucible of the British problem', thought Conrad Russell (1991:532)), then in Lowland Scotland.[19] Within this complex, a substantial though not precisely knowable number of Protestants in Ireland adhered to the Stuart cause in the 1640s, and smaller but still not negligible numbers did so in 1689.

   The end result was not only the creation, finally, of a consolidated British overrule in Ireland but also of key subsequent historical reference points for Ireland's different traditions. For Unionists and Ulster Protestants, these were the massacres of 1641 (which actually claimed perhaps 6,000 lives, but which Protestant contemporaries asserted and may even have believed to have had 200,000 or more victims), the exaggerated heroism of the 1689 Siege of Derry, and William's victory at the Boyne.[20] For the Catholic Irish, the matching touchstones are of course Cromwell's atrocities (the slaughters of Drogheda and Wexford, unlike those of Ulster Protestants in 1641, were massive enough to need little subsequent propaganda inflation: though they were far from unusual by the contemporary standards of European warfare), the defeat at Aughrim and subsequent surrender at Limerick.[21] The impact of this long war was more drastic, and probably bloodier, for Ireland than for any other part of the archipelago. One contemporary observer, Cromwell's Physician-General William Petty, believed that from 1641 to 1652 alone 616,000 died, and that in the following few years another 140,000 emigrated or were transported (Berresford Ellis 1988:25). The figures may well be overstated—though Petty had no obvious incentive to exaggerate a dispossession from which his own pockets benefited greatly—but certainly there was a major demographic shift.[22] The final defeat in 1691 saw a further exodus, especially of men of military age, the 'Wild Geese' who took service in the armies of France and Spain. The Protestant population, by the end of the wars, had expanded from roughly 5 per cent of Ireland's total to 20 per cent, owning almost 80 per cent of the land. Within a few more decades, Protestant landholding had expanded to 85–90 per cent of the total. Crucially, however, they did not become a majority of the population anywhere except the north-east and a handful of towns elsewhere: the flow of migrants from England and Scotland constantly disappointed the expectations of its projectors (Barnard 1998:310–11). Indeed land intended for new settlers, in the 1650s and no doubt also later, was overwhelmingly bought instead by those already long resident (ibid: 314).

Ireland's era as fully-fledged British colony, then, begins (if the term is appro-priate for any era) with the long series of military defeats from Kinsale to Augh-rim—even if not one of these ranged an ethnically 'English' army against an 'Irish' one.[23] More particularly, it begins from the British-Irish civil wars of 1640–91. A fully-fledged, fairly secure United Kingdom political authority over the entire archipelago was only finally achieved with the end of the Williamite war—or, some would say, only with the suppression of the Jacobite Highland clans after 1746. The most profound impact of these events, beyond the imme-diate political and demographic shifts, was perhaps cultural, with the Irish language starting its long retreat, the religious faith of the majority embattled and subordinated, and the customs and social institutions of 'Englishness' strongly identified with status, wealth and power.

We shall return in more detail to the theme, and the rhetorics, of cultural colonialism and its opponents. But it should be underlined that in late-seventeenth- and eighteenth-century Ireland as in other colonial contexts these patterns were always complex and contested, rather than forming a mere manichean opposition of colonisers and colonised—as a glance for instance at the careers of such diverse figures as Swift, Sheridan, Goldsmith or Burke will suggest.[24] As Andrew Carpenter and Seamus Deane succinctly put it, trans-planted 'English' culture:

was profoundly affected by its new environment, even to the point of transformation. Not Gaelic and yet not wholly English, it had to discover either what it was or what it could become. By a remarkable transition, the English living in Ireland in the eighteenth century gradually learned to create a new identity for themselves by recollecting the frag-ments of the Gaelic tradition and transmuting them into an English that itself was a transmutation of the English civilisation from which they derived. (Field Day 1991, I:961)

Culturally, and perhaps psychologically, the Ireland of the eighteenth century was thus an English colony.[25] But it was one where, as in all colonies but earlier and perhaps more intensely than most, various modes of cultural hybridity and syncretism developed: including not only the Ascendency intellectuals whom Carpenter and Deane seem to have mostly in mind, but the very different adap-tations made by the Catholic peasantry—Daniel Corkery's 'hidden Ireland'

(Corkery 1925, Maume 1993)—the Catholic 'underground gentry' among whom (so Breandan O Buachalla (1992, 1995) and Kevin Whelan (1996a ch. 1) argue from the perspectives of literary and social history respectively) Jacobitism remained strong throughout the century, and the distinctive world-view of Ulster Dissent, whose radical traditions Marianne Elliott (1985), Flann Campbell (1991) and Tom Paulin (Field Day 1991, III:314–79) have sought to recuperate.[26]

It is surely anachronistic to describe any of these emerging worldviews as either 'imperialist' or 'nationalist': though Thomas McLoughlin (1999) has recently and forcefully argued otherwise. Opposition to the new order, whether expressed in Gaelic poetry or in sporadic attempts at political organisation, used mainly the rhetoric of Jacobitism, and occasionally that of the Counter-Reformation, not of anticolonial nationalism. As to the position of the 'settlers', Nicholas Canny's view judiciously balances its judgement. Insofar as they had substantial material privileges and were antinationalist in ideology, they remained 'colonists according to our modern definition of that term', as were their counterparts in North America. Yet as they became 'firmly anchored throughout the country, not only in the north-east corner' and were fiercely attached to the land and locality they 'have as much right as any other element of the population to be described as Irishmen'. (Canny 1988:140) The 'teleolog-ical view' of Irish history preferred by traditional nationalists has, Canny concludes, been decisively faulted *inter alia* by its 'attempt to ignore the contri-bution made by the settlers to Ireland's historical development.' (ibid: 138) Each new wave of incomers had to adjust to prior patterns of settlement, administra-tion and culture: as Barnard says 'Ireland . . . never resembled "a white paper" on which immigrants could inscribe whatever they pleased. The residue from the past settlements stained the supposedly white sheet, so that the crude geom-etry of the new plantation, when not obliterated, was blurred as the earlier con-figurations showed through.' (Barnard 1998:326) Indeed some recent work, like that of Sean Connolly (1992, 1996) and C. D. A. Leighton (1994) has suggested that the notion of an 'ancien regime' rather than that of a 'colonial society' best fits eighteenth-century Ireland.[27] As Connolly suggests:

It was a pre-industrial society, ruled over by a mainly landed elite, in which vertical ties of patronage and clientship were more important than horizontal bonds of shared economic or social position . . . It was also, like the rest of Europe, a confessional state, in which religion remained a central aspect of personal and political motivation, and in which differences of religious allegiance were a cause of fundamental conflict. (1992:2)

This is not to deny the unusualness, if not uniqueness, of some aspects of Irish social conflict: aspects which derived heavily from the legacy of conquest and which 'gave Ireland some of the features of a colony.' (ibid: 113). But these did not, so Connolly concurs with Ellis, include fundamental 'racial' divisions. 'The barrier created by the penal laws could be crossed, in a way that no barrier based on colour could ever be . . . Geography and ethnography ensured that the indigenous population, at any social level, could not in the long term really be treated as the native peoples of colonies generally were.' In any case 'race, language and culture were not in themselves the basis on which that dispossession, or the subsequent exclusion of a large majority of the population from power and privilege, were carried out.' Comparisons with apartheid are thus, Connolly insists, deeply misleading (ibid: 113–14). And as Toby Barnard among others has underlined, the identity of the Anglo-Irish—usually prosperous, and strongly tied to England—should not be taken as identical to that of the much wider category of Protestants in Ireland, far more diverse in their economic status as in their political allegiances, and for whom 'Ireland was more often the physical (though not the mental) limit of their world.' (Barnard 1990:82)

Economically, the historical picture of eighteenth-century Ireland has long been overcast by the dark shadow thrown back from the 1840s Famine. Yet here too modern 'revisionist' historiography has sought to show that the eighteenth-century Irish economy was both more dynamic and less abjectly dependent on British dictates than had long been thought. British discrimination against Irish agricultural imports is itself backhanded testimony to the relative success of rural capitalism in some parts of Ireland. Certainly, despite early legal restrictions, Ireland was not shut out from Atlantic trade but participated vigorously in it (R. C. Nash 1985). Even though Ireland was less able to benefit from expanding colonial markets than was Scotland, and although Irish colonial trade was dominated by English capital and intermediaries, its failure to take optimal advantage of new opportunities probably owed more to the legacies of internal political and religious conflict than to British restrictions and discriminations (Bartlett 1998:258–9).

Yet development was dramatically uneven, with proto-industrialisation in Ulster through linen production coexisting with regions of extreme and perhaps growing poverty, exacerbated by population growth—which was substantially faster in Ireland than in Britain, across the eighteenth and earlier ninetenth centuries.[28] Emigration was already substantial, though it was probably heaviest among Ulster Protestants—the later 'Scotch-Irish' of Britain's North American colonies. Recent estimates suggest that between 1700 and 1775, 66,100 migrants went from Ulster to the thirteen North American colonies, as against 42,500 from the rest of Ireland (Horn 1998:32). To these must be added possibly another 30,000 emigrants to North America in 1775–1800, roughly 40,000 migrants, mainly as indentured servants, from Ireland to the Caribbean, and perhaps 10,000 convicts transported first to the Americas, later to Australasia (Bartlett 1998:256).

To a degree, the growth of cultural syncretism too reflected these economic realities. Although between 1691 and the 1720s a wide range of 'penal' laws discriminating against Catholics was passed, the most drastic of these were—as most historians now recognise—unenforceable and unenforced (Wall 1989). Despite much of the rhetoric of the time, the real aim was not to destroy Catholicism as such, but to exclude Catholics from political office and large-scale landholding: it was as much a matter of a *class* consolidating its position as of a nation, let alone a religion, doing so. And even in this it was far from wholly successful. In the west especially, a Catholic landowning class survived, albeit often under the cloak of pretended conversion; and as the century proceeded a new urban, commercial and professional Catholic stratum emerged with some vigour. (S. J. Connolly 1992 *passim*, R. F. Foster 1988:153–6, 203–7, Whelan 1996a). Certainly, as several recent studies have indicated, Catholic economic activity was vigorous enough for Protestant and Anglo-Irish fears at economic as well as demographic 'swamping' by Catholics to be recurrent through the eighteenth century (Thomas Bartlett 1992, S. J. Connolly 1992, McCoy 1994).

Politically, the country was a dependent kingdom with a subordinate Dublin parliament from which Catholics and Dissenters (as well as women and propertyless men) were excluded. In theory Ireland's status as a separate kingdom, and possession of a fully-fledged parliament rather than the mere Councils or Assemblies which the western Atlantic colonies could at best boast, gave it greater autonomy than the latter. In practice, though, the Irish legislature probably had less freedom of action than did those of many American colonies. Ireland's sheer physical proximity, naturally, had much to do with this. There was however not only debate, but deep uncertainty, about its constitutional status. Essentially London had opted, as it was to do where conditions allowed elsewhere in its Empire, for indirect rather than direct rule. After much doubt and division, it had chosen the Protestant elites of Ireland as its main partners (or, if one prefers, clients or sub-contractors) in the process. The choice was in significant part prompted by the remaining Catholic elite's hostility to such cooperation, as demonstrated through the long wars of the seventeenth century: but exclusion in its turn, inevitably, perpetuated and intensified that hostility. And this was still not, at least in the first half of the eighteenth century, a division between 'pro-Union' and 'Irish nationalist' beliefs. Sean Connolly argues that even the Irish patriotism which emerged ever more strongly during the century 'can, to some extent, be seen as no more than the application to Irish conditions of the principles of civic virtue, active citizenship and a commitment to close parliamentary scrutiny of the executive that characterised English "Country" politics.' (1995:196–7) Protestants continued 'to refer to themselves as Englishmen, using "Irish" as synonymous with "Catholic".' (ibid: 197) Irish patriotism 'was more British than it looked' (197). And this was even more true of the dominant political ideology among Catholics, at least up to the 1750s, Jacobitism. This was 'by its very nature a British political ideology, shared with some Englishmen and many Scots, and concerned with restoring a Scottish dynasty to the combined thrones of England, Scotland and Ireland.' (197)

The drive for greater legislative autonomy, if not full independence, gathered pace from the 1750s. It was given a militant edge by the Volunteer movement but was always led and mostly supported by the Protestant, and especially Dissenting, middle classes. Among them, a sense of collective identity and thwarted aspiration coalesced which some historians have seen as at least proto-nationalist, directly analogous to that simultaneously growing in Britain's North American colonies.[29] Yet as Thomas Bartlett underlines, it was—at least until the emergence of the United Irish movement—not pressing for secession, nor was it hostile to Empire. Rather, eighteenth-century Irish Patriots wanted a bigger share for Ireland in Britain's overseas expansion and its profits (Bartlett 1998:260–1). In 1782, taking advantage of British preoccupation with the American war and itself substantially inspired by the example of the American colonists, this Protestant elite 'Patriot' grouping headed by Henry Grattan wrung from London the concession of a semi-independent legislature.

Some of the Patriots advocated abolition of the Penal Laws and were prepared to move cautiously towards Catholic enfranchisement. Their links of political alliance or sentiment with the rural Catholic poor were, however, tenuous in the extreme. Catholic agrarian discontent was mobilised instead by the parallel but antagonistic Defender movement, strongest in Ulster, and the more anarchic, spontaneous, less politicised rural violence of Whiteboyism and other 'underground' movements. Not for the first or the last time, shared antagonism to British rule was crosscut and substantially overridden by internal political, economic and above all religious rivalries.[30] Such rural rebels, so most who studied them concur, were not 'anticolonial' proto-revolutionaries. Their protest was localised and sporadic, defensive and backward-looking, better characterised by ideas of 'moral economy' (Thomas Bartlett 1987, Clark and Donnelly eds 1983, Magennis 1998) than by any affiliation to nationalism—they were in these, as in most, respects very like their counterparts elsewhere in pre-industrial Europe including England. Indeed in the 1760s the Whiteboys explicitly proclaimed their loyalty to George III (S. J. Connolly 1996:23).

Thus modern historical research depicts an eighteenth-century Ireland economically more dynamic, socially and culturally more variegated, politically more pluralist, with fewer effective discriminations against Catholics, and less oppressive power wielded either by landlords or by London, than had previously been believed. It was utterly unlike the manichean images of colonial society purveyed both by classical nationalist history and by the latterday proponents of an Irish Fanonism.[31]

Yet religious antagonisms persisted and in some respects grew sharper. This was also the era of the foundation of the Orange Order, in County Armagh in

1795, emerging out of the increasingly bitter—and increasingly sectarianised—local agrarian clashes between rival armed gangs, Protestant 'Peep O'Day Boys' and Catholic Defenders (D. W. Miller ed. 1990). Even the anti-sectarian and republican United Irishmen did not wholly overcome these schisms. Indeed one recent account (A. T. Q. Stewart 1993) emphasises the specifically Presbyterian republican—and largely Freemason—milieu shared by almost all the movement's founders; though other recent work has re-emphasised its socially radical dimension.[32] As they sought French aid (an alliance traced in Elliott 1982) and lower-class Catholic support, the potential for internal schism, whether between revolutionaries and reformers or on sectarian lines, was always great. They were, moreover, subject to the attentions both of an often brutally effective repression, and of numerous spies, informers and double agents. Thus their projected national revolution with French aid materialised instead as a series of largely disconnected regional revolts; notably in eastern Ulster, where the relative levels of involvement by (and degree of unity achieved between) Catholics and Dissenters have been lastingly controversial,[33] and in Wexford where a mainly Catholic peasant rising took on, among some participants, violently anti-Protestant overtones. Early histories of the revolt, notably that by Sir Richard Musgrave, quickly established an abiding tradition of seeing it as both anarchic and sectarian.[34]

By contrast and indeed in virtual mirror-image, Catholic writers from the 1870s onwards sought in effect to claim 1798 as their own, downplaying or ignoring Protestant participation and greatly overstating the role of priests in the leadership. As Kevin Whelan suggests, that new 'Faith and Fatherland' image can be found perpetuated in many of the sentimental ballads about the revolt, which proliferated in the 1890s and largely replaced the songs sung by the rebels themselves, and even in such modern literary productions of Thomas Flanagan's *The Year of the French*, Seamus Heaney's 'Requiem for the Croppies', and Brian Friel's *Translations*. (Whelan 1996a:169–73)[35]

(iii) Unions and Disunities

The failure of the United Irishmen, with the continuing fear of French invasion, ushered in legislative Union with Britain. For the next 120 years Ireland was, legislatively, to be part of a unitary Kingdom: on a constitutional level at least the never clearly defined 'colonial' status of Ireland had ended. In fact in the fierce Irish debates on Union in 1799–1800, and indeed thereafter, its advocates persistently stressed that it would enable Ireland to play a fuller and more equal role in the affairs of the subject Empire (e.g. Bartlett 1998:271–2). Yet on other levels and by other definitions the country's position as a subordinated part of the British imperial system was intensified, not ended, by Union. At the heart of all perceptions of the situation as a colonial one lay the question—or rather the myriad questions—of culture. In this language played a diminishing role. English became not only dominant but near-universal, despite the late-century drive among some Irish intellectuals for Gaelic revival; but religion retained or even increased its centrality, augmented by both rural and later urban economic grievances. The rhetorics of 'race', too, had an increasing salience whether in English stereotypes or Irish assertions: though as discussed below their precise modality in Anglo-Irish relations remains contested. Perhaps above all, the political language of nationality itself, gaining strength everywhere in Europe and eventually beyond, sustained a growing perception of Ireland as unjustly subordinated to Britain—even though this was not yet ordinarily expressed in terms of colonialism and anticolonialism. It could not be: that language did not yet exist.

Some British statesmen had always wanted a more conciliatory and integrative strategy towards Ireland than was actually pursued. Pitt, for instance, initially hoped to combine the Act of Union with Catholic emancipation; but was unable to carry either the Crown or the Lords with him. It is tempting to speculate what might have been the course of Irish history, either if London had refused to concede self-government in 1782—thus perhaps provoking a fullscale independence movement on the American model; or if it *had* conceded full Catholic rights two decades later—opening the possibility of Ireland being integrated into the British state perhaps as fully as Wales and Scotland had been.

As it was, the state which emerged under the Union was a curiously hybrid one. In formal political terms the administrative machinery of Dublin Castle, with the institution of the Lord Lieutenancy which was a fairly evident direct successor of the Viceroyalty, remained as the most clearly colonial feature of the Irish landscape. There was still a separate Irish legal system, though in many respects it was more formally distinct from the British than it was substantively different. The police force, armed and under central rather than local control, was also markedly different from those of Britain. Otherwise the institutions of government and law in Ireland were—at least after Catholics were admitted to Parliament in 1829—in many ways less distinct from the English than were those of Scotland or even the Isle of Man. If this was colonialism then, on the strictly political level, it was firmly *internal* colonialism (cf. Hechter 1975). It remains, however, possible to argue that even if Ireland's juridical status, cultural complexion and so on were not colonial ones during the nineteenth century, nonetheless important aspects of British policy-making treated it as part of the external imperial system: this contention is explored further in chapter 5 below.

Economically, what followed the Union was not integration but, in important respects, increasing divergence. Broadly and crudely, parts of the north-east—especially Belfast—shared fully in British industrial development whilst the remainder of Ireland remained overwhelmingly agrarian, with low growth rates and a heavy dependence on exporting agricultural goods, especially live-stock, to Britain. This agrarian economy was itself sharply divided, between areas where a relatively prosperous capitalist farming economy flowered (much of the east, northeast and midlands), and those where an impoverished small-tenant economy was overwhelmingly and in the event disastrously reliant on a single crop, the potato. The latter, in the west and southwest, were also the regions where Gaelic and other aspects of pre-conquest culture remained strongest, and where the social divisions between the peasantry and an Angli-can, often absentee landowning elite were sharpest. Contemporaries, and each generation of subsequent historians, argued fiercely about which, if any, of the Irish economy's misfortunes should be attributed to the Union itself.[36]

This picture, and consequently the political map also, were dramatically shaken up by the Famine of 1846–51. As a direct or indirect result, in the region of a million died and up to three million emigrated. There remains much dis-pute over the figures, and over the degree of responsibility which British policy should bear for the disaster.[37] There is little argument, however, about certain of the effects, apart from the human cost and suffering: that the Famine and emi-gration quickened the pace and sharpened the temper of Irish nationalist asser-tion, including the soon to be important sympathy movements in the USA and other emigrant destinations; and that they immensely hastened the decline of Gaelic rural culture by depopulating the very regions where it remained strongest.[38]

The Famine, and especially British responses to it, continue to be controver-sial and emotionally charged issues. Conservative British commentators still express outrage at tendencies to describe it as an act of genocide by Britain, or as comparable to the Nazi Holocaust. And they in their turn still bend the stick wildly the other way, to produce a picture of British virtue that is just as dis-torted: the sesquicentennial produced an outpouring in London newspapers of surprisingly emotive defences of the 1840s British government record (e.g. Wyatt 1995). In fact no serious Irish historian has ever proposed a 'genocidal' interpretation (among recent works, Liz Curtis 1994:56–9 perhaps comes clos-est to it); though it has recurred in the rhetoric of some politicians (e.g. Living-stone 1989:144), of Irish-American commentators and organisations (see several of the contributions to Hayden ed. 1997, and the caustic commentary in Toibin 1998), and in at least one major comparative historical study. Theodore Allen, polemically comparing British rule in Ireland with North American racial slavery, and citing sources which do not in fact support his claim, still refers to 'the deliberateness of England's genocidal policy' (Allen 1994:277 n. 90)[39]. In reality British government reactions to the famine were certainly not motivated by some genocidal impulse, but were at best insensitive, inefficient and ineffective. Ministers and officials were ill-informed, slow and inconsistent in their reactions, riven by internal schisms and hobbled by dogma: free market dogma which insisted that state intervention must be counterproductive, providentialist religious dogma which saw famine as punishment for sins, and cultural-cum-racial dogma which blamed the supposedly idle and feckless Irish peasantry for their own ills. Emergency relief and public works schemes were frequently a shambles, and food often did not reach those most in need. Many died, quite simply, because of bureaucracy.

The experience of famine was regionally very uneven, striking hardest in the west and southwest. Conversely, it seems clear that excess mortality and emigration rates in 1845–9 were lower in the northeast than elsewhere: though the suffering and the deathtoll were great in Ulster too. Between the censuses of 1841 and 1851, Ulster's (the nine counties') recorded population fell by 374,493 (Vaughan and Fitzpatrick eds 1973:15). Nonetheless, regional differentiation was evidently reinforced by the experience of the 1840s—and, still more, regionally varying intensities of collective memory about the Famine soon crystallised, with Ulster Protestant historical narratives effectively 'forgetting' the events. This was to have important later political effects.

Socially there was substantial change as the nineteenth century proceeded. Catholic educational and income levels rose steadily. But this was mostly a matter of increased entry into the ranks of the *lower* middle class, with further progress very much the exception. Big business, large-scale landowning, the top professions, and above all the senior reaches of the bureaucracy itself, remained mostly Protestant. And, in a pattern replicated across much of Europe as later through colonial Asia and Africa, the growth of educational opportunity and partial social mobility fostered rather than deflected the growth of political nationalism. Those British statesmen who, misled by the intensity of agrarian grievances and conflicts, believed that solutions to these would 'kill Home Rule', were rapidly disabused.[40] The conjunction, temporary though it was to prove, of Home Rule agitation and agrarian unrest in the era of the 'Land War', 1879–82, helped cement a more lasting association, between nationalism and Catholicism. And in Ulster, Protestant fears at Catholic advance—however limited this might still be—fuelled an increasing militancy of sectional organisation. As Paul Bew comments, 'Unionists had succeeded—and they were helped in this by injudicious nationalist tactics—in stigmatising the programme of the land movement, which had substantial initial appeal for the Protestant tenantry of north-east Ulster, as merely the cover for nefarious separatist objectives' (1987:3) and helped produce the characteristic pattern of recurring urban riot and accompanying evictions of 'the wrong sort' from mixed residential districts. Such outbreaks took place in 1857, 1864 and 1872, and as later were concentrated in West Belfast; though other locations such as Lurgan and Portadown also earned a reputation for particularly sharp sectarian antagonisms, which they have never since lost.[41]

The emergence, or rather recasting, of discourses of Irishness during the nineteenth century was evidently shaped by several other developments. These included not only the Irish nationalist challenge itself, but the rise of pseudo-scientific racism, the 'new imperialist' ideologies of the century's last three decades, the ideas about Hebraism, Hellenism and Celticism most famously articulated by Matthew Arnold, and the elaboration of a mythos of Anglo-Saxonism in English history (MacDougall 1982, Simmons 1990, Melman 1991). Within this complex, a particularly important part was played by both British and Irish ambivalences about the relationship of Irishness to Britishness; to the status of the Irish as 'marginal Britons' (Boyce 1986). It is arguable that a concerted attempt to create a British national identity was a product specifically of the late nineteenth century, and was a response to the relative decline, especially in trade, manufacture and technology, which London politicians were then beginning to apprehend. A full account of this reformation of Britishness would require systematic attention to the parallels and interrelations between Irish, Welsh and Scottish political developments: a task well beyond the scope of the present study.[42] We may, however, note that Ireland's relationship to this identity-formation was problematic and contestatory from the start. British statesman such as Lord Salisbury and ideologues like A. V. Dicey proclaimed the formation of the United Kingdom to have been not only a beneficent and progressive, but in some sense both a necessary and a natural process, whose calling into question would undermine every aspect of Britain's power and prosperity. But they were doing so in a context where an already vigorous Irish nationalism, increasingly fuelled by Gaelicist cultural appeals, was repudiating any idea that 'Britishness' extended to Ireland.

Undoubtedly, and inevitably, all strands of Irish nationalism worked with and through, even as they reacted against, English and British ideas, traditions, beliefs, and discourses. Donald Jordan's compelling study of the 1880s Irish National League suggests, for instance, how there developed 'a dynamic and tense interplay... between traditional and more modern conceptions of justice, as well as between culturally sanctioned beliefs in entitlement to land and the right to subsistence and the notion of property as a commodity' (1998:171). Rural protest drew both on 'moral economy' traditions, and on notions of justice and law which derived directly from English legal norms. Around the same time and higher up the social scale, the Gaelic Revival owed a great deal to the English Arts and Crafts movement (Moffat ed. 1998, Samuel 1998:28–9, 63–4). A little later, as Richard English emphasises (albeit with perhaps too sharp a polemical edge), the dominant influences on such Irish revolutionaries as Ernie O'Malley were overwhelmingly British ones, on every level from thinking about nationhood itself to ideas about military heroism—where John Buchan and, less surprisingly, Shakespeare were crucial touchstones, and England's literary traditions more generally an inescapable, all-pervasive, indeed deeply *loved* ambience (English 1996a, 1997, 1998).

Yet even those who did vigorously proclaim themselves simultaneously Irish and British, as most Unionists did through the nineteenth century, felt increasing strains in this dual identification. The crux of the issue, in a sense, was whether Britishness could effectively be separated from Englishness, the United Kingdom become a state which adequately recognised its own multinationality. Liberal advocates of Home Rule for Ireland (or of what contemporaries sometimes called 'Home Rule all round', for Wales and Scotland too), and many Irish leaders such as Isaac Butt or later John Redmond—but not apparently Parnell—thought that it could. Revived Irish legislative autonomy might even make it so. 'Was home rule then to be a means, not of fulfilling a distinct Irish destiny, but of strengthening a wider sense of Britishness, making Ireland at last a contented province of Britain?' (Boyce 1986:236)

The answer, of course, was 'No', even if John Redmond and the Irish Parliamentary Party wrestled with those contradictions in a more thoroughgoing, sophisticated and independent-minded way than later nationalist historiography ever gave them credit for doing. The view has gained ground in more recent historical reassessment that by 1914 they had within their grasp at least as much as was to be achieved, after so much bloodshed, in 1921. Certainly they had mapped out the achievable far more clearly than had the architects of the 1916 Rising, or those who inspired the losing side in the Civil War. Given the strength and relative cohesion which Ulster Unionism had already amassed— far more, so recent historiography suggests, than earlier views of it as merely a makeshift, late substitute for all-Ireland Unionism implied—more could simply not be had.[43] Moreover, their Sinn Fein rivals had, as Paul Bew comments, forgotten the emphasis on conciliation which had so crucially formed one side of Parnell's complex political character (Bew 1987:217–22). As Bew has also shown, Redmondites and Unionists, even in 1912–16, sustained a genuine, serious, sincere debate with one another: their successors too often degenerated into mere name-calling (Bew 1994). Bew urges too the renewed contemporary relevance of Redmondism: 'Ever since Lemass started to unpick the elements of economic nationalism in the 1950s we have moved back into the world of Redmond . . . with Brussels to some degree playing the role Redmond envisaged for London' (Bew 1994:158).

The development of these contending identities and assertions, and the long history of their attempted resolution by the various actors and by all means from land reform and devolved government to revolution, are far beyond our present remit. It is enough for the moment to mark that the bulk of the island gained legislative independence, though not as yet full formal sovereignty, in 1921–2. This was accompanied by Partition, and by civil war in the newly self-governing South—which soon thereafter, however, settled into peaceable constitutional politics accompanied, less happily, by what many came to view as economic stagnation and cultural parochialism. Six Ulster counties, also after a spate of localised violence, remained within the United Kingdom under a devolved legislative authority which instituted a *de facto* one-party Unionist state. Debates over colonialism and its legacies immediately took on new forms; ones which differed sharply between the two parts of the island. Before examining these, we must turn to look at the political languages of emergent nationalism itself, and at the use it made of ideas about colonialism and decolonisation.

4

Irish Nationalists and the Colonial Image

(i) Nationalists, Race and Empire: 'The Purest Breed of Men'

John Hutchinson has recently and forcefully argued that Irish historians, whether 'nationalist' or 'revisionist', have entirely failed to understand Irish nationalism. This is because of their insularity: 'Whether they are aware of it or not, most Irish historians are methodological nationalists since they tend to take for granted the nation as the proper unit of analysis. Revisionism as a tendency can be seen in various ways as an attempt to broaden the definition of the nation, to qualify its pervasive appeal by reference to other factors or to liberalise the practices of the nation-state. But nationalism is a global phenomenon and cannot be explained in any one country by local peculiarities.' (Hutchinson 1996:101)

Despite this salutary and accurate complaint, contemporary scholarship has massively enhanced, complicated and disaggregated our view of the nationalist tradition. We can now see it as extending less far back in time (e.g. S. Ellis 1986), more strongly imbued with religious currents and of often limited popular appeal without these (P. O'Farrell 1971), more localised (Rumpf and Hepburn 1977, Hoppen 1984, 1989), more class-specific in its aims and patterns of support (Bew 1978, 1987, Garvin 1987), more heavily shaped by English and by continental European influences (O'Day 1994, Hutchinson 1987 respectively) than previously believed, and so on. What such scholarship has not on the whole done is expand our knowledge of Irish nationalism as anticolonialism. This is for a very simple reason: across most of the history of nationalist thought there was no such thing, and the search for it (a search in which, as we shall see, many historians and even more literary theorists have engaged) is largely an anachronism.

Anyone seeking to sketch a history of Irish anti-imperialist discourse soon finds it to be, until one reaches the very recent past, a surprisingly thin subject. Over the longer historical period the material is scanty in quantity; most Irish nationalists before the 1960s did not use the colonialism/anticolonialism model in describing their situation. In the past three decades or so this model became far more extensively marshalled, being the common discourse of the Republican movement, its intellectual sympathisers and of much of the international left's views of Ireland, as well as of many contemporary cultural nationalists. Yet in this mass of recent writing, quantity is frankly not matched by quality. On the whole, the argument equating the Republican struggle with an anticolonialist 'national liberation movement' has been in the form of rather superficial sloganising, with little serious attempt to trace the relationships between the Irish situation and either anticolonial movements elsewhere or global theories of imperialism.

Even the most intellectually sophisticated pro-Republican writers took few steps beyond this superficial polemicising. In a broader nationalist intellectual milieu, arguments of greater rigour and originality have been proposed, from figures such as Raymond Crotty, Desmond Fennell, and D. R. O'Connor Lysaght, and more recently from literary analysts of 'colonial discourse'. Such writing, shifting from a position where the underlying assumptions about imperialism—so far as they were clearly articulated—were based on an economic and usually Leninist model, to one where culture, 'race' and nationalism are the primary referents, has opened up the space in which the colonial model can be employed from a rather wider range of political positions, and in more subtle ways, than the older economic versions had been. Yet these newer arguments too, as will be shown, have had some serious intellectual flaws.

Early Irish nationalists hardly ever identified their situation or cause with that of other, non-European subject peoples in the British Empire or beyond. John Mitchel had angrily rejected any suggestion of analogy between the Irish plight and that of slaves in the Americas, and was himself a keen supporter of slavery, even fantasising about a future independent Ireland possessing her own slave plantations (McVeigh 1992:38). The racist basis of Mitchel's case for Irish rights has become notorious. Lamenting the tragedy of the Famine, he appealed: 'Can you picture in your mind a race of white men reduced to this condition? White men! Yes the highest and purest blood and breed of men.' ('The Last Conquest of Ireland (Perhaps)' 1861; in Field Day 1991, II:181), Mitchel was a bundle of contradictions: regarded not only by British authorities but by many of his own colleagues as a wild extremist, this Ulster-born Protestant admirer of Carlyle united numerous incompatibles in himself. They included not just a mass of racial prejudices but a capacity to rejoice at the massacre of Paris workers in 1848, and a view of socialists as 'worse than wild beasts'.

But Mitchel, if idiosyncratic, was not unique. Arthur Griffith, founder of Sinn Fein, thought it nonsense to compare Ireland with Britain's non-European subjects, scorning the idea that 'excuse were needed for an Irish nationalist declining to hold the negro his peer in right.' (Quoted McVeigh 38; see also C. C. O'Brien 1974:65). Frank Hugh O'Donnell raged at Yeats's play *The Countess Cathleen* for supposedly disparaging the Irish peasantry by depicting them as 'just like a sordid tribe of black devil-worshippers on the Congo or the Niger.' (quoted R. F. Foster 1997:209) Douglas Hyde, similarly, indignantly insisted that the Irish were *not* to be compared with 'a savage tribe' or 'Red Indians'. Erskine

Childers, in his 1911 *Framework of Home Rule*, argued that 'Ireland is no colony. She has no claim based on colonial rights . . . Her leaders in 1782 repudiated any right or claim on colonial grounds.' (quoted Richard Davis 1974:108)[1]

There was evidently a 'racial' factor in this refusal. The Irish were described as an ancient, cultured European people who could only be demeaned by comparison with non-whites. But there was also a directly political calculation. There was as yet hardly any influential voice within Britain calling for Britain's non-white subjects to be self-governing. Even for the colonies of white settlement the limit of conceivable reform was usually thought to be what, after Canada achieved partial self-government in 1867, began to be called Dominion status. Since so many Irish political figures wanted, if not complete independence, at least something more far-reaching than Dominionhood, their cause would only be weakened by linking it to colonial parallels. Griffith for some time floated the idea of Ireland not freeing itself from the British Empire, but rather becoming a more equal partner in it: a partner, that is, in dominating the non-European peoples (Richard Davis 1974:106–8). This was wholly consistent with his advocacy of an Austro-Hungarian style Dual Monarchy as a model for Anglo-Irish relations. In adopting this source of political inspiration, Griffith was arguably 'blind in his failure to see that the Hungarians were an aristocratic caste whose oppression of the Serbs and Croats in the years before the 1914–18 War was notorious throughout Europe.' (ibid: 108) Overall, as Richard Davis suggests, Mitchel and Griffith, over-reacting to 'the popular 19th-century English and American nativist belief in the Irishman as a white nigger', adopted 'an aristocratic conception of Irish liberty akin to that of the Greek, Roman and American slaveholders.' (ibid: 107, 109)

There is of course another side to the story, with some nationalists adopting more generous internationalist attitudes. Daniel O'Connell was a fierce opponent of slavery, refusing to visit the USA because it was a slaveholding society, and repeatedly raising the issue even at the cost of damaging the American support network for Irish freedom. He also launched some sharp attacks on the brutalities of colonial expansion, especially in Australia and New Zealand— though, like all but a tiny handful of his contemporaries, he cannot be called an opponent of colonialism *tout court*—and became a leading campaigner for Jewish emancipation. (MacDonagh 1989:19–22) O'Connell's stance was linked to a wider current of Irish support for abolitionism; though this was by no means necessarily so broadly shared among Irish-Americans (Theodore Allen 1994 chs 7 and 8). Even Mitchel's support for the Confederacy in the American Civil War may have owed more to a misplaced analogy between the South's cause and that of Ireland than to specifically racist motives. And it was not shared by all his co-thinkers: Fenians, like other Irish-Americans, fought on both sides in the Civil War, for very mixed motives. Young Ireland leader Thomas Francis Meagher raised an Irish Brigade for the Union side, which was shattered (by the guns of the also mostly Irish Confederate Louisiana regiments) at Fredericksburg. As a further indication of the complexities of nineteenth-century Irish-American politics, it might be noted that both a remarkable proportion of the Union's leading generals, and on the other side all the founders of the Ku Klux Klan, were of Ulster Protestant—or as it was then called in the USA, 'Scotch-Irish'—descent. (Wade 1987:31–5[2])

Parnell on several occasions condemned British imperialism in general terms, as for instance in proclaiming in 1877, during the debate on South African confederation, that 'History showed that England always neglected the interests of her colonies. She annexed Fiji for example, then introduced the measles, and then taxed the people to pay the expense of the annexation.' (quoted Kee 1993:145) Yet the context of this intervention was argument over the rights of white settlers in South Africa, rather than of the native population; and Parnell and other Irish members were using the dispute mostly if not entirely to draw comparisons with and attention to *Ireland's* grievances (ibid: 145–50) By contrast a few years later, in the 1881 Anglo-Boer conflict, Parnell's colleague (and third point in one of history's most famous love triangles) Willie O'Shea, far from condemning Britain's war against the Dutch settlers, was complaining at inefficiency in its prosecution (ibid: 348, 358); whilst in the 1885 Sudan crisis the Parnellites voted with the Tories (Liz Curtis 1994:123–4). Later Michael Davitt, with such largely forgotten figures as Irish Socialist Party founder Frederick Ryan, espoused sympathy for a range of international causes from that of Egyptian independence to the plight of Jews in Czarist Russia. (Feeley and O'Riordan 1984) Yet even Davitt, in his commentary on the Boer War, confined his solidarity to the Afrikaners, viewing the native majority as 'savages'. In his book *The Boer Fight for Freedom* (Davitt 1902, and see Moody 1981), which was undoubtedly the most substantial Irish nationalist consideration of the conflict and was based partly on an extended stay in southern Africa and on close contacts with Boer leaders, he regarded any claim that the Afrikaners oppressed indigenous peoples as hypocritical and irrelevant, gave no indication that he thought the latter had any rights at all—and was predisposed credulously to swallow any and every story of British atrocities.

Indeed in relation to colonial questions in the British House of Commons, Bernard Porter is probably not wrong to complain that 'The Nationalists rarely looked further than their Irish noses; they saw everything from the point of view of the Anglo-Irish dispute.' (1968:312) He even suggests that some Irish Nationalist MPs felt that British agitation against the brutalities of King Leopold's rule in the Congo stemmed merely from Protestant dislike of a Catholic monarch—and notes that the only English MP thus uncompromisingly to back Leopold's tyranny was the reactionary, anti-Semitic Catholic Hillaire Belloc. (ibid: 300)

Yet this too is a tale with two sides. Parnell expressed sympathy with the Zulu cause in the 1879 war, though again (as Porter's comment implies) from a somewhat Hibernocentric perspective, complaining that 'At least half the regiments now at the Cape are composed of young men from Connemara . . . sent to Zululand to become the holocaust of that imperialism which has lately become so much the fashion.' (quoted Kee 1993:186) The 'holocaust' which concerned him was apparently the deaths of Irish soldiers rather than of Zulus (though he also protested at the latter in the Commons a little later (ibid: 190)); the 'imperialism' he decried was—in accordance with most contemporary usage—an expansionist *attitude* rather than the structure of colonial power itself. Some Irish nationalists expressed strong sympathy for Maori resistance to colonisation in New Zealand (Richard Davis 1980). One of the two greatest campaigners against the Congo 'Red Rubber' horrors was the Irishman Roger Casement—later to pay with his life for his espousal of Irish independence. (The other was the Belgian-descended E. D. Morel.) Casement emphasised time and again that it was his Irishness that drove him to combat colonial oppression in central Africa. Congolese exploitation was, he wrote to one correspondent 'a tyranny beyond conception save only, perhaps, to an Irish mind alive to the horrors once daily enacted in this land.' To another he said 'it was only because I was an Irishman that I could understand *fully*, I think, the whole scheme of wrongdoing at work in the Congo.' (Casement's letters to Alice Stopford Green and William Cadbury, quoted Bernard Porter 267). On a popular level, though we as yet know very little about mass attitudes to colonial questions in Ireland or in Britain, there seems to have been a somewhat indiscriminate Irish nationalist willingness to applaud anyone or anything that was seen as standing against the British. Thus, for instance, at a mass meeting at Westport, County Mayo in 1879 which Parnell addressed, cheers were apparently called with equal enthusiasm for the Zulus, for the French Revolution, and for the Archbishop of Tuam (Kee 1993:188). Although the subject still awaits detailed research, it would appear that nineteenth-century Irish nationalists and Home Rulers were no 'worse', if perhaps also no better, in their racial and colonial attitudes than their contemporaries among English Radicals, Chartists and early socialists.

Yet perhaps O'Connell remains a more representative figure than Mitchel or Griffith. Certainly, as Roediger says, 'the Irish were not race-conscious in the sense that Irish-Americans would be . . . the evil "race" that plagued the Irish Catholic imagination was white and British, not Black and African.' (1991:137–8) Despite the Parnellites' incoherent line on colonial questions, in the late nineteenth and early twentieth centuries the Irish Parliamentary Party voted fairly consistently, together with the British Radical-Liberals, for colonial self-government and against schemes of further imperial expansion.

A certain elective affinity between Irish nationalism and the young Indian National Congress became apparent from the 1890s: though one finds considerably more, and more generous, acknowledgements of this affinity from the

Indian side than from the Irish.[3] Griffith, according to the most detailed study of his social thought 'was keenly aware of contemporary Indian nationalism and exchanged information with several Indian patriotic journals.' (Richard Davis 1974:92–3) He on his side, Nehru and Gandhi on theirs, were interested in parallels between their movements: though Nehru was more inclined to stress similarities, Gandhi differences. Davis suggests that Griffith's writings were 'apparently' translated into a number of Indian languages (ibid: 93), and Brasted (1985:32–3) cites some examples of this, though fewer than Davis's claims imply. Writings by Frank Hugh O'Donnell, too, were published in Indian nationalist periodicals (Brasted 1980:50–3). Later the Indian Communist (and for a time British MP) Shapurji Saklatvala, seeking to convince Gandhi of the need for a more militant anticolonial approach, pointed to the Irish struggle as a model to be followed (Communist Party of Great Britain 1927). Overall, though, it would seem that the non-violent strategies of Parnell or Griffith had far greater impact in India than did insurrectionary ideas: the Bengal 'terrorist' movement and its analogues drew on quite different, more indigenous inspirations than that of Sinn Fein. So far as more mainstream Indian nationalists were concerned, T. G. Fraser's judgement is that they 'looked to Ireland as an example of opposition to imperial control and were grateful for expressions of Irish interest and support', but neither expected nor received much practical aid from that source, while some of them were perturbed by the 'extremism' of Irish nationalist politics (1996:92).

One must certainly view with scepticism, then, the frequently expressed claim by Irish nationalists and Republicans that—as Sinn Fein's Gerry Adams put it—'The Irish nationalist movement had played a leading role in the international development of the struggle to overthrow colonialism . . . In India and Africa, the Irish revolutionary tradition had been one of the strongest influences in the anti-colonial movements.' (Adams 1996:280–1) The most extreme expressions of such a supposed Irish place as role-model for anticolonial movements worldwide, indeed, ventured into the self-aggrandisingly fantastic. Thus it was claimed in West Cork that the locally important but comparatively tiny armed clash at Kilmichael in 1920 'jerked the people of India to a new appraisal of their position. Egypt stood amazed. It ultimately pervaded darkest Africa . . . Most impressive of all, it has been reported that when the Japanese army captured Singapore, they marched in singing "The Boys of Kilmichael".' (Hart 1998:22) Such influences were in reality fitful and tenuous. There were even, it may be noted, intellectuals from other oppressed or colonised peoples who regarded the lessons to be learned from Irish experience as almost entirely negative ones. Thus the pioneer Afro-American thinker Alexander Crummell took Irish nationalism as a dreadful warning to black America, a demonstration of the fatal results of dwelling obsessively on one's disadvantaged state.

For a century and more they have been indulging in the expensive luxury of sedition and revolution . . . The mind of the whole nation has been dwarfed and shrivelled by morbid concentration upon an intense and frenzied sense of political wrong, and an equally intense and frenzied purpose of retaliation. And commerce, industry, and manufacturing, letters and culture, have died away from them. (1891:16–17)[4]

Among the Irish, recognition of any such affinities, positive or negative, was the exception rather than the rule. Irish influence on Indian nationalism may have been significant, but the converse was not the case.[5] Such manifestations of Irish-Indian pan-nationalist solidarity as historians have noted seem to have been mainly for US consumption (e.g. Liz Curtis 1994:314–16). The aspiration of members of the British Indian Association, to persuade Irish Home Rulers to sponsor Indian candidates for some Irish seats, came to nothing (Brasted 1985:38, n. 35). Contemporary historians' attempts to trace interconnections through the careers of individuals often seem tenuous in the extreme. Such is Catherine Candy's jargon-ridden sketch of the 'richly intercolonial experience' of Irish-born Theosophist and suffragist Margaret Cousins. Her experience, according to Candy (1994:590), 'suggests the efficiency of the automation [sic?] of nationalist, imperialist and feminist epistemological systems'—a claim which founders on the failure to demonstrate that Cousins was at all involved in nationalist politics in either Ireland *or* India!

(ii) Shifting Stereotypes

The wider relationship between discourses of 'race' and those of colonialism and imperialism has been a complex, contested one in the Irish as in other contexts. A substantial body of writing has argued that British colonial discourse stereotyped and maligned the Irish in ways directly analogous to those employed against Africans or Indians—and indeed still does so.[6] Hostile images and stereotypes of Irishness, as carried for instance by important sections of the British press in the first half of the nineteenth century, have been suggested to have had an important impact on policy, notably during the 1840s Famine (e.g. Peter Gray 1993, de Nie 1998, and in more sweeping terms Scally 1995).[7] Theodore Allen's comparative study goes further, arguing for very close structural parallels between 'racial oppression' in Ireland and in New World slave societies. In doing so, though, he is mainly reliant on dated and highly partisan sources; his footnotes include a mass of nineteenth-century nationalist historical polemics, and very little contemporary Irish historical research. (Allen 1994) He swallows whole, for instance, romantic Catholic nationalist myths about the nature of early Irish society, about the viciousness and effectiveness of the Penal Laws, and so on, while his view of Ulster history and the background to Partition is solidly Connollyite.

'Revisionist' historiography, meanwhile, has sharply disputed this racialised view of British-Irish relations, with Sheridan Gilley (1978) in particular arguing that 'racism' is not an applicable label for English attitudes to the Irish. In Gilley's view English views of the Irish involved primarily *cultural* rather than 'racial' stereotypes, by no means all of them negative, and assumptions of a fixed biological difference and hierarchy between 'Anglo-Saxon' and 'Celt' were rare. Gilley's argument does, though, seem to rest in part on a rather disconcerting assumption that English prejudices against blacks were somehow more natural than those against the Irish, for the former rested on more 'real' racial differences. Roy Foster, drawing on Gilley's work, has been aggressively scornful of 'half-baked "sociologists" employed on profitably never-ending research into "anti-Irish racism", determined to prove what they have already decided to be the case' (in Field Day 1991, III:584). And Sean Connolly suggests that the emphasis on continuity of English attitudes identified by Lewis and Liz Curtis is misleading, for during the eighteenth century 'The wild Irishman rampaging at the frontiers of English settlement gave way in English folklore to the comic provincial.' (Connolly 1992:113)[8]

Here the debate intersects not only with wider arguments about the role of 'race' in colonial discourse, but with those over the history of 'race' relations in Britain, the USA and elsewhere. Several historians have explored the triangle of Irish–Black–WASP interaction in the United Kingdom and, in more detail, in the USA. They have uncovered patterns of Irish disadvantage and negative stereotyping somewhat analogous with those suffered by blacks; including a standard trope in anti-Irish rhetoric which was precisely to compare the Irish with Africans.[9] Yet they have also traced ways in which Irish-Americans participated in hostility to and subordination of African-Americans—driven both by job competition and a wider ideological climate to insist desperately on their own whiteness and the rights this gave them.[10] Within Ireland itself, there has indubitably been a racist strain in the political culture, including antisemitism (most notoriously manifested in the 1904 Limerick riots which are sometimes, if hyperbolically, described as a 'pogrom'), and latterly a considerable currency for prejudice against travellers or gypsies.[11] And some have wished to insist that there was always a qualitative difference between the kinds of prejudice directed at Africans and that experienced by the Irish. Thus African-American historian Thomas Holt argued of one of the most persistently-cited 'anti-Irish racists', Thomas Carlyle, that:

His public and private correspondence show consistent denigration of blacks, whereas some of his best friends were Irish. Blacks were his emblem of degradation, of the level to which whites could sink. (Holt 1992:282)

Furthermore, patterns of anti-Irish prejudice, as of migrants' adaptation, assimilation and social mobility, varied greatly between the different destinations of Irish emigration. Whilst there is still relatively little fully comparative work in this field (for surveys see Akenson 1996, Belchem 1992, O'Day 1996, van Duin 1994), the general impression seems to be that upward mobility and social acceptance came more readily in America and Australia than in Britain, using the networks of city 'machine' government in the former, trade unions and Australian Labor Party in the latter, strong emphasis on education in both.[12] In Britain, the available evidence—patchy as it is—suggests a stronger persistence of disadvantage, with Irish migrants and their children suffering disproportionately high levels of unemployment, mental illness and concentration in unskilled and insecure work—and quite startlingly, life expectancies well below the UK average.

However, evidence on anti-Irish discrimination and prejudice in Britain remains highly ambiguous. In the later 1990s a major research project on this theme was sponsored by the Commission for Racial Equality (Commission for Racial Equality 1997). The findings were contradictory: noting some significant indices of Irish disadvantage in Britain, and also finding (though unable in any significant way to quantify) manifestations of prejudice, it failed to explain the links, if any, between these phenomena or to explore their relationship with the simultaneously observable trends of substantial integration and upward mobility. The very notion of anti-Irish racism aroused resistance or even ridicule in some quarters: sections of the tabloid Press subjected the CRE project to vehement scorn. And it must be added that the two senior members of this project operated with a notably simplistic understanding of the prior literature on Irish history and race relations, and of such concepts as 'assimilation'. (Hickman and Walter 1995, Walter 1986) They appeared simply to assume, rather than argue for, the relevance of the idea of 'colonial racism' to Irish experience in Britain (Hickman and Walter 1995:9), and that the operations of the Prevention of Terrorism Act have necessarily been racist (ibid: 11; see also Hillyard 1993). They also seemed, like so many writers about the Irish diaspora worldwide, to equate 'Irish' with 'Catholic', whereas all the available evidence suggests that Irish Protestants migrated to Britain, Australia, New Zealand and elsewhere in proportions equivalent to their numbers within the Irish population as a whole. In North America, meanwhile, a *majority* of those who identify themselves as of Irish descent are Protestant.[13] Insofar as clear differences in patterns of social mobility and success did emerge between the different destinations of Irish migration, 'racial' prejudice may well not have been the major factor: it would be hard to argue, for instance, that the nineteenth-century USA was a less racist society, or one where anti-Catholic animus was less strong, than Britain.

It should be recognised too that there may not be such compelling reasons as most of this contemporary writing seems to assume, to believe that the emergence of racial discourses—anti-Irish or any other—was intimately or necessarily linked to colonialism. Perhaps evidently enough, one could have racism without colonialism, as a great deal of European history (above all the history of anti-semitism) demonstrates.[14] Conversely, one could—if perhaps more unusually—have colonialism without racism. And even if the two coexisted, as apparently they did in much of the record of Anglo-Irish relations, it may be over-hasty to presume some intimate or strongly causal relation between them. In particular, we should not automatically assume a causal link between cultural stereotyping and politico-economic domination. As Terry Eagleton, perhaps surprisingly in this context, asserts:

If women are oppressed as women, are the Irish oppressed as Irish? In one sense, surely not: it was never of much interest to British imperialism whether the Irish were Irish or Eskimo, white or black, whether they worshipped tree gods or the Trinity. It was not their ethnic peculiarity but their territory and labour-power which have entranced the British. (1988:10)

Eagleton thereafter immediately half-disowns his own claim by describing this scepticism about the relationship of colonialism to culturalist racism as 'In another sense . . . abstract cavilling' (ibid.), but the injunction is nonetheless telling for his own ambivalence about it. Undoubtedly there was a distinct strain of English writing and imagery which caricatured, scorned or dismissed supposed Irish characteristics. Some of this was explicitly racial in form, and a small part did indeed directly transfer the same denigrating images from black to Irish. For instance the 'Irish Frankenstein', taking over the figures of Mary Shelley's monster and his creator which had already been extensively used in anti-African caricature, became a widely deployed idea in mid-Victorian periodicals: most notoriously in *Punch*. It was brought forward in reaction to O'Connell's agitation in the 1840s, to the Fenians in the 1860s, and the Phoenix Park murders in 1882 (Malchow 1993:124–5). Such stereotyping of a supposedly innate and atavistic Irish propensity to political violence inevitably revived in every period of Irish conflict or bloodshed, and has thus received a new lease of life since 1969. To some extent this may have replaced earlier, more religiously based forms of hostility, which one scholar has argued always formed the sharpest focus of anti-Irish bigotry. (J. A. Jackson 1963:154) Still more routine was hostility based around images of drunkenness, fecklessness, unintelligence, unfair labour market competition, and criminal or motiveless rather than politically directed violence (cf. J. A. Jackson 1963 and Colin Holmes 1988 *passim*). This last, too, has found contemporary resonances, including its use as a pseudo-explanation for political unrest, even in reputable academic writing—as the following passage from A. T. Q. Stewart's acclaimed *The Narrow Ground* may indicate:

Violence would appear to be endemic in Irish society, and this has been so as far back as history is recorded . . . What has always been noted about the Irish is their capacity for very reckless violence, allied to a distorted moral sense which magnifies small sins and yet regards murder as trivial. Their kindness and hospitality are legendary, but so too is their reputation for hypocrisy and cruelty. (Stewart 1977:113)

'Legendary' is, perhaps, truly the operative word: it is somewhat unclear how far Stewart himself endorses the stereotypes he describes.[15]

An increasing body of feminist-inflected scholarship has further emphasised how the discourses of 'race' and colonialism were imbricated, in Irish as in other contexts, with those of gender. In particular, it is emphasised how British writers and administrators came to view the land and/or the people of Ireland as feminine, with the implications of something passive, to be possessed and even violated.[16]

Where it is not so much colonial *populations* as colonised *land* which is identified as having been feminised in imperialist perceptions, much of this writing has failed to note the rather basic fact that there may be little or nothing specifically colonial about the identification. It rested on, and may not in its colonial applications significantly have transformed, a prior discursive conceit which identified land (especially agricultural land) as such with the feminine (see e.g. Patricia Parker 1987). Unless specifically colonial or racial reformulations of this ancient and transcultural identification are specified, there is little if any analytical force in such vague claims as that of Daphne G. Watson that 'England's past and present relationship with Ireland has been consistent with a subconscious defining of Ireland as a feminine "Other" subject to an imperious male.' (Watson 1991:40).

For Ireland, this whole structure of identification has been perhaps most famously evoked by a male poet, Seamus Heaney, in his 'Act of Union':

> . . . I grow older
> Conceding your half-independent shore
> Within whose borders now my legacy
> Culminates inexorably.
> And I am still imperially
> Male, leaving you with the pain,
> The rending process in the colony,
> The battering ram, the boom burst from within.
>
> (Heaney 1975:49)

Conversely, the Irish nationalist discourse that emerged from the early 1840s onward habitually imagined Ireland as a woman.[17] Arguably these equations have fed, more or less surreptitiously, into more recent writing from ostensibly feminist perspectives which has in practice subsumed its feminism almost entirely within an uncritical obeisance before nationalist or Republican shibboleths (see below pp. 188–91).

Across the Victorian era, not only British but also Irish nationalist thought— almost inescapably in that time—used the language of race. Contrary to what is

suggested by modern commentators like Luke Gibbons (on whose sometimes anachronistic notions about the nineteenth-century legacy see below,
pp. 63, 126–7) it did so when it was repudiating, just as when it was affirming, a
narrowly Celticist vision; as the words of Young Ireland leader Thomas Davis
indicate. Irish nationalism, said Davis:

must contain and represent all the races of Ireland. It must not be Celtic; it must not be
Saxon; it must be Irish. The Brehon law, and the maxims of Westminster, the cloudy and
lightning genius of the Gael, the placid strength of the Sacsenach, the marshalling
insight of the Norman . . . these are the components of such a nationality. (Quoted in
Cronin 1980:67)

Thus even one of the most inclusive, generous versions of the nationalist ethos
deployed unquestioningly the stereotypes of 'racial' characteristics. Such attitudes shaded later, in one of their several lineages, into the 1930s racial agitation
of Eoin O'Duffy and his Blueshirts, the pro-fascism of such diverse if mostly
marginal figures as Oliver St John Gogarty, J. J. O'Kelly, 1940s TD Oliver Flanagan and Limerick IRA leader Sean South, and the clerical antisemitism which,
as Jim Kemmy's 1970s Limerick battles over it showed, remained a live issue
until very recently. None of these were dominant currents in twentieth-century
Irish nationalist culture—but nor were ecumenically internationalist, anticolonial or anti-racist discourses. Modern-day Sinn Fein's rhetoric of identification with the ANC, PLO and other 'liberation movements', whatever its
limitations, was a new development rather than the continuation of a long
tradition.

There was a complex contest within Irish nationalist discourse between those
espousing an exclusivist, racially defined sense of Gaelicism and 'Irish Ireland'
and those seeking more generous and inclusive definitions. This debate, which
sometimes—but again, perhaps no more than its equivalents elsewhere at the
time—used the language of biology and pseudo-scientific racism, intertwined
with the dispute between cultural provincialists and universalists, and that over
the place of Catholicism in national consciousness.[18] And although the language of biologistic racism may be discredited, the cultural and religious disputes evidently remain alive and bitterly contested in modern Ireland. This
helps account for the still highly charged atmosphere in which the character of
nineteenth-century nationalism is discussed; as also does the fact that whereas
attitudes to Africans and Asians were peripheral to these debates, stances
towards Irish Protestants were and still are central. Thus critical reappraisals of
early nationalists' racial, cultural and religious attitudes still carry a fiercely controversial political burden—perhaps most self-evidently in the writings of
Conor Cruise O'Brien.[19] We shall return to these themes in more detail when we
examine contemporary cultural debates on colonialism and postcoloniality in
Ireland.

(iii) **Global Irishness: Exiles, Empire-builders and Antagonists**

The Irish role in British imperialism has been a subject even less researched than has Irish anti-imperialism.[20] It was of course substantial, with large—perhaps disproportionately large—numbers of Irish settlers, administrators, traders and above all soldiers and missionaries operating throughout the British Empire.[21] The contribution of Anglo-Irish Protestant families to Britain's imperial officer caste was especially great, from Wellington to Montgomery, but Irish Catholic soldiers and officers also served, fought and died in vast numbers wherever the Union flag waved (see Jeffery 1996b).

Almost everywhere in the global reach of British conquest, rule, migration and domination, and throughout the centuries of their expansion and consolidation, the Irish—Catholic and Protestant—were minorities. They found their places, often though certainly not always disadvantaged or marginalised ones, within imperial and colonial systems whose dominant, and usually majority, element was English and whose political, legal, religious and cultural structures were predominantly those of the English Crown and then the British state.[22] There were two intriguing exceptions: Ontario in Canada, where the Irish were by some margin the largest population group until the end of the nineteenth century; and the tiny Caribbean island of Montserrat, which at the end of the twentieth century remains, devastated by a recent volcanic eruption, as one of the few surviving fragments of Britain's Crown Colony system. In the latter, colonisation was a more thoroughly Irish exercise than anywhere else in the New World (or more so than any other successful enterprise: there were failed colonial projects by Irish entrepreneurs on the Amazon and elsewhere), and a substantial majority of the European settler population was and remained Irish—though an overall population majority came to be of enslaved African origin. Donald Harman Akenson (1997) has used these two places as ways into the intriguing question of what distinctive Irish contribution there may have been to the character of new colonial societies—or, as he more strikingly puts it, how different would things have been if the Irish ran the world?

Ontario is, Akenson believes, too large, and Irish cultural influence there too intermingled with that of other groups, to provide a good 'laboratory specimen' for answering such questions. His discussion of it is thus fairly brief and speculative, though he does feel able to suggest that such marked characteristics of Ontario society as intense respect for the law and state, tolerance of dissent and of minorities (supplanting a formerly pervasive religious sectarianism) and 'a strong and consensual sense of public decorum' derive substantially from the Irish legacy. Ontario is in Akenson's view 'a civilized, gentle place, the kind of world that the Irish might have created, the earth around, had they had a bit more power' (1997:5)—not to mention one which, in his description, directly controverts certain abiding negative stereotypes about the Irish. But Montserrat's place as an Irish-dominated enclave within the first British Empire is in Akenson's opinion a far clearer and more manageable test-case: and the conclusions he draws from it are rather less flattering.

It is, Akenson urges, misleading to generalise about 'the Irish' in the colonial diaspora. One must at the least disaggregate the group into the four broad categories recognised by seventeenth-century contemporaries: 'native Irish', 'Old English', 'New English', and 'Ulster-Scots'. One must note religious divisions (from at least the 1640s until the 1840s, Protestants formed a significantly higher proportion of the emigrants from Ireland than they did of the island's population); while also remembering that as Akenson has elsewhere argued at length (1988) the economic, social and cultural differences between Irish Protestants and Catholics were often quite marginal. Perhaps above all, Irish colonial settlers included many wealthy merchants and landowners—some of them slave-traders and slave-owners—as well as impoverished indentured servants. There is simply no reliable evidence, from Montserrat or elsewhere, that the former were any more humane as colonisers or as slavers than those of any other ethnicity; while it is equally ahistorical to see the latter either as existing in a slave-like state (the distinctions between indentured and slave status were real and sharp) or as displaying significant political solidarity or cultural interchange with the slaves (the notion that interaction and intermarriage between Irish indentured labourers and African slaves produced Montserratians' distinctive, and to some ears Irish-tinged, accent is apparently doubtful). This leads to Akenson's most politically charged point:

Thousands of African slaves on Montserrat . . . were during the course of the seventeenth, eighteenth and part of the nineteenth centuries owned by Irish slaveholders, and still others experienced the fierceness of an Irish overseer . . . Oliver Cromwell at his bloodiest did not indulge in the sadistic methods of torture through which we saw errant slaves being put to death for crimes as minor as stealing an item worth a single shilling.

None of this is pleasant to record. But if the self-replicating cycle of abuser-abused-abuser-abused is to be broken, the Irish polity, through the historians who are the keepers of its collective memory, must cease to view the emigrants from Ireland as forever-passive victims, and therefore as persons who were incapable of hard dealing. One of the fundamental stories of the Irish diaspora is of Irish emigrants choosing to do unto others what others had already done unto them. In neither case was that a matter of kind and tender mercies. (1997:174–5)

(iv) Republicans and Empire

The only really major expression of Irish Nationalist enthusiasm for a colonial struggle came with the second Anglo-Boer war in 1899, when much cultural nationalist opinion in particular—like its counterparts in most of continental Europe—passionately backed the Boer republics. An Irish Brigade under John MacBride fought with the Transvaal forces; though its 300 men were mostly Irish-Americans. (Meanwhile, at least 25,000 Irish-born men were fighting on the other side, in the British army.) Nationalist support for the Boers was matched by virtually complete silence about the indigenous majority of Southern Africa. This too has been enduringly controversial, redeployed in current arguments: one may note for instance how, in 1992, Graham Walker responded to Joseph Lee's description of Ulster Unionists as a 'herrenvolk' by recalling 'Irish Nationalist admiration for the Afrikaaners (a real "herrenvolk")' (1992a:66). But once again, Irish nationalist pro-Boerism and blindness to the fate of black South Africa, far from being unique, was the common currency of radical and socialist movements, and of small-nation nationalists, throughout Europe at the time.

   Although pro-Boer agitation was heavily Dublin centred, this was apparently not just a concern of the urban nationalist elite. Micheal O'Suilleabhain, born as the war ended and in 1921 a rank-and-file IRA man in West Cork, recorded that his earliest political memories were of stories about the South African conflict: 'The handful of farmers who stood up against an empire and humiliated it set an example for the oppressed and downtrodden of the world. The example was not lost on the militant-minded in our own country.' (O'Suilleabhain 1965:22) But O'Suilleabhain's lament in his 1960s memoirs for the Irish who died in Britain's other colonial wars surely reflects a purely retrospective political perception; or at most one which was shared by only a small minority in his youth, as well as a shaky sense of South African geography: 'Alas for the poor lads who died in the Tugela valley fighting against the Boers, against Zulus and other weak peoples. If only they had fought for those oppressed peoples.' (ibid: 24) And O'Suilleabhain's suggestion of the ubiquity of pro-Boerism and its centrality to nationalist consciousness is also questionable. A few other Republican veterans mention formative childhood memories of the Boer War, as does Dan Breen's autobiography (1981:8), but they are the exceptions. Tom Barry, slightly older than O'Suilleabhain and leader of West Cork IRA's famous Flying Column, mentions the South African conflict only in passing in *his* memoirs, and as an adult political influence rather than a childhood memory. (Barry 1962:108; see also the diatribe about the 'slaughters and massacres' of Britain's imperialist wars in ibid: 111–12, and its faintly absurd insistence on the military incompetence of all British armies throughout history.) None of the Republican veterans interviewed in Uinseann Mac Eoin's *Survivors*, almost all born in the 1890s, invokes it or any other non-Irish colonial question; not even those of them like Sean MacBride and Peadar O'Donnell who were actively involved in the 'anti-imperialist' politics of the postwar era. (Mac Eoin 1980)

Opposition to the Boer War helped transform nationalist politics, providing a forum in which hitherto rather disparate currents including labour organisation could coalesce: it was, as Roy Foster suggests, 'nearly as crucial an event for Irish nationalism as the death of Parnell.' (1988:448) But it did not lead to the generalisation in nationalist circles of a perception of their own situation as a colonial one, analogous or linked to movements elsewhere in the British Empire. Rather, the parallels to which the emergent leaders of Sinn Fein and the Irish Republican Brotherhood, like their predecessors, looked were overwhelmingly European ones. Davis, with his aspiration to a multi-ethnic nationality, had focused on Switzerland, Belgium and the United States. For Arthur Griffith the model was Hungary (see Field Day 1991, II:354–9 and Richard Davis 1974, esp. 113–19). For Yeats, Ibsen's Norway and Wagner's Germany were classic examples of cultural nationalist revival. Others focused on the nationalisms of Italy and Greece.

A few Republicans did evince a more meaningful engagement with Indian and other colonial questions. This was most evidently the case with the man who was, after James Connolly's death, the seemingly most socially radical figure in the Republican leadership, Liam Mellows. As his highly sympathetic socialist biographer C. Desmond Greaves notes, Mellows had come into close contact with Indian nationalists in the USA and had worked with the 'Friends of Indian Freedom' there (Greaves 1971:205, 208). In the bitter debates over the Anglo-Irish Treaty, Mellows—with Constance Markiewicz—invoked the 'colonial question' as a part of the reason for rejecting an agreement which would leave the Free State as at least formally part of the British Empire. 'We are going into the British Empire now to participate in the Empire's shame, and the crucifixion of India and the degradation of Egypt. Is that what the Irish people fought for freedom for?' asked Mellows in the Dail on 3 January 1922 (Greaves 1971:278). And in his famous 'Jail Notes', written while imprisoned by the Free State government and before his execution by them on 8 December 1922, he not only urged that the Republican movement enter into 'closest touch' with Indian nationalism (ibid: 368) but more generally, and very unusually, pressed that 'imperialism' in general should become a major theme of Republican propaganda:

Imperialism. What the rejection of it by Ireland means. What its acceptance by Ireland means. This should be fully explained. What imperialism is, what Empires are— what the British Empire is—its growth. How it exists and maintains itself. Colonies (Irish Free State as a colony)—India, how oppression and possession of it is essential to the maintenance of B.E. [British Empire]. Money, Trade, Power, etc . . . What Ireland's connection with Imperialism (however much apparent gain) means to her future. No use freeing Ireland to set her up as a State following the footsteps of all the rotten nations of Europe today—what Ireland's rejection of imperialism means etc. (ibid: 365)

There is very little sign, however, that subsequent Republican propagandists even tried to carry out the ambitious programme so hastily sketched by Mellows. As more acerbic commentators than Greaves, like Henry Patterson (1997:24–8) and Richard English (1994a:52–5) suggest, the neo-socialism of which Mellows's anticolonialism was part was neither a coherent political programme, nor one which had much of an influence among his contemporaries. Only well after his death did Mellows's writings come to be seen as pre-eminent among the founding documents of socialist Republicanism.

In the post-Treaty era, some political groupings within the Irish Free State associated themselves, to a degree, with international anticolonialist politics. The main protagonists were the socialist Republicans grouped at various times in such bodies as Saor Eire, the Republican Congress and Cumann Poblachta na h'Eireann, as well as operating within the anti-Treaty IRA and in Dublin's successive small pro-Moscow parties. Even in these circles, though, such international involvement was small-scale and seemingly almost tokenistic. Sean MacBride retrospectively referred almost dismissively to the League Against Imperialism (the Comintern-dominated international lobby formed in Brussels in 1927) as 'one of those high sounding organisations that we felt we had to support in pre-Hitler days.' (Mac Eoin 1980:122: for a general account of the League, see Howe 1993:71–7). The major—if not sole—recorded activity of the League's Irish branch, a mass College Green, Dublin meeting on 10 November 1930, seems to have been an occasion mainly for Anglophobic rhetoric of a decidedly insular kind, rather than expressions of solidarity with Indian or African strugglers against colonialism (English 1994a:113). Its holding on the eve of Armistice Day, on the doorstep of the traditionally Anglophile Trinity College, was obviously no accident.[23] Far from being instances of a consistent internationalist anti-imperialism, such activities were more part of the wildly eclectic if not merely opportunist inter-war Republican attempts to find external allies, a search that took them from Boston to Madrid, from Stalin's Moscow to Hitler's Berlin.[24]

Subsequently some Irish writers, especially in the north, have sought to trace links both of colonialism and anticolonialism between Ireland and the 'wretched of the earth' which are not only forced, but positively plaintive in their appeal to wishful thinking. Thus Bill Rolston, drawing stretched analogies and connections between the conquest of Ireland, Columbus's voyages and later colonial expansions—connections supposed to establish a case for Irish experience as 'the training ground' for all colonialisms everywhere—concludes by urging its case as the original training ground for anticolonialism too (Rolston 1993:17–19). He goes on:

I must say that I find the notion—infrequent as the occurrences might have been—of Irish servants joining with black slaves in joint rebellions an exhilarating one. I would like to believe that the long years of apprenticeship were worth something, that colonialism had bred a sense of justice and a rejection of oppression that was not merely confined to personal experience. I would like to believe that their long experience of oppression had led the Irish to oppose oppression wherever they found it.

I wish the evidence to support those beliefs was more widespread than it is. (ibid: 19)

The open avowal of faith over evidence here is refreshingly honest.[25] Rolston's argument becomes more problematic when he turns to contemporary matters:

There is the real potential that Ireland could become a training ground once more, this time for decolonisation rather than colonisation. Such a process starts with decolonising the mind, rejecting the racism of the coloniser. And it leads to decolonising the structures of this country, of which, I would argue, the most obvious is the running sore of a border created by Partition. (ibid: 23)

The 'training ground' idea has found numerous proponents, if few detailed or elaborated accounts. Kevin Toolis puts it in stark form, as an explicit defence of the morality of the IRA's cause—despite his having earlier narrated a troubled and sceptical account of the latter:

It would be simple here to hedge and qualify the issue of the morality of the IRA's struggle, but I won't. A great historic injustice was perpetrated in Ireland in the seventeenth century—the blueprint for all future campaigns of conquest, dispossession and colonization by the Crown. Ireland was the first English colony and it will be the last. The natives always resisted their subjugation violently, savagely; the land was always troubled. Ireland remains troubled today, not just through the burden of this history but by the failure of the Crown to relinquish its final hold on the provinces of Ireland. (Toolis 1995:369)

Gerry Adams, similarly, proclaims that 'Irish republicans had a natural, instinctive and deep affinity with the oppressed black majority in South Africa and with the ANC.' (1996:281)[26] Such notions are very 1990s ones, extremely distant from the thought of earlier Irish patriots—as well as exhibiting a mildly megalomaniac evaluation of Irish nationalism's global importance. So far as 'imperialism' was invoked at all by Irish nationalists as a general explanatory category beyond Ireland's own shores, it was not as a set of expansionist practices, forms of exploitation or institutions of colonial rule but as an attitude of mind, a popular enthusiasm to be combated among the Irish just as among the British public. In this, too, they were at one with English Radicalism. (See Bernard Porter 1968 and Howe 1993)

Yet despite the absence of an articulated view of British imperialism as global phenomenon, Irish nationalists evidently had a set of strong assumptions about the operations of British overrule in their own case. This differed sharply from the dominant wisdom of the late twentieth century in seeing formal political control as crucial, indeed all-determining. Only retrospectively—long after independence—did Irish nationalists, taking their usually unacknowledged cue from Marxist theories of imperialism, come to point the finger at informal empire, neocolonialism, British economic or cultural hegemony and similar concepts. For that matter, even Partition only came well after the fact to be seen as the crucial limitation on (or in the Republican version, negation of) Irish decolonisation. In the arguments of 1921–2 which issued in civil war, and for years afterwards, it was not the status of the six counties but the issue of formal sovereignty—Dominion, Free State or Republic?—which most divided opinion.

Thus nationalists before 1921 generally believed that for the fate of the Irish economy, what mattered was not British domination in general but the Union itself, Ireland's *political* status, as Robert Mitchell Henry argued:

The trade, commerce and industries of Ireland which had flourished during its brief period of independence [i.e.under Grattan's Parliament] had dwindled since the Union and from causes for which the Union was directly responsible . . . Nothing but the removal of the cause could arrest this spreading decay. (Henry 1920:42–3)

Nationalist economic thought remains relatively underresearched: subsequent scholarship has largely reproduced the movement's own overwhelming emphasis on constitutional, and even more on cultural, questions. Political economy had been a novel and vigorous intellectual enthusiasm in Ireland in the 1820s and 1830s, symbolised by the foundation of a Chair in the subject at Trinity College in 1832 and the proselytising activities of the Dublin Statistical Society. Some saw it as a cure-all: in a divided country 'consensus was sought in the new discipline . . . claiming to be scientifically impartial and to be an incontrovertible form of knowledge which transcended all divisions.' (Boylan and Foley 1992:xii) This popularity, however, soon waned. In particular, the Famine shattered its prestige: 'Irish nationalists were suspicious of an "English" science used to explain away the Famine.' (ibid: 159) And this led to a wider intellectual shift, among both nationalists and Unionists:

Roman Catholicism, Irishness, and engrained familial ideology, all perceived as economically regressive forces, not only resisted the onslaught of political economy but forced the establishment into a moral and sociological critique of its absolutism . . . Contemporary evolutionary views were used to validate the notion that Ireland was insufficiently developed to come under the full rigorous sway of political economy . . . The decline in prestige of political economy was concomitant with the increased emphasis on Ireland's difference from England. Ireland had to be governed by 'Irish ideas'. It was, it transpired, a short step from historical to 'national' economics. (ibid: 160)

Arguments asserting the damaging economic effects of the British connection had a long pedigree; dating at least to William Molyneux's *Case of Ireland Stated* in 1698, and given programmatic form by Henry Grattan's mercantilist assertions in the eighteenth century. But it was the Famine and consequent discrediting of orthodox liberal economics which opened the way to their hegemony. The basic ideas owed much to the German nationalist economic theorist Friedrich List. They were renewed by Isaac Butt and other Victorian Home Rulers, invoked in more elaborated guise by Arthur Griffith and Thomas Kettle, adopted as virtually unquestioned wisdom by Sinn Fein during the independence struggle.[27] Perhaps their most fully articulated form was given in 1918–21 in the trilogy of books by nationalist economic historian George O'Brien.[28] Yet even O'Brien, in his post-1921 role as key adviser to the new Free State Finance Department, was to prove a pillar of orthodoxy—liberal economic, not nationalist, orthodoxy—in his advocacy of an export-oriented strategy, free trade, and fiscal stringency.

This tradition of nationalist critiques of the British economic connection is not in any serious sense intellectually alive in modern Ireland. Insofar as it is referred to it is usually only by way of out-of-context quotations plundered for propagandistic purposes. But then this has been the modern fate of much earlier Irish nationalist writing: to be selectively or misleadingly cited in order to make the authors sound more socially radical, and more anti-imperialist by late-twentieth-century criteria, than they were. Polemicists like Vincent Tucker have, for instance, sought to present such unlikely figures as Pearse and even Griffith as precursors of modern 'Third World' anticolonialist and socialist thought (Regan and Sinclair eds 1986:31; see below p. 146). Most famous, or notorious, is the recurrent misquotation of Wolfe Tone's reference to Ireland being liberated with the aid of the 'men of no property' in order to suggest, falsely, that Tone was a social egalitarian providing apostolic sanction for the association of nationalist and socialist causes.[29] Nor was Tone any kind of generalised anticolonialist: he had urged that Britain conquer the Sandwich islands from Spain and establish colonies there, and bemoaned the fact that Ireland had no colonial possessions of her own (Elliot 1989:55–9).

The real ancestry of modern Irish left-wing 'anti-imperialism' begins not with Tone but with James Connolly. Other earlier Irish socialists, like William Thompson, seem to have given no attention at all to such questions. And Connolly's thoughts on imperialism have been misinterpreted and inflated almost as comprehensively as have Tone's on social equality.[30] Connolly, an autodidact scholar in the scanty time he could snatch from political and union activism, had read widely in Irish history—but not beyond. He played no role in the general debates of the international socialist movement before 1914, including those on imperialism; and there is no sign in his writings that he was aware of the theories of imperialism developed by Rosa Luxemburg, Rudolf Hilferding, Nikolai Bukharin or, nearer to home, J. A. Hobson. Nor is there any indication that he—or almost any other Irish radical of his generation—was aware even of the existence of anticolonial nationalist thinkers outside Europe: of Rammohun Roy or Bankimchandra Chattopadhyay or Rabindranath Tagore, of Li Ta-Chao or al-Afghani or Edward Wilmot Blyden. Austen Morgan's observation that 'Connolly's support for Irish statehood did not make him an advanced critic of imperialism in the late 1890s (as is often claimed)' seems just (Morgan 1988:37). Morgan has traced just twelve references to overseas dependencies in Connolly's writings, almost all ephemeral, and suggests that these 'did not breach a Eurocentric and indeed racist view of world politics . . . The people of the "non-civilized" world are totally missing in Connolly's writings'(ibid: 210).

Yet claims that Connolly anticipated almost all subsequent radical thought about Ireland, including culturalist analyses of colonialism, continue to be made, as has been done recently by Luke Gibbons. Connolly's thinking on history, according to Gibbons, derived not from the Second International's 'mechanistic socialism' but from the 'far-reaching' nineteenth-century Irish debates on political economy. (Gibbons 1994:30) This is somewhat fanciful. There is no evidence that Connolly was responding to or even substantially aware of these debates, as Gibbons suggests. Gibbons claims too that Connolly's historical writings 'are of interest because they point to the cultural mediation of market forces, an awareness that economic necessity does not operate in the same way in the undeveloped periphery (particularly under colonialism) as it does in the metropolitan heartlands.' (Gibbons 1994:30) Such arguments are, quite simply, not to be found in Connolly's writings, but are rather projected onto them by Gibbons. As it happens, we know a certain amount about Connolly's reading and his sources for *Labour in Irish History*. He was primarily reliant on the works of Alice Stopford Green—which were products of an extreme romantic nationalism, and were almost entirely political as opposed to social or economic chronicles. Far from displaying a sophisticated version of Marxist theory far ahead of its time (prefiguring Raymond Williams, according to Gibbons[31]) Connolly shows no evidence of being influenced by any Marxist writing beyond the *Communist Manifesto*, which he quotes as providing the 'key to history', and *Capital* vol. 1, which he quotes as a primary source on wage rates in Ireland and the struggles over working hours of Irish bakers (James Connolly 1917:15, 204–6).

Far from representing an avant-garde synthesis of Irish and global anticolonialism, and of economic and cultural analyses, as such anachronistic assertions suggest, Connolly's writings were marked by a double blindness: towards the Unionism of the Ulster working class, and towards the changing social structure of rural Ireland.[32] The former oversight, carried over by the social Republicanism which adopted Connolly as its patron saint, was in the long term to prove the more serious. The latter, though—ignoring the development of a substantial rural Catholic middle class with a real stake in self-government—set the tone for subsequent analyses of independent Ireland as neocolonial. As Henry Patterson says, Connolly's:

catastrophist view of the future of Irish agriculture ignored, as Marx did earlier, the economic and social weight of the Irish rural bourgeoisie, which was far from doomed to extinction. It led inevitably to the view that the only substantial bourgeoisie, in Catholic Ireland at least, was urban and comprador in nature, with a limited form of Home Rule as its ultimate political ambition. Thus Connolly was able to provide an optimistic prognosis for the coming Irish revolution ... If the bourgeoisie was so integrated in the existing nexus of economic relations with Britain, any 'true' nationalist would see that real independence necessitated a social revolution. (1989:9)

Conversely, since there had been no social revolution in 1916–21, it followed necessarily for those who adopted Connolly's assumptions that the Free State was not truly independent.[33] This perception, though, was slow to grow. Only after the Treaty—indeed only from the 1930s onward—did the notion of Ireland as a victim of informal imperialism or neocolonialism gain ground: that is, the belief that irrespective of its formal political and constitutional status, the island had been and the 26 counties still were victims of British economic and cultural hegemony. Distinctively socialist or 'Connollyite' versions of such a belief were yet more narrowly supported—essentially confined in the 1930s and forties to a handful of individuals like George Gilmore, Peadar O'Donnell, Michael Price, Frank Ryan and Connolly's daughter Nora. After 1969 they seemed to revive, first in the Official, later the Provisional Sinn Fein-IRA: only to be abandoned again by the leaderships of both, with Gerry Adams' former Provisionals discarding this strain of 'anti-imperialist' rhetoric rather unceremoniously as they turned to a negotiated settlement in the 1990s. Concepts of *cultural* dependency had a longer and more continuous history, as we shall see: but economic imperialism was an idea whose time came—mostly but not exclusively in Republican circles—long after the keys of Dublin Castle were handed over. We shall explore these themes further when we turn, in chapters 8 and 9, to explore the various uses of colonial models for understanding the contemporary Irish Republic and Northern Ireland.

5

British Imperialists and Their Critics

(i) Imperialists and Federalists

If Irish nationalist thought, even in the last decades of the Union, included very little sustained engagement with imperial and colonial questions or Ireland's place in these global frameworks, what of the other side of this coin? That is, to what degree did Victorian and Edwardian British official, and public opinion perceive Irish questions in an Imperial and colonial context? To cut a complex story short, it did so far more, more intensely, more systematically, more overtly, than was ever the case among Irish nationalists. When 'defence of the Empire' emerged as a major electoral issue in 1880, and was so again on several subsequent occasions, it was not the fate of Australia or India, still less of such uncontentious enclaves as Guiana or the Gold Coast, that was at issue. It was mainly the Irish Home Rule question, for which Empire became virtually a synonym. It would be tempting to conclude from this that modern Irish theorists of colonialism are right, and earlier Irish Nationalists were merely blind in not seeing that theirs was quintessentially a colonial situation.

But such an easy equation would miss a central point; that the discourse of Empire in this period fused more fully than at any time before or since with that of nationality itself. In speaking of Home Rule as threatening the Empire, its opponents did not assimilate the status of Ireland to that of Britain's transoceanic colonies. Quite the reverse: they associated it with the integrity of the British state itself. 'Dismemberment of the Empire' as ultimate fear played upon by Salisbury or Chamberlain in successive Home Rule crises did not denote that losing Ireland would be 'as bad' as losing Kenya or Jamaica. They knew how few electors would lose sleep over the latter. Rather, it specifically proclaimed (and no doubt for most of its invokers sincerely meant) that breaking the Union with Ireland would destroy the entire state and social order. The distinction remained clear, for instance, in the absolute refusal of the British political system, unlike the French, to allow any kind of colonial representation in its own Parliament: whereas Ireland was, more or less equally, represented there (in fact for much of the period of the Union Ireland was, by ratio of electors to seats, overrepresented). It became clear in a different way when, amidst the first Home Rule crisis, some British commentators began to argue that ideas of 'imperial patriotism' were to be preferred to those of 'Britishness' and 'British patriotism', precisely because the latter did not sufficiently, organically incorporate the Irish. (On this see Koebner and Schmidt 1964:168–71)

J. R. Seeley, in his hugely influential lectures on *The Expansion of England*, remarked that 'If Greater Britain in the full sense of the phrase really existed, Canada and Australia would be to us as Kent and Cornwall.' (1883:63) Seeley believed that such a Greater Britain could, should and would come into existence. So far as Ireland was concerned, in significant part, it already did. For much of the British body politic Cork and Kerry were, if not quite 'as Kent and Cornwall', then at least—in most moods, for most purposes—as Strathclyde or Swansea. Thus the man who popularised and voluminously analysed, if he did not invent, the term 'Greater Britain' itself, Sir Charles Dilke, did not include Ireland in his three weighty volumes on the theme (1868, 1890), for what would have seemed to him the near self-evident reason that it was part of a securely existing Union rather than a possible or desirable future one.

Nonetheless, the language used itself contained profound ambiguities—reflecting, among other things, the ambiguous status of Ireland itself, neither clearly colonial nor fully integrated into the United Kingdom. As Koebner and Schmidt point out, the words:

Imperial as well as Empire . . . had been applied to the United Kingdom only as recently as the early Victorian period; and so it could happen that during the Home Rule debate the defence of the Imperial Parliament meant the legislative authority of the United Kingdom, while the defenders of imperial unity also thought of the British Empire in its wider and more recent connotations. (ibid: 170)

It is intriguing in this context that the earliest use of the term 'imperialism' in an Irish context traced by one major authority on the subject is an *approving* use. The *Spectator* in January 1868, in the course of an attack on the anticolonialist (though also antisemitic) Goldwin Smith, wrote of 'Imperialism in its best sense', which it identified with 'the consciousness that it is sometimes a binding duty to perform highly irksome or offensive tasks, such as the defence of Canada or the government of Ireland.' (quoted Koebner and Schmidt 1964:24–5)

Nineteenth-century official British perceptions of Irish questions as colonial ones may, so a few historians argue, have extended beyond the particular context of late-century debates on Home Rule or imperial federation to a wider pattern of intellectual and policy interconnection. A recent study by S. B. Cook is perhaps the most extended attempt to make this case, focusing on land policies and arguing for a close interaction between attitudes to Ireland and those toward India. The 1885 Bengal Tenancy Act, the core of Cook's analysis, is suggested convincingly to have been heavily influenced by the experience of Irish agrarian conflict. (Cook 1993: the general discussion of whether Ireland was conceived of as part of the Empire is at pp. 17–26). The English historian John Turner—unlike, it would seem, most contemporary specialists—agrees that the relationship with Ireland was or had become conceived of as a clearly colonial one:

Westminster-inspired 'solutions' of the Irish 'problem' were delivered by an imperial metropolis to a colonial dependency, whether they were straightforwardly oppressive . . . or socially palliative . . . At the same time the Catholic Irish, whether they lived in Ireland or in England, whether they were peasants, migrant labourers, professionals or politicians, were treated by the English political elite as an inferior race. (Turner 1995:260)[1]

It is not surprising therefore that Turner should believe that 'the retreat from the Irish Union was seen *even at the time*, as a process of decolonisation rather than as a dismemberment of the integrity of the United Kingdom.' (ibid: 265) Yet this is to fly in the face of the evidence accumulated by dozens of other specialists in the issue, writing from many places and political views, who concur that 'the break-up of the United Kingdom' was indeed what was felt to be at stake by almost all involved.[2] Turner's view that British Conservative—or 'Unionist'—politicians proved not to care one bit about the Union but rather about preserving and enhancing their hegemony in England, seems to read the alignments of the 1990s back onto the 1860s, 1900s or 1920s.

There should be little surprise that historians have found it difficult to place British thought about Ireland in the context of a general discourse of Empire—for it might be said without exaggeration that there was no such discourse. Neither British colonialism as such nor the ways it was represented formed a coherent political or cultural system with distinctive, homogenised symbolic codes. It might even be doubted, if one wished to take an extreme nominalist position, that there was in any real sense a singular 'British Empire' at any one time, let alone across time (for historians often refer to the 'First', 'Second', 'Third' and sometimes even more British Empires in chronological succession). At its greatest extent just after the 1914–18 war, Britain's overseas possessions included Crown Colonies (mostly without significant European-descended populations) across Africa, the Caribbean and South-East Asia, self-governing Dominions mainly inhabited by people of British or other European ancestry, numerous islands and enclaves around the globe held mainly as strategic bases, like Malta, Aden, Gibraltar and Singapore, former Turkish and German colonies held under various kinds of League of Nations Mandatory authority, the vast Indian territories which were in themselves an extraordinarily complex patchwork of forms of rule, and so on.

The structures and discourses of British politics during the era of the Union, then, did not and could not usually assimilate Irish questions to some generalised colonial model; nor did they, conversely, integrate them wholly with the political management of Britain itself. Both tendencies existed—and as I have suggested, they were by no means necessarily *opposite* tendencies, at least in the era of rhetorical and to a degree material efforts to forge a 'Greater British' identity encompassing most overseas dependencies, especially those of white settlement. But while both colonialising and integrating discourses were in play—as they had been at least since the sixteenth century—neither dominated. Again, they could not: the model of internal self-government within an imperial framework, that which in the later nineteenth and early twentieth centuries appeared to be operating with marked success for Canada, Australia, New Zealand and the Cape, had perhaps been foreclosed for Ireland already by the events of 1798–1801. Even if not, it expired some time between the death of Parnell and that of the Archduke Franz Ferdinand. The solution of full integration, never whole-heartedly embraced in any case, foundered on British fears of entrenching Irish schisms even more securely at the heart of their own polity than had proved to be the case in the 1880s. Either way, not only the strength of nationalist sentiment but, perhaps more decisively, the growing intensity of Ireland's internal divisions blocked each successive attempt to improvise a new consensus.

The efforts of imperialist discourses to negotiate these tensions towards the end of the Victorian era, to combine its authors' awareness of rising Irish nationalist sentiment with their conviction of the essential loyalty of Ireland to the Empire, would make a fascinating study in their own right. A general survey would, again, be beyond the present remit. We can over-crudely summarise by saying that, especially in the late nineteenth and early twentieth centuries, Ireland was a sphere of ambiguity, tension, transition, hybridity, between 'national' and 'imperial' spheres—but if it was perhaps the longest-standing, the most contested such area of ambiguity, it was not the only one. Canada and Cardiff, Auckland and Aberdeen, also partook of the blurred and shifting negotiations of identity and sovereignty between a global Greater Britain and an insular but still compound Britishness. As Robin Wilson wrote, between 1880 and 1930 recurrent Irish crisis 'was a central, integral factor in the crises of Westminster governments and the British state.' (1985:151) But simultaneously it was part of a discourse of imperial crisis: Cabinet discussions in 1918–21 persistently associated Irish nationalism with anticolonialism in India and Egypt, with a perception that Irish independence might be the first domino to fall in a generalised collapse of Empire (ibid: 168–9). Yet it remains difficult to assess how important British withdrawal from most of Ireland was in influencing the eventual decolonisation of Britain's Indian, African and other colonies—despite the sweeping claims made on this score by some Irish nationalists.[3] This is so, in large part, because we do not yet have a satisfactory overall explanation for Britain's imperial decline: Ireland's place in the jigsaw cannot be clear until the picture as a whole has a sharper focus than the current state of historical research allows. Even in relation to specific aspects, such as the relation between the British experience of policing and counter-insurgency in Ireland and practices elsewhere in the Empire, very diverse and speculative judgements remain possible.[4]

The United Kingdom has never been a federal system, though a federal Union rather than one in which England incorporated other regions was what many Scots had argued for in the debates leading to Anglo-Scottish parliamentary fusion in 1707 (see e.g. Kendle 1997:1–11), and what Irish Patriot politicians claimed and to a limited degree achieved between 1782 and 1798. Ireland under the Union was, as we have seen, a strange constitutional hybrid: quite unlike any part of the subject Empire in that it was represented—on the whole, fairly represented, proportional to population—in the Imperial Parliament, but unlike any other part of the Kingdom in the presence of 'colonial' institutions headed by the Lord Lieutenancy. Irish (and Scottish) Home Rule campaigns across the nineteenth century repeatedly threw up ideas of resolving the anomaly by creating something close to a fully-fledged federal structure, perhaps embracing the white-settled Dominions as well as the countries of the UK. Perhaps the most elaborated attempt was Isaac Butt's *Irish Federalism* (Butt 1874). As the Home Rule issue became ever more central to British political debate in the last decades of the century, and as concurrently ideas of a wider Imperial Federation were in the air, more substantial schemes were voiced from a wide range of political stances (Kendle 1989, 1997:58–78). Once again Ireland's hybrid status made it the hinge between debates on domestic politics and those on the future of the Empire. But federal solutions, in any of the forms then put forward including the mixtures of 'devolution', 'federalism' and 'colonial self-government' that Gladstone's Home Rule Bills represented, satisfied none of the key political actors. For a growing number of Irish nationalists, they went nothing like far enough, while for British constitutional conservatives (who, then and since, were by no means all to be found in the Conservative Party) their challenge to the doctrine of undivided parliamentary sovereignty was unacceptable. It bears underlining that it was this doctrine—the cornerstone of Britain's uncodified constitutional order—rather than any specifically or directly colonial ideology which was seen to be most under threat in these long-running debates. As John Kendle stresses, most of those who did advocate what they called federal ideas in 1880–1914, or in 1918–21, were actually proposing devolutionist rather than truly federal arrangements—the same might be said of debates over Wales and Scotland in the 1990s—while hardly anyone gave serious attention to the relationship between their constitutional proposals and issues of culture or ethnicity (Kendle 1997:74, 77). The 1920 Government of Ireland Act contained what may be called weak federalist elements; but these were never operated in practice. The federal idea—or at least its ghost—may however be said to have appeared again in 1998, with the proposal for a

'Council of the Isles' as part of Northern Ireland's constitutional agreement in the spring of that year.

In terms of high politics, British policies towards Ireland in the post-Union era have been widely and ably dissected (though the coverage becomes notably thinner, and often more unhelpfully polemical, when dealing with the very recent past) and no attempt will be made to replicate that analysis here.[5] We can, however, summarise the consensus of serious historical work on British policy by saying that as the twentieth century proceeded British statesmen perceived themselves to have ever fewer crucial economic, strategic or political interests in Ireland which would be significantly damaged by changes in the constitutional status of Ireland or, later, of the north. The claim, which has attained the status of cliché, that Britain has retained sovereignty over the six counties of Northern Ireland only in default of being able to find some acceptable means of disengagement, is at best too simple, but it encapsulates more of the reality than does the opposed cliché of a continuingly crucial British 'imperialist' stake there. The rhetorical flourishes one still occasionally encounters, like Liz Curtis's invocation of 'Britain's colonisation of Ireland, and desire at all costs to hang onto it' (Curtis 1994:viii) seem detached from reality. Even among the Conservative politicians who had seemed prepared, especially in 1911–14, to risk constitutional breakdown or indeed civil war in order to preserve the Union, there seemed thereafter to be a surprising rapid and painless readjustment. As Stephen Evans (1998) has recently argued, the dominant conception of Unionism quickly shifted from a territorial to a populational one, emphasising now not the physical unity and integrity of the Kingdom but rather preservation of social peace, especially as between classes. Certainly the willingness of the British public to pay any cost at all in order to 'hang on' to Northern Ireland today is extremely weak—matched in its feebleness, perhaps, only by any willingness of the Irish public to incur costs in order to incorporate the north.

On the level of public opinion, what has become most striking is the lack of British popular support for the Union—equalled only by lack of enthusiasm for unification among the Republic's voters. Successive polls from 1981 to 1993 seemed to indicate that the British public's preference was for an independent Northern Ireland—favoured by 35–41 per cent. Far fewer—between 24 and 28 per cent—wanted the status quo. They were almost matched by the proponents of a united Ireland, who ranged between 15 and 24 per cent of the total across the decade (Cochrane 1994:387). In the Republic, a November 1993 poll indicated that only 19 per cent of respondents would be willing to pay higher taxes as a price of unity. Another showed just 24 per cent favouring 'no role' for Britain in Northern Ireland's future. Maybe most significantly of all, a third survey found a mere 21 per cent declaring themselves 'very interested' in the issue of unification (Cochrane 1994:392–4).

So far as rulers' attitudes are concerned, there has been little if any sign that successive British governments have attached overriding significance to the Union with Northern Ireland, or associated it with compelling ideas about national greatness, strength and will—as they so evidently did, for instance, in relation to the Falklands islands in 1982. It seems at least since 1970 to have been recognised that the government of the Irish Republic had a special and legitimate claim to involvement in Northern Irish affairs, even before that recognition was made explicit in the 1985 Anglo-Irish Agreement and subsequent statements. Unlike France in Algeria—and unlike British political debate over Ireland before 1914—the Union has neither been conceptualised as crucial to national pride, nor become an important battleground of party politics in the metropolis. Even within the Conservative Party, the 1970s and 1980s witnessed a slow death of 'British Unionism' in relation to Northern Ireland. The IRA's murder of Tory MP Ian Gow in 1990 removed the last really influential and able exponent of such a stance.[6]

The nature of British economic interests—if any—in Northern Ireland is increasingly hard to discern. It may well be that, at the time of Partition, it was economically rational and advantageous for Britain to retain sovereignty in the six counties of Northern Ireland—which were then responsible for the great bulk of Ireland's non-agricultural exports. It does not follow, however, that this was in fact the reason for Partition: most historians of the period, whatever their nationality and ideology, concur that directly political pressures from Northern Unionists were the overwhelmingly important factor. Still less does it follow that economic advantages to Britain persisted into the 1960s or after (McGarry and O'Leary 1995:71–8 summarise the relevant economic data). Almost no one has tried in recent years to argue that Britain profits from the continuation of the Union. The subvention from London, it is generally agreed, amounts to nearly one-third of Northern Ireland's total GDP. Economic arguments from Nationalist or Republican viewpoints have resorted to an assortment of claims. It can, of course, be asserted that the heavy British subsidy to Ulster is a reason why Britain should want to withdraw, or *would* want to do so if political considerations did not intervene, or why it should 'join the persuaders' coaxing Unionists into a united Ireland. It can be argued that a successful peace process leading to unification would enable massive savings on security-related public expenditure, produce a substantial 'peace dividend' in increased inward investment, tourism and enhanced business confidence, that significant economies of scale, removal of the need for wasteful duplication of services and facilities, and other advantages would ensue from unification, and (in echoes of older arguments) that the 'dependency' of both parts of the island on Britain with the alleged associated damaging consequences would be ended.[7] Unionists, by contrast, have been able to argue that the subvention makes a united Ireland utterly impracticable; any major shift in constitutional arrangements would have disastrous economic consequences for Northern Ireland and perhaps also for the

Republic.[8] The Unionists' main point is undoubtedly accurate: that Northern Ireland is heavily subsidised by the taxpayers of the rest of the UK, and that it is hard to imagine the Irish Republic being able or willing to take over that burden. Beyond this, the dispute is perhaps mainly evidence of how the same economic statistics can, in ideologically rival hands, be made to bear totally opposed interpretations.

As all serious studies of Northern Ireland as an issue in British politics have stressed, the province has been considered, from its foundation, as a place apart. Successive Home Secretaries saw no reason to challenge the convention that Northern Ireland's affairs were a matter for Stormont, not for action from Whitehall or debate at Westminster. Between partition and the late 1960s, the House of Commons averaged two hours' Northern Irish business per annum (Norton 1996:129–30). Reluctance to intervene in any way was motivated not only by indifference and ignorance, but (so many commentators suggest) by a more positive desire to keep so potentially contentious an issue out of British political debate, after the embittered experiences of partisan conflict over Irish Home Rule between the 1880s and 1921. Positive commitment to the Union was never so evident as was a more passive acceptance of the strength of Ulster Protestant enthusiasm for it—though the Second World War may have brought greater conviction of the Union's value to some British political circles (Fisk 1983, Barton 1996). The more sophisticated analyses of British state strategies and aims since 1969, moving away from a simplistic view of 'British imperialism in Ireland' have depicted policy formation as generally short-termist, reactive and often bemused.[9]

The decision of the British Conservative Party to establish itself in Northern Ireland in 1989 was reluctant, tokenistic and followed by no serious effort actually to organise there: the other major British parties have not even gone so far. There has been no sign since the 1920s that senior British politicians have felt that 'playing the Orange card' (or the Green one) might bring electoral advantage, nor that they believed Northern Ireland to have significant strategic, let alone economic, value for Britain. Full integration of Northern Ireland into the British political system has never been mooted as an option in core London political circles, even when there has appeared to be widespread support for it within Northern Ireland, and even when all other possibilities have seemed to fail.

(ii) Critics and Obituarists

The comparatively very small part which the wider, indeed global, questions of imperialism and decolonisation played in Irish thought between 1801 and 1921 was, if anything, undercut by the place awarded to Ireland and Irish questions in the thought of the major early international theorists of imperialism themselves: for the place was, by and large, nowhere at all.

The scattered thoughts on Ireland in the writings of Marx and Engels—predominantly in private letters and occasional journalism (collected in Marx and Engels 1971)—have been picked over pretty exhaustively by subsequent, more or less pious, exegetes. Whilst they exceed in bulk, by some margin, their commentary on any other nationalist movement or colonial question, they in no way add up to a detailed investigation or theorisation of the issue. Still less did they amount to placing the Anglo-Irish question in some general theory of imperialism or of international relations: something which, in any case, neither man ever essayed. Anthony Coughlan's claim (1994:291–2) that it was from observation of Ireland that Marx and Engels formulated their theory of imperialism is entirely false, for they had no such theory (Marx apparently had vague plans to discuss imperialism in volume Six of the vast project which never actually got past volume one: *Capital*). The founders of Marxism were generally in favour of Irish independence; but more because it would weaken British power and, they sometimes hoped, even pave the way for the socialist revolution in Britain, than for any reason intrinsic to Ireland itself. It perhaps deserves to be recalled, moreover, that the young Engels at least had had a rather low opinion of the Irish, and of the claim that Ireland's woes were wholly Britain's fault:

Irish distress cannot be removed by any Act of Repeal. Such an Act would, however, at once lay bare the fact that the cause of Irish misery, which now seems to come from abroad, is really to be found at home. (Engels 1969(1848):299)

Their work cannot be taken even as the starting point for an overarching theory of imperialism in Ireland, and even their most orthodox Irish followers have rarely sought to pretend that it can.[10]

J. A. Hobson's *Imperialism* (1902) first formulated the theory of a specifically capitalist imperialism, driven by the search for new fields of investment—a theory which became dominant on the political left, worldwide, in the succeeding decades and still lies behind an enormous amount of modern thinking on the subject, in Ireland as elsewhere. Yet Hobson clearly did not think of Ireland as being a part of the phenomenon he was dissecting. His only reference to the country is a passing one, as part of a promiscuous list of *European* nationalities engaged in conflicts over sovereignty, along with the Poles, Finns, Hungarians, and Czechs. (ibid: 2) In the major work of Hobson's most important direct successor among the Radical–Liberal critics of imperialism, H. N. Brailsford (1915), Ireland does not receive even this much notice. Indeed the general lack of interest in Irish questions among the New Liberal intellectuals, with the exception of J. L. Hammond, was striking. Hobson, L. T. Hobhouse, Graham Wallas and the rest spent their formative and most active years through the recurrent crises of Home Rule and then Partition, but none of them devoted significant writings to the question. Nor was it a major focus of their political activities, though Hobhouse, with R. H. Tawney and Basil Williams, did join the Peace with Ireland Committee which Hammond instigated at the height of the 1920–1 war (Peter Clarke 1978:213–14).

After Hobson, and somewhat derivative of him, the most influential radical work on imperialism was that of Lenin. His *Imperialism, the Highest Stage of Capitalism* (1917) attained canonical status within the Communist movement, in Britain and Ireland as elsewhere. Lenin's main purpose was not, as was so often subsequently assumed, to explain European colonial expansion, but to account for the origins of the First World War and to assert that it marked the last gasp of a dying capitalism. Ireland plays no part in the analysis; and as Bew, Gibbon and Patterson among others point out (1979:19–25) the very concept of imperialism used by Lenin bears little relation to that presupposed by later Irish Marxists. The few scattered remarks that Lenin did make on Irish issues—remarks which, like those of Marx and Engels, were endlessly picked over by later exegetes—relate essentially to tactics rather than theory, and fell under the rubric of debate over national self-determination rather than of imperialism. It is evident that under the *specific* circumstances of 1916–21 Lenin believed in the revolutionary and anti-imperialist potential of Irish revolt: but that like Marx and Engels, he did so mostly because of its effects in weakening a major capitalist power. 'We must support every revolt against our chief enemy, the bourgeoisie of the big states, provided that it is not the revolt of a reactionary class', he urged in 1916 (Lenin 1971:124). He never extended from this observation to any general analysis of British aims and policies in Ireland. Bukharin's *Imperialism and World Economy* (1918), second only to Lenin's little book in the Communist pantheon on the subject (at least until Bukharin's disgrace and execution by Stalin) follows Lenin in making no reference to Ireland at all. Later Marxist analyses of Ireland in terms of imperialism were to have roots other than the classic Communist texts; as they had to have, in the absence of substantial relevant material in them.

Non-Communist sources were little more helpful. Perhaps the most widely read critique of imperialism between the wars, apart from Lenin, was Parker Thomas Moon's *Imperialism and World Politics* (1926). This too, a sweeping survey and indictment of colonial policies worldwide, written in heavily-Irish New York so soon after Partition, makes not a single mention of Ireland. And although some of the major radical critics of British colonialism from the 1880s through to the 1960s also had engagements with Irish questions, these were almost entirely parallel with but separate from their concerns about Britain's colonial Empire. Hardly a one of the numerous books such critics produced attacking colonial power discussed or even mentioned Ireland.[11]

The virtual exclusion of Ireland from the analyses of classical theorists of imperialism has been replicated by almost all modern historians of the British

Empire. Peter Cain and Anthony Hopkins, in the most widely discussed contemporary work on British imperialism, make just three passing references to Ireland, effectively making it just an entry in lists of places where English authority was consolidated during the eighteenth century (Cain and Hopkins 1993:90, 96, 97). Of the major synthesising overviews produced in recent years, D. K. Fieldhouse's *The Colonial Empires* (1982), Ronald Hyam's *Britain's Imperial Century* (1993), Denis Judd's *Empire* (1996), the *Cambridge Illustrated History of the British Empire* (Marshall ed. 1996), Jan Morris's *Pax Britannica* trilogy (1968, 1973, 1978) and Bernard Porter's *The Lion's Share* (1984), only Judd's and Morris's books could really be said to incorporate Ireland as an integral part of the story. Only Morris includes the Famine or other aspects of Irish society as such as a significant theme, in the least scholarly though perhaps most vivid of these works, while Judd's scattered Irish references are among the least well-informed parts of his book. The Cambridge volume suggests early on that: 'Questions about Ireland also became imperial questions . . . The ambiguous situation of Ireland is thus a major theme in British imperial history' (Marshall ed. 1996:9) but the subsequent chapters do not in fact treat it as such—the few relevant references are mostly to the Irish as participants in empire-building. In most other overviews, so far as Ireland is a theme at all, it is this participation, plus Home Rule as an issue in British and imperial politics and sometimes Irish nationalism as precursor to post-1945 anticolonial agitation, which are stressed. None of the significant contemporary theorists of imperialism, Marxist or otherwise—Frank and Wallerstein, Amin and Rey, Arrighi and Emmanuel—incorporate Ireland in their models. The most noteworthy break from this tradition of effectively excluding Ireland from British Imperial historiography is the multi-volume new Oxford History of the British Empire, whose first two volumes (Canny ed. 1998, P. J. Marshall ed. 1998) include fairly extensive discussion of Ireland in the contexts first of English medieval and early modern 'internal colonialism', then of Britain's Atlantic activities in the seventeenth and eighteenth centuries. Treatment of Ireland in the project's later volumes is perhaps less successfully integrated into the global picture. There is little discussion of the notion of Ireland as colony: rather, the focus is mainly on the Empire-building activities of the Irish diaspora (D. Fitzpatrick 1999) and, for the twentieth century, on the Free State's relations with the Commonwealth and Dominions (McMahon 1999, Harkness 1999, following the lead of Harkness 1969, 1970).

6

Chroniclers and Revisionists

(i) Histories: Green, Pink and Grey

Ireland's formal status in relation to the English Crown, and to the complex constitutional web of the United Kingdom and British Empire, shifted numerous times from the first Norman incursions onwards. On this political level, recent historical work has tended, as we have seen, to stress discontinuity, complexity, ambivalence and hybridity in British-Irish relations rather than the more traditional nationalist narratives of '800 Years of Crime'. Yet recognition of discontinuity has by no means resolved debate over the relevance of colonial models to understanding Ireland's past: rather, it has complicated it. And increasingly, debate has engaged with the concepts of colonialism, imperialism and postcoloniality not only as political phenomena, but as social, economic, psychological and above all cultural ones. Not only have exponents of many different academic disciplines become involved, but we find also intriguing differences of emphasis between, as well as within, the disciplines. On the whole economists and economic historians have not followed the colonial model, which has found more support among political scientists, though still only that of a minority in recent years—and among them there are some, like Steve Bruce, who apparently think invocation of the colonial image, at least for any period after the early eighteenth century, is simply a matter of nationalist apologetics (Bruce 1994:129–31). Historians have been most sharply divided on the issue; and it is their disputes which have had the widest political and public resonances. Among them so-called revisionists, most of whom either deny the relevance of colonialism as a category for understanding modern Ireland or question its significance, have held most of the high ground in recent times. The counterattack against 'revisionism' has come above all from cultural and literary theorists; and it is in their ranks that concepts of colonialism and postcoloniality have been most widely and interestingly used for Irish studies.[1]

It has sometimes been argued that some versions at least of academic social science and historiography have simply been unable to perceive the significance of colonial and neocolonial influences on Ireland, because of their own ideological or methodological blinkers. This is especially often alleged in respect of what has been labelled revisionist historical writing.[2] Here disputes over interpretation of the past have become associated, not only in the intellectual community but to some considerable extent in the popular mind, with political agendas and even social class. Thus critics have identified historical revisionism with 'Dublin 4'—shorthand for a nexus of politicians, broadcasters, media commentators and academics who are claimed, by those like Desmond Fennell who believe themselves unfairly excluded by it, to form a kind of anti-national mafia (Fennell 1993, esp. ch. 10).[3]

Occasionally one does indeed encounter work which, largely as a result of its adherence to the straightjacket of (usually American) theoretical models, appears to justify such a charge. Thus for instance an essay surveying an Irish 'party-building cycle' whose phases appear to have nothing at all to do with the radical and violent shifts in the country's political status over the past century (R. K. Carty 1993), appears more than a little myopic. More generally, it is some-what frustrating that, as John Whyte comments in regard to studies of Northern Ireland, those scholars who have not employed the colonial model have usually not explicitly examined and rejected, but simply ignored, it (Whyte 1990:178).

Disputes over 'Ireland's story', and the place of colonialism within it, are thus intensely politicised. But some would question the very idea of a singular story. It is perhaps salutary to note how much of Irish history, or rather how many Irish histories, and cultures, are entirely uncaptured in the national-level argu-ments and narratives. This can be indicated through the words of two American historical anthropologists, who when beginning research in the rural commu-nity of Thomastown, County Kilkenny, were puzzled to find no reference in local sources to many supposedly crucial historical events—no United Irish-men, no Land War, no Famine, and so on:

seemingly, Thomastown lay outside Irish history. The historians (to whom they pre-sented their puzzle) were somewhat amused. They knew, and readily admitted, that so-called Irish history was an amalgam of local and regional events combined to create a unified and coherent whole held together by nationalist (and later, revisionist) ideology. They did not find it surprising that a particular local area or region never experienced all or even any of the events that later became part of so-called Irish history. (Silverman and Gulliver eds 1992:6)

In somewhat related vein, the pre-eminent historian of folksong in these islands, A. L. Lloyd, has traced (1978) the seemingly near-inextricable mixture of history, folklore, nationalist myth and popular memory associated with one particular incident of the Land War—and does so merely by compiling, collage-like, without commentary, documentary record, ballad lyrics, and interview material. The result indicates both how extraordinarily vivid, and how impos-sibly protean, have been popular representations and refigurings of the 1878 killing of Lord Leitrim—and, by implication, of much of the narrative of Irish history. A yet more compelling, extended demonstration of the same message comes in American ethnographer Henry Glassie's magnificent, moving study of folk-history, community and memory in rural Fermanagh, *Passing the Time in Ballymenone* (1982). Glassie's small Fermanagh village has a strong local historical sense, a rich and complex narrative built from songs, fireside storytelling, and folklore. Events like certain battles of the seventeenth century, and of the nineteenth, are powerfully present in the community's archive, rich in detail and resonance: but neither recalled in ways that match the scholar's reconstruction (most of the eighteenth century, for instance, seems to have dropped out of the story), nor imbued with any strong sense of belonging to a *national* narrative.

In part responding to such findings, in part to wider international scholarly trends, an increasingly substantial body of Irish historical work has taken a localist focus, and sought to explore specific local roots for the different courses which ostensibly national conflicts took in different parts of the country. Major examples would include Theo Hoppen's work on nineteenth-century politics (Hoppen 1984, 1989), Erhard Rumpf's and David Fitzpatrick's on the early twentieth century and the Civil War (Rumpf and Hepburn 1977, Fitzpatrick 1978), and the writings of historical geographer Kevin Whelan (see esp. his 1993).[4] In this a strand of Irish 'revisionism' (though Whelan, for one, would certainly repudiate the label) resembles its counterparts in other contexts, like the wave of county-based studies of the English Civil War which did so much to call into question earlier orthodoxies about the character and supposed inevitability of the conflict. By analogies elsewhere, one would expect this current of scholarship to continue growing—pushed as much by the ever increasing specialisation and compartmentalisation of historical research as by any more ideological impulse. And one may confidently predict that future 'revisionist' accounts of the post-1969 northern violence will also seek localist explanations, perhaps especially in relation to such rural conflict zones as South Armagh, finding the roots of enmity in microhistories of landholding, familial traditions, and inherited parochial grievances.[5]

If much Irish historiography has arguably been excessively national in not being local enough, a great deal more has been too national in another way. The development of thinking about Ireland's history, society and politics has all too often persisted in a pervasive myth of Irish exceptionalism, to which the rather insular focus of most modern history-writing has contributed heavily.[6] One form of this is a tendency to *assume* the Irishness of particular phenomena which actually have non-Irish origins or parallels—often multiple ones—elsewhere. A symptomatic case is the use one skilful but romanticising recent reporter makes of something he took to be an Irish popular tradition. Kevin Toolis's *Rebel Hearts*, a much praised investigation of the contemporary IRA, recalls a play he saw as a child, a Victorian melodrama entitled *Murder in the Red Barn*. This was, he says, 'the usual woeful Irish tale . . . Irish history is an endless nightly rerun of *Murder in the Red Barn*.' (Toolis 1995:368) But in fact the play was based on a famous *English* murder case, the killing of Maria Martin by William Corder which took place in 1827 at Polstead, in Suffolk. In other words, what the story of *The Red Barn* and its survival in the popular theatre of County Mayo in the 1960s actually indicates is the 'archipelagic' nature of folk culture across the former United Kingdom. That cross-fertilisation could be exemplified from many other sources: for instance, the vast number of 'traditional' songs which exist in both English and Irish variants. The astonishing thing is that Toolis *knows* of the English origins of the 'Red Barn' story, as he tells us in a footnote (ibid: 371), but this does not prevent him from pressing it into the service of a maudlin narrative of Irish violence, Irish tendency to repeat the past, Ireland's special sorrows.[7]

To understand what follows, and the immense political weight which differing interpretations of the past have borne, it is necessary to go beyond such clichés of a peculiarly Irish 'obsession with history' and briefly to trace the history of Irish history-writing itself. The master-narrative which the Irish historical profession has constructed here is of the gradual supplanting of a teleological nationalist account by more discontinuous, nuanced and complicated interpretations.

If we ask against what the nationalist narrative was itself reacting, the answer is that it was not, on the whole, some previous reigning orthodoxy within historical writing, but something far more diffuse and largely outside it. If we expect to find—as historians of, say, India or southern Africa have found—a fully-fledged imperialist historical discourse more or less openly serving as ideological justification for Ireland's conquest and colonisation, and *preceding* some later nationalist *response*, we shall be confounded. We can obviously point to texts, from the sixteenth century to the nineteenth, which offered a view of past events (recent or distant) supportive of the English Crown's claims over Ireland, of Anglo-Scottish settlement, of Protestantism as against Catholicism, or indeed which stigmatised the 'Old Irish' and their culture. Some such texts, like Spenser's *View of the Present State of Ireland* (*c.*1596), the various Irish references and possible allusions in Shakespeare, or—a more recent target of latterday anticolonialist critique—Milton's *Observations upon the Articles of Peace* (1649), have been intensely worked over by modern critics seeking to anatomise a colonialist ethos (e.g. Burnett and Wray eds 1997, Patricia Coughlan ed. 1989, Hadfield 1997, Tracey Hill 1993, Maley 1994, 1997, Bradshaw *et al.* 1993). Of properly historical writing dedicated to such viewpoints, however, there is surprisingly little that could be regarded as foundational. Stretching a point or two, we might possibly place Macaulay's *History of England* (1848 *et seq.*) or Hume's *History of Great Britain* (1754 *et seq.*) under the rubric of 'colonialist' historiography in relation to Ireland, but little else of lasting substance.[8] Indeed historical chronicles, like that of Geoffrey Keating (Seathrun Ceitinn)—as well as

more numerous poetic efforts—in Gaelic and then English decrying the conquest and asserting proto-nationalist themes emerged at least as early as
attempts by English writers to justify the colonial incursion.[9] And aggressively
anti-Catholic and anti-Irish works by Protestant crusaders such as Sir John
Temple, Henry Jones and Richard Lawrence drew immediate counterblasts,
not least from Irish fellow-Protestants such as Vincent Gookin (Barnard
1990:51–72).

Thus a complex and politically charged dialogue was evident from the very
beginning of Irish historical writing. A pro-British account like Edward
Ledwich's *Antiquities of Ireland* (1790), which in Oliver MacDonagh's view marks
the birth of modern Irish historiography, was already reactive, already engaged
in battle against nationalist interpretations. Ledwich 'had discerned a dangerous association of Gaelic, Catholic and radical political views, and was proceeding to take his counter-measures.' (MacDonagh 1983:2) In the immediate
aftermath of the Union, historical sketches seeking to undermine its validity,
like Denis Taafe's, were as quick to appear as those upholding it, like Francis
Plowden's (R. F. Foster 1988:290). Hostile accounts of the United Irishmen, like
Musgrave's *Memoirs*, contended in the wake of the 1798 revolt with apologetic
ones—and ones seeking to vindicate particular factional positions among the
rebels' fractious leadership. The most fiercely anti-Irish historical narratives,
like J. A. Froude's *The English in Ireland in the Eighteenth Century* (1872) were yet
more evidently responses to rather than predecessors of the emergence of
nationalist accounts.

Indeed as historical scholarship in anything like the contemporary sense
began to develop during the nineteenth century, it was predominantly nationalist from the start. Its story has often been told, from varying viewpoints: how
a group of predominantly Protestant scholars, antiquarians and, sometimes,
mythologists, many of them prominent in the Young Ireland movement and its
culturalist successors, created the first major narratives of the country's past.
Men like Sylvester O'Halloran, Charles O'Conor and Charles Vallancey in the
eighteenth century were in no small degree fantasists, proposing Phoenician
descent and all manner of mystic virtues for the ancient Irish (Leerssen 1988,
Hutchinson 1987:55–67). Their successors in the era of Gaelic revival, headed by
Douglas Hyde and Eoin MacNeill, were by contrast many of them very considerable and sober scholars; but the political purposes of the different generations' work had much continuity (Sheehy 1980). And they were accompanied
by a substantial strain of more popular historical writing, massively imbued with
romantic nationalism, bitter anti-British sentiment, and frequent assertions
that the chains Britain loaded on Ireland were in the words of one such writer
'heavier and more galling than any forged for any nation before'. (Henry 1920:2)

It may be added that—a strain of overtly racist diatribes, to which we shall
allude later, aside—the supposedly colonialist historiography was rarely quite

so single-minded in defence of 'its side' as the nationalist counterpart was in glorification of its. Few British chroniclers could pretend that Britain's record in Ireland was one of unalloyed virtue. David Hume's work (arguably the first in European history-writing to give economic determinants their due, anticipating Adam Smith and Karl Marx even if long preceded by Ibn Khaldun in this) is an interesting case in point. Although Hume depicts the settlement of Ireland as the most positive achievement of James I's reign, he does so in the context of a thoroughly damning appraisal of England's general record in Ireland:

Most of the English institutions, too, by which that island was governed, were to the last degree absurd, and such as no state before had ever thought of, for the preserving dominion over its conquered provinces . . . Rapine and insolence inflamed the hatred, which prevailed betwixt the conquerors and the conquered: Want of security among the Irish, introducing despair, nourished still further the sloth, so natural to that uncultivated people.

But the English carried still farther their ill-judged tyranny. Instead of inviting the Irish to adopt the more civilized customs of their conquerors, they even refused, tho' earnestly solicited, to communicate to them the privilege of their laws, and every where marked them out as aliens and as enemies . . . Being treated like wild beasts, they became such; and, joining the ardor of revenge to their yet untamed barbarity, they grew every day more untractable and dangerous. (1970:118)

It is hard to tell who comes off the worse in this account; the Irish in their barbarity or the English in their ill-judged tyranny. For Hume, Irish laws and customs are primitive and uncivilised, the people lazy and violent—but these traits are attributed not to innate national character or racial essence, but to Ireland not having experienced the modernising impact of Roman rule like the rest of Europe (ibid: 119), and to reaction against English oppression. So far as the notion of an English 'civilising mission' is unquestioningly accepted, and associated especially with James's plantations in Ulster, then Hume may fairly unproblematically be categorised as a colonialist historian. But insofar as the difference between conquerors and conquered is not typed as racial or immutable, the record of the conquerors is itself seen so damningly, and the work of civilisation explicitly counterposed against the 'vain and criminal glory of conquests' (ibid: 122) then Hume escapes or troubles the category of the purely colonialist chronicler.

The greatest Victorian historian of Ireland, W. E. H. Lecky, also cannot readily be placed in either a 'nationalist' or an 'imperialist' camp: politically committed to the Union, he was equally committed to Catholic rights and proud of Irish cultural achievement. Such figures as Matthew Arnold were just as complex, combining faith in England's civilising mission and (like Lecky) hostility to the extension of democracy with panegyrics to 'Celtic genius'. Given the sheer weight of nationalist historiography, then, there is more than a hint of double-think in such claims as Ernie O'Malley's, when (after describing a childhood suffused with nationalist consciousness, tales of past resistance, the formative influence of reading Tone's *Autobiography*) he could still assert that 'Irish history had not been written; it was the history of the underdog.' (O'Malley 1936:59)

Early and Victorian Irish nationalist historical thought (which as the Field Day anthology and other recent work seeks to show, was in fact more interestingly heterogenous than often thought) thus provided the basis for a kind of emerging orthodoxy in the earlier decades of this century. It was entrenched especially in popular chronicles such as *Speeches from the Dock* (Sullivan and Sullivan 1890/1968) and in school history textbooks such as Christian Brother J. M. O'Brien's *Irish History Reader* (1905), Hayden and Moonan's *Short History of the Irish People* (1921) and James Carty's *Junior History of Ireland* (1932). On more advanced level, works by Daniel Corkery (e.g. 1925) and later, more left-wing accounts by T. A. Jackson (1946) or Desmond Greaves (1961) as well as Frank Gallagher's *The Indivisible Island* (1957), whose publication was it seems surreptitiously financed by the Irish government (Akenson 1995:132; see also Graham Walker 1992b) reproduced many of the same pieties. In the classroom itself—especially, some have suggested, the classrooms of Christian Brothers schools throughout Ireland (Coldrey 1988 esp. 113–49; C. C. O'Brien 1994:9, 24–8)—the romantic nationalist orthodoxy will have been yet more heavily, and perhaps crudely, emphasised than in the printed texts. Early directives on primary education in the new Free State urged that the main aim in history teaching should be 'to inculcate national pride and self-respect . . . by showing that the Irish race has fulfilled a great mission in the advancement of civilisation.' (quoted R. F. Foster 1988:518) And in some milieux at least, familial and other influences outside the formal educational process reinforced the same version of the past. Eamonn McCann (born 1943) evocatively sketches the idea of history he acquired during a Derry childhood:

One learned, quite literally at one's mother's knee, that Christ died for the human race and Patrick Pearse for the Irish section of it . . . The oppression against which the political heroes of the past had fought was, we learned, primarily oppression of the church. (McCann 1980:9, 13)

Denis Donoghue recalls that at his Christian Brothers school in the 1930s–40s:

[W]e were encouraged to regard the history of Ireland as unfinished business, a great story that lacked only a noble resolution. It was our duty to maintain a sense of Ireland, to learn the language and speak it, take part in national and never in foreign games, practise the old customs of Ireland, and above all keep alive the great consanguinity between Ireland and the Catholic Church. (1990:156–7)[10]

Such memories are naturally in part caricatures. Yet they point to the genuine problem of an intellectually narrow, politically and religiously constricted historical consciousness. The recollections of a myriad other products of Irish Catholic schooling, in the south and (perhaps more particularly) in the north, from the 1900s to the 1960s, from Paul Durcan and Patrick Kavanagh to Gerry Adams and Bernadette Devlin,[11] evoke similar images. In political terms, the educational orthodoxies of cultural nationalism and of the Free State may have succeeded in their aims—and they may have done so in large part, as Gabriel Doherty suggests, because they corresponded to genuine popular feelings and desires. A 'teleological spiritual meta-narrative', in Doherty's terms, dominated by 'belief in an inner spirituality of the Irish people, demonstrated by their abiding fidelity to the twin ideals of Catholicism and political freedom' was not just imposed from above by cultural nationalist ideologues, but derived its power from 'its coincidence with popular opinion.' (G. Doherty 1996:326, 342, 349[12]) For all its inadequacies—and it was, Doherty believes, neither as monolithic nor as lacking in support from professional academic historians as is often thought—this vision of history served important state-building, cohesion-affirming and psychologically comforting functions in a weak and insecure new polity.

The development of an alternative to and critique of this vision, and the entry of Irish historical writing into the mainstream of western historiography, started already from the 1930s, when T. W. (Theo) Moody and Robert Dudley Edwards began their academic careers. There had, as Joseph Lee points out, been significant historical scholars in Irish universities before this, like Eoin MacNeill and Edmund Curtis, but the wider impact of their work was slight and most of their energies went either into teaching or, as with MacNeill, into politics. The turning point was the first appearance in 1938 of the journal *Irish Historical Studies*. It deliberately emphasised its ethos of professionalism, its adherence to international standards of evidence and scholarship (an insistence which in itself, in some hostile eyes, was evidence of 'neo-colonial' intellectual servility) and avoidance of nakedly political controversy. This eschewal of politics was manifested in the journal's refusal, until very recently, to publish articles on twentieth-century themes.[13]

Dublin—both the traditionally Protestant Trinity College and more particularly the newer, initially Catholic University College (UCD)—was the main seedbed of the new history. Over the water, significant roles were played by London's Institute of Historical Research and by Cambridge, especially Peterhouse (which, as anti-revisionist critics were later to mutter conspiratorially, has also nurtured many of Britain's most conservative major historians). Almost as important as Dublin, though, was Queen's University Belfast. Queen's may, as Cornelius O'Leary trenchantly argues, have failed the communities it served by sponsoring (until recently) little if any research on constitutional abuses or religiously based discrimination in Northern Ireland (C. O'Leary 1993), but in historical work its contribution was second only to UCD's. In this sphere, the Border was no barrier to intellectual interchange.

Methodologically, the new history was thus very much part of a transnational disciplinary mainstream. In some ways, then, it could come to be seen—especially from the 1960s—as conservative: and such charges have been launched in recent years, ironically, in the service of pleas for a return to older nationalist conceptions. Thus, in critiques to which we shall have occasion to return later, Brendan Bradshaw (1989) urged that the notion of 'value-free' research, supposedly espoused by the 'revisionists' and derived from the 1930s writings of Herbert Butterfield, was untenable; whilst Seamus Deane (1991a) alleged archaism and epistemological naivety in failure to take account of postmodernism, the 'linguistic turn' and the ideas of Hayden White.[14]

And certainly the work produced in and around *IHS*'s circles included until recently little social history, very little that was influenced by Marxism or the *Annales* school, and almost nothing on the history of women or of 'marginal' or 'subaltern' social groups.[15] In all this it reflected or even moved behind the orthodoxies not so much of the international, as specifically of the Anglo-Saxon historical profession. Sometimes it seemed to move very far behind the orthodoxies, relying on gurus who had become notably unfashionable elsewhere. The great touchstone in philosophy of history for Robin Dudley Edwards, Theo Moody and Ronan Fanning was Herbert Butterfield (see Moody 1994:86, Fanning 994:154, 158, O Grada 1994b:278, 285). Brendan Bradshaw, as well as seeking to turn Butterfield against the founding 'revisionists' (Bradshaw 1994:199–201, 210–14), brought R. G. Collingwood to bear (ibid: 215–16). And as late as 1996 one could find the injunctions of Geoffrey Elton (regarded as downright antedeluvian by most younger British and American scholars) put forward, by a young and energetic historian of Ireland, as ones 'most skilled Irish historians' would 'have little difficulty in endorsing' (English 1996b:223).

To that degree, the historians' nationalist and left-wing critics had a telling point: except that what many of the latter posed as an alternative was something even more methodologically retrograde. It could also be charged that the successive waves of historical 'revision' remained static in one crucial regard: the high degree of insularity generally displayed. Neither conceptual boldness in integrating Irish themes into wider international currents, nor comparative work of any degree of sophistication—as we shall have occasion later to observe in more detail—has been much in evidence. An implicit or explicit belief in Irish exceptionalism seems widespread even among the scholars most critical of nationalism. Revisionism has been an attempt to broaden the definition of the nation, to qualify its appeal, or to liberalise it, not to supplant it or step outside it altogether. The other side of this coin perhaps follows naturally: that modern Irish historical writing has had little international influence. There has been no Irish Braudel or Foucault, no Edward Thompson or Hayden White, no equivalent to *Subaltern Studies* or *Past and Present*. The monographs and the journals seem to be read only by those involved in research on Ireland itself, hardly at all by those with comparative or theoretical interests. One will search in vain the literatures of historical 'revisionism' in relation to the Arab–Israeli conflict or the German 'Historikerstreit', for example, for reference to Irish historiography.

In terms of the wider public function, including the political impact, of history a greater omission than any of these was the reluctance of the first generation or two of modern professional historians to attempt major works of synthesis; especially, as might be expected given the *IHS*'s embargo on contemporary topics, ones including the twentieth century. The first such effort was not the work of an academic, but of newspaper editor Tim Pat Coogan (1966)—the author also of an important history of the IRA and a biography of Michael Collins (1990). Coogan's book was vivid and entertaining, but perhaps inevitably impressionistic, and largely adhered to the received nationalist wisdoms. It was followed by weightier efforts from John A. Murphy (1975) and, commanding the field over the past decade, J. J. Lee (1989), as well as F. S. L. Lyons's chronologically wider-ranging *Ireland Since the Famine* (1973). Lee's massive book, which may in some respects be seen as combining 'revisionist' emphases and sophistications with more classically nationalist sympathies, has been both widely admired and widely controversial. Stormier by far, though, was the reception given another work of synthesis, which sought to place twentieth-century experience in the context of a narrative starting in 1600, Roy Foster's *Modern Ireland* (1988). Foster's book, accompanied by numerous shorter, more specialised or polemical pieces and by its author's high media profile, has become seen as the flagship of 'revisionism' and the central flogging-horse of attacks on that supposed school. Foster's own view, though, was that the efforts of previous decades of 'revisionist' history had had rather little general impact: 'by 1972 new textbooks were being used in schools and universities, and new questions were being asked. But what might seem most striking is how little this affected the popular (and paradoxically Anglocentric) version of Irish history held by the public mind.' (ibid: 595) As Gabriel Doherty—from a position less friendly to 'revisionism'—concurs, the efforts of the professional historians could only chip away at the edifice of popular historical belief, not undermine its foundations (1996:349).[16]

Arguably the strongest early challenges to simplistic nationalist ideas of the past, in terms of public impact, came not from the academic community of professional historians but from two figures who in very different ways stood outside it. One was a Jesuit priest, Francis Shaw, whose highly combative essay 'The Canon of Irish History: A Challenge' was published in 1972 in *Studies*, the ecumenical and intellectually impressive journal of the Irish Jesuits. The other was Conor Cruise O'Brien, whose book *States of Ireland* appeared in the same year. The significance of O'Brien, perhaps the most recurringly controversial of all modern Irish thinkers, is discussed further below. Father Shaw's challenge, however, requires brief attention here.

'The Canon of Irish History' had in fact been written for the fiftieth anniversary of the Easter Rising in 1966, but judged inappropriate for publication amidst the celebratory atmosphere of the commemoration. Its appearance six years later, after the author's death, still aroused storms, including front-page and editorial coverage in the *Irish Times*; and it has subsequently itself been canonised or stigmatised as the founding text of revisionism.[17] Shaw's polemic was a somewhat uneasy mixture of historico-moral critique of nationalism, and specifically religious condemnation of Pearse's blood sacrifice rhetoric, the Rising itself, and physical force insurrectionism generally. In the latter vein, it could be seen as reconnecting with the dominant tendency of the Catholic hierarchy before 1921 to proscribe militant nationalism as anti-Christian: a stance which had led to the senior clergy being viewed as pro-British under the Union. Thus far, Shaw's attitudes could be typecast as conservative and backward-looking, as they duly were by nationalist critics. Yet the condemnation of nationalist political violence, and even more of the allegedly idolatrous Pearsean idea of sacrifice to the national ideal, as abhorrent on theological grounds also looked forward both to later recurrent clerical censures of the IRA and to an end of the post-Treaty symbiosis between Catholic and Irish nationalist pieties. The ever-growing gulf between the two was reflected in several later works, notably in *Studies* itself, assaulting the Pearsean tradition from specifically religious premises.[18]

In terms of the historical debate on nationalism, what marked Shaw's essay as distinctive was its wholesale repudiation of the dominant nationalist idea as such. The reigning historical canon, Shaw charged:

> stamps the generation of 1916 as nationally degenerate, a generation in need of redemption by the shedding of blood. It honours one group of Irishmen by denying honour to others whose merit is not less. In effect it teaches that only the Fenians and the separatists had the good of their country at heart, that all others were either deluded or in one degree or another sold to the enemy. This canon moulds the broad course of Irish history to a narrow and pre-conceived pattern; it tells a story which is false and without foundation. (Shaw 1972:117–18)

It could be counter-charged that Shaw's argument itself sought to impose a 'narrow and pre-conceived pattern', writing out British policies, social and economic conflicts, and the social content of nationalist movements themselves in order to present nationalism as merely a kind of false religion, to be fought in the name of the true, Christian one. The idea of nationalism as a religion, or as akin to one, is by no means evidently trivial or false, as Carlton Hayes and Benedict Anderson remind us. But clearly the very various movements and ideologies grouped together as nationalist, across the past few centuries of Irish history, cannot very usefully be categorised *only* in such terms. Although Maurice Goldring's dismissal of Shaw's article as 'naive, crude, prejudiced and almost entirely lacking historical foundation' (Goldring 1993:87) is in its turn grossly overstated, it is Shaw's depiction of nationalism which provides sanction, if any does, for claims like Luke Gibbons's that revisionism itself created the monolithic nationalist ideology which it claimed to combat.

For over two decades now Conor Cruise O'Brien has been the most famous and influential Irish critic of Irish nationalism. His nationalist critics have indeed often accused him of hating Ireland and the Irish. He sometimes sounds as though he does: but that may have been his greatest service to them. One of Lawrence Durrell's characters in the *Alexandria Quartet* asserts that: 'It is the duty of every patriot to hate his country creatively'.[19] By that standard at least, O'Brien could be counted among the foremost Irish patriots of the century.

O'Brien's intellectual career pursued a long trajectory of development, from fairly orthodox nationalism, towards not only accepting but celebrating the legitimacy of Ulster Unionism, and viewing the Catholic-Nationalist ideology as steeped in original sin. This culminated in 1996 with his joining and seeking election on behalf of Robert McCartney's new United Kingdom Unionist Party. Its earlier stages, and greatest continuing influence, came in 1972 with O'Brien's book *States of Ireland.* This mixed autobiography, history and political analysis in a manner O'Brien had already essayed in *To Katanga and Back* and was to repeat in most of his later writing. It was an unsystematic and even a disorderly book; but perhaps in part precisely because of its lack of rigour, it not only founded one strand of 'revisionism' (that identified by Desmond Fennell as anti-nationalist revisionism) but anticipated, at least in passing, most major themes in subsequent discussion of the Northern Ireland problem and the Irish Republic's relations to it. O'Brien was keenly aware of potential colonial analogies for Irish affairs—he had, after all, worked in the Congo and Ghana, and had written a small *tour de force* of a book on Albert Camus, the French-Algerian novelist—and placed the analysis of Ireland's position as a colonial one at centre stage, only to expose its limitations. Invoking that latterly most popular of colonial images in relation to Ireland, Frantz Fanon's manichean dichotomy between colonisers and colonised, he immediately urged that this, though suggestive, was 'too simple for the [Irish] situation, and for most others.' At the start of the century, he believed, at least six contending groups could be identified in Irish cultural politics, rather than Fanon's starkly opposed duo (O'Brien 1974:71). He also explored differing conceptions of Irishness, some including and some excluding the Protestant populations—and argued that the founding figures of romantic and physical-force nationalism, including not only Pearse but also James Connolly, entirely failed to think seriously about Protestants or about Ulster, and in practice adopted definitions of the Irish nation which excluded them. This was, at the time, still largely a novel and certainly a scandalous proposition, with the criticism of Connolly (ibid: 89–97) especially

perturbing for the Irish left to which O'Brien belonged. O'Brien charged that
what he considered a resultant endemic confusion about the very concept of
Ireland, a blindness and self-deception over who was truly part of the Irish
people, and over the relationship between religion and nationality, bore a significant part of the blame for the north's descent into violence after 1969.

As the years went by, O'Brien moved ever more decisively and stridently to
the view that Irish Catholic nationalism must bear *all* the blame for that violence. In his much later book *Ancestral Voices* (O'Brien 1994), accompanied by a
mass of 1990s journalism making the same case, O'Brien's argument is simple;
and is far cruder than the attitudes he had expressed while his disengagement
from Irish nationalist thought was still in process. In Ireland over the last century, religion and nationalism have become inextricably intertwined, to the
detriment of both. Nationalism has taken on all the worst characteristics of religious fanaticism, while the Catholic Church in Ireland has become deeply
embroiled in nationalist politics (see also, for O'Brien's views on the intertwinement of religion and nationalism, his 1988b). His 1990s view is that the
awful, bigoted mixture which he calls sacral nationalism continues to shape Ireland's political culture, and is the driving force behind the policies not only of
Gerry Adams, but of John Hume, Albert Reynolds and Dick Spring. (After
Reynolds's replacement by John Bruton, O'Brien unsurprisingly found him too
to be cast from the same mould, while *his* successor, Bertie Ahern, was adjudged
as even worse.) From this it follows that the Irish 'peace process' is actually
nothing of the kind, but is rather the continuation by other means of an unbroken Holy War against Britishness and Protestantism.

In these more recent writings, the political argument is again interlaced with
autobiography and with family reminiscences. O'Brien's parents and other
immediate relatives represented among them every variety of response to Irishness and Catholicism. Almost all Ireland's major literary and political figures,
many of them by now mythical characters—Yeats and Joyce, Patrick Pearse and
Maud Gonne, De Valera and Lady Gregory—were family friends. The 'ancestral
voices' which haunt modern Ireland are, for O'Brien, also the voices of a personal ancestry. Clearly he has come to feel himself, in old age, in some sense
betrayed by it.

O'Brien undoubtedly presents an overly monolithic picture of Irish nationalist traditions. Analysing the mystical and dogmatic rhetoric of a D. P. Moran
or a Pearse, he does not see these as representing one extreme within a varied
spectrum of nationalist thought. Rather, such voices are viewed as expressing
the hidden truth of *all* Irish nationalism—those who appear more moderate,
secular, democratic or non-sectarian than they, are in O'Brien's eyes merely less
honest. This is often quite evidently unfair; as when O'Brien claims of John
Hume that his 'actual attitude to Ulster Protestants is the implacable and relentless hostility of the seventeenth century' (1994:92). O'Brien does not entirely

ignore the more generous, ecumenical, strands of Irish nationalism, but he does hold the fixed view that those who propounded such relatively attractive versions of what he thinks at heart a bigoted creed were and are mostly fools or frauds.

If consistency can be found in O'Brien's thought across the decades, it lies in his particular brand of cosmopolitan liberalism. This has itself been subject to the varying, buffeting crosswinds of international politics, in its relations to anticolonial nationalism (in its African, Arab and Zionist as well as Irish variants), to the Cold War, to socialism and to religion. Broadly, O'Brien has become ever more passionately convinced that his kind of liberalism—increasingly closely linked to Edmund Burke's kind, even if O'Brien's first major biographer, Donald Harman Akenson (1995) goes overboard in proclaiming a near-mystical filial relationship between the two—is incompatible with socialism, with nationalism and with organised religion. He himself claims, though, a further 'underlying consistency and continuity.'

I was brought up to detest imperialism . . . As a servant of the United Nations, I combated a British imperialist enterprise in Central Africa in 1961: the covert effort to sustain secession in Katanga in order to bolster the masked white supremacy of the then Central African Federation. From 1965–1969, in America, I took part in the protest movement against an American imperialist enterprise: the war in Vietnam. And from 1971 until now I have been combating an Irish Catholic imperialist enterprise: the effort to force the Protestants of Northern Ireland, by a combination of paramilitary terror and political pressure, into a United Ireland they don't want. (1994:5)

Despite all this it may well still be—as Ernest Gellner argues in one of the few extended critiques of O'Brien's work other than internalist Irish ones—that O'Brien remains 'not only an analyst, but also a victim, of nationalism.' (Gellner 1994:60) This is because he remains wedded to the idea that: 'the nation, whatever that be, is the natural political unit . . . He has not come to see that this is a contingent, historically limited condition, and not a universal, self-evident verity.' (ibid: 60) Gellner also rightly points to the lack of discussion or even reference, in O'Brien's writings on nationalism, to almost any of the modern non-Irish literature on the subject. O'Brien is clearly not parochial in his concerns, in the usual sense: his knowledge of international affairs, and his comparative allusions, are substantial. But the major intellectual influences on him remain local ones (above all that of Edmund Burke). He has apparently not considered that Irish experience might be illuminated by reference to Benedict Anderson or Eric Hobsbawm, Karl Deutsch or Elie Kedourie, Anthony Smith or Miroslav Hroch. In that he is all too typical of modern Irish historical writing.

Merely to list such names and works as those mentioned above and in the previous chapter, is to indicate the huge variety of perspectives as well as research themes among so-called Irish historical revisionists, even confining oneself to those whose writing has focused on the past century. Amongst those who have produced large-scale overviews of modern Irish history, for instance, Roy Foster and Joseph Lee have extraordinarily little in common, either methodologically or politically. And if one delves further back to the origins of British rule in Ireland, then it becomes virtually meaningless to lump together, say, Ciaran Brady and Steven Ellis as fellow 'revisionists'.

In purely academic terms, then, one could dismiss the whole 'revisionist— anti-revisionist' dispute as an irrelevance: almost all serious practising histor- ians are in the former camp, and they have too little in common to form an identifiable school or movement. As has more than once only half-jokingly been said, if a historian is not in some sense a revisionist then she must be a pla- giarist. It might then seem obvious to propose, as Tom Dunne does in the *Irish Review*, that the wave of the future lies beyond this increasingly sterile debate, in a 'post-revisionism' which 'involves a new focus on vital areas (marginalised in the nationalist account) such as women's history or local history, and the many other narratives of ordinary life' (Dunne 1992:11).[20] Several other historians have come to describe themselves as post-revisionist (e.g. Kevin Whelan 1996a:x) or have complained rightly at the 'rather jaded' character of an aca- demic historical debate obsessed with the 'revisionist' label (Liam Kennedy 1996:222).

But the whole point, in a sense, is that this has not been and could never yet be—to ironise my own words a few lines back—a debate 'in purely academic terms'. One of the reasons why not is underlined, albeit in a formulation which over-emphasises the distinction between the academic and the political, by Fionnuala O Connor's remarkable book of interviews with Northern Irish Catholics:

Attitudes to the South are not lightly placed on record. People preferred to talk about what they took to be Southern opinions of Northerners, even though these were unpleasant, rather than about their own feelings. Those who were best informed became passionate about one aspect alone: revisionism. Not the academic business of re-examining history, 'revisionist' was instead used angrily to mean 'anti-Northerner' in general. (O Connor 1993:228)

The active Republicans among O Connor's interviewees, unsurprisingly, gave such sentiments a harder edge. A prominent Belfast IRA man, inevitably anonym- ous, suggested that: 'There's an intellectual poverty in the South as a result of partition, a crisis within what should pass for the intelligentsia because of the Northern conflict. The worst spewing by academics is all revisionist—all because of the state's own need for preservation.' (ibid: 240) And Gerry Adams expressed the underlying anxieties in a way that is, perhaps, unconsciously revealing:

What revisionism has done is tell people they can't be satisfied with what they come from. That's putting things you thought of as constants under attack: the effect's like a family trauma, like discovering you've been adopted . . . all that is where revisionism has had a political effect, where people can't be contented and confident with what they are. (ibid: 246–7)

What is more surprising, perhaps, is to find rather similar sentiments, of resentment at being deprived of a comforting version of one's history, echoed by a then very prominent academic who was soon to attain a political prominence far greater still: Mary McAleese, then Director of Belfast's Institute of Professional Legal Studies, subsequently elected President of the Irish Republic. She told O Connor of her encounter with the symbolically charged figure of Conor Cruise O'Brien thus: 'Here was this extraordinarily arrogant man, in the process of revising everything that I had known to be a given and a truth about Irish history—and who set in motion a way of looking at Northern Ireland that we are only now beginning to grow up and grow out of.' (ibid: 263) 'Revising everything that I had known to be a given and a truth'—this is not the statement of a critical mind which detects falsehood, but the lament of a religious believer whose faith is questioned.[21]

'Revisionism', then, is apparently associated in many Northern Irish Catholic minds with those in the Republic who, they think, view them and their problems as simply a nuisance or an embarrassment, an obstacle on the road to Ireland's modernisation and Europeanisation (or, in the eyes of some nationalists, its further neocolonialisation).

Daltun Ó Ceallaigh, for instance, believes that revisionism amounts only to the 'portrayal of nationhood as a myth' after which demolition job 'what is left is not an enriched and positive rendition of Irish history but a stark abnegation.' (1994:12) Alluding to the 'revisionist' tendency to highlight the exclusivist and sectarian currents within Irish nationalism, he proclaims that:

Probably the same type of critic, confronted with Nazi crimes in the Germany of the 1930s, would have been quick to opine that the Third Reich was not without its Jewish bigots. (ibid: 15)[22]

In a metaphor which may be unintendedly revealing of Ó Ceallaigh's emotional roots, he describes revisionism as 'like a dispoiled church full of smashed images' (22), and believes that 'if this overweening and callous enterprise were to be taken fully to heart, Ireland would be left mentally supine and prey to political bullying and cultural hegemony from without.' (22) Even the far more intellectually flexible and ecumenical Terry Eagleton could still be found, in 1998, caricaturing revisionism as being all about 'shutting up about the Famine so as not to annoy the Brits . . . revising Irish history in order to sanitise colonialism and slander republicanism' (1998b:132).[23]

The political implications of historical 'revisionism' provoked sharp public

exchanges already in the early seventies, fuelled by the outbreak of serious violence in the north. Their tenor was well exemplified by John Hume's famous
Irish Times review of *States of Ireland*, a review which some see as having been
deliberately designed to break O'Brien's political career (Akenson 1995:378–82).
Only much more recently, though, did such political controversy over Irish history become more generalised and ambient. There have been episodes when
attempts have been made directly to associate the wider historico-political
arguments with quotidian party conflict, perhaps especially in the early 1980s
when supporters of embattled Fianna Fail leader Charles Haughey alleged that
his critics sought to topple him because of their Anglophile resentment at his
Republicanism. Thus Fianna Fail deputy Niall Andrews claimed that a well-
organised pro-British lobby threatened Ireland's sovereignty, and that 'revisionist' historical writing and attempts to indict Haughey and his associates for
corruption were merely two wings of the same sinister movement. Andrews
named Conor Cruise O'Brien, *Irish Independent* writer Bruce Arnold, and
Limerick socialist politician Jim Kemmy (all three historians as well as political
figures) as ringleaders of this anti-national conspiracy. (Joyce and Murtagh
1983:251–2)[24] Such directly partisan assaults on the 'revisionists' have, however,
been unusual—except, perhaps, from the pens of Northern Republicans (e.g.
Rolston 1992b)—though some academic commentators have appeared to associate revisionism quite directly with political conservatism and with Unionism
(for instance, Kevin Whelan 1991).

Some others would also reject the 'revisionist' label largely for political
reasons, as does Nicholas Canny. He fears that although the growing professionalism and sophistication of Irish historiography has led to its fuller acceptance into international Anglophone debate: 'the price of acceptance has been
absorption. By this I mean that scholars working on Ireland now not only feel
the need, as did earlier authors, to make reference to current publications on
England, Wales and Scotland, but also feel obliged to dovetail their work with
the preoccupations and prejudices of the leading historians of Britain.' (Canny
1996:246)[25]

It has been rare in the Irish context—by comparison with the rhetorics of cultural nationalism in, for instance, the African diaspora and South Asia—to present nationalist history overtly and selfconsciously as necessary myth, as the
counter-narrativisation of the oppressed and excluded's 'writing back'. Ordinarily nationalist historiography has contested with revisionism on the ground
of 'the facts', or of claim and counter-claim about ideological distortion. In its
more fundamentalist forms, indeed, it asserts that historical writing from any
political perspective other than its own represents ideologically driven apologetics, while it alone remains true to the factual record (for an unusually 'pure'
contemporary variant of this stance, see the work of Brian P. Murphy). The
voice of the self-proclaimed mythographer, though, is increasingly heard in

Ireland too. Usually it takes its cue, as parallel movements elsewhere do, from poststructuralism. But it also has more 'traditional' variants, as for instance from someone who has been first and foremost, through all his ideological vagaries, a Catholic nationalist writer, Desmond Fennell:

Every nation in its here and now, the people who make up the nation now, have needs with respect to their national history. They need for their collective wellbeing an image of their national past which sustains and energises them personally, and which bonds them together by making their inherited nation seem a value worth adhering to and working for.

Thus Ireland needs 'historians whose passion for factual truth, and for conscientious moral judgement, is equalled by their piety for their nation's pattern of historical meaning, and their regard for what their fellowcountrymen, and they themselves, need from their national history for their minds and hearts' (Fennell in Field Day 1991, III:588–9, orig. pub. 1988). As against such pious paragons, revisionism is 'the historiography of the Irish counter-revolution.' (ibid: 587)

A similar, and similarly impassioned, anti-revisionist call came almost simultaneously from historian Brendan Bradshaw. He not only denounced the 'cynicism' of those who refuse to endorse 'the controlling conception of nationalist historiography, the notion of a "national past" of Irish history as the story of an Irish nation unfolding historically through the centuries.' (Bradshaw 1989:345) He actually argued that the nationalist master-narrative should be protected from such attacks even if it is wrong, because it is a 'beneficent legacy'. (ibid: 347–8)[26]

This rallying-cry is to be encountered in numerous national contexts. It is the demand for a usable past, for history as necessary myth: usable and necessary in the service of national identity. What gives the demand its perceived legitimacy, its moral credit, is the belief that the identity thus served is an oppressed one, defending itself against threat rather than threatening others. Thus it is crucial, in the Irish as in other 'postcolonial' cases, not only to assert that the national past whose integrity, continuity and heroism is being proclaimed was one of resistance to colonial oppression, but also to insist that the nation's *present* is menaced by and struggling against colonialism. Non-nationalist, postnationalist and 'revisionist' historical interpretations—or even ones which cast doubt on the infinite malevolence and destructiveness of the former rulers[27]— are thus seen as playing into the hands of the nation's enemies and helping perpetuate the colonial stranglehold. That is why it is evidently important, emotionally and politically, for Brendan Bradshaw to insist on the 'catastrophic dimension' of Irish history (1989:341), and elsewhere to speak of Protestants imposing 'apartheid' in early modern Ireland (Bradshaw 1978:502; see also the critique by Canny 1986). Bill Rolston, in equally polemical vein, makes the same unexamined South African analogy: (Rolston 1993:15). There are marked resemblances to what Edward Said (1993) has described, and deplored, as the 'rhetoric of blame' in numerous postcolonial cultural nationalisms.

Another striking point of comparison between these Irish disputes and arguments over the nature of historical understanding in other arguably postcolonial contexts lies in supposedly contending ideas about the nature of historical time itself. An increasingly widespread trope in postmodernist/postcolonial discourse about the status of 'History', as a discipline and a conceptual category, has been a claim that 'non-western' or colonised peoples reject linear, progressivist, developmentalist and rationalist notions of history, which are seen as very specifically European and colonialist in origin and intent, and especially associated with the Hegelian legacy.[28] Attempts to apply this dichotomy in its currently theorised forms to Irish experience—most notably made by David Lloyd (see below pp. 128–31) have been rather schematic and derivative. But we can find some intriguing precursors, as for instance in Ernie O'Malley's characteristically allusive mixture of landscape, mythography and the minutiae of guerrilla war. In 1921, in County Mayo, an IRA unit waits to fight—in a district whose inhabitants harbour a legend of a once-and-future battle fought there between the Irish and their foes:

From their vantage point on the peak, the seven IRA men were able to identify the islands . . . Below them, glistening in the reflected light, as far as they could see, was the whole history of the district. Some of them could supply memoried fragments which in a folklore territory went back to medieval times.

Time there brought past, present and future together. The British would solve a problem as if time were a matter of temporary expediency, but it would be difficult for them to relate the past and present and future in an indivisible unit. (Ernie O'Malley 1982:177)

The same antithesis resonates through numerous imaginative works, as for instance in Thomas Flanagan's acclaimed novel about 1798, *The Year of the French* (1979). Oliver MacDonagh, in more analytical vein, suggests something rather similar. He believes that one can discern two sharply opposed conceptions of historical time, dominant respectively in Irish and in English attitudes. The first involves an apprehension of the repetitiveness and cyclical character of historical events, indeed the simultaneity of all historical time. MacDonagh suggests that this is a specifically Christian (non-predestinarian) belief—though to some readers it may recall also the ideas of Walter Benjamin at his most Judaically mystical; ideas which have recently gained a somewhat modish popularity among those who want excuses for not taking history seriously.

Negatively, it may be described as an absence of a developmental or sequential view of past events. Positively, it implies a mode or habit of judgement and apprehension outside a chronologically calibrated, or indeed any, time scale . . . Such a view appears to me to approximate to the concept of the past which infused Irish historiography at its modern commencement and which still infuses the historical assumptions of most ordinary Irish people. (MacDonagh 1983:6–7)

Such a conception was fertile ground for the defence of prejudice, ignorance and anachronism; but also for historical interpretation in terms of transcendent ideals of law and morality. The passage of time did nothing to soften past injustices or lessen the need for their redress. It is a view, MacDonagh believes, as entrenched among Unionists and Protestants as Nationalists and Catholics. He sees it operating in the language of Carson and the Covenant, of O'Connell, Parnell and Redmond, O'Neill, Faulkner and Hume:

Whether it is 1778, 1782, 1793 or 1825 the same forces operate in the same fashion. There is a constant relationship between the oscillation of coercion and conciliation on the part of the overlord and the oscillation of negotiation and the threat of violence upon the part of the subjected. (ibid: 9)

The dominant English conception, by contrast, was that of 'beneficial development' (ibid: 9). Its locus classicus lies in the Whig view, where:

past evils were weighted according to the lesser potentiality for evil which existed in simpler circumstances. Here was a view of time in which the march of reason, of knowledge and of compassion was steadily diminishing the relative power and extent of immorality . . . The corollary of such moral expansionism was a corresponding diminution of any sense of responsibility for the past. (ibid: 10–11)

But although classical Whig progressivism may be largely dead, its essential components—history as development, relativism, the steadily declining significance of the past as its events themselves recede chronologically—remain in MacDonagh's view pervasive. He insists that these contrasting historical assumptions have not been 'either innate or universal' (ibid: 11). It is tempting, however, to see the disputes discussed here as replaying the antitheses yet once more, as with the thinly disguised Whiggery of a Roy Foster and its vehement repudiation by Fennell and Bradshaw. And as we shall see, postcolonial cultural theory in Irish as in other contexts has sought to resuscitate an idea that the contrast *is* innate, universal, civilisational—and normative, with progressivism and rationalism identified as innately imperialist. Postmodernism has given the anti-developmentalist stance a new lease of life, or at least draped it in modish new robes.

(ii) Histories: Orange

Unionist historical narratives in modern Ireland have evolved in parallel—and, increasingly though still too incompletely, in dialogue—with nationalist versions. They have, however, been far less studied or debated than the latter,

with the general tendency being to assimilate Irish, and then Ulster, Unionists'
historical consciousness either to the melting-pot of Britishness (and hence,
primarily to Englishness) or to the emblematic caricatures of bowler hat, fife
and lambeg drum. Theo Moody, in his famous dissection of nationalist myths
in Irish historiography—a founding moment in 'revisionism'—also noted
some especially important Unionist myths. These, though, were not his main
focus, and subsequently the development of Unionist historiography has been
relatively neglected by modern historians—though this is an omission Alvin
Jackson, Brian Walker, Ian McBride and others are now seeking to rectify.

The main thrust and abiding problem of Ulster Unionist historical thinking,
at least since Partition and in some ways already during the previous century,
has been to match time with place: to express or create a sense of Ulster itself
(whether in six- or nine-county incarnation) as the subject of a coherent historical narrative. No one doubted that Ulster was, in some significant ways, different from the remainder of Ireland; but attempts to project this
distinctiveness far back in time have seemingly had little to support them.
Archaeologists, ancient and medieval historians find that no clear cultural divisions can be discerned between Ulster (however its boundaries are defined:
these have 'always been very much a moveable feast' (Mallory and McNeill
1991:325)) and the rest of the island. Archaeological remains 'have often empha-
sized either regionalism within Ulster itself or the fact that Ulster participated in
the same type of cultural behaviour that we often find outside its borders.' (ibid:
325) The evidence for a separate Iron Age Ulster kingdom is limited and
ambiguous: the picture presented in the 'Ulster Cycle' of heroic tales, of kings
ruling from Emain Macha (Navan Fort near Armagh) over the whole of the
modern nine counties, may reflect the boastful aspiration of an actually much
more restricted rulership, rather than historical reality. Similarly, it is by no
means clear what kind of political, let alone cultural, boundary was represented
by the 'Black Pig's Dyke' and other major linear earthworks in south Armagh,
Donegal and Monaghan which have usually been seen as defences of an ancient
Ulster against invaders or raiders from the rest of Ireland. (Mallory and McNeill
1991:150–3, 164–71[29]) The modern geographical boundaries of Ulster—nine- or
six-county—'are nothing more than the legacy of Queen Elizabeth's map-
makers.' (ibid: 326) In terms of population, for Ulster as for the rest of Ireland,
the major basis and in all probability the main ancestry of today's inhabitants
lies with the Neolithic migrants who first brought agriculture to the island: 'no
subsequent immigration to Ireland is ever likely to have contained anywhere
near the number of people as were already settled in Ireland before they arrived.
Whether we accept the putative movement of Bronze Age peoples or a variety of
Iron Age Celtic populations, subsequent Vikings, Scots, Huguenots, or English,
each was invariably only an intrusive minority to the already existing population of Ulster.' (ibid: 326) Identification of an Ulster with a very long historical

pedigree is thus extremely problematic. Moreover, even perception of long-existing Ulster distinctiveness by no means necessarily implies support for partition in the twentieth century: thus for instance the great historical geographer Estyn Evans was a strong proponent of the former, but regarded the latter as a tragedy (see Crossman and McLoughlin 1994).

Nonetheless, attempts to project Ulster distinctiveness far back in time have been politically significant. Recent attempts to provide historico-mythographic underpinnings for Unionist and Loyalist political projects, though less elaborately developed and less widely endorsed than their Catholic-nationalist counterparts, share many of the same features and the same intellectual flaws. The classic instance of this is Ian Adamson's mythography of the Cruthin, designed to provide ancient historical underpinnings for a militantly separatist sense of Ulster identity, and in many respects a mirror-image of Sinn Fein's invocation of ancestral Gaelic virtues (Adamson 1974, 1982, 1991, 1994, Hall 1986, 1993, 1994a, b). Adamson's claim is that the 'Cruthin' (or 'Pretani') were the original inhabitants of both Ireland and Scotland, and it was in Ulster that they held out longest against the invading Celts. The Scottish planters who migrated to Ulster from the sixteenth century were, therefore, merely reclaiming their ancestral homelands. Ulster's cultural distinctiveness, then, has extremely ancient roots as well as much underrated glories.[30] Adamson's attempt to show the European or even global significance of ancient and medieval Ulster intellectual life, centred on the sixth-century monastery of Bangor, directly parallels the exaggerated claims routinely made by Catholic nationalists for Gaelic Ireland's religious learning and missionary endeavours; though Adamson takes the trait to peculiar extremes, describing little Bangor in one of his tracts as the 'Light of the World' (Adamson 1979).

Adamson himself, and his co-thinker Michael Hall, have been anxious to repudiate sectarian appropriations of their work. The Cruthin, according to Adamson, are not just the ancestors of Ulster's Protestants but form a large part of the heritage of all the region's people. He sharply dissociates himself from those 'who have tried to use my work in their efforts to justify a sectarian position . . . a "we were here first" mentality' (1991:xiii). His theories provide, he believes 'proof of the common identity of the Northerners . . . the facts of their history, for once, offered the hope of uniting the Ulster people at last.' (ibid: 104) Hall, similarly, describes as 'blatant misrepresentation' any idea that contemporary Protestants are descended from the Cruthin, Catholics from the Gaels (1994a:23). Hall also argues that Ireland's present population, Protestant and Catholic, is mostly descended from pre-Gaelic inhabitants. This is probably correct: as we have just noted, professional archaeologists tend to concur. In Ulster specifically, the historical-political message is clear: 'Throughout history Ulster and its people have exhibited a distinctive identity.' (1993:19)[31] This is, moreover, seen as an identity which escapes nationalist claims to become part of a shared Europeanness, with for instance the Ulster Saint Columbanus 'the patron saint of those who seek to construct a united Europe.' (Hall 1994b:13)

Adamson and Hall's polemical and popularising intentions were evident. Their books and pamphlets can be found very widely available—certainly not only in specialist bookshops—across Protestant Northern Ireland. Their populist efforts extended to a sword-and-sorcery style comic book treatment of the Cuchulainn story, complete with both soft porn spicing and an Ulster nationalist subtext (Hall and Hamilton 1989), and to numerous articles in the Ulster Defence Association newspaper *Ulster*. Hall was explicit about his propagandist aims, saying of his *Ulster: The Hidden History* that 'I don't see it as a book, I see it as a weapon'(quoted Belfrage 1988:343), and scorning 'merely academic' historians (Hall 1994a:10–11). Adamson's themes have had some significance for the Loyalist militants of the UDA, but their actual political impact was rather limited, even within such circles (McAuley 1991:55–7; Bruce 1992:235–6).[32] Nor have their ideas found much favour among professional archaeologists or historians. Indeed as the most authoritative contemporary overview of Ulster archaeology says:

Whether any of this is true or not is hardly discussable since the Cruthin as a distinct ethnic group are archaeologically invisible, that is, there is not a single object or site that an archaeologist can declare to be distinctly Cruthin . . . [I]f the Cruthin are imagined to have been early medieval descendants of the original Neolithic population of Ireland, then . . . attributing to them a common all-Irish much less an Irish-Scottish identity up until the arrival of the Celts is quite remarkable . . . about the only thing the Cruthin hypothesis does emphasize are the continuous interactions between Ulster and Scotland. (Mallory and McNeill 1991:177–8)

The relative lack of appeal such ideas have had amongst ordinary Unionists, or possibly even the rank and file of the Loyalist paramilitaries, is obliquely suggested also in Bill Rolston's survey of political murals in Northern Ireland (Rolston 1992a). Not one of the Loyalist murals he reproduces alludes to prehistorical or mythic themes (though subsequently several have appeared in Belfast, depicting mythical figures like Cuchullain who supposedly 'defended Ulster against the Irish'). What they *do* show provides an intriguing window on a popular Loyalist sense of historical reference points. Of those which take historical topics, the overwhelming majority depict William III. Five take the Somme as their theme, two the siege of Derry, one the battle of Aughrim, and just one depicts Sir Edward Carson. On the Republican side, murals with historical themes are overall less common, enabling Rolston somewhat tendentiously to claim that popular art shows how Loyalism looks only to the past, Republicanism to a hoped-for future (ibid: v). Among the backward-looking Republican images, however, Celtic symbolism features prominently—other popular historical themes being pictures of Connolly, Pearse and above all the 1981 hunger strikers.

Neil Jarman's survey of images on Orange Institution banners in the 1990s points in rather similar directions. He photographed a total of 578 images on 336 banners between 1990 and 1996. 221 of these depicted Williamite scenes, 196 being the familiar representation of William III himself on his white horse. Against this, only sixty-three showed other historical scenes: twenty of these illustrating the Somme, just four the signing of the Ulster Covenant, thirty-nine images from Protestant history from both Ulster and beyond, including twelve of the Oxford 'martyrdom' of Cranmer, Latimer and Ridley. Far more—147 in total—had biblical and other religious images; though fifty-three of these combined religion with patriotism by depicting Crown and Bible together. Sixty showed local places and buildings, forty-three portraits of past Orange dignitaries, thirty-five were specifically British or imperial, displaying portraits of monarchs, Britannia or 'the Secret of England's Greatness' (Jarman 1997: Table 8.1). The banners of the Royal Black Institution were far more single-mindedly religious in theme: 250 of a total 326 images were biblical or other Christian ones, only two Williamite (ibid: Table 8.2). Jarman's far smaller sample of banners carried by Catholic paraders, the Ancient Order of Hibernians and Irish National Foresters, indicates that these characteristically link religion and cultural nationalism, with St Patrick, the 'Maid of Erin', and various historical Irish saints and martyrs featuring far more heavily than the handful of figures from the secular nationalist pantheon like Pearse, O'Connell or Patrick Sarsfield (ibid: 192–205 and Table 9.1).[33]

All this suggests a Loyalist historical imagination overwhelmingly fixated on the seventeenth century and secondarily on the 'blood sacrifice' of the Ulster regiments at the Somme,[34] with the 1912 Home Rule crisis playing a surprisingly small part. This emphasis on the period 1640–92 as being formative of all subsequent Unionist perceptions is also that proposed by A. T. Q. Stewart (1977) and Brian Walker (1992, 1996): though Stewart tends to see it as having been handed down across the intervening centuries, Walker (surely more accurately) as being largely a late-Victorian creation. The remarkable pervasiveness and persistence of myth about the era may be indicated by the way the prominent DUP figure Sammy Wilson, in interview with Tony Parker, repeated the figure of 150,000 Protestants massacred in 1641—a figure which was the product of contemporary propaganda and, as we have seen, is at least twenty times the real deathtoll. (Tony Parker 1993:139–40)[35]

In related if yet more strident—if not paranoid—vein, a contributor to the UUP's *Ulster Review* in 1997 saw Nationalist opposition to Orange marches as merely 'a milder variety of the same spirit as underlay the boycotts, the border genocide, the Munster Pogroms of the 1920s, the Whiteboy massacres of 1798 and the Bann massacres of 1641—a simple sectarianism.' (Sam Gray 1997:13) Catholic Nationalist behaviour thus appeared to be seen as the expression of a malevolent, invariant, essence whose founding ethos lay in the events of the 1640s and has never really altered.

Alvin Jackson, however, argues persuasively that images of and myths about
Carson and Craig, the Ulster Covenant, the UVF and their gun-running, have
become the seminal reference points for modern Unionism and Loyalism. He
notes especially the recurrent attempts by Ian Paisley to don Carson's mantle,
the centrality of this historical moment to such formations as the Ulster Society,
and he suggests that if Irish Catholic families treasured portraits of the Pope and
the Kennedies, 'the Unionist household gods were the king-emperor, William
III, and—above all—Carson.' (Alvin Jackson 1992:172) In some respects at least
this too has been, as Jackson also acknowledges, a recent historical appropriation: an image of 1912–14 first appeared in Loyalist wall-painting, he believes,
only as late as 1987 (ibid: 178).[36] It was in significant part prompted by the
renewed sense of threat and potential betrayal experienced by Unionists during
the 1980s, and especially with the Anglo-Irish Agreement: 'the isolation of 1914
became the isolation of 1985' (177). In this context, its power and sincerity
should not be underrated—in which regard Jackson draws an intriguing comparison with the 'counter-revisionist' writings in Irish historiography, which
have reminded historians of the importance of empathy in interpreting the past
(178). And the resonance for today of the Unionist mobilisations of 1912–14 is
better understood when it is noted that the latter were, for the first time in
Ulster's history, fully modern (led by commercial and industrial elites rather
than landlords) and fully participatory (involving substantial numbers of
urban workers and other non-elite groups, and doing so in ways going far
beyond mere passive assent). Thus it can be figured as an appropriately direct
precursor of contemporary Paisleyite or other *levées en masse*. (Jackson
1989:320–6, 1992:183–5).

For all that, memories of 1912–14 or 1690 proved, in Jackson's view, all too
feeble a basis for an identity. He refers dismissively to the 'constrained historical
vision of loyalism' which in turn derives from 'the limitations of Unionist ideology—a monochrome present created from a monochrome past.' (1992:185) And
the poverty of historical imagination, Jackson believes, had powerful modern
political effects, contributing substantially to the collapse of Unionist rule itself
in 1972:

Unionist Ulster failed in 1972 partly because Northern Ireland had never been a coherent aspiration, and partly because the ideology and ceremonial of the state, the history
exploited by the Unionist movement, illustrated this fact with a brutal clarity. Unionist
Ulster failed partly because it was failed by its own past. (ibid: see also Jackson 1994,
1996a)

Brian Graham, similarly—though with symptomatic cursoriness, as if the
point had no need of discussion—proclaims that 'the traditional poverty of
Unionist historical awareness' has necessarily led to 'cultural incoherence and
political impotence' (1997a:39). And Terence Brown reaches for exactly the

same language, charging that the Unionist historical imagination is 'impoverished'. (1985a:8)

Graham moreover sees the Unionist historical sense as marked not only by 'traditional poverty' but by a lack of an overarching, coherent, developmental narrative. Instead:

[S]ingle events, often of sectarian hue, substitute for the powerful cultural synthesis that Nationalists derive from the meshing of place and past. Set outside place, and indeed time, these events lack any continuity of theme, a narrative that might connect them together. Above all, they singularly fail to provide a coherent text of place. (1997a:40)

Graham's emphasis on the supposed absence of a sense of place in Unionist visions of the past is questionable. It might be argued, on the contrary, that popular historiography, as displayed for instance in Loyalist song, is unusually replete with specific location, landscape and placenames: just to list a sample of songtitles, think of 'Derry's Walls', 'The Boyne Water', 'Green Grassy Slopes of the Boyne', 'Tandragee', 'Aghalee Heroes', 'Ducks of Magheralin', 'Battle of Garvagh', 'Dolly's Brae', 'Enniskillen Dragoons', 'Star of the County Down' . . .

The claim about a lack of narrative synthesis may have more force. Certainly it is true that official Unionist self-presentations did not come to include a fully-fledged, consecutive historical narrative—as opposed to a series of tableaux focused on specific, mostly seventeenth-century, historic episodes—of the sort normally accompanying and legitimating nationalist state-building and so prolifically generated by Irish nationalism. Calls for a Stormont-sponsored 'official' history of Ulster were several times made, but never acted upon (see Loughlin 1995:144–5). The nearest Stormont came to producing such a book was a pamphlet, Hugh Shearman's *Northern Ireland: Its History, Resources and People* (1946, updated 1950 and 1968). Naturally it was a pro-Unionist account, one identifying 'the Ulster community' with Protestants only, but it fell very far short of providing a full-blown, legitimating genealogy for the Northern Irish semi-state. Nor did any sympathetic British writer move to fill the gap. The popular English historian Arthur Bryant, with his close personal interest in Ulster, was very active from the 1930s in pushing for a better 'mainland' understanding of what he saw as Ulster's essential Britishness (Loughlin 1995:101–3), but Bryant was an exceptional figure in this, and even he never produced the major historical account of Ulster for which his Northern Irish friends hoped. In addition, as an associate of various extreme-right groupings before 1939, Bryant was not perhaps Ulster's ideal international defender. Only as late as 1992, two decades after the fall of Stormont, did a major synthesising narrative treatment of Ulster's history from prehistory to modern times finally emerge, with Jonathan Bardon's monumental work: and this was very far from being the apologetic account for which Unionist politicians had earlier canvassed. On the contrary, as most critics from varying political positions concurred, Bardon's was a remarkably even-handed survey: its 'bias', if any, being not so much Unionist or Nationalist as mildly Labourist.

There appeared, then, to be an endemic defensiveness and insecurity, but also pervasive inconsistencies, about Ulster Protestants' place in a wider world. These emerge even in the perhaps unlikely setting of the coffee-table book which accompanied a 1989 Channel 4/Ulster TV historical documentary series on the 'Scots-Irish' experience. *The Scots-Irish Epic* sets itself up at the outset to dispell myths: the myth of a monolithic, bigoted, historyless Ulster Protestant community (Rory Fitzpatrick 1989:1), the myth that Ulster Protestants were a privileged population not sharing the 'primitive living conditions of their Catholic fellow countrymen' (ibid: 57), and the 'greatest of all the myths . . . the non-existence of the Ulster-Scots as a separate people' (274). Yet alongside this, and alongside a celebration of the Ulster-Scots contribution to world and especially North American civilisation, is a set of claims insecurely fastening on archaic notions of race. There are repeated invocations of 'the Scots-Irish race' (e.g. 274), and of '[t]he racial position of the Ulster Scots' (272). There is the notion that 'it is they [the Scots-Irish] and not the so-called "native Irish" who are the truly Celtic people' (274), the latter being 'mostly English' as a result of successive waves of migration (272). The title of the book and TV series, *God's Frontiersmen*, turns out to be less self-reflexively ironic than might have been expected.[37]

Popular Unionist versions of the past crystallised in a particular institutional form in the Orange Order, and may be traced not only in banners and parade routes, but in its journal the *Orange Standard*.[38] Three major kinds of historical reference point have been repeatedly invoked there in recent decades: the history of Orangeism itself, that of Protestant Ulster (with particular emphasis, naturally, on the events of 1688–91), and the history both locally and internationally of the Protestant and especially Presbyterian faith. Just as in Irish nationalism, there is emphasis on the transcendent importance of a correct historical understanding: 'The Orange Institution frees us from a corrupt interpretation of the past and from an ideological cult which uses murder as a political lever' (Editorial, July 1987).

In a general sense, not even just the essence but all of Orangeism is a celebration of its own past: whether repeatedly commemorating the triumphs and tragedies of Ulster Protestant history, or marking the lives and deaths of venerable, long-serving officials of the Order, the Orange Institution spends most of its time and most of the wordage of its publications marking its own history. More specifically, the *Orange Standard* frequently reminded readers of the Order's past, recalling its birthpains at the Battle of the Diamond (March 1975, February 1991), tracing its early history from origins (April 1975), through attitudes to the Act of Union (May 1975) and struggles against the insurgent 'Ribbonmen' (June 1975) to Victorian semi-respectability (July 1975). Particular local Orange traditions were also highlighted, like that of Portadown (September 1985). Orangeism abroad, past and present, was frequently profiled, with especial attention to the more exotic Lodges like those in Ghana and Togo, or among Canada's Mohawk Indians ('Red Indian Chief who was an Orangeman', November 1993). It was recalled, no doubt to many readers' surprise, that New York had once had active Orange Lodges, which engaged in vigorous contestation with the city's Irish Catholics in the post Civil War years (June 1978).

The general who was the real architect of William's victory at the Boyne, Frederick Schomberg, was twice profiled (February 1979, May 1982): *The Orange Standard* called him 'the forgotten hero', but evidently he was not to be forgotten by Orangemen. William III himself, naturally, received more coverage than any other historical character, even aside from the *Standard*'s hundreds of reproductions of his image on banners and in commemorative re-enactments of his triumphs: in 1988 a huge six-part series traced his career as leader of 'the Struggle for Civil and Religious Liberty' (March–September 1988). The Boyne battle was refought with regularity (e.g. July 1990), and more interestingly a contemporary 1690 report (from the *London Gazette*) of William's reception in Dublin was reprinted (May 1979: one of three substantial historical pieces in the same issue).

The Protestant agitator and reviver of Victorian Orangeism William Johnston of Ballykilbeg was repeatedly profiled, as 'A Loyalist Folk Hero' (May 1988), a 'Charismatic Orange leader' (March 1991), and as one who set an example for the present (August 1975, and December 1982/January 1983). Almost as important, apparently, was the revivalist preacher (and outspoken sectarian) 'Roaring Hugh' Hanna, profiled in an expansive three-part biographical sketch as the 'Lion of Presbyterianism' (March, April and May 1979). The defenders of Londonderry were, as one would expect, frequently recalled, with another three-decker minibiography devoted to the Rev. George Walker (October and November 1989, December 1989/January 1990) and hymns to the 'Brave Thirteen' who closed Derry's gates against the aggressor (July 1979).[39] Some rather more obscure heroes were also highlighted, such as Thomas Waring, a County Down Unionist MP in 1895–98 (February 1975) or William Willoughby Cole, Lord Enniskillen (February 1988). Local history publications were very frequently reviewed and praised, mainly those by amateur historians both Orange and non-Orange (but, it seems, always Protestant and Loyalist), issued by local presses in smaller Ulster towns. The icons of twentieth-century Unionism too received hagiographical treatment, as with 'Lord Craigavon—Ulster's Founder and Father-figure' (December 1990/January 1991) and Sir Edward Carson (a relatively massive three-page spread, including the front page, in October 1982).

The third theme is the one which has been most neglected in academic discussion of Unionist views of history: the specifically religious strain. Religious figures of historic import were frequently profiled in the *Orange Standard*: some with specific Ulster associations like seventeenth-century Archbishop of Armagh James Ussher (May 1987) or his Victorian successor the 'Primate and Poet' William Alexander (February and March 1984); some the European and especially the British heroes of Protestant Reformation, with a five-part hagiography of Martin Luther (March, May, June, October and November 1983); a three-parter on John Wesley (June 1984, April and June 1985); and separate articles on John Wycliffe (May 1979), Hugh Latimer (June 1988), Thomas Cranmer (October 1988) and the collectivity of 'Protestant Martyrs' under Queen Mary (July 1988). There were efforts to reclaim Saint Patrick from Irish nationalism (June 1981, May 1986), and homage to a possibly unexpected exemplar of Protestant virtue, 'John Charles Royle, First Bishop of Liverpool' (May 1986).

Other motifs were more fugitive and varied: Ulster's contribution to the development of the USA, from frontiersmen to numerous Presidents (June 1978, April 1986, June 1992); the lessons to be learned from the 1605 Gunpowder Plot (December 1981/January 1982); the manly virtues exemplified in the history of the Boys' Brigade (April 1983). Robert Kee's BBC television history of Ireland was attacked for nationalist bias—the historical variant on the Orange Order's apparently fixed obsession with being misrepresented by the BBC (April 1981). The history of Irish nationalism received surprisingly little attention, but when it did the tone was predictable—scorn for the vainglory surrounding memories of Easter 1916 ('The Myths about a Skirmish in Dublin' June 1992), or insistence on the recurrent murderousness of 'The Blood Tradition of Irish Republicanism' (April 1993).

Some crucial historical episodes are strangely un- or under-represented in popular Loyalist historiography. The 1798 Rising, and the politics of the movements which sponsored or opposed it, have remained ideologically intensely charged. Occasionally contemporary Loyalists, especially those Belfast UDA and UVF militants attracted to socially radical ideas, have invoked the memory of the United Irishmen in positive fashion (Richard Davis 1994:83–6); and the nature of the 1998 bicentenary commemorations offered some further signals pointing in that direction (Howe 1999a). The dominant Loyalist perception of 1798, however, appears to remain that of an official Orange Order publication in 1996. Partially reprinting an extremely partisan nineteenth-century account, by Canadian Orange Order Grand Master Ogle Gowan, its story is of a United Irish movement initiated by well-meaning but utterly misguided Dissenters but then taken over by wild pro-French revolutionaries and Catholic sectarians, and degenerating into genocidal pogroms against Protestants in Wexford. The main credit for suppressing the revolt, in Ulster as well as in the southeast, is given to the Orange Order (Gowan 1996).[40] Unfortunately, no substantial new Orange or Loyalist interpretation of 1798 seems to have appeared for the revolt's bicentennial. There are indeed some skilled professional historians who are members of the Orange Order, but to my knowledge none who is an 'Orange historian' in the sense either of specialising in the history of the Order itself or of openly avowing Orange principles in their scholarly work. One might suggest that, if the Order and other Loyalist institutions are to achieve the 'modernisation', the adaptation to a more inclusive ethos, of which many have spoken in recent years, an essential foundation is a more critical analysis of their own history.

If the 1790s are oddly neglected, the 1840s are seemingly almost entirely a blank in Loyalist popular memory. Until very recently, few studies of the Famine have focused closely on Ulster.[41] Undoubtedly, however, it was experienced differently in the northeast from the way it was elsewhere in Ireland— and, in a contrast far sharper than that of actual lived experience, it was *remembered* differently there. In 'inner Ulster' (east of the river Bann), to a greater extent than in most of the rest of Ireland, there existed non-agricultural sources of employment, especially weaving, which enabled rural communities to soften the worst blows of the crisis. Indeed employment opportunities in such fields grew quite rapidly in the Famine years, and even if this meant that survival was bought by intense labour exploitation, this in itself held potential for interpretation in terms—congenial to Calvinist tradition—of personal salvation through strenuous labour. Farming itself, too, was less overwhelmingly potato-dependent than further south and west, and tenants on the whole had more and better-defended rights. Landlords in Ulster, as elsewhere, came under attack for their failures to provide more relief for the hungry; but their influence and legitimacy were far less thoroughly undermined than in the west. The long-term effect was 'probably to reinforce the growing sense of sectional identity of "Ulster"' (Wright 1996:109), though only later was this difference in famine-era experience turned into a sectarian trope, with Protestant industry contrasted to Catholic idleness and held to account for the north's less savage devastation. Increasingly in the following decades, northern Protestant spokesmen made that equation when they mentioned the Famine at all—which they rarely did, as it came ever more to be invoked in furtherance of nationalist claims. The contrast has persisted into the present. In 1995–6, at the 150th anniversary of the outbreak, the mural painters of Catholic West Belfast produced a large number of often powerful works on Famine themes. In the city's Unionist districts, there were apparently none at all, even though there is little reason to believe that their inhabitants' ancestors actually suffered less in the 1840s than did their Catholic neighbours' forebears.

It has been usual to contrast Ulster Unionist visions of history with those current elsewhere in the United Kingdom (or even, by extension, elsewhere in the industrialised world) in one of three ways. One is a perception that the historical past is simply more important for people in Ulster (who thus supposedly share in a wider, stereotyped Irish trait) than those in other, more sensible places. A second is the claim that they conceive of history in strongly religious terms, whereas in most 'civilised' places the sense of the past has been substantially secularised. A third, expressed with vehemence by commentators like Brian Graham and with a kind of sadness by Alvin Jackson, is that the Unionist historical sense is unusually impoverished and incoherent.

All three views need hard questioning. Ulster Protestant historical imaginings are more varied, and in any serious comparative perspective less aberrant, than all of them presume. If, for instance, Unionist fixation on the Glorious Revolution of 1688–9 as founding myth seems strange and anachronistic in a British context—for the public discourse of mainland Britain, which once accorded 1688 the same revered status, has long since abandoned it—it should appear far less odd when viewed from the USA, where 1776, the Revolution and resulting Constitution still play such a ubiquitous, mythic, quasi-religious role in all public debate, underpinning the undiminished force of American exceptionalism; or indeed from France, where 1789 fulfilled at least until very recently very similar if more internally divisive functions. The central role for religion in public memory, too, may seem idiosyncratic by comparison with England— but the latter has one of the world's lowest rates of religious observance, and so this is again a distorting comparison. Ireland, north and south, is by no means unusual in this regard when measured against many continental European countries, let alone African, Asian or Middle Eastern ones. The third suggestion, that Unionist historical consciousness is peculiarly debilitated, is most often linked to Unionists' ambivalent senses of national identity. We shall therefore return to that theme in a more detailed discussion of contemporary Northern Irish group identities, in Chapter 10.

7

Colonialism, Criticism, and Cultural Theory

'When are you going to tell the truth?'
For there's no such book, so far as I know,
As *How it Happened Here,*
Though there may be. There may.

Paul Muldoon: 'Lunch with Pancho Villa'
(1986:20)

(i) Postcolonial Studies and Ireland: From Politics to Culture and Back Again

Much of the popular, and even some of the academic, historiography of both nationalist and Unionist traditions, as we have seen, has engaged in the making and remaking of myth: more or less elaborate, more or less deliberate, more or less well intentioned. In this chapter we return to the theme of history as mythography; and we turn to the contemporary politics of culture. Here too the colonial model re-emerges: not, as in the disputes dissected in the previous pages, as an economic or political phenomenon, but as a cultural one. Irish cultural and literary history has become a major site for the elaboration of ideas about colonialism and postcoloniality. Their proponents are mainly associated with the political left, and include many of the most influential, innovative cultural and intellectual figures in modern Ireland. They include applications to Ireland of colonial discourse analysis, and often of Fanonian liberationist rhetoric, by (to select from a rapidly growing list) Seamus Deane, Declan Kiberd, Luke Gibbons, David Lloyd, David Cairns and Shaun Richards, Gerry Smyth, Clair Wills, Cheryl Herr, Richard Kearney, Carol Coulter, Kevin Collins, and C. L. Innes.[1] A growing number of monographs have studied particular major Irish writers through the prism of postcolonial theory, or denounced the anti-Irish racism and colonialism of major figures in the English canon like Milton and Spenser.[2] There are also the relatively superficial insertions of Ireland into wider arguments about imperialism and decolonisation by internationally celebrated cultural theorists like Edward Said (1988; 1993), Fredric Jameson (1988) and Terry Eagleton (1988; 1989).[3]

This new explosion of work has often set out to be inter- or trans-disciplinary;

but coming mainly from literary analysts, it has been perceived by some historians as producing new barriers or clashes between disciplines instead. Nicholas Canny complained in a *History Ireland* interview that often today, when students come into history classes 'they have already been packaged a version of what the historical experience was by people who are involved in post-colonial theory . . . we find that students have pre-packaged versions of the past designed by post-colonial theorists with present and future agendas. As a result we are encountering undergraduates who really have no respect for the past because the people who taught them haven't any respect for the past. Lecturers in literature, the social sciences, etc. are colonising history as their own, and these are people who seem . . . to have simplistic answers supported by a limited amount of historical evidence.' (Canny 1998a:55) Canny objects also to the political implications often drawn from such literary work: 'What offends me is that people who might read a piece of mine on Edmund Spenser suddenly zoom from that to talk about the recent IRA campaign and would say that this was fully justified because of what Spenser said.' (1998a:53) One upshot of this chapter's discussion of postcolonial theory in Ireland will be to attempt judgement on how far Canny's charges—made by a historian who has himself, as we have seen, been one of the strongest advocates of analysing the Irish past in colonial contexts—are accurate.

This Irish work has formed a part—indeed often a rather derivative offshoot—of a far wider 'colonial discourse' and 'postcolonial' intellectual trend in recent years. It is necessary, therefore, to situate it in the context of the claims and shortcomings of this broader current. Here that can only be done in abbreviated and rather peremptory terms.[4]

In the past decade or so, a major new paradigm for studying colonialism has emerged: what has become known as colonial discourse analysis. Such theories tend to see colonial power as an all-embracing, trans-historical force, controlling and transforming every aspect, every tiny detail of colonised societies. The writings and attitudes of those involved with empire are seen as constituting a system, a network, a discourse in the sense made famous by Michel Foucault. It inextricably combines the production of knowledge with the exercise of power. It deals in stereotypes and polar antitheses. It has both justificatory and repressive functions. And, perhaps above all, it *is* a singular 'it': colonial discourse and by extension the categories in which it deals (the coloniser, the colonised, the subject people, etc.) can meaningfully be discussed in unitary, abstract, unsituated terms.

Much current writing in this vein thus treats colonialism as homogeneous and all-powerful, and uses the term to denote patterns of domination, or even merely of transregional contact, which actually preceded, succeeded or indeed were substantially disengaged from periods of actual conquest, possession and rule. Calling all these sorts of things 'colonial' systematically denies or underrates historical variety, complexity and heterogeneity. In part what is wrong has a disciplinary origin: the presumption that the tools and techniques of literary criticism can stand in for those of historical, social, and economic analysis. It is, to the historian, an evident methodological absurdity to base general claims about colonial mentalities on a single text. Yet the few individual colonial texts and incidents discussed in such work are often used not even as 'symptoms' of wider social phenomena (a problematic enough procedure in itself, which has been the general besetting sin of what has been called 'new historicism' in literary studies), but as perfunctory pegs on which to hang sweeping assertions about a generalised colonial situation. Claims initially made about the forms and reception of specific literary texts are thus illegitimately generalised into claims about the historical and political situations from which such texts derive. The texts are characteristically assumed to express a shared colonial, or anticolonial, mentality. Relationships between forms of knowledge, whether literary, artistic, historical or scientific, and colonial power are either seen in crudely and ahistorically instrumentalist terms, or (sometimes, quite inconsistently, by the same authors) collapsed into indeterminacy by a vulgar-Foucauldian claim that knowledge and power are identical. And it is very widely assumed or asserted that not only do all these forms of knowledge stand in equal proximity to directly political and ideological projects, but they are all in some sense equivalent to one another. At the extreme (an extreme now famously parodied and dissected by Alan Sokal and Jean Bricmont (1998)), no distinctions can or should be observed among different kinds of writing in respect of their correspondence to reality: a novel, a historical monograph and a mathematical proof are all equally good, or bad, ways of establishing their authors' claims.

Even more obvious, and deriving heavily from the disciplinary backgrounds and social milieux of the scholars concerned, is an overwhelming culturalist bias: indeed a cultural reductionism which is a mirror-image of the economic reductionism typical of some parts of the Marxist tradition. Despite the debts to Marxism proclaimed by many exponents of colonial cultural studies, there is rarely any apparent interest in the economics of colonial or postcolonial relations—and where passing references are made to these, they are often by way of ill-understood claims derived from dependency theory. Insofar as it is at all theoretically explicit, other than about its relations to earlier *literary* theory, such work again takes much of its inspiration from the later Foucault, with his rejection of attention to the state as privileged source or instance of power. Much poststructuralist theory goes further, spurning not only the state but society as an object of analysis. Here colonial discourse analysis connects with the 'linguistic turn' in social and historical studies more generally in its rejection of social explanation and very often of totalising explanation *tout court*. Or rather, its ostensible rejection; for in fact very sweeping kinds of general claim about 'the colonial situation' are characteristic. In the more rigid kinds of colonial discourse analysis, colonialism is not only often homogenised and endowed with agency, rationality, ubiquity; it is granted a kind of trans-historical intentionality. Contemporary scholars, especially those in literary and cultural theory, very frequently assume that European colonialism was a wholly willed phenomenon (the main exceptions are traditional, orthodox Marxists who see it as an inevitable stage in the development of world capitalism). The assumption may seem natural enough, but it is made without argument or evidence. It typically fails to consider the extent to which colonial rule in general, and the British Empire in particular, was a patchwork quilt, an enormously varied set of forms of rule and domination, largely the product of improvisation and full of internal contradictions and strains, rather than a deliberately constructed global system. Ideologies of empire were far more often *ex post facto* rationalisations for acts of expansion undertaken for a very wide range of reasons, opportunistically driven by crisis, or by the availability of new means of domination (technological and other), rather than by the ideology itself.

(ii) Fanon comes to the Foyle: The Field Day Writers

Perhaps the most forceful and cohesive focus for the new Irish cultural studies of colonialism has been the Field Day group. Founded in Derry by playwright Brian Friel and actor Stephen Rea in 1980 to launch Friel's play *Translations*, the Field Day company rapidly moved beyond its initial theatrical role to a wider cultural, and increasingly political, intervention. On the way it acquired an editorial board including Seamus Deane, Seamus Heaney and Tom Paulin, published a series of pamphlets, and embarked on its most ambitious undertaking, the production of a monumental anthology of Irish writing. Latterly it has begun publishing a series of substantial monographs on Irish history and culture under the title 'Critical Conditions', by authors including Luke Gibbons, Kevin Whelan, Terry Eagleton, and the remarkable Dutch cultural historian Joep Leerssen. Meanwhile individual group members have continued to produce major works: some relatively distant from the group's early preoccupations, like Paulin's study of William Hazlitt (1998), others very much within them, like Deane's *Strange Country* (1997).

The Field Day endeavour produces intense reactions. W. J. McCormack even claimed, fairly early in the group's career, that they were unprecedented reactions. The group members were, he suggested, 'a tightly structured team of polemicists' responsible for 'alliances and antagonisms new to Irish literary debate.' The group's enemies 'review a Field Day pamphlet as if it were some edict imposed on defenceless readers by an unstable and treacherous Fate'. (McCormack 1986:17) Overall, however, Field Day writings have been more varied and ambivalent on directly political questions than charges by critics like Edna Longley, Francis Mulhern, and Shaun Richards, to which we shall refer later, would suggest. The group's publications and activities have not formed a cohesive political project, though in the process of producing the great *Anthology of Irish Writing* something like a 'party line' may have emerged. Certainly it was not monolithic: pamphlets the group has published included work by Richard Kearney, Terence Brown, Marianne Elliott and prominent Unionist Robert McCartney, all of whose arguments were very far from any obvious nationalist, let alone Republican, consensus. Kearney's highly critical dissection of the language of sacrifice and martyrdom in nationalist discourse, underpinning and legitimating the 1981 hunger strikes (1984), offended some widely held Republican beliefs—though his understanding of the hunger strikers and their supporters as imprisoned in a mythologised past was later substantially to be confirmed by Padraig O'Malley's massive analysis of the strikes, *Biting at the Grave* (1990). O'Malley's work not only quoted Kearney with approval (ibid: 57–8, 116): his own extensive interview and archival researches documented the pamphlet's claims.

Programmatic statements on behalf of the group have appeared to point in somewhat different directions. One emphasis, shared by Friel with Kearney, was to speak of a cultural 'Fifth Province' transcending the divisions between and within the existing Ulster, Leinster, Munster and Connaught. Friel called this a 'transcendent location'. Deane, however, implied something more directly political, and nationalist: 'the cultural, social, political unification that is possible in Ireland between all the different groupings and sects.' He also said, in the same interview, that he hoped Field Day would be remembered in future as having 'made a contribution towards the achievement of the peaceful, non-sectarian society that emerged in Ireland somewhere in the next century'.[5] The obvious problem was that a route to that objective premised on 'unification', even if this is seen as being as much cultural as political, would have little appeal to people in Ireland who conceive of their identity as essentially British. As Shaun Richards remarks, even if the main objective is a new cultural state from which a political state might follow: 'It is the nature of that political state, effectively predetermined by the cultural state which precedes it, which poses substantial problems.' (1991b:141) Another Field Day director, Seamus Heaney, especially in his most recent work, has seemed to take such concerns deeply to heart, speaking approvingly of ideas about flexible and plural identities, the virtues of 'two-mindedness' (1994:14). Heaney has also expressed considerable reservations about the characteristic emphases of colonial discourse analysis. He has insisted that alongside his belated recognition of how Christopher Marlowe's drama, for instance, was shaped by its Elizabethan context of aggressive English expansionism, he still wants to:

find a way of reaffirming the value and rights of Marlowe's poetry in our own post-colonial time . . . it is necessary to find a way of treating the marvellously aspiring note of his work as something more than a set of discourses to be unmasked . . .

We have been forced to cast a suspicious eye on the pretensions of Renaissance humanism by having its sacred texts placed in the context of their authors' participation in such brutally oppressive escapades . . . But even so, it still seems an abdication of lit-erary responsibility to be swayed by these desperately overdue correctives to a point where imaginative literature is read simply and solely as a function of an oppressive dis-course, or as a reprehensible masking. (1995:22–4)

Is Field Day's project posited, as a whole, on the colonial model for Ireland's past or Northern Ireland's present? We have noted the group's internal variety, and that publications under its auspices, in the pamphlet and 'Critical Conditions' series, have offered a fairly wide range of views. Yet Edna Longley (1992, 1994) and Shaun Richards (1991b), in sharp polemics, have suggested that it is so posited, in ways that are intellectually and politically limiting, indeed damag-ing. Some programmatic statements, especially from Seamus Deane, have pointed in the same direction. Thus Deane has pronounced that: 'Field Day's analysis of the situation derives from the conviction that it is, above all, a colo-nial crisis.' (1990:6) Richards argues that Field Day's reading of Northern Ireland as 'unambiguously colonial . . . informs, and problematises, the whole Field Day undertaking.' (Richards 1991b:139–40) He accuses the company of, in effect, censoring work which does not fit nationalist preconceptions, eviden-cing particularly Frank McGuinness's *Observe the Sons of Ulster Marching Towards the Somme*[6] and David Rudkin's *The Saxon Shore* (ibid: 142–3). Cer-tainly some Field Day writers have adopted the colonial model wholesale—but then Richards himself, in his coauthored book *Writing Ireland* (Cairns and Richards 1988) had appeared also to do so. The colonial interpretation is expli-citly that adopted by several leading members and associates of the group—Seamus Deane, Tom Paulin, Declan Kiberd and Luke Gibbons—as we shall see in some detail later.

In the 'General Introduction' to the *Field Day Anthology of Irish Writing* Seamus Deane sets out an ambitious model both of Irish history and of ways of representing that history. Both are avowedly pluralist. Indeed the proclaimed openness, variousness, refusal to 'fix' monistic interpretations, of Field Day's practice is counterposed to the habits of 'Historians of limited philosophical resource' who naively, or dogmatically 'long to answer the question, "What really happened then?"'. (Deane 1991b:xxi) And Ireland's history is presented as one of conquest and colonisation, but one where these things have been mul-tiple; not apparently reduceable to the simple polarity of oppressor and oppressed:

Ireland has been colonized through conquest and invasion several times and in several ways . . . by pre-Christian invaders, Christian missionaries, the Normans, the pre-Reformation English, the Elizabethans, Cromwellians and by the Williamites . . . But other, internal conquests took place as well, deriving from and modifying the supervening realities of colonial rule. Versions of Ireland and its history and culture were created by many groups within the island—colonists and colonized (ibid: xx).

Yet no sooner has this plural play of cultures and interpretations been established (Field Day's open field: Deane cannot have been deaf to the echoes from Milton and from Robert Duncan the idea evokes) than Deane begins hedging and ditching, creating boundaries (an activity also with its local poetic resonances, from Seamus Heaney and John Montague). This he does partly by way of the thinly veiled polemic against 'revisionist' historians, who are presumably also those of limited philosophical resource, which snakes throughout the remainder of the essay. The pretence to 'objectivity' is viewed as merely a disguise for anti-nationalist political animus (ibid: xxii). 'Revisionist' periods in Irish history display, he says:

an anxiety to preserve the status quo, to lower the political temperature and to offer the notion that historical processes are so complex that any attempt to achieve an overview cannot avoid the distortions and dogmatism of simple-minded orthodoxy. This is a powerful antidote against criticism and rebellion. Since rebellion is, of its nature, devoted to a simplified view of a complex situation, its proponents can be accused of indulging in historical fantasy, of intellectual narcosis and uneducated convictions. (ibid: xxiii)

The view that the rebel is necessarily a simplifier, that stress on complexity and the need for accuracy serves the status quo, is a peculiar or even mystificatory one. Diderot or Paine, Marx or Gramsci, DuBois or Nehru, would not have agreed. One may speculate, for that matter, that if Wolfe Tone or Connolly had lived their natural spans and looked back on the simplifications and errors in their early views, they would not have gloried in these as a necessary part of rebellion, but lamented the lack of time and of accurate information which produced them, and resolved to do better. The focus on historical detail and complexity has hardly been always an alien, or apparently a reactionary, value for Deane himself: poems like 'History Lessons' or 'Christmas at Beaconsfield' (in Deane 1983) are magnificent exercises in recalling the fine grain of the past for present purposes. Deane might usefully have recalled how Hugh MacDiarmid, poet, cultural critic, and rebel, identified himself with those:

> . . . who waste no words
> On manifestoes but are getting down
> To the grim business of documentation,
> Not seeking a short cut to the universal
> But with all their energies concentrated
> On gaining access to the particular.

And he might have found equally apposite the thought a few lines further on in the same minor poem:

> If all the world went native
> There would be a confusion of tongues,
> A multiplication of regionalisms.
> *Partikularismus*, however,
> Is hostile to nationalism
> And friendly to internationalism.

('I Am with the New Writers' in MacDiarmid 1978, I:653)

For having issued a manifesto for cultural plurality, Deane's essay then seems to slide back towards presenting a simple bifurcation in Ireland's cultural history—and, by implication, its present—between colonialism and nationalism:

When colonialism is successful, it reconciles the colonized culture to its own. When it is unsuccessful, it enforces itself by violence—slaughter, confiscation, the demonizing of those who resist it. Nationalism, cultural or political, is no more than the inverted image of the colonialism it seeks to replace. It too is an act of translation or even of retranslation. (Deane 1991b:xxv)

This is, self-evidently, hardly an apologia for nationalism: though it leaves quite open the question whether it is only the reactive nationalism of the anticolonial moment that is colonialism's reflection, whether (as earlier Field Day writings had seemed to suggest) a new, more plural, more inclusive, more self-reflexive Irish nationalism can escape the traps of the past. Are all translations equally acts of appropriation, repression, dispossession? This trope, which resonates not only through Deane's 'Introduction' but throughout the Field Day project, derives from Brian Friel's play *Translations* (1981; also in Field Day 1991, III), in which the act of mapping the Irish landscape, undertaken by British Army Engineers and involving the Englishing of Irish place-names, is a symbol of colonialism. Near the end of Friel's play we are told that 'it is not the literal "facts" of history that shape us, but images of the past embodied in language.' (ibid: 1234)[7] Translation is never simple or innocent, but always involves the creation of a new discourse and thus a new view of the world (cf. also, on translation and colonialism, Cheyfitz 1991; Niranjana 1992). Such claims can be read as a 'strong' anti-realist case (there is nothing outside the text . . .) or as a 'weaker' claim about the necessarily but variably limiting or distorting effects of particular discourses, particular translations. I have elsewhere traced the ambivalences on this issue of Said, Spivak and other colonial discourse theorists (Howe 2000b, c, *passim*). Deane appears similarly ambivalent; though apparently shifting gradually towards a 'stronger' version of the claim, with which Declan Kiberd—though not necessarily other Field Day writers—also seems to align himself. The uncertainty is significant partly because it leaves open the question of whether Field Day's project is, as Stephen Regan suggests, 'sustained examin-ation of the nationalist rhetoric and mythology' about the Irish past (1992:26), or the attempt to replace past myths, 'bad' rhetorics and translations, with new and more liberatory ones. If the latter, then not only is historical 'truth' an irrele-vant chimera; but it may be, as Deane had appeared to suggest, that the simpler the counter-myths are, the better.

The great mythographies at issue are, inevitably, those of colonialism and nationalism: in contesting them, Deane and other Field Day writers have arguably remained trapped within their assumptions. In *Celtic Revivals* Deane had appeared fairly dismissive of the Irish nationalist tradition, suggesting that:

It was and is so imbued with the sense of the past as a support for action in the present that it has never looked beyond that. This is particularly true after . . . 1921. Once nation-alism, although only partially triumphant, was faced with the future, it became little more than a species of accommodation to prevailing (predominantly British) forces. Its separation from socialism left it ideologically invertebrate. (1985a:15)

Even here, however, Deane's main complaint is that nationalism was insuffi-ciently militant or socialist; that it accommodated too much with Britain—as of course the anti-Treaty Republicans of 1921 and since also believed. In other words this was a *neocolonial* nationalism: one created, as the celebrated discus-sion of W. B. Yeats in *Celtic Revivals* suggests, largely by Protestant Ascendancy figures and rejecting the hard questions of modernity, class, economics and government for the misty totalities of spiritual and racial essence, of an im-agined aristocracy and peasantry (ibid: chs 2 and 3). In the light of this polemic and ignoring Deane's other writings one could perhaps find sanction for Hazard Adams's otherwise puzzling judgement that the Field Day agenda is a 'Marxist and internationalist' one (H. Adams 1991:175).

Yet if Deane is not exactly *for* nationalism, at least in the hegemonic forms it had assumed in Ireland, he is evidently *against* what he takes to be the anti-national: against liberalism and cosmopolitanism. This hostility is coded in the 'Introduction' to *Irish Writing*, far more overt in his essay 'Wherever Green is Read' (Deane 1991a) in *Revising the Rising* (Dhonnchadha and Dorgan 1991), an angry assault on Roy Foster's revisionist historiography and, through that, on all modern Irish critics of the nationalist tradition. The essay drew on American 'metahistorian' Hayden White (whose famous, highly formalistic analyses of selected historical texts had argued for their irreducibly literary character, and were widely interpreted as denying any essential distinction between historical and fictional narratives[8]) to validate its anti-realist claims. Yet Deane's decon-structive reading of a passage from Roy Foster's *Modern Ireland* seemed rather half-hearted, petering out after a few paragraphs as Deane reverted to directly politico-polemical mode. He proclaimed that 'revisionism' amounts, ever more nakedly, to nothing more than purely Unionist apologetics: 'their pseudo-scientific orthodoxy is so obviously tailored to match the prevailing political climate—especially in relation to the northern crisis—that its claims to "objectivity", to being "value-free", have been abandoned as disguises no longer needed.' (ibid: 91) Deane's view of historical writing seemed curiously unstable, asserting within a few sentences that it 'owes its allegiance to fact, however select-ive, however organized', but then that historians 'do not write about the past; they create the past in writing about it', and that history 'is a slippery discipline.' (ibid: 101) Elsewhere, Deane proclaimed in the same vein but with unusual dog-matism that 'There is no such thing as an objective history, and there is no inno-cent history. All history and literature, as far as I understand them, are forms of mythology.' (1992:26) This appeared to involve a startlingly false antithesis: many, perhaps most, historians are wary of the notion of absolute objectivity, and probably few regard their work as 'innocent' (whatever that may mean in the context), but equally few believe this reduces it to mythology.

Amidst all this, there was rather little evidence that Deane had actually read much of the 'revisionist' writing he attacked: apart from his main target, Roy Foster, his only historical references were to Ruth Dudley Edwards's biography of Pearse, John Hutchinson's work on nationalism and, peculiarly, Ian Adam-son's *The Cruthin*. There was, however, a nice irony in Deane's attacking Foster for his lack of attention to postmodernist theory; for soon thereafter Terry Eagleton (1994) was to assault Foster from a similar political angle to Deane's—but by way of accusing him of being a shamefully modish postmodernist![9]

Returning to the assault in the closing pages of his major 1997 book *Strange Country*, Deane referred to a somewhat wider range of historical writing: the recipients of his negative criticism now included Theo Moody, L. M. Cullen and F. S. L. Lyons. His renewed attack on the historians formed a curiously anti-climactic finale to a wide-ranging discussion of literary-political representa-tions of Irish 'national character'. The strangeness of Ireland, in these representations, lies in its oscillation between civilisation and barbarism, between being part of the British political and cultural system and something utterly alien to it. British and pro-Unionist discourse trying to negotiate these tensions is 'remarkably hostile' to theory—and in his conception of 'theory', Deane appears to lump together French revolutionary ideas, Irish nationalist ones, and academic constructs—'always featuring it as abstract, systematic, and deeply involved with atrocious violence.' (1997:18) That tradition of hostility to theory, in Deane's account, is founded by Edmund Burke: historical revision-ism is its modern inheritor. Deane's preferred alternative, however, appears not to be a complex discourse of theory but a fairly crude manicheism: historic Irish underdevelopment must be, straightforwardly, either 'produced by Irish national character' as the British allegedly always believed, or 'a structural problem produced by the colonial relationship between the two countries.' (ibid: 27–8; see also 32–3)

Not only is revisionist history the latest incarnation of a banal, rationalistic conservatism incapable of understanding either Ireland or revolution, it is purely and directly colonialist and Unionist:

The rhetoric of revisionism obviously derives from the rhetoric of colonialism and imperialism. It defines its nationalist opponent always in terms of an irrationality for which it is the saving alternative. It has to deprive nationalism of agency, of self-consciousness, envisaging it as a mystification, a mythology, an impulse by which its adherents are driven; although almost any passage from any revisionist historian would reveal this charge to be applicable to itself, revisionism remains happily ensconced not only in ignorance of its own theory but the more happily so because it regards such ignorance as the badge of its peculiar notion of professionalism. (ibid: 193)

Yet more remarkably, in Deane's eyes the historians are knowingly complicit in Loyalist violence: 'Revisionism legitimates those Irish cultural formations that wish to adhere to the British system, even if by violent means; it refuses legitimacy to those who wish to break from it, especially if their means are violent.' (ibid: 193) It is difficult to believe that Deane really wishes to suggest that historical revisionism, however defined, 'legitimates' the activities of 'King Rat', the Shankill Butchers or the Red Hand Commando—but that is what he appears to be saying here.

It may be suggested that the most debilitating fault in Deane's view of the historical and political world lies mainly in his refusal to differentiate between the epistemological (or indeed emotional) stances appropriate to some kinds of intellectual task, and those suitable to others. This was already indicated by the terms of Deane's 1977 critique of Conor Cruise O'Brien:

The kind of humanism which Conor Cruise O'Brien sponsors is precisely that . . . which, though welcome from a rational point of view, renders much of what he says either irrelevant or simply wrong . . . The very clarity of O'Brien's position is just what is most objectionable. It serves to give a rational clarity to the Northern situation which is untrue to the reality. In other words, is not his humanism here being used as an excuse to rid Ireland of the atavisms which give it life even though the life may be in some ways brutal? (quoted Akenson 1995:361)

Or in still other words, you have to share in the murk, to be part of it, in order to understand it—and presumably, to do anything about it. For the maker of fictions, such a stance (or empathy with it) may be necessary: where would Deane's own extraordinary, part-autobiographical 1996 novel *Reading in the Dark* be without its atavisms, its murk, its titular and essential darkness, its refusal of rationalist kinds of clarity? But to extend such protocols to attempts at historical or political analysis is, surely, to reject the possibility of any analysis whatever: quite apart from any particular judgement on Deane's and O'Brien's respective political positions (though the latter has at least been argued for, with the clarity which Deane dislikes, over the years), or the fact that Deane's real objection seems not to be to O'Brien's 'rational clarity' as such, but to the fact that it appeared to push him towards ever greater sympathy for Ulster Unionism.[10]

Such claims perhaps represent a certain 'greening' of Deane's thought over the years. Certainly there is, in his more recent writing or in that of some other Field Day contributors, no hint of the search for alternatives to nationalism itself, for which MacDiarmid—or in the Irish context the 'regionalism' of great Ulster poet John Hewitt[11]—had called. MacDiarmid—a glorifier of Scottishness to the point of anti-English racism, and a mythologist of pan-Celticism to the point of enlisting Stalin as an honorary Gael—did not live up to his own programme. But the programme itself, allying regionalism and internationalism against the claims of nationality, will be to many people more attractive than even Deane's liberationist brand of nationalism.

It remains unclear how Deane thinks it possible to attain that for which he attractively called in one of the first Field Day pamphlets: 'new politics, unblemished by Irishness, but securely Irish.' (Deane 1985b:58) The implication is apparently that 'Irishness' was a colonial creation, the product of English stereotyping and essentialising of 'the native'—and presumably also of the counter-essentialism of cultural nationalist Gaelicism. To be 'securely Irish', by contrast, is to attain a conception of identity that is self-fashioned, free from the neuroses of cultural colonialism. But it may well be implied—as Terry Eagleton suggests in a later Field Day tract—that in order to get to the desired new identity it is necessary to go 'all the way through' the old one first. To suppose otherwise, to think one can dispense with collective identities and communal solidarities, is in Eagleton's view 'to play straight into the hands of the oppressor.' (Eagleton 1988:5) Elsewhere, in the Introduction to the published text of his Field Day play *Saint Oscar*, Eagleton refers repeatedly to 'colonial oppression', the 'colonial oppressor' and 'the colonial subject' and concludes ringingly that 'small nations will not rest until they are free.' (Eagleton 1989:x–xii) Does this mean that the political project supposedly inscribed, preordained in the colonially created identity of Irish Catholic Nationalist—the project of enforcing British withdrawal and Unionist surrender, of achieving unification—must be completed before the liberation of being 'securely Irish' can be enjoyed? Eagleton's answer, in 1989 if not necessarily later, is an unequivocal, militant affirmative. Deane's is unstated. It is very clear what he is against. Among other things, he is against people who are against nationalism. It is not so clear what, politically, this leaves him standing for.

All this suggests how a culturalist nationalism, rather than offering more imaginative and inclusive visions of the future than a purely political one, as the Field Day writers proposed, might actually end with something narrower. As the leading French scholar of modern Irish history, Maurice Goldring, argues:

Ironically enough, cultural nationalism contributed greatly to an ethnic definition of the nation whose main drawback is not that it closes the external frontiers, which after all, is the purpose and function of nation-states, but [that it] also closes them on the inside . . . Those who do not share the values considered as vital for the country are asked where they were born, as Jim Larkin was in 1913. How, with his socialist ideas, could he be a true-born Irishman? (Goldring 1993:178)

A further major problem with the Field Day project has aroused intense controversy but cannot fully be addressed here. This is the significant underrepresentation of women writers in the *Anthology*, and its alleged general inattention to questions of gender. Widespread complaints at this imbalance led to the commissioning of an additional, later fourth volume of the anthology, focused especially on women's writing.[12]

Francis Mulhern, while raising this concern at gender imbalance, also registers a wider objection to the *Field Day Anthology*. He proposes that behind the editorial emphasis on plurality, 'micro-narratives' and so on lies a continued commitment to a fairly traditionally conceived nationalist ethos. Mulhern's strictures are especially sharp against Luke Gibbons's contributions to the second and third volumes. But he believes that Gibbons is not a 'maverick' within the project as a whole; rather he 'is perhaps best viewed as giving unusually intense, and unguarded, expression to a wider tendency.' (Mulhern 1993, 27) Gibbons's words on Thomas MacDonagh, that Irishness was for him something to be achieved by concerted cultural effort, are seen as symptomatic of the collective's aims:

These words reiterate the familiar theme of 'prospective' nationalism: there never was an Irish nation in any of the canonical senses, but it is possible and necessary to achieve it in the future. Here, if anywhere, is the motivating conviction of the anthology.

And from this follow damaging political as well as cultural consequences:

The ideal of a common, consenting 'Irishness' is crucially ambiguous: open to the extent of acknowledging historical complexity, yet confining in that it prescribes an order of legitimate cultural initiative. Field Day takes its distance from one after another version of cultural nationalism but holds on to the axiom that founds them all: the proposition that the sovereign cultural concern of the Irish population is its national identity. To a nationalist this is self-evident truth.

But this—in the end—narrow nationalist focus 'undermines the very sense of cultural projects whose engagement with the country's realities, while taking all due account of a specific situation, follows bearings other than those of national identity.' (Mulhern 1993, 27) And it is here that Mulhern's critique undergoes its most interesting twist, for he identifies the source of these omissions and distortions as being essentially geographical. Field Day was a

Derry initiative, Derry being conceived of as the symbolic capital of the Northern Ireland crisis; and 'it is from there that all of Ireland is effectively seen.' (27)
In the view from Derry, the Republic 'is rendered marginal to itself. The data of
its specific politico-cultural history are centred or marginalised, lit up or
shadowed, cued or cut according to a vicarious monocular "northern" scheme.'
(27)[13] The rapid tides of socio-economic change, conflicts over the Church's
position, the massive literary production of Catholic institutions themselves,
the struggles of feminists, the abortion and divorce referenda, all are ignored,
squeezed or stretched on the Procrustian bed of the 'national question' as
viewed from the north.

Mulhern's own geographical trope is perhaps over-simple: Irish culturo-
political geography cannot be reduced to Derry versus Dublin, any more than it
can adequately be characterised as an overfed and cravenly Anglophile Dublin
4 pitted against the Plain People of Ireland. Yet his complaint at Field Day's
Derry-centrism points acutely, if perhaps one-sidedly, to a persistent tension in
culturo-political projects between north and south. Earlier Seamus Heaney,
reflecting on his youthful discovery of Patrick Kavanagh, had underscored one
very important aspect of this tension:

Without being in the slightest way political in its intentions, Kavanagh's poetry did have
political effect. Whether he wanted it or not, his achievement was inevitably co-opted,
north and south, into the general current of feeling which flowed from and sustained
ideas of national identity, cultural otherness from Britain and the dream of a literature
with a manner and a matter resistant to the central Englishness of the dominant tradition ... So there I was, in 1963, with my new copy of *Come Dance with Kitty Stobbling*, in
the grip of those cultural and political pieties which Kavanagh, all unknown to me, had
spent the last fifteen years or so repudiating. (Heaney 1988:9–10)

The views of the Field Day and other Irish 'postcolonial' theorists are deeply
ambivalent in their attitudes to nationalism. In some places it is almost uncritically celebrated or, as with Deane on Yeats, the tradition's luminaries criticised
only for being somehow not quite nationalist *enough*. At others, a much harsher
view is taken or implied, seeing the 'national renaissance' as a flawed or at best
incomplete project, still awaiting consummation in a future 'liberationist'
philosophy which was prefigured by some great artists but whose arrival was
denied by conservatism, provincialism, clericalism and a supposedly 'neocolonial' form of semi-independence. But the nature of this liberation, this full
decolonisation, too remains unclear. Is it to be a fuller, more complete nationalism, somehow more 'securely Irish' (to use Seamus Deane's phrase) than
what's gone before? Or is it rather (as the widespread invocation of Fanon
would imply[14]) something *beyond* nationalism?

(ii) Postcolonials from Connaught to California: Declan Kiberd, Luke Gibbons and David Lloyd

Another prominent Field Day contributor, Declan Kiberd, gives Deane's arguments an even sharper political edge. He is insistent on the literally boundless capacity of British colonialism to remake or create the objects it then controls: even those which are apparently the results of nationalist self-fashioning. It is not only a stereotypical 'Irishness' which is a colonial creation, as Deane had argued, but Ireland itself:

The English did not invade Ireland—rather, they seized a neighbouring island and invented the idea of Ireland. The notion 'Ireland' is largely a fiction created by the rulers of England in response to specific needs at a precise moment in British history. (Kiberd 1985:83; also in Field Day 1991, III:637)

The notion of Englishness being formed through 'not-Irishness', and vice versa, is a central theme of Kiberd's thought. It is, however, surely overplayed. In particular, it makes Ireland sound simply more important to England and Englishness than it was. Most historians who have studied such matters, I think, would suggest that 'being English' was formed more by being 'not-French' than by being 'not-Irish', both in the Medieval period and again in the era of the French Revolution. The great continental enemy was a more significant 'Other' than the Irish or other conquered peoples (cf. Colley 1992, Newman 1987, Samuel ed. 1989). Kiberd, significantly, never suggests even in passing what Britain's 'specific needs at a precise moment' may have been in inventing Ireland.

Yet this direct transposition of the Orientalist paradigm to Ireland at least has the apparent merit of resolving Edward Said's classic ambivalence—is 'the Orient' a purely discursive construct or does it (mis)represent some real object?— in favour of the former assertion. It also enables Kiberd to engage in forthright and sweeping condemnation of every aspect of contemporary Irish life. The Irish, he argues, 'no longer live in a country of their own making, but in a kind of tourist's filmset' in which the past has become 'deadening', an 'oppression' (Kiberd 1984:11–12). The 'no longer' is puzzling; since the thrust of Kiberd's argument is that 'the Irish', being a colonial invention, *never did* live in a country of their own making. And there is a certain rhetorical sleight of hand in shifting from assertions about the colonially-imposed character of the national predicament to damning *in toto* the culture of independent Ireland, without any attempt to show in detail how this or that feature derives from the colonial past. Yet Kiberd's next move is if anything even more remarkable: to blame the supposed inadequacy and weakness of the 'Irish personality' on a colonially induced distortion of family structures. Irish fathers have been 'emasculated' by colonialism; their subjection to mothers raises the child—though Kiberd immediately, and revealingly, slips from saying 'child' to 'son'—as an irresponsible, backward-looking 'rebel' rather than a confident 'revolutionary':

> Weak fathers lead to clutching mothers who raise rebel sons. If the father does assert himself, the child may begin the task of achieving a vision of society as a whole and the even more exhilarating challenge of framing an alternative. (1988:51)

Kiberd's apparent enthusiasm for traditional gender roles, and laments for a supposedly colonialist masculinisation of women and feminisation of men, are disconcerting from someone who proclaims a sympathy with feminism.[15] The contrast drawn between patriarchal values and 'proper manliness', with the assertion that patriarchy is the product of 'weak men', ignores the feminist claim that patriarchy is structural, not just the outcome of this or that individual male personality type.

Kiberd's magnum opus, *Inventing Ireland* (1995), however, offers a more complex and nuanced stance. The discussions of particular authors are often acute, illuminating and powerful—some, especially perhaps the treatment of Yeats, are indeed superb. It is also, nonetheless, a deeply flawed work; notably in the general political and historical framework which it proposes. The dominant impression is of a text marked by deep internal instability, a pervasive uncertainty about what, in the end, the author really wishes to say. In some places, such as the Introduction and the section on the Easter Rising, Kiberd celebrates the nationalist tradition, even in its most romantically culturalist, and its most militarist, manifestations. Elsewhere, he damns it and appears to suggest that the philosophy behind it, a cultural nationalist essentialism, is precisely what he thinks must be overcome. Yet simultaneously he appears nostalgic for if not still wedded to just such an essentialism. And he will also denounce, in the most unnuanced terms, those he regards as backsliders from the anticolonialist cause, such as Vidya Naipaul or Conor Cruise O'Brien (Kiberd 1994:105–8). Nonetheless, *Inventing Ireland* is the most extensive and detailed attempt thus far to apply ideas about colonialism and postcoloniality to Irish culture, certainly stronger as well as longer than related efforts, to be discussed below, by Luke Gibbons, David Cairns, and Shaun Richards, or David Lloyd; though Kiberd does not have the range and subtlety of reference to 'postcolonial' cultural theory that, say, Lloyd has. Rather, he relies heavily and somewhat uncritically on Edward Said and Frantz Fanon.[16]

Kiberd wants, as in his earlier essays, to attribute to the colonial impact a whole series of social attributes, especially relating to gender roles, which one would really need to *show* as significantly deriving from colonialism. This he does not do, in *Inventing Ireland* (e.g. 44–6, following Ashis Nandy) or elsewhere. Whilst Foucault, for instance, has been much and justly criticised for entirely ignoring imperialism in his account of the formations of sexuality, it is rash, to say the least, to rush to the opposite extreme and without argument or evidence, attribute a huge range of interpersonal, familial and sexual relations to Empire.[17] Kiberd refers also to 'the imperial strategy of infantilizing the native culture.' (1995:103, and similar formulations at 104 and elsewhere). Certainly there was much colonialist writing which either infantilised or feminised subject peoples—but one cannot simply collapse these different things together. By no means all colonialist thought did this—for instance British Indian 'martial races theory' imagined some groups as feminine (e.g. Bengalis), others as ultramasculine (Sikhs, Pathans). And on other levels there is an intriguing absence of feminine stereotypes of the Irish—the 'Paddy' image is not often accompanied by a corresponding 'Biddy' in British popular racism, though it may more frequently be so in the American version.[18]

In other respects too, Kiberd appears to attribute not only an all-determining power but a quite unreal degree of instrumentality to the 'colonial' rulers: 'one of the objects of colonial policy was to maintain conditions in which the production of serious works of literature describing a society in all its complexity was well-nigh impossible.' (1995:50) At the most rhetorically extreme, not only is colonialism presented as seeking to destroy Irish culture, but as making the place itself disappear: 'Ireland after the famines of the mid-nineteenth century was a sort of nowhere, waiting for its appropriate images and symbols' (115). The notion seems to be that Ireland was unique in nineteenth-century Europe in having very few archival or institutional sources for the construction of nationalism. Supposedly, some European peoples like the French have constructed themselves, defined their national identities, from within, while colonialism has forced the Irish to build their identity negatively, in reaction against English pressures and stereotypes. The contrast is at best overdrawn, and indeed elsewhere (e.g. 1995:135) Kiberd seems to draw back from it.

The single-minded insistence on reading most major Irish writers as colonial or postcolonial, though far more nuanced and detailed in execution than in Kiberd's earlier work or most other exercises in the genre, persists throughout *Inventing Ireland*. Yeats and Walt Whitman are described as 'the first artists of the decolonizing world' (117)—the implied claim about Whitman's America, a state then just beginning to flex its own imperial muscles, is as problematic as that about Ireland. Fanon's Algeria is seen as 'an analogous situation' to Yeats's Ireland (163). Yeats's writings of 1908 are 'one of the first Irish articulations of the dialectics of postcolonial liberation' (165). The structure of Synge's *The Playboy of the Western World*, Kiberd says, 'corresponds very neatly with Frantz Fanon's dialectic of decolonization, from occupation, through nationalism, to liberation.' (184) Synge is thus 'arguably the most gifted Irish exponent of the three phases of artistic decolonization later described by Fanon.' (186) Later the Fanonian associations shift, without explanation, from text-microcosm to state-macrocosm: 'The history of independent Ireland bears a remarkably similarity, therefore, to the phases charted by Frantz Fanon in *The Wretched of the Earth*.'

(551–2) Brendan Behan is 'one of the first post-colonial writers to impinge on the consciousness of post-war Britain.' (529) Beckett's *Murphy*, similarly, is seen as 'one of the earliest novels of immigrant life in Britain.' (532–3) The education system in the Irish 'post-colony' is depicted as having very close African parallels, and illuminated through the words of Ngugi wa Thiong'o and V. S. Naipaul (552–7). Insofar as a subsequent literary generation has abandoned this supposed anticolonialist focus, it is to Kiberd a cause for bitter regret. Dermot Bolger and other younger Dublin writers, he laments, 'took a line [on Northern Ireland] even more conservative than that favoured by the Dublin establishment . . . an obsessive, sometimes paranoid, search for elements in southern culture which might be complicit in the northern carnage.' (ibid: 610)[19]

This picture is sometimes—perhaps rather inconsistently—more varied than in Kiberd's earlier essays. Ireland's 'invention' is now depicted as having some things in common with those of other European countries, but others—more important—with Africa and Asia. Irish cultural and language debates 'anticipated those which would later be conducted in Africa and Asia.' (135) Still: 'If in certain cultural respects the Irish experience had much in common with that of other emerging states in Asia and Africa, in more directly political terms it was a very representative European country.' (475) 'Within Europe itself a country such as Greece (the other former colony [sic]) betrayed far more of the classic symptoms of underdevelopment.' (476) The dream of a future boundless, utopian state of liberation persists: 'Nationalism and Unionism are but one another's headache; those who insist that art must be either English or Irish are boring; but a nation having defined itself by passing through opposites, may see those opposites acquire and engender. When this happens, an end will come to that restless arraignment of the English Other and to the consequent purging of heresy within: instead there will emerge a self-creating Ireland produced by nothing but its own desire.' (124) The optimism is boundless: 'in a Europe filled with countries which have a glorious past, the Irish are among the few still exercised by the prospect of an interesting future, by a belief that everything in the country might yet be remade.' (579)

Colm Toibin, in a sharp critique of Kiberd, sees his literary and theoretical sophistication, all his playing with fixity, as 'at times, a mask for some very old-fashioned views on Irish nationalism and Irish history.' (Toibin 1996:14) He even, in Toibin's eyes, adheres 'to the story we all read in the schoolbooks, which he is the last to believe.' (ibid: 15) Toibin's objections are mainly political, but he dislikes too Kiberd's placing of all literary creation into a narrative of 'inventing Ireland': he would prefer 'a book called 'Not Inventing Ireland' in which Joyce and O'Casey and the writers of the Blasket Islands lead to Kavanagh and McGahern, with Beckett and Banville nearby; in which writers ignored the idea of Ireland and . . . made the whole idea of Irish nationalism a sick joke or a burden or a lie.' (ibid: 16)[20]

This is unfair, for much of what Kiberd writes troubles or contradicts that textbook story. It is tempting, however, to see Kiberd as merely incorrigibly inconsistent on such matters. In his Field Day essay 'Anglo-Irish Attitudes' he had insisted on the need for a serious study, a 'pragmatic analysis', of Ulster Unionist culture. Yet that culture is entirely unexamined in his subsequent writing. Kiberd's view of Northern Ireland itself seemed fairly straightforward, at least in the mid-1980s, when he reached for the familiar Algerian analogy by saying that British intellectuals 'will be only too well aware that the collapse of the French government in 1958 occurred when the military became embroiled in a similar "no-win" colonial situation.' (Kiberd 1985:104) In criticising F. S. L. Lyons, he had attacked the latter's exclusive focus on culture, saying that changes in both Unionist and Republican politics have been fundamentally economic in nature. He even suggested that fixation on cultural rather than politico-economic explanation was a peculiarly English failure to understand Ireland. Yet everything else Kiberd has written has been, despite one or two caveats, near-exclusively cultural in attention, with barely a reference to economic determinants. The major exception was a more journalistic essay on the theme of Irish postcoloniality, in the *Sunday Business Post*. Here he pointed to Ireland's then low growth rates, high unemployment and emigration, cutbacks in public services, and indebtedness as classically postcolonial ills—as if these were not features of many European societies in the past decade. He also lambasted what he called a 'regime of mimic-men' in Dublin's government and media, and suggested (in an argument that might win assent among many who would not accept his wider case) that Charles Haughey as Taoiseach was 'far more "Third Worldly" than any of his predecessors . . . reminiscent of a Juan Peron or an Indira Gandhi.' But even here Kiberd's polemic ended with a focus on the cultural, urging Ireland's economic and political actors to emulate the daring of its writers, with 'a similar experimentalism, rather than accepting the inherited and calcified colonial forms.' (Kiberd 1991a) Once again literature is in the vanguard, and in command.

The message which Deane suggests in nuanced and elliptical ways, and Kiberd adumbrates in yet more ambiguous fashion, is more forcefully announced in Luke Gibbons's contributions to the Field Day anthology, and his other writings. He seeks to enlist a combination of postcolonialism, poststructuralism and more traditional cultural nationalism against 'revisionism'—which he apparently identifies with everything from the 1959 opening of the Irish economy and later EU membership, to current historical scholarship. Gibbons thus seems to have a dual purpose: to rehabilitate the nationalist legacy by demolishing hostile 'revisionist' views of it, and to press the case that Ireland's position remains essentially a colonial one. In the *Field Day Anthology* this project is pursued, in the sections Gibbons compiled, with an explicit didacticism at odds with the tone of most of the rest of the anthology.[21] The argument itself is nonetheless interesting and sometimes original: especially in Gibbons's section of Volume II: 'Constructing the Canon: Versions of National Identity' (Field Day 1991, II:950–1020), which successfully (even if with an all too evident political purpose) makes the point that conceptions of Irishness in nineteenth-century nationalist thought were very diverse. Gibbons's polemic in Volume III, 'Challenging the Canon', is less convincing. Historians and political writers critical of the nationalist tradition are repeatedly suggested—though on rather little evidence—to be caricaturing and denigrating it (III:563–6). The very notion of a continuous and relatively homogeneous cultural nationalist tradition is argued to be itself a creation of the 'revisionists', rather than of those they were 'revising' (III:568). And it is asserted that 'The fact that the modernization project has lost its way in Ireland is clear to all who are willing to disengage themselves from fantasy, "bourgeois humanist" or otherwise.' (III:567)

It is an argument that Gibbons has been repeating for some time. In his contribution to Richard Kearney's *Across the Frontiers* he had similarly urged that 'The equation of urbanization and industrial development with enlightenment values of progress, secularization and cosmopolitanism proved no longer viable' in the Ireland of the 1980s. (Gibbons 1988a:207)[22] It was the crowds that gathered to welcome John Paul II, not those who marched against tax increases, who were 'a portent of things to come', showing the capacity of 'traditional Ireland to emerge from the ashes.' (ibid: 218) Gibbons evidently welcomed this; though what political conclusions were supposed to follow—or how they might be compatible with his proclaimed leftism—remained less clear. In a rather related vein was Gibbons's hymn of praise for Edmund Burke (1997), where Burke's celebration of tradition was endorsed, but coupled with a very forced attempt to turn Burke into a kind of 1990s cultural nationalist-cum-postmodernist. Burke, Gibbons suggested without textual evidence 'had little sympathy for triumphalist versions of Britishness which sought to trample on the rights of other cultures, and which would construe any badge of difference—the Irish language, Catholicism, or in our own time, even Gaelic games—as a form of subversion.' (1997:22) 'In emphasising the primacy of culture, Burke strikes a curious modern (or postmodern) note' (ibid: 22) Thus it was possible to assert Burke's abiding contemporaneity, though only through a reading that is itself 'curious' in its anachronism: 'Burke's rethinking of the relation between past and present, culture and commerce, aesthetics and politics, extend beyond his own era.' (ibid: 25)

Similar claims are pressed on behalf of the 1790s United Irish movement (Gibbons 1998). Gibbons has proposed that the thought of the United Irishmen, insofar as it departed from the eighteenth-century European republican mainstream of Enlightenment universalism and rationalism, did so by being in advance of it. So far in advance, indeed, as to offer a startling anticipation of 1990s postcolonial theory. Supposedly, United Irish thinkers espoused avant-garde conceptions of cultural pluralism. They held the view that cultures as such, not just individuals, have rights. They repudiated the imperialist assumptions of most Enlightenment thought, 'refracting the Enlightenment itself through the prism of cultural diversity' (1998:127). They did not, as usually claimed, scorn appeals to the past or tradition and set their sights firmly on a utopian future. Rather, it was only the British past—with its insistence on the innate superiority of the ancient constitution and the Protestant religion— which they rejected, while warmly embracing ideas of Irish and Gaelic trad- ition. This is a stimulating argument, but one ill-anchored in historical evidence: in the (admittedly abbreviated) version that has thus far appeared in print, Gibbons offers not one citation or quotation from any United Irishman in support of any of these claims about their thought.

Gibbons is thus concerned to press not only a postcolonialist, but a post- modernist and 'post-humanist', though also in many ways surprisingly trad- itional, view of Irish culture. Writing in the Field Day anthology, he urged that:

While liberals of a secular persuasion were announcing the death of God in Ireland, philosophers on the Continent such as Michel Foucault and Jacques Derrida were pro- claiming the death of man. The revisionist enterprise in Ireland, based as it is on a liberal-humanist ethic, was faced with an intractable dilemma as it gradually became apparent that a belief in a human condition, transcending all historical and political divisions, belonged to the kind of cultural fantasy that Sean O'Faolain associated with nationalism, except that it was now a humanist rather than a Gaelic mystique. (Field Day 1991, III:567)

Francis Mulhern has argued, in a harshly phrased critique, that Gibbons exhibits 'an inability to think of Ireland except in terms of nationality, or of nationality in other than the special terms of national*ism*.' (Mulhern 1995:30). His obsessional reference back, in debates over the present state of Ireland, to clichés about the 'colonial' past derives from this inability (ibid: 32) and typ- ically ignores the fact of Irish nationalism's historical success:

To describe the culture and society thus created as 'postcolonial' is either platitudinous or—more interestingly—tendentious . . . [T]o reassert the actual history, the accom- plished colonial fact, as the defining crux of Irish culture today—*three generations after Independence*—is tantamount to suggesting that indigenous propertied classes and their politico-cultural elites are not really responsible for the forms of exploitation and oppression they have conserved or developed in their own bourgeois state, and that rad- ical social critics must acknowledge a continuing, mitigating 'national' ordeal. The name for this is postcolonial melancholy. Its political implication, like that of any nationalism prolonged beyond its validating political occasions, is confusionist and, at worst, reactionary. (ibid: 32: emphasis in original)

With Gibbons as with Kiberd, while the philosophical or literary-theoretical underpinnings of the arguments advanced may be sophisticated (Gibbons is,

among other things, steeped in Wittgensteinian thought; though this has surfaced little so far in his published writing), the politico-cultural alternatives are
crudely polarised. If modernisation, cosmopolitanism, liberal humanism and
'post-nationalism' have all failed, what is left except for colonialism and anticolonial nationalism to resume the integrity of their quarrel? Responding to the
criticisms of Francis Mulhern, he appeared to identify any scepticism about the
historical nationalist project with 'indifference to any form of cultural specificity' (Gibbons 1994:29). Such scepticism seems also necessarily to be linked, in
his mind, with sympathy or subservience towards the 'Protestant Ascendancy'
and 'the might of the British Empire.' (ibid: 28) The dominant fact about contemporary Ireland is unequivocally that it is 'a culture still trying to come to
terms with centuries of colonial domination.' (ibid: 31) Thus invocations of a
literary-critical avant-garde serve mainly to underpin a return to a somewhat
old-fashioned politics.

The work of literary historian David Lloyd has a similar, if often more
nuanced, intellectual thrust to Gibbons's. Drawing on the mixture of Frantz
Fanon and Jacques Derrida already made familiar in international postcolonial
theory—interestingly if eclectically supplemented, in his case, with ideas drawn
from Kant, Levi-Strauss, Deleuze and Guattari, Ricoeur, and latterly a promiscuous mixture of postcolonial 'subaltern' historians and theorists—Lloyd
wishes to contest not only the supposedly universalising, homogenising narrative of Enlightenment-as-imperialism but also the traditional cultural nationalism which is seen as merely, if unconsciously, integrating Irishness into an
assigned subordinate place within that narrative. 'Bourgeois' nationalists, contesting only the political (not the cultural or discursive) authority of colonialism in the name of a unitary, mythicised national spirit, reproduced the very
universal narratives which legitimated the wider imperialist cultural project.
The story which the Young Irelanders and their ideological successors told was
one of an ancestral national spirit, once expressed in precolonial Gaelic culture
but now available, translated, only through the linguistic and cultural work of
the revivalists themselves. Their project, then, was premised on the destruction
of the ancient culture which had resulted from Ireland 'undergoing the transition to hegemonic colonialism far earlier than any other colony' (Lloyd 1987:3—
the Welsh, the Caribs, Maltese and many others might perhaps dispute the
chronological claim).[23] This meant that cultural nationalism, as it developed
after a certain (ill-defined) point, was inherently inauthentic, conservative and
backward-looking. More, it meant necessarily inscribing Ireland into a universalist tale of advance from primitive community to modern nation-state—precisely imperialism's own self-justifying story and one in which Ireland had to be
a belated and dependent participant (ibid: *passim*; also Lloyd 1989).

This has echoes of Deane on Yeats; but Lloyd differs not only in his far more
systematic and self-conscious integration of specifically Irish concerns with

poststructuralist theory, but in inserting them within a meta-story of imperialist universalism versus resisting Otherness. Lloyd, long resident in California, has increasingly sought to integrate his ideas on Ireland with a more global conception of cultural politics, alluding also to the Philippines, India and the role of 'minority discourse' in continental Europe and the USA, among other sites of argument (e.g. JanMohamed and Lloyd 1990, Lloyd 1996, 1997, Lloyd and Thomas 1998). In another essay of Lloyd's, this almost oxymoronic insistence on assimilating Irish particularism into the general story of racism and colonialism goes to the peculiar lengths of ascribing to the English the view that in the natural order of things the Irish, as colonial subjects, *should* be black. Colonial discourse supposedly dealt with the 'disturbance in the visual field' caused by Irish people's stubbornly observable whiteness by insisting that somehow they *were* really black. The sole evidence for this is two overworked quotations from Charles Kingsley and Thomas Carlyle (Lloyd 1991: 76–7).[24] In Lloyd's studies we encounter again, as in much self-proclaimedly postmodernist and post-structuralist thought, the paradox of a grand historical narrative ostensibly premised on denial of the possibility of such narratives. And again we see sweeping claims about colonialism as a homogeneous entity, seemingly unsupported by any extensive reading of colonial history. In one of the few places where Lloyd acknowledges the fact that colonial practices differed in different places, he does so by citation from a source notably marginal to this subject, Renate Zahar's book on Fanon; and even this token recognition is immediately undermined by the claim that 'the structure of assimilation remains largely the same' across these differences (Lloyd 1991:92 n. 29). Latterly Lloyd has proclaimed that: 'Any serious analysis of Ireland's complex relation to colonialism must draw on the international histories and analyses of colonial processes and ideologies, not in order to throw up facile analogies but in order to comprehend more deeply the differentiated processes of domination and the insistence of alternative structures of cultural practice.' (1997:91) He has fiercely attacked others, including Terry Eagleton, for alleged neglect of the work of postcolonial and 'Third World' theorists, and has proclaimed that critiques of the colonial model for understanding Irish history 'have come mostly from people who have spent little time investigating the global dynamics of colonialism and are largely ignorant of contemporary discussions of the global networks of capitalist colonialism.' (1997:87) Yet much of his own published work appears vulnerable to similar strictures.

Lloyd himself seeks to avoid nationalist romanticism, and indeed proclaims himself to be no great friend of nationalism or of identity politics. In his first book he had suggested that nationalism, 'a progressive and even a necessary political movement at one stage in its history . . . tends at a later stage to become entirely reactionary.' (1987:x) Yet, once again, this seems to apply only to 'hegemonic' kinds of nationalist movement, not subaltern, resisting ones. Evidently he believes that so far as the twenty-six counties at least are concerned, that later stage was long since reached:

In post-independence Ireland, the historical 'victor' has clearly been a politics predicated on the constitution of national identity, with as its consequence sixty years of conservative republican rule and the perpetuation of economic dependency. (ibid: xii)

It is for this reason, he argues, that the philosophical critique of identity thinking, which 'may appear, in "metropolitan cultures", to be an apolitical intellectual luxury, is here a task preliminary to any rethinking of radical political options.' (ibid: xii) And that in its turn is presumably why, in a very harsh assessment of Seamus Heaney's work, it is the poet's alleged identitarian illusions on which Lloyd fastens most savagely (Lloyd 1993:13–40).

   The basic claim that Irish nationalism in many respects resembled the 'imperialism' against which it ranged itself, is hardly as original as Lloyd seeks to make it sound: historians like Paul Bew, utterly opposed to Lloyd in their methodological, disciplinary and political presuppositions, had already observed as much in relation to the new culturalist nationalism of the later nineteenth century (Bew 1987:6). Yet in Lloyd's work even more than in the other authors discussed here—and precisely because of his unequalled breadth of reference—a highly sophisticated theoretical apparatus is deployed in the service of what is, in the end, a fairly crude and manichean politics. Thus he can, in a notably elaborated text of literary-theoretical readings, refer without qualification or contextualisation, to 'the continuing anti-colonial struggle in Northern Ireland' (1993:3). Elsewhere, he airily dismisses 'imperialist and, perhaps much the same thing, revisionist histories' (ibid: 125): thus, as we have seen, consigning most modern Irish historical scholarship to the dustheap.[25] Addressing readers of *Subaltern Studies* he makes explicit the general implication that to categorise Ireland as 'post-colonial' means that 'that portion of the island under British rule is, properly speaking, still colonized.' (1996:262) His work 'take(s) as its premise that Ireland has been and remains a site of colonialism and anti-colonial struggle' (ibid: 262). Ireland has, as in the most unreconstructed kind of romantic nationalist chronicle, suffered 'continual subjection from the Tudor period to the present.' (1997:87)

   A kind of Marxism appears to lurk behind the poststructuralist tropes, and despite the avowed debt to Gramsci (1993:9, 126–8), or Lloyd's recent coauthored attempt to construct what might fairly be called a cultural-determinist theory of state formation (as opposed to classical Marxist economic determinism) (Lloyd and Thomas 1998), it is a fairly old-fashioned kind. He continues to have occasional recourse to such unelaborated phrases as 'the bourgeois ideology of the state' (1987:208) under which 'the democratic subject' and 'the colonial subject' seem more or less interchangeable. Nationalism merely 'repeats the master narrative of imperialism' (1993:54), and all it creates is 'the ensemble of institutions which ensures the continuing integration of the post-colonial state in the networks of multinational capital.' (ibid: 113) Yet in Northern Ireland an 'anticolonial struggle' continues, which Lloyd appears to support—perhaps in the same spirit that he celebrates the 'unrepresentable' agrarian violence of nineteenth-century Ireland for its very anarchy, its escape from the embraces of the state and hegemonic nationalism. (ibid: 125–62)[26] Such celebration would certainly be consistent with the scorn for 'bourgeois' democracy Lloyd else-where evinces, as well as his predictable hostility to European integration and to the 'absorption—ever more inevitable though this often seems—of Ireland into European modernity.' (1996:263)

Similarly homogenising tactics are pursued in the work which is, with Kiberd's and Lloyd's, probably the most extended discussion of cultural imperi-alism and its resistances in Ireland: the writings of David Cairns and Shaun Richards. Yet their assumptions about a generalised colonial and postcolonial situation are less damaging to their case than are Kiberd's, Gibbons's or Lloyd's, because they claim less for them. Their invocations of a general colonial model function largely as a kind of scene-setting rather than a rigid interpretive frame for the investigation as a whole; and their work is free of the dehistoricising thrust of mainstream deconstructive poststructuralism (see esp. Cairns and Richards 1988:1–8, 12–17; Richards 1991a:120–2). Theirs is theoretically a simpler stance than Lloyd's, deriving essentially from three (alas, rather predictable) sources: an application to Ireland of Said's protocols from *Orientalism*, Grams-cian notions of hegemony, and Foucault's discourse analysis. Frantz Fanon too is inescapably invoked, more especially by Richards writing alone: his 1991a:120–2 opens with ringing invocations of Fanon, Amilcar Cabral and a rather out-of-context Partha Chatterjee on the need for cultural decolonisa-tion. This Fanon, like Benita Parry's (Parry 1987), is the political militant of the first part of *Wretched of the Earth* rather than the pseudo-Lacanian analyst invoked by Homi Bhabha and by David Lloyd.

Cairns and Richards' relatively simple theoretical framework is however accompanied by a breadth and depth of empirical reference greater than that essayed by almost any of the other writers discussed here. It is a predominantly literary reference: underlining once more the near-universal assumption in all these debates that inventing a new Irish identity takes place today, as it did dur-ing the Revival, in and through the work of novelists, playwrights and poets. It is also, one may note, a considerable narrowing of focus compared to the ideas of discourse employed by Said or Foucault and the notion of culture held by Gramsci. Thus Cairns and Richards engage in close readings of Samuel Fergu-son, Thomas Davis, Standish O'Grady, Pearse, Yeats, Joyce, O'Casey and Heaney: valuable in themselves, but very much congruent with the widespread tendency we have noted, of using a handful of canonical texts as supposed substantiation for claims about national trends in society and mentality. This

concentration on literary high culture, which is thus made to bear more interpretive weight than should be placed on it, is accompanied by a further
homogenisation, this time of the category of 'the people', which is accomplished
by simply transposing Gramscian categories from class to nation, and sits oddly
with the authors' insistence that such essentialism is itself a colonial product.
Their conclusion explicitly aligns them with Deane, especially his hope that cultural renewal will as in the past lead the way to a new politics (Cairns and
Richards 1988:152–4); but also and in my view less convincingly, his apparent
conviction that the roots not only of the contemporary northern bloodshed but
of the south's past economic traumas can be found in British colonialism. Elsewhere, however, Richards has (as we have seen) appeared far more critical of
Deane's and Field Day's use of the colonial model (Richards 1991b).

Some other Irish appropriations of the manichean image of colonial relations are less historically grounded than are Cairns and Richards's. A good
example of its ahistorical elaboration would be James Knapp's discussion
of Lady Gregory, in a major American collection on the 'macropolitics' of
nineteenth-century literature. Knapp sees Lady Gregory's depiction of Irish
peasants as partaking of an anti-imperialist worldview, but simultaneously as
representing primitivism and primordialism. Yet, astonishingly (at least, it
would be astonishing to someone not acquainted with the clichés of colonial
discourse analysis) Knapp does not see this 'romantic primitivism' (Knapp
1991:299) as the integral part of the cultural nationalist worldview which it so
evidently was. Rather, he chooses to present it as a reflection of Gregory being
'both colonizer and colonized . . . a member of a threatened class' struggling 'to
contain that revolutionary change which she feared as well as urged.' (ibid: 300)

Other exercises in the genre similarly amount in effect to little more than a
mechanical transposition and 'application' to Irish contexts of themes from the
internationally influential literature of postcolonial theory, as with Colin Graham's reading of Edgeworth's *Castle Rackrent* by way of Homi Bhabha's essays.[27]
Bhabha's concept of 'sly civility', in Graham's view, 'describes with some degree
of accuracy the textual tactics at play in *Castle Rackrent*, and these tactics insist
in this case on a paralleled linkage [sic] between a coloniser-colonised relationship and the gender relationships of marriage.' (C. Graham 1996a:22) Here, as in
so much of the by-now vast global literature 'applying' colonial and postcolonial cultural theory to a huge range of specific texts, the all-determining colonial context is merely assumed rather than argued for, as equally is the authority
of the particular theorist (in this case Bhabha) whose ideas are subject to no
kind of interrogation whatever.[28]

Several of the critics adhering to such perspectives argue for a radical historical—and cultural—distinction between different kinds of nationalism. This
division is perhaps most clearly and extensively drawn in the writings of David
Lloyd and Luke Gibbons (see esp. Lloyd 1993, Gibbons 1992). On the one hand

lies state-centred nationalism, dominant since Independence but representing a direct continuation and copy of many traits identified by the critics as specifically colonial. It is seen as not only state-worshipping and repressive, but associated with masculinist and patriarchal values and (in a clear if often unspecific invocation of Marxist arguments) with 'bourgeois' rule and the dominance of multinational capital, culture, and media. On the other hand lie various oppositional kinds of nationalism: decentralised, non-hierarchical, even anarchic, fragmentary and fugitive in expression, associated with peasant, proletarian, female, local and minority resistances.[29] Favoured sites for its operations include the various agrarian 'secret societies' of Irish history—Whiteboys, Ribbonmen, Defenders, and so on. It is sometimes stated, and more often apparently hinted, that Sinn Fein and the IRA in some sense belong to or are inheritors of this alternative, oppositional tradition. A somewhat promiscuous range of non-Irish sources is drawn upon for the framework, notably Fanon, Said and the *Subaltern Studies* historians. Rather predictably, however, the range of historical reference is less impressive. Both Gibbons and Lloyd rely on fairly scanty reading about Irish agrarian movements, and a serious dearth of comparative material on similar movements elsewhere.[30]

It is also sometimes argued—most clearly, again, by Luke Gibbons and David Lloyd—that specific aesthetic features correspond to these political divisions. Metaphor and symbol are the preserve of the dominant, the colonial and statist, metonymy and allegory correspond to the anti- and post-colonial, the resistant, oppositional and non-statist. Sharply criticising these claims, Kevin Barry describes them as an 'especially dynamic, obsessive and influential' current in Irish studies. (1996:2) He argues to the effect that the alleged division in rhetorical and aesthetic strategies simply cannot be sustained from the evidence. One can find close parallels to the Whiteboys and other Irish agrarian protestors in English and other contexts (as for instance in the Windsor 'Blacks' classically analysed by E. P. Thompson (1975)); not only in their activities, but in their rhetorics including reliance on allegory (ibid: 5–8). And one can find allegory in a wide range of official state representations, as for instance in the designs of banknotes (ibid: 8), while of course it is central to such writers as Edmund Spenser, 'arch-colonist and arch-allegorist'(ibid: 11). Thus there is very little substance to:

the claim of any post-colonial theory that the nation-state is supported by symbol and opposed by allegory . . . The nation-state may, in each instance, employ an aesthetic mode which is precisely the mode attributed by Lloyd and Gibbons to those who would oppose the state. (ibid: 8)

Still less can one sustain claims that the traits supposedly identified are specifically colonial or postcolonial ones. Lloyd echoes as a received truth an assertion that is no less contestable for being so widely repeated: that colonial conditions induce a very particular melding of the cultural and the political. And he then, leaping from the globally portentous to the locally sectarian, dismisses any notion of a distinct and respect-worthy Unionist culture more totally even than any recent Sinn Fein pronouncement has done:

> [T]he very division between politics and culture that is the hallmark of liberal ideology is conceptually bankrupt throughout the colonial world, for which cultural incommensurability is the rationale for racist domination and the stimulus for native refusal and resistance. Under colonial conditions, there is no transcendence either of the political state or of culture. Liberal attempts that pretend to an Irish multiculturalism or models of two (or more) traditions are simply dishonest to the extent that they ignore the asymmetrical and violent relations that have structured Ireland historically and contemporaneously. (1997:88)

(iii) Originators, Imitators, and Assailants

If Frantz Fanon has been an increasingly ubiquitous father-figure for analyses of an Irish 'colonial situation', then a more immediate but almost equally influential presence here as throughout the new field of postcolonial studies, a kind of elder brother to the Irish theorists, has been Edward Said. Said's massively influential disquisitions on Orientalism and cultural imperialism did not, until relatively recently, take explicit cognisance of Ireland. When he began to do so, first in a Field Day pamphlet (Said 1988) and then with a reworked version of the same material in his *Culture and Imperialism* (1993) it was in the context of a new attention not so much to Orientalist discourse itself as to resistant, nationalist and liberationist counter-discourses. He sought especially to place W. B. Yeats in this framework, in a fashion which was more than a little procrustean.

Said described Yeats's earlier work as more or less unproblematically 'anti-imperialist', as being part of the global movement of 'great nationalist artists of decolonization and revolutionary nationalism like Tagore, Senghor, Neruda, Vallejo, Cesaire, Faiz, Darwish.' (Said 1988:8) The poet is seen as 'restoring a suppressed history, and rejoining the nation to it' (ibid: 22) in a way directly analogous to that for which Fanon had called. And although Yeats does not make the full breakthrough into a post-nationalist imagining of 'liberation', his work remains 'a considerable achievement in decolonization none the less.' (ibid: 24)

In the later, revised version of this essay which appeared in *Culture and Imperialism*, Said somewhat qualifies his claims for Yeats. The last phrase quoted, for instance, becomes 'a considerable achievement in *cultural* decolonization' (1993:288. My emphasis)—a rather less sweeping judgement. Yet he retains the dubious suggestion (based solely on a recollection by Pablo Neruda, for which the most plausible explanation is simply that Neruda's memory was at fault) that Yeats supported the Spanish Republic's cause against Franco. (On Yeats's actual 1930s politics, which shaded towards fascism, see C. C. O'Brien 1988a, Cullingford 1981.) And while he emphasises more strongly than before his conviction that Yeats's later reactionary and mystical views 'cancelled out' his earlier revolutionism (1993:283; earlier this had been 'to some extent cancelled out' 1988:21) still Said remains wedded to the idea of at least the younger Yeats as a revolutionary nationalist, and one moreover whose proper historical context is not so much European as within the milieu of twentieth-century 'Third World' anticolonialism and decolonisation.[31]

Indeed in *Culture and Imperialism* Said is considerably more emphatic than before in placing Irish experience—past and, apparently, present—in the colonial mould. As he baldly asserts:

It is an amazing thing that the problem of Irish liberation not only has continued longer than any other comparable struggles, but is so often not regarded as being an imperial or nationalist issue; instead it is comprehended as an aberration within the British dominions. Yet the facts conclusively reveal otherwise. (1993:284)

The confident appeal to 'the facts' would be hard put to survive a reading of Irish history more extensive than the rather limited range revealed in Said's footnotes (though it should be acknowledged that Said's general historical reading has certainly been wider than that of most cultural theorists of colonialism).[32] Greater attention to the historical record would also at the least qualify Said's claim that 'reductive and slanderous encapsulation of Irish actualities . . . had been the fate of the Irish at the hands of English writers for eight centuries' (ibid: 286): a claim which is itself strikingly reductive. It would further render unsustainable such judgements as that 'The Irish experience and other colonial histories in other parts of the contemporary world testify to a new phenomenon: a spiral away and extrapolation from Europe and the West.' (ibid: 288) For even leaving aside the rather basic fact that Ireland is by most reckonings a part of Europe and rather far West, if any one theme, apart from the violence in the north, has dominated contemporary Irish life it is not an 'extrapolation from' but an increasing economic, political and cultural *integration* with the rest of Europe.[33]

David Lloyd's and Luke Gibbons' (1991:95–104, 112–3) attempts, drawing on such Saidian claims, to insert British-Irish relations into a narrative of colonialist racial theory based on visual signs of Otherness—the racial difference, even the essential if elusive blackness, of the Irish—are evidently fraught with difficulty. Kiberd's psychiatric model of neocolonial dependency, both ahistorical and in places sexist, is even more so. A more promising avenue of enquiry is perhaps to focus on language as the key to cultural imperialism: in the contexts both of the fate of Gaelic, and of Irish accents and dialects as signs of inferior otherness. The 'language question' was, as is well known, central to the successive projects of cultural nationalism from Young Ireland to the early policies of the Free State. It has gained renewed salience in the culturo-political debates of recent years. But it is not quite the same question. A minority current continues to frame the issue in the old terms of the revival of Gaelic against the colonialist imposition of the English language. This is, most obviously, the thrust of Sinn Fein's cultural wing, for whom the revival of Gaelic is associated with recovery of romanticised traditional values:

Our traditional Gaelic culture held values of human dignity, of cooperation, of social- ism which are directly opposed to the materalism, consumerism, individualism, com- petitiveness which predominate in the Anglo-American culture of today. (Padraig Ó Maolchraibhe, quoted in Wills 1991:33)[34]

Both Luke Gibbons (1988b) and Clair Wills (1991) have developed arguments linking representations of language and of political violence—and in Gibbons' case the romanticised silences of the Irish landscape and its people—in modern Irish history. Best-known and most influential, however, has been Tom Paulin's 'A New Look at the Language Question' (in Paulin 1984), where he advocates a 'federal' concept of Irish-English, both granting proper place to regional dialects and achieving enough homogeneity to challenge the hegemony of the 'neocolonial' standard English.

The political implications are evident, and attractive, enough: an Ireland which has achieved full cultural independence, which is politically united, but which preserves and encourages full cultural diversity including the distinct traditions of Ulster Protestants. But as Clair Wills points out, there is a tension or contradiction here between 'a view of language as expressive of national, regional or racial identity (i.e. inherently bound up with certain values), or alternatively as a political tool in the creation of a community resistant to an imperial cultural hegemony.' (Wills 1991:33) What Wills does not say is how sharply this tension centres on Ulster. For many of the north's people the notion of their cultural traditions as part of a federation explicitly designed to be *resist-ant* to Britishness would be extremely uncongenial. Edna Longley (1986, also excerpted in Field Day 1991, III:648–54) makes just this point. She accuses Paulin, Deane and Co. of adopting such a programme only by default of hopes to revive Gaelic: which, she believes, their resistance to linguistic colonialism actually logically requires. Paulin's argument, she charges, is not only crudely propagandistic, but 'creates division where unities already exist' and is even totalitarian in its implications (ibid: 651). Deane too is accused of 'atavised rationalism' and, in effect, of having a hidden Catholic-Republican agenda (ibid: 652).

Such charges are clearly exorbitant, but serve at least to underline just how much is at stake in these debates, where even a plea for the separation of politics and poetry (which is Longley's central ostensible aim) demonstrates an intense politicisation of literary or linguistic argument. Somewhat similarly, Wills's and

Gibbons's interventions, overtly centred respectively on theories of language and on cinematic romanticism, both turn into arguments about reason, representation and political violence. And both are concerned to attack those who would deny all rationality, and all representativeness, to Republican violence (Wills 1991:46–55; Gibbons 1988b:230–3; and see also John Hill's essay in Rockett, Gibbons and Hill 1988). Such concerns are less evidently foregrounded in Wills's more extended reworking of her ideas, in her book *Improprieties* (Wills 1993). The main focus there is on close readings of three Northern Irish poets; Tom Paulin, Medbh McGuckian, and Paul Muldoon; and especially on themes of sexuality in their work. Yet this too is framed within a meta-narrative in which postcoloniality and present colonialism—the two terms never clearly distinguished—are simply assumed to be the dominant realities of Irish and/or Northern Irish life.

Perhaps the most systematic attempt to elaborate and explicate a theoretical framework for Irish cultural 'postcolonialism' is Gerry Smyth's recent book *Decolonisation and Criticism* (1998). Leaning on the ideas of Deane, Kiberd, Gibbons and Lloyd—and behind them Bhabha and Spivak (though Smyth's grasp of the latter pair's admittedly often obscure thought is, to be blunt, not very precise[35])—he derives from them a rather rigid binary model of cultural 'decolonisation'. It has always been either 'liberal' or 'radical'. The former, mainly associated with 'Anglo-Irish' writers and critics, proclaims Irish *equality* with the former colonisers, but in doing so is essentially imitative, and remains trapped in colonialist categories. The latter, which became the Free State's and Republic's dominant discourse, insists on its own Otherness and difference; but thereby also imprisons itself in reactive collusion with colonial culture (ibid: 15–19). All Irish critical thought, at least until the very recent past, was caught in this binary opposition: though Smyth gives a detailed account only of the 1950s, and even for that period has a narrower focus than he implies. Thus although he makes sweeping claims about the character of Irish historical writing and even of 'scholarship' in general, his references are only to a handful of *literary* histories (ibid: 123–31, 191–8). Only now, with the adumbration of postcolonial thought in Ireland, can one escape from those categories into 'the difficult and dangerous freedom imagined by contemporary postcolonial theory' (190) and 'a genuine postcolonial politics of displacement' (207).

The colonial model is simply assumed, never argued for or supported by evidence. 'The assumption upon which this study is based is that a colonial relationship obtained between England and Ireland since the twelfth century . . . as a *first* principle I shall assert that "colonialism" continues to be a useful *general* term (that is, in Ireland and elsewhere)' (9; emphases original). Thereafter that model, and Smyth's simple picture of the 'two forms' of decolonisation, are shored up merely by a remarkable degree of repetition. Thus the writing, mostly from the 1950s, which he examines is 'compromised by its engagement with', 'structured in terms of', 'contributing to the maintenance of', 'increasingly implicated in', 'fully implicated in', 'fully implicated in', 'enabled the practices of', 'heavily implicated in', 'fully implicated in', again 'fully implicated in', 'did nothing to undo', 'a symptom of', 'thoroughly implicated in', 'implicated, as fully as the radical discourse it ostensibly opposed, in', 'implicated in', yet once more 'fully implicated in', 'unlikely to amount to much of a challenge to', 'in complete accord with', and 'trapped within the terms of' colonial discourse and pseudo-decolonisation (ibid: 95, 114, 122, 123, 123, 126, 128, 132, 133, 138, 141, 162, 167, 170, 172, 175, 187, 196, 206). There is the usual failure to substantiate the colonial model by looking at *any* colonial or postcolonial country other than Ireland, or any non-Irish postcolonial writing beyond the narrow, stereotyped, approved lineage of Fanon, Memmi, Nandy, Said, and the most famous of the current colonial discourse analysts. The whole of 'the rest' of the British Empire is represented solely by Partha Chatterjee's *Nationalist Thought and the Colonial World* (1986), and the argument even of that is distorted by transposing what Chatterjee had said about political leaders like Gandhi and Nehru onto the positions of Irish literary critics (Smyth: 27, 78, 224). Understanding of Irish history itself is reduced to a tiny handful of almost exclusively literary texts (there is, as usual in this genre, almost no reference to modern Irish historical scholarship) and a scattering of inaccurate clichés about Ireland's 'classic colonial encounter between three communities—native Gaelic, settler Anglo-Irish, offshore English' and 'legislative and cultural apartheid' (54).

And in a manner which has become familiar, all Smyth's anti-essentialist gestures coexist with a very traditional essentialisation of Irish identity and uniqueness, and a yet more traditional association of Irishness with Catholicism. Thus he repeatedly refers to the 'problematic' national status of certain writers, apparently because of their Protestantism (e.g. 161, 171, 176), with the evident implication that for some other types of person a non-problematic national identity existed. Non-Irish (or non-'Irish') writers are, repeatedly 'foreigners' or even 'the off-shore Subject' (183). As with Kiberd, Lloyd and so many other Irish postcolonialists we have looked at, behind Smyth's attempts at theoretical sophistication lies a manichean politics: a proclamation of radicalism which leads him to expect that his book will be 'attacked by those who have an interest in maintaining the status quo, be they publisher, academic-lecturer or intellectual-ideologue' (x). Approaches other than his own are 'fundamentally apolitical and ahistorical . . . the most reactionary research' (38). And, with wearying predictability, there is reference to 'the artificial political divide between certain parts of the island' (132–3).

All these arguments—even at their most extensive and elaborate, as in Kiberd's *Inventing Ireland* or Smyth's *Decolonisation and Criticism*—are structured around two great absent centres. One is the definition of colonialism itself. Although the concept is repeatedly invoked, it is very rarely pinned down by reference even to a dictionary definition, let alone to any of the substantial body of historical writing that seeks to clarify and demarcate the term. In failing to define what they mean by it, the cultural theorists constantly imply that Ireland's position was or is exactly the same as that of all Britain's African, Asian or Caribbean colonies. Such a homogenising implication only has to be stated to be seen as erroneous. They also presuppose, as George Boyce points out, that Ireland is, in the British Isles' experience, 'unique, apart, the product of the collision—or is it collusion—of native and colonising forces'. (1991a:12) Insofar as such a view implies the determining effects of a 'racial' division, especially in Ulster, then as Boyce shows, it collapses: for 'racially' the inhabitants of South Wales or of Wexford are as various as those of Northern Ireland. Thus:

national differences, 'Celts' and 'Saxons' or whatever, clearly do not explain the existence of the Northern Irish problem any more than they account for the lack of a South Walian or Wexford problem. (ibid: 18)

The theorists we have examined are mostly interested in the supposed cultural and psychological effects of colonialism, especially as reflected on by major literary figures, rather than the political or economic ones: indeed many of them appear virtually blind to debate on the latter. These cultural and psychological effects are specifically linked by Deane, Kiberd and others to the history of English/British political domination of Ireland, but are not confined to it, since the effects of psychological dependency are argued to persist long after the ending of formal British rule. This relationship, too, is assumed or asserted by way of rhetorical flourishes, not substantively argued for (see, for an attempt to make such an argument about psychological legacies, Moane 1994).

The fuzziness about the meanings of colonialism extends, perhaps inevitably, to *anti*colonialism too. Although Kiberd, Lloyd and others have had enlightening things to say about submerged anticolonial themes in some key Irish literary works (for instance Kiberd's discussion of *Ulysses* in his 1995), this at times drifts towards a tendency to see virtually any critique of anything at all as a critique of imperialism. And noting, as Kiberd does in his massive *Inventing Ireland*, a handful of articles and speeches, most of them directed to US audiences, in which Irish nationalists expressed solidarity with Indian and other anticolonial movements is not sufficient to make the case for a serious 'united front' against imperialism. As we have seen, such expressions were spasmodic if not exceptional.

The second great absence follows obviously from this: failure to engage in any way with the politics and culture of Unionism. Even Kiberd, who certainly does not ignore Irish Protestantism and its role in nationalist thought (*Inventing Ireland* might be thought if anything to overemphasise it, finding 'Protestant spirituality' in some rather surprising places including Pearse's writings) has almost nothing to say about any Unionist or non-nationalist literary or cultural figure. Luke Gibbons refers to Unionist and Loyalist traditions only by way of comparisons between their 'colonising' efforts and those of 'proponents of the frontier myth in the new world'. These are, he insists, 'not just analogies but . . . part of a shared historical experience of colonization.' (1996:14; see also ibid: 151–2) That, apparently, is *all* that Unionism amounts to: it is certainly not part of the 'Irish culture' Gibbons's work surveys. Deane's *Celtic Revivals* has just one passing reference to Ulster Unionists, who are identified only by their 'clamant imperialism' (1985a:66); while in discussing Derek Mahon's poetry, he notes Mahon's northern Protestant origins and suggests that his 'most deeply felt poems derive from his sympathy for its (the Protestant community's) isolation and its fading presence rather than from straightforward repudiation of its stiff rhetorical intransigence.' (160) Deane would, it appears, have preferred Mahon to engage in 'straightforward repudiation'; but since he takes it for granted that Protestants are 'fading' anyway, Mahon's work can be read and contained as elegy. David Lloyd offers a sketch of what Protestantism has supposedly meant in contemporary Ireland:

In Northern Ireland . . . the figment of Protestant identity, with all its racial overtones, immediately masked certain internal differences of sect and geographical origin as well as of economic interest. More importantly, 'Protestantism' acted for bourgeois politicians as a means to divide Protestant and Catholic workers along sectarian lines . . . the border played a crucial role in externalizing the threat of difference, placing it outside the Protestant community and the ideally Protestant state, and permitting the definition of the Catholic population as alien. (Lloyd 1993:18–19)

In the *Field Day Anthology*'s substantial section on 'Northern Protestant Oratory and Writing 1791–1985' no representative of Ulster's liberal, labour or socialist traditions is included: the only contemporary (post-1945) Unionist political figures featured are Ian Paisley and Harold McCusker. The anthology's section on 'Political Writings and Speeches 1900–1988' is devoted almost entirely to different kinds of nationalism, with the last four texts and thus main representatives of contemporary political rhetoric being from Charles Haughey, John Hume, Sean MacBride and Gerry Adams: hardly a broad cross-section of modern Irish political thought. There is nothing of substance on social or economic debates, nor on feminism: 'Irish Politics' is exclusively the politics of Catholic, male nationalism.

There are in all this writing very few overt allusions to the concept of settler colonialism, or to the strong contemporary political consequences which follow from a belief that Northern Ireland is a settler-colonial regime. It seems however, from numerous passing comments, that Deane, Gibbons, Kiberd, Lloyd and others do hold that belief. Even apart from the scattered favourable references to contemporary Northern Ireland Republicanism in their writings, it might be thought logically to follow, if one thinks that the Union was purely and simply imperialism, that Unionism today is by nature imperialist, and nothing more need be said of it. Thus Gibbons, Kiberd, Lloyd, the Field Day authors and indeed most others in this milieu reproduce the myopia of those they examine and often celebrate. The contemporary political implications of this hardly need further underlining. As John Wilson Foster suggests—albeit in an argument which is both frustratingly sketchy and uncritically reliant on Memmi's psycho-social portrait of 'the coloniser'—the colonial model itself can be double-edged, with northern Unionists viewable both as colonists and as themselves fearing colonisation from the Catholic South (J. W. Foster 1988).[36]

Perhaps the culturalist theorists of Irish colonialism and postcoloniality represent in the end not so much a theory as a mood. Certainly one observer of what was probably the biggest and most intellectually prestigious gathering discussing such themes, the May 1992 'Gender and Colonialism' conference in Galway, claimed to discern such a mood as all-pervasive there. Clara Connolly noted the overwhelming dominance of literary and cultural as opposed to historical or political-economic approaches among the 300–plus attenders and eighty paper-givers. This, she argued, partly accounted for the dominance of 'a clear pro-republican stance, opposed equally to the "bourgeois nationalism" of the Irish state, and to the "liberal revisionists".' The anti-revisionism was symbolised—or self-caricatured—by Barbara Harlow of Texas allegedly attacking the historians as 'the strip-searchers of academia'. (Clara Connolly 1993:105) It related also to the prevalent 'anti-Enlightenment' rhetoric of the conferees: summed up in its most extreme form in Luke Gibbons's reported dismissal of the concept of citizenship as 'a form of ethnocide'—a view echoed, if more cautiously, by David Lloyd (ibid: 109). Carol Coulter, it was reported, lauded the shared commitment to 'communal values' of Rana Kabbani and Desmond Fennell as against the 'liberal Ayatollahs' of Dublin and London, and argued that any feminism which did not ground itself in such values, which were a refuge against colonialism, was doomed in Ireland (ibid: 107).[37]

In Connolly's view, then, avant-garde literary theory and its fashionable anti-humanism merely reinforced 'an *exclusive* focus on the creation of a national identity' which 'confines "culture" to its narrowest definition of "ethnicity", and prevents the possibility of addressing other divisions in Irish society, at least as significant, such as those created by gender and class.' (ibid: 110) This brings her critique close to Mulhern's; and both note the affinities between such rhetorics and those of militant Republicanism.

There is evidently a danger of the classic 'slippery slope' fallacy here: the risk that critique of any political, cultural or intellectual position broadly describable as nationalist may slide into associating such positions, perhaps quite wrongly, with unreconstructed Republicanism or the IRA's campaigns. Such a slide has been ever more apparent, for instance, in the writings of Conor Cruise

O'Brien. At worst, it may issue in the kind of 'Irish McCarthyism' of which Bill
Rolston has complained (Rolston 1992b). But as we have seen, equally in evidence has been the converse intellectual slither by which all positions broadly
definable as revisionist, postnationalist or even just condemnatory of Sinn
Fein's Republicanism or IRA violence are dubbed anti-national, Unionist or
neocolonialist. And there is also what one might call the reflexive slippery slope;
by which complaints at false accusations from one side turn almost impercept-
ibly into counter-accusations from the other.

The intensity of these culture wars, the unusually high profile of literary politics in Ireland and its intricate intertwinement with arguments over historical
interpretation, national identity and politics itself in the more narrow and conventional sense, help explain the sharpness of the contestation. They help
explain why, for instance, Colm Toibin can, in the course of a discussion of literary history, suddenly burst out apropos of the Easter Rising and by extension
of Irish nationalism generally: 'I loathe everything about it, every single
moment of it.' (Toibin 1996:16) Such explosions of rage are lurking, barely concealed, beneath the surface of much of the writing we are examining, from all
sides of the arguments.

The preceding pages have been sharply critical of almost all applications of
the colonial model to Ireland, including theories of neocolonialism and applications of colonial discourse theory. None of this, nor recognition of the shortcomings of Field Day's and others' revived cultural nationalism, implies that
there are easily adoptable alternatives. The difficulties in framing such alternatives, from within the paradigm of debate on Irish culture, may be suggested by
examining a writer who has taken a very different route from those discussed
above, Richard Kearney. Kearney initially analysed modern Irish culture by
counterposing in familiar ways the traditional and the modernist; identified
respectively with the national and revivalist, and the discontinuous and foreign
(Kearney 1988, esp. Introduction). Rather tentatively, he proposed a transi-
tional mode of cultural creation mediating between these and identifiable in
some (not very clearly delineated) sense with postmodernism. Kearney's guiding star here was the hermeneutical tradition of European philosophy, and
within it above all Paul Ricoeur. At the same time, however, Kearney in his early
writings still seemed wedded to certain essentialist, cultural nationalist, themes.
The very title of a collection he edited, *The Irish Mind* (Richard Kearney 1985),
and the tenor of his Introduction, partook of that ideology in fairly pure, if
sophisticated, form. It was also one of the earlier deployments of the 'postcolonial' trope in Irish cultural criticism, flourishing the Fanonian rallying-cries
and the references to non-nationalist writers as exhibiting 'post-colonial servility' which were soon to become commonplace.

From the end of the eighties, Kearney then moved to a fully-fledged celebration of postmodernism as twin to and facilitator for postnationalism: the

former's fragmentation of identities and narratives, its celebration of pastiche and *bricollage*, enabling a parallel breakdown of nationalist solidarities and frontiers—but allowing (he implies) the recuperation of local and national loyalties as politically harmless nostalgia, even kitsch. (Richard Kearney ed. 1990: Introduction; 1997 ch. 4)

The resultant ambiguities are still evident in Kearney's more recent collection, *Postnationalist Ireland* (1997). In position papers co-written with Robin Wilson for the Opsahl Commission and the Dublin Forum for Peace and Reconciliation, he offers a vision of Northern Ireland's future as a European region, with a shared-sovereignty Council for Britain and Ireland. But in essays on the philosophers George Berkeley, John Toland and John Tyndall, he seeks for an elusive if not mythical distinctively Irish cast to their thought, very much in line with the tendencies in his earlier *Irish Mind* collection. In between these poles, Kearney will at some points urge, as in his earlier writing, that the future lies inevitably beyond the nation-state: 'The shibboleths of both Irish and British nationalism begin to come undone when exposed to the razor of contemporary change.' (1997:11) The breakdown of traditional conceptions of sovereignty, the coming of a new European order both transnational, federal and regional, is both fated and felicitous.

Yet Kearney continues to insist, repeatedly, that this vision does not involve him in blanket hostility to nationalism: he can maintain the belief that 'the history of Irish nationalism was itself a relatively noble one—with the exception of the IRA campaign after the 1960s' (1997:57), as if there were no moral ambiguities in the earlier history, and no connections between it and the modern IRA. And he can repeat the historically very dubious claim that religious sectarianism in the nationalist tradition was 'not so much a product of republican nationalism in Ireland as a product of British hostility to it.' (217, n. 29)

Kearney's oscillations underline how strong certain nationalist anxieties and insistences remain even in the minds of some of those, Irish or British, who believe themselves to be fully postnationalist. It has often been commented that there is in Ireland a 'double minority problem'—Catholics as a minority in Northern Ireland, Protestants a minority in Ireland as a whole. Many of the cultural critics implicitly conceptualise Ireland as a 'triple minority' dispute; the third minority being the Irish as an embattled, disadvantaged group within the north Atlantic archipelago. Such a perception is not today widely held in the Irish Republic: political culture and debate there have moved on far from the 'colonial' insecurities engendering it. Some intellectuals, inspired at least as much by North American academic fashions as by Irish realities, have been working hard to revive the anachronistic neurosis. Their assumption is that history can be forced into repeating itself: an idea all the more readily proclaimed by those who do not believe in history anyway. Charles Peguy famously suggested that everything begins with mystique and ends as politics. In Ireland, instead, it sometimes seems as if everything begins with politics, becomes mystique, and ends as literary theory.

Some may still hope that the cultural nationalist counterposing of myth against history need not necessarily have regressive consequences. Even the mythos of the Easter Rising might, as Gearóid Ó Crualaoich argues, be freed from its more damaging associations. 1916 is, Ó Crualaoich says:

paradigmatic for me in ways that profoundly resist assertions of continuity between 1916 and today's Provisional Republican Movement. Mythic discourse which allows great events to be symbolically re-enacted or to be ever-present in a timeless and mythic *now*, enriches every human life it touches, rather than defiling and even destroying it with the bullet and the bomb, resorted to in the profane temporal. Symbolic and mythic re-enactment can never be replicative of bloody sacrifices contained in 'original' sacred or dream-time events; claims to the contrary violently distort the values that lie, in different ways, at the hearts of the historical and the mythic processes. (Ó Crualaoich 1991:54–5)

Ó Crualaoich is extremely vague about what these values might be—though they are strongly national ones (ibid: 63). His is an attempt, somewhat resembling Kearney's, to dissociate nationalist myths which hold for him important emotional truths from what he sees as their perversion by contemporary Republicanism. He wishes to retain 'liberatory' myths by distinguishing them from regressive ones. But it is a doomed exercise, for—like, say, Lyotard with his peculiar and politically disabling misreading of Kant (cf. Benjamin ed. 1992, Drolet 1994)—he has deliberately evacuated the ground of judgement on which one could meaningfully make such distinctions. In the end, from this anti-foundationalist, relativist and mythophiliac perspective, what is left for someone like Ó Crualaoich who disapproves of paramilitary violence except to say that he finds it aesthetically displeasing? In such registers the contemporary celebration of myth and the irrational—Nietzschean, Heideggerian or postmodernist—connects with the anti-rationalist heart of both cultural nationalist and physical force republican traditions. The image of 1916, and above all the thought and legend of Pearse, are redressed in the clothes of central European philosophy and transatlantic literary-critical fashion.

However, all has not been loss in this mushrooming of invocations of colonial parallels. The reference points chosen might often—as I have argued—be inappropriate, distorted or politically self-interested ones. Nonetheless, one might argue, a misleading comparative method is better than a total absence of comparative thinking, better than national solipsism. A decade ago, W. J. McCormack complained of a general 'failure to see Irish affairs in relation to anything else, anywhere.' (1986:11) He went on:

[T]he response has been to acknowledge the violence of the present as irrefutable evidence of an inescapable past, a past which determines the present whether through the agency of British policy, republican tactics, or loyalist rhetoric. Not many have considered the possibility that violence in Irish society—in Dublin or Belfast, political in its vocabulary or otherwise—is part of a broader pattern in Western society. The result has been that the debate on Irish affairs is conducted in a remarkably inward fashion—even the term 'the Troubles' carries with it a sense of intimate possession . . . your Troubles are your own. (1986:14)

Such a complaint would be less plausible in the late 1990s, and that at least is an advance. There still remain the tasks of reinserting Irish history, including not least the histories of its radical, socialist and feminist movements, into the myriad stories of the North Atlantic archipelago, of Europe, of the Atlantic world, as well as of a genuinely rather than rhetorically comparative colonial and postcolonial historiography.

8

The Irish Republic as 'Postcolonial' Polity

(i) Ireland after 1921: Decolonisation, Dependency or Dynamism?

Since the 1920s, and especially since the 1970s, a substantial body of writing both agitational and academic has sought to analyse the Irish Free State and later Republic either as 'neocolonial' (that is, overwhelmingly dependent on the United Kingdom or some other foreign power), or 'postcolonial' (i.e. substantially shaped and determined still by the legacies of British rule). The terminology involved is, once again, near the heart of the difficulties with such analyses. The term 'neocolonial' has functioned far more as a sign in political polemic than in analysis; whilst 'postcolonial' is used in two almost diametrically opposed senses, depending on whether the emphasis is placed on the 'post' or on the 'colonial'—on the break from colonialism or on its continuing influence. These ambiguities have haunted the Irish debate as they have so many others.

One version of the case for seeing independent Ireland as wholly shaped by classically colonial forces was put with polemical force by Vincent Tucker of University College Cork at a symposium on British-Irish relations. Tucker described Ireland as a 'microcosm' of the Third World, and continued:

Much of what is regarded as unique in the experience of Ireland is common to other colonial and ex-colonial countries. There is a marked reluctance . . . to view Ireland as a 'Third World' country. (Regan and Sinclair eds 1986:29)

Despite this supposed reluctance, Tucker asserted that Ireland's historic syndromes of underdevelopment, external interference, the nature of the anti-British struggle and of the 1920s civil war (which Tucker, oddly, saw as a class conflict), the successes and failures of development programmes, the non-aligned stance—all were viewed as paradigmatic of colonial and postcolonial patterns. Ireland was thus seen as having pioneered 'Third Worldism', with Connolly, Pearse and Griffith anticipating 'nearly all' subsequent Afro-Asian socialist thought (ibid: 31). A few years later, much of the same rhetoric was to be reproduced in slim volumes by Kieran Allen (1990), Therese Cahery and others (1992), Carol Coulter (1990) and Kevin Collins (1990), and by former Irish professional soldier and senior civil servant Jack O'Brien (1993).[1]

The argument that Ireland's economy and society have, through all their transformations under and since the Union, retained a 'neocolonial' character has however found little scholarly support. Indeed the dominant contemporary view in Irish historiography and social science has been, whilst noting the inevitable asymmetry of relations between a relatively large (and formerly globally dominant) state and a very small one, to urge that earlier nationalist writers grossly overestimated the role of British political domination or its later economic hegemony in determining Ireland's fate. In particular the allegedly damaging effects of the Union, to which nationalist economic thought so forcefully drew attention, have been reappraised with much scepticism by recent economic historians. It has even been possible to argue, albeit on a polemical rather than evidentiary basis, the counterfactual proposition that had Ireland remained within the Union after 1918 it would have had far higher growth rates, lower taxes and public debt, better services and less emigration than it did (see e.g. Arthur Green 1988).

Theorists of neocolonialism might naturally respond that this actually supports their argument: that it merely underlines how empty political self-government, whether before 1801 or after 1922, is when not accompanied by true economic and cultural sovereignty. If the Union as such was comparatively unimportant economically, this was because British imperialism in a wider sense obviously existed in and dominated Ireland for several centuries before full political unification, and equally obviously survived its demise. The economic 'neocolonialism' case depends, however, not only on a claim about persisting Irish dependence and British exploitation, but on another counterfactual hypothesis: that Ireland's economy would have performed better, developed and probably industrialised more rapidly, and avoided the extremes of emigration and depopulation, without Britain's interference.

A rough approximation to testing this claim came when some of the prescriptions implied by the nationalist diagnosis were implemented by De Valera's governments after 1932.[2] The drive for protectionism, hostility to foreign investment and a degree of autarky in those years did not, however, stem by any means exclusively from the indigenous nationalist economic tradition. This was an era not only of global depression but of protectionist policies on a world scale: even the British state, despite its long global evangelism for free trade, imposed substantial import controls and tariff barriers in this period. And the new policy coincided with strained Anglo-Irish economic relations—called, hyperbolically, by some contemporaries the Economic War—sparked by disputes over annuities on pre-independence land acquisition. Almost as soon as this dispute was settled, the Second World War intervened to disrupt world trade. Thus it could plausibly be said that the 1930s, forties and early fifties, the era of protectionist economic nationalism, were not a 'fair test' of the policies which Irish economic nationalists would advocate. They could, furthermore, argue that a strategy of 'delinking' simply was not attempted in anything like radical enough fashion. After all, even at the height of the Economic War, 91 per cent of Irish exports still went to the UK. Alternatively it could be argued, as Republicans especially were wont to do, that Partition made effective economic nationalism impossible, and was perhaps designed specifically to do so.

Certainly Ireland from the 1930s did not witness the growth and development which theorists of dependency or neocolonialism postulate should result from even partial 'delinking' from the world economy, and which Andre Gunder Frank, for instance, asserts was achieved through such policies by some Latin American countries in the era when they, like the Irish, opted for protectionism (Frank 1969, 1972). To the contrary: growth rates were notably low, and Ireland's relative position in the European economic league table became steadily worse.[3] Ireland's failure to share in the rapid expansion of most western European economies in the 1950s prompted pressure for a change of course, which was signalled in the two famous White Papers of 1958, *Economic Development* and *The First Programme for Economic Expansion*. Sean Lemass's government and its successors pursued an 'open door' trade and investment policy, accompanied by strong emphasis on state-sponsored industrial development; and the era also witnessed dramatic social and cultural changes (cf. Bew and Patterson 1982). The latter, often referred to as the 'modernisation' or 'Europeanisation' of Ireland, has been taken up in Chapter 7's look at arguments over culture and colonialism.

This is not the place to debate the economic balance sheet of the succeeding decades, the impact of EC and EMS membership, or the causes first of renewed economic crisis then reinvigorated growth during the 1990s. Our concern is solely with the nationalist critique which has argued that, through all these changes, the Republic's economy has remained, or become ever more profoundly, a neocolonial one. Again, academic orthodoxy has had little time for such views. Dermot McAleese describes them only as 'a strong body of sentiment, buttressed by flimsy but suggestive economic reasoning.' (1986:89) That critique has indeed, it must be repeated, been on the whole an unsophisticated one. On a world scale the 1960s and 1970s witnessed a veritable explosion of Marxist-influenced theories of neocolonialism, dependency, unequal exchange and the 'development of underdevelopment', in which the most prominent theorists included Andre Gunder Frank, Samir Amin, Arghiri Emmanuel, Oswaldo Sunkel, Theotonio Dos Santos, F. H. Cardoso and Immanuel Wallerstein. Arguments substantially analogous to those of Irish economic nationalists gained massive if often shortlived influence in the study, and to some extent the politics, of Africa, Asia and Latin America.[4] But the Irish nationalist argument remained indeed *analogous* to, rather than fully integrated with those global intellectual movements. There is little sign that Irish economic publicists during these years related to such ideas elsewhere, which might have been thought to support their case, except in the most superficial ways. By the time substantial references to the theories of Frank

and Co. began to be made in Irish political discourse (including that of Republicans), during the 1980s, these theories and the prescription for 'delinking'
based on them, had already received devastating criticism and been abandoned
by most African, Asian and Latin American specialists. Samir Amin is one of the
very few major theorists to have retained faith in a substantially unaltered version of this set of beliefs; though even he has become sceptical about the
prospects of an autarkic 'delinking' from the world capitalist system (see his
1990a, b).

The dependency model saw the economies of some countries or regions as
decisively and damagingly conditioned by the development of others, to which
the former are subjected; the former, 'peripheral' economies can expand only as
a reflection or side-effect of growth in the latter, 'core' ones. (Or, in a 'harder'
version of the theory, growth in the advanced countries can only, inevitably,
produce further underdevelopment in the periphery.) The dependent states or
regions produce a narrow range of goods, concentrated on primary products or
raw materials and on the export market. Their economies are thus 'heterogenous' in that sectors with widely different levels of productivity (on the one
hand peasant agriculture, on the other the export sector) exist side by side; and
'specialised' in that the modern export sector exists as an isolated enclave creating few linkages. This pattern is opposed to the 'homogeneous' (that is, having
high productivity in almost all sectors) and 'diversified' central or dominant
economies. Between these two poles, then, there is a clear international division
of labour which operates massively to the advantage of the central economies,
and which tends to reinforce and accentuate the differences between centre and
periphery. This accentuation takes three main forms:

i) The heterogeneity of production generates growing unemployment, as surplus population is drawn from the agricultural sector into the export sector;
which is unable to absorb this population at viable levels of productivity or
wage-rates;
ii) Specialisation of production generates balance of payments deficits, because
given the concentration of the modern sector on a few (mostly exported)
products, demand for manufactured goods can only be satisfied through
imports—and there is a high income elasticity in demand for such goods;
iii) From these follows a tendency to deterioration in the terms of trade, as both
the pressure to absorb surplus population, and the need to pay for manufactured imports, lead to expansion in primary product exports faster than
increase in demand for them. Prices thus fall, and this is passed on in lower real
wages. Thus the disparity in real incomes between centre and periphery keeps
growing.

Within the dependent economies, there is dramatic income inequality—
typically far greater than in the 'core' states—and much profit is expatriated,

so that the domestic consumer market remains small. Such modern, high-productivity industrial activity as there is, whether in the export sector or in import-substitution, is capital- rather than labour-intensive. Thus it creates little employment: ever more of the population is marginalised—unemployed, pushed into the 'informal sector' (which means anything from market traders to robbery or prostitution), trapped in low-productivity traditional activities, or forced to emigrate.

Meanwhile, the relatively small economic elite has tastes and consumption patterns copied from richer countries—their disproportionate share of national income thus goes overwhelmingly on goods which are imported, capital-intensive, or both, worsening all the above problems. And they are, according to the dependency theory, enthusiastic partners in increasing foreign control of the economy—they become what the Latin American left called a 'comprador bourgeoisie'. For both provision of the goods and services demanded by the local elite, and control of the high productivity, capital intensive enclaves of export-oriented and import-substituting activity, are heavily and increasingly in the hands of multinational companies.

The multinationals' operations are argued to have a whole series of damaging consequences. They tend to monopolise rather than diffuse skills, knowledge and technology. Multinationals are increasingly 'vertically integrated'—flows of capital, information, training, promotion and so on take place within firms rather than between sectors of national economies. By taking over local firms and displacing local entrepreneurs, multinationals not only block but actively retard indigenous initiative and possibilities for development. The sorts of 'complete package' of capital, skills, and productive techniques they offer are not likely to be complementary with local factors of production, but instead act further to distort them. And of course they are argued not only to meet, but to feed, to influence, indeed to create the distorted, damaging consumption patterns already mentioned, through the power of their advertising.

It is very widely accepted, even among many former 'dependentistas' themselves, that the above schema does not work as a global theory—the post-1960s experience of some South-East Asian economies, for instance, pretty thoroughly controverted it on the predictive level. In any case, little of the picture thus drawn ever fitted modern Ireland very well. Although Ireland's per capita income levels at independence, and thereafter, were substantially below those of Britain, they were not only well above those of any of the tropical colonies which gained independence in the following decades but (despite the almost masochistic conviction to the contrary of many Irish nationalists) were around average for western Europe between the wars and substantially higher than those for most of eastern and southern Europe. In 1910 Ireland's per capita Gross National Product stood at 62 per cent of the United Kingdom level, as against 70.3 per cent for Germany, and was above the levels for Norway, Sweden, or Italy—let alone any eastern European state (Lee 1989:513). At independence in 1922 Irish infant mortality rates, at 69 per thousand live births, were among Europe's lowest; comparing, for instance, with 156 for Austria, 90 for France, 207 for Romania, 101 for Scotland (B. R. Mitchell 1978:42–3). A literacy rate of virtually 100 per cent compared with around 70 per cent in Poland and Bulgaria, 50 per cent in Yugoslavia, just 20 per cent in Albania (Lee 1989:76). On indicators from private car ownership to beer production, Ireland's per capita levels stood well above European averages (B. R. Mitchell *passim*). In relation to India or to any African state, the gap was so huge as to make comparison absurd. Liam Kennedy points out that, even before independence, the bulk of productive economic assets, of the press and the educational system were indigenously owned and controlled (1996:174, 176). The distribution of income followed a fairly typical western European, rather than a 'Third World' pattern, and the pattern of employment did not reflect a 'heterogeneous' or 'specialised' economy: already as early as 1911, 25 per cent of the Irish workforce was in industry, 43 per cent in agriculture, as against typical African and Asian levels of under 10 and over 75 per cent respectively (ibid: 168–9). Over time Irish real wage rates tended to increase, income disparities to diminish, and the economy's dependence on primary commodity exports to decline: all the reverse of the dependency theorists' picture. As playwright John Arden caustically suggested two decades ago (1977:119) invocation of Ireland as a Third World state might have won some applause among Dublin intellectuals, but would have evoked only puzzled resentment in the supposedly most 'Third-Worldish' segments of Irish society, the rural poor.

If there was little to support a case for Ireland's post-independence economic structures as classically neocolonial, a stronger argument could perhaps be made in relation to the political system. Probably the most influential and thorough attempt to analyse modern Irish politics as postcolonial has been the earlier work of Tom Garvin (1978, 1981). Noting how atypical Ireland's party system and political culture have in his view been within western Europe, Garvin suggests that it has more in common with the postcolonial new states of the developing world, although unlike most of these it has retained stable democratic politics:

An important source of confusion in interpreting the politics of the Republic is the habit of either treating the country as hopelessly unique or, at best, as a rather peculiar Western European country. The Republic is only a fringe member of the European group, as few of these countries have had extensive experience of external rule[5] ... modern Ireland is culturally hybrid and represents a successful, if not totally harmonious, synthesis of native and British cultural themes ...

A joint product of an emergent, peasant people and of colonial administrators, its combination of traditional nationalist symbolism with underlying newness is typical of many post-colonial states. (Garvin 1981:2–3)

Garvin's argument involves a heavy emphasis on continuities of political culture and alignments between pre- and post-independence eras:

Fianna Fail and Fine Gael are, structurally and historically, not different political parties, but internal factions of the old pan-nationalist party which still exists in 'ghost'
form; the nineteenth-century Irish party system haunts, or underlies, its successor in the
independent Irish state. (ibid: 161)

This challenges the previously dominant self-image, both in political rhetoric
and in academic study, which had stressed the absolute sharpness of the break
in 1921–2 and of the Civil War as bloody birthplace of the modern party system
(e.g. Manning 1972: and note too that Hechter 1975 drops southern Ireland after
1921 from his discussion, implicitly suggesting that 'internal colonialism' ended
with self-government). Without the schism over the Treaty, John Whyte specu-
lated, Sinn Fein might have remained the overwhelmingly dominant party
rather as Congress had long been in India (1974:620).[6] Yet Garvin's emphasis on
continuity, tradition and—in this very specific and narrow sense—colonial
legacies has been broadly supported by other political scientists: by Basil Chubb
and Ronan Fanning with reference to public administration (Chubb 1982;
Chubb and Fanning in Drudy ed. 1986), Brian Farrell for political culture (1971),
Michael Gallagher for the party system (1985).

   Yet Gallagher has also underlined the limitations of this model for Ireland in
particular, and indeed of the concept of postcoloniality itself. Ireland today, as
he asserts, may be a relatively poor member of the group of 'western liberal
democracies', and in its party cleavages and political culture an atypical one, but
'the country still has much more in common with this group than with any
other.' (1985:147) It is, as he wryly suggests 'decadently wealthy' in comparison
with almost all 'Third World' countries in per capita income, industrialisation,
literacy, technology and communications. And its political system and institutions are clearly 'First World' ones in almost every respect. Distinctiveness lies
perhaps, if anywhere, in the continued powerful role of organised religion, the
relative lack of strong social bases for party alignments, and the salience of
'nationalist' issues in politics. Yet none of these makes it unique or even unusual
in Europe, especially when the new political systems and religio-nationalist
conflicts of eastern and southern Europe after 1989 are taken into account; and
even the national question is, as often noted, rather marginal to electoral choice.

Moreover, the 'post-colonial' label can be applied to such a wide variety of states that it
is questionable whether those so labelled have anything in common other than that they
were once colonies of European powers . . . it seems that the description retains little
power to enable us to separate political systems for analytical purposes. (ibid: 147)

   Liam Kennedy, however, argues that a certain commonality of experience *can*
be discerned among 'Third World' postcolonial states in terms of economic and

social patterns—but it is a shared situation with which Ireland has nothing in common. He compares statistics for Ireland's economic and social develop-ment with those of major selected 'Third World' states and finds that the latter reveal a pattern from which Ireland, whether early this century before independ-ence, or more recently, deviates dramatically: whether in employment struc-ture, per capita GDP, rates of literacy or of infant mortality (Liam Kennedy 1993, 1996 ch. 7).

The postcolonial model may also lead political analysts to discern a supposed Irish exceptionalism where actually its experience is far less remarkable or odd than is supposed. This lies in Ireland's post-independence attainment of liberal democratic pluralism, which is contrasted with the fact that so many other new states emerging from European colonialism were marked by endemic authori-tarianism, dictatorship and/or instability. Yet it may be—as has perhaps most systematically been argued by Bill Kissane (1995)—that this is misleading both in the points of comparison chosen and in the dominant theoretical approach. Authors such as Tom Garvin and Jeffrey Prager (1986) tend to assume that it is above all political culture which determines democratic prospects, and that important aspects of Irish political culture militated against the establishment of stable democracy. For Prager these were what he labels 'Gaelic-Romantic values and norms' (1986:42–50), which he identifies solidly and too simply with Fianna Fail and the anti-Treaty side in the Civil War, but which were fortunately defeated by those adhering to 'Irish-Enlightenment values and norms' (38–42).[7] The losing side, however, later successfully reintegrated itself, (most of) its fol-lowers and hence the romantic nationalist legacy, into the democratic struc-tures which the winners had established (185–214), securing future stability. Kissane argues, by contrast, that attention should be focused on earlier changes in Irish social structure which meant that 'Ireland was already a modern society by 1921.' (1995:64) Even if sections of elite and public opinion harboured pre-modern cultural values or aspirations, the social and economic preconditions of stable democracy were in place at Independence.

If Ireland is seen not in a postcolonial frame but instead in the context of other new European states emerging in the aftermath of the First World War— with Czechoslovakia, Finland, Poland and the Baltic Republics—then it will be seen to have been typical rather than otherwise in its establishment of parlia-mentary institutions (see Coakley 1986, 1987, Jorstad 1990). Even though many of these latter, especially in the 1930s, succumbed to varying degrees of authori-tarianism, this also does not distinguish them clearly from other European states. Descent into authoritarian rule, in the thirties, was quite obviously the fate of much of Europe; there is little reason to think that newly founded states were more prone to it than others; indeed the most extreme and brutal instances of the syndrome (such as Italy, Romania, Spain and most obviously of all, Ger-many) were in relatively well-established nation-states. Little if anything about

Ireland's post-1921 political fate is anomalous. It may also be noted that the other clearest instance of a European society subject to modern British over-rule, Malta, has since its independence in 1964 also maintained competitive democratic politics.

The most developed critical analyses of the Republic's political economy, whilst often motivated by both a nationalist and usually a socially radical impulse, have had little in common with theories of neocolonialism or with even modified versions of Republican economic nationalism. Thus J. J. Lee's lament for Irish economic failure views postcolonial dependency as an essentially *psychological* rather than economic condition, a failure to mobilise intellectual resources deriving from 'the dependency syndrome which had wormed its way into the Irish psyche during the long centuries of foreign dominance'(Lee 1989:627). The origins of the syndrome may be colonial, but its persistence and possible overcoming are now domestically determined. Similarly Breen, Hannan, Rottman and Whelan, in their major synthesis of research on Irish state development and social structure, see modern Ireland as falling firmly into the category of advanced capitalist societies (1990:7–11): and, drawing on theoretical frameworks developed by Anthony Giddens and Theda Skocpol, regard the internal dynamics of state and class as the central explanatory variable. Although in its early decades, and perhaps especially under De Valera, the Republic's economic position and political culture were they think in many ways underdeveloped and 'postcolonial', and although the country remains 'semi-peripheral' and 'dependent' within the western European economic system (ibid: 8–9), Ireland has been 'truly transformed' by rapid state-sponsored economic change since 1958 (ibid: 17). From about 1960 onwards 'the dynamic elements in the society's social structure were those characteristic of the advanced capitalist societies: industrialisation and urbanisation.' (ibid: 7) Very much the same picture is suggested by Bew, Hazelkorn and Patterson's neo-Marxist sketch of *The Dynamics of Irish Politics* (1989). The authors urge the need to focus mainly on 'the complex and changing *internal* balance of economic and political forces' (1989:12; emphasis in original) as opposed to looking to external sources for Ireland's ills. They too place central emphasis on the extent of 'modernisation' since the 1950s, building on an earlier work by two of the co-authors which surveyed the career of that modernisation's key architect, Sean Lemass (Bew and Patterson 1982).

It is questionable whether there is any necessary connection between assessment of 'modernisation's' success in the Irish Republic, and attitudes to the Northern Irish conflict. Yet there has undoubtedly been an elective affinity between views judging positively the former, and those critical of traditional nationalist claims over the latter. Nowhere is this more evident than in the work of Bew and his various co-authors, who argue that a relegation of the 'national question' to relative unimportance was an indirect or unintended consequence of the great policy shift from the late 1950s, and that this was 'undoubtedly Lemass's most progressive legacy.' (Bew and Patterson 1982:196)[8] In part this is because they argue, in the classical Marxist tradition, that economic development brought in its train political realignment towards a more class-based, and thus typically European, setup. This in its turn 'threatens finally to consign militant republicanism to the ghettoes of Northern Ireland.' (1989:224) Further, the capacity of the Irish state so radically to change policy direction is held to demonstrate the genuineness of its sovereignty, contrary to the perception of it as inextricably tied to UK policy interests (ibid: 11).

If there is little objective basis for seeing Ireland as a 'Third World' country in any but the most loosely rhetorical terms, a better case can perhaps be made in terms of subjective beliefs. To some degree the perception of Ireland as a postcolonial, even Third World state entered into the official discourse of the Irish Republic, especially at the United Nations, in the post-1945 era. Thus the Foreign Minister in 1960, Frank Aiken, said that:

We know what imperialism is and what resistance to it involves. We do not hear with indifference the voices of those spokesmen of African and Asian countries who passionately champion the right to independence of millions who are still, unfortunately, under foreign rule . . . More than eighty years ago the then leader of the Irish nation, Charles Stewart Parnell, proclaimed the principle that 'the cause of nationality is sacred, in Asia and Africa as in Ireland.' That is still the basic principle of our political thinking in Ireland today, as it was with those of my generation who felt impelled to assert in arms the right of our country to independence. (quoted F. S. L. Lyons 1973:594)

The era of active anticolonialism in Irish foreign policy was, however, a fairly brief one; roughly from 1957 to 1960 when Aiken (by background a traditional Republican) was Foreign Minister and Conor Cruise O'Brien Ireland's UN representative. It was always ambivalent and subject to numerous cross-pressures; analysed with great acuity though not of course perfect disinterestedness by O'Brien himself in *To Katanga and Back* (O'Brien 1962:12–39; see also Akenson 1995:149–83 on this period in O'Brien's life). There O'Brien also produced one of the most eloquent expressions of an Irish nationalist anticolonial sensibility; the kind of view which he was himself later to repudiate with ever growing sharpness:

This is not just a question of 'brooding on the past'—although it is hard to read history without doing some brooding on the past—but of a present-day contrast rooted in history. Ireland is still a relatively backward country, next door to a highly advanced one. The culture of the advanced country has almost completely destroyed, but only partially replaced, the culture of the backward one. The replacement can only be partial, for the conquered can never properly assimilate one central element in the conquering culture: the psychological attitudes of racial superiority. True, the *language* of racial superiority has been taboo among enlightened adults since the rise of Hitler, but the thing itself is still with us, as not only West Indians or Irish labourers in Birmingham, but any Irish boy at an English school can testify. (ibid: 30–1)

Yet such perspectives, however passionately held, clearly did not result in a strongly or consistently 'Third Worldist' Irish foreign policy. A detailed recent study of this subject, written for Trocaire, the Catholic Agency for World Development, found that Ireland's bilateral 'Third World' links 'have developed in an ad hoc and sporadic manner' and that relations with postcolonial states 'have never been a priority' in Irish foreign policy. (Michael Holmes *et al.* 1993:19, 20). Ireland had no embassies at all in the 'Third World' until one was opened in Argentina (a rather questionably 'Third World' country: though later the one which Declan Kiberd (1991a) was to argue was most similar to Ireland) in 1947, followed by Nigeria in 1960 and India in 1964. Only with the entry into the European Community was there substantial expansion of diplomatic links in Asia and Africa and the first beginnings of a bilateral aid programme. Foreign policy has been dominated by relations with Britain and the USA on one level, EC and UN involvement on another. 'Third World' links and issues have been 'something of a poor relation.' (31) The legislature—which lacked even a standing foreign affairs committee until 1993—has never paid much attention to issues of the postcolonial world (37–9). Policy towards refugees and migrants has, until very recent liberalisation, been ungenerous: in 1986–90 only twenty-three applications for political asylum were approved (43). The Irish Trade Board has no offices in Africa or Latin America (46).

As a member of the European Union, Ireland has participated fully and uncomplainingly in protectionist policies which discriminate against 'Third World' producers, while its development aid budget, as a proportion of GNP, has been below the western European average (Liam Kennedy 1996:180–1). Whilst Ireland has played an especially prominent role in UN peacekeeping operations, most notably in the Congo and Lebanon, studies of UN General Assembly voting patterns on decolonisation issues found Ireland's votes conforming to the pattern of a European bloc—albeit, with Denmark, Sweden, the Netherlands and later Greece, on the 'liberal' wing of that bloc—rather than a Third World or postcolonial alignment (Hurwitz 1976; Rosemary Foot 1979). Irish government attitudes to such issues, as on South Africa (Brigid Laffan 1988), have certainly been consistently less conservative than those of Britain, France, or the USA; but their similarity to those of several other European states raises doubts over whether there is anything specifically 'postcolonial' about this. Certainly Ireland's strong orientation to a European bloc, including EU membership, has been found by academic analysts heavily to qualify the view that its foreign and security policies have been 'neutral' or 'nonaligned' in the postwar era (Salmon 1989).

It is by no means clear that Irish organisations' or individuals' views on the question of Northern Ireland have correlated with stances toward Third World issues. Frank Aiken's Third Worldism has been interpreted as stemming from his Republican background; but it was Garret FitzGerald, perhaps the least traditionally 'green' of modern Irish statesmen, who pioneered concern for 'Third World' development issues (Holmes *et al.* 1993:37). Possibly a left-right division, rather than that over the national question, has been most significant. Among the Republic's political parties, Labour has apparently devoted most time and effort to postcolonial and development matters (ibid: 48–50). Similarly, the Irish Congress of Trade Unions has a specific Third World Committee, whilst the employers' and farmers' associations do not (51). Only perhaps in Belfast Republican circles have efforts been made vigorously to link an 'anticolonial' Irish nationalism with concern for 'Third World' issues[9]—though the 1995–6 commemorations of the 1840s Irish Famine were turned to this end in a few quarters.

This is not to say that Aiken's or O'Brien's rhetoric was wholly empty. Holmes, Rees and Whelan suggest that:

the colonial past has given the country considerable sympathy for decolonisation struggles elsewhere and has contributed to a lingering suspicion concerning the activities and motivations of more powerful states. The Northern Irish situation creates a particular awareness and appreciation of the complexities involved in any conflict or border dispute. And the country's own economic problems encourage a degree of understanding on issues such as demands for a New International Economic Order, although they may at the same time lessen the desire to act on these demands. (ibid: 29)

The establishment of aid and diplomatic links with countries such as India was argued to stem at least in part from shared colonial experiences (82–90, 103) and later Ireland developed a 'special relationship', on a limited scale, with certain Arab countries (100–2, 159–60); though some have suggested that aspects of this, like the relationship with Iraq, concerned business deals of dubious morality rather than more principled considerations (182–3, and see O'Toole 1995). A perceived colonial legacy has, one might generalise, helped induce sympathy with the 'underdog' in various international disputes—even where this has involved conflict with other policy aims. Thus, as Michael Gallagher points out, Irish nationalists (those who have considered such questions at all) have mostly sympathised with Tibetan nationalists against China, and Western Saharan ones against Morocco, even though Chinese and Moroccan territorial claims over Tibet and Western Sahara have clear historical analogies with those of the Republic over Northern Ireland (M. Gallagher 1990:22–3).

Perhaps the most significant international network of all has been the religious one—itself in great measure a product of Irish participation in the British Empire, since as Thomas Bartlett comments, ' "Ireland's Spiritual Empire" was roughly coterminous with the British Empire.' (1998:273) Over 5,000 Irish priests and nuns are active in eighty-five Third World countries, many of them involved in development work and some even in more directly political circles devoted to ideas of 'liberation theology', as in the Philippines (Michael Holmes *et al.* 90–1, 93–9); though in other cases their political influence, so far as it has existed, may have been more conservative (ibid: 51–4; Hogan 1990). As in most western European countries, there has also sprung up, especially since the 1960s, a wide range of non-governmental aid agencies, both religious and secular; as well as of solidarity groups among which the Anti-Apartheid Movement, strikingly vigorous given the size of the country, has been most prominent and was able significantly to influence state policy (Brigid Laffan 1988). Overall, it has been suggested that both Irish and Third World leaders and peoples have preferred to remember Ireland's formerly colonised status and struggle for independence, rather than the major Irish role as soldiers and administrators in British colonial domination worldwide. (Michael Holmes *et al.* 180) Nonetheless, Irish 'Third Worldism', especially on official level, has not been a particularly let alone a uniquely vigorous growth since the 1920s.

(ii) Rhetorics of Subjection: Nationalist and Socialist Critics of the Republic

Thus it seems that, given the very rapid transformation of the Irish economy and social structure in the past three decades, and given all the respects, from constitutional structures and foreign policy orientation to literacy levels, in which Ireland is evidently an advanced capitalist democracy, arguments asserting the continued neocolonial or postcolonial nature of Ireland must now be reduced to two forms. Either they can seek to show that the changes which have taken place, even in and through all their 'developmentalist' and 'modernising' character, have nonetheless retained or intensified a distinctively dependent or neocolonial pattern. Or they can shift the main ground of argument from economy and political institutions to culture. Both these moves have indeed been made: the first primarily on the pro-Republican and Marxist left, the second by a wider range of commentators including both traditional cultural nationalists and poststructuralist practitioners of colonial discourse analysis. In some discourses, as in that of Sinn Fein, the two approaches are combined.

The economic case for seeing Ireland as a neocolony and Northern Ireland as a colony has always been secondary to the political and cultural one. Its first full expressions were formulated by Irish and British Communists in the 1920s and 1930s culminating in the red-green syntheses of T. A. Jackson's *Ireland Her Own* in 1946 and C. Desmond Greaves's editorship of the London-based Connolly Association monthly *The Irish Democrat*. Jackson had been a leading member of the British Communist Party since the early 1920s, and one of its most important theoreticians. Yet *Ireland Her Own*, like so much even of the best nationalist-inflected writing on Ireland, was not so much theoretical or analytical as it was a polemical narrative of the tragedies of Irish history. Embedded in the narrative, however, is an argument that Irish underdevelopment after 1921 was induced by subservience to British policy and, above all, by Partition (T. A. Jackson 1946 *passim* esp. 400–23).

It was also from Connolly Association—London Irish Communist—circles that a socialist-nationalist critique of the Republic as neocolony came to Ireland itself. Two former Association members, Roy Johnston and Anthony Coughlan, returned to Dublin in the early 1960s. Through a discussion group called the Wolfe Tone Society, they began to exert a major influence on the ailing Republican movement. Their role in turning Dublin Sinn Fein and IRA leftwards, and thus in helping produce the 1970 split in the IRA and eventual evolution of the Workers' Party, was a major one and has recently been extensively analysed.[10] For our present purposes, their importance lies in the novel theoretical line they introduced to Republican thought. It was novel not so much in its theses themselves, most of which were fairly direct transpositions of orthodox Communist thought on imperialism, as in its relative sophistication: to the growing irritation of traditional Republicans, Johnston and Coughlan constantly hammered home the previous theoretical 'illiteracy' of the movement.[11]

Connolly apart, certainly there had been little elaborated theory or ideology among even the leadership, let alone the rank and file, of earlier nationalist rebels.[12] Every serious study of the ideas and motivations of ordinary volunteers in the 1916 Rising, the 1919–21 guerrilla conflict and subsequent Civil War suggests that beyond a romanticised interpretation of Irish history strongly shaped by the nature of post-1908 school instruction (Augusteijn 1990:26–7) there was little doctrine involved among them. 'It appears that thorough, well developed ideologies did not play a great part in the struggle. The widespread demand for an independent Ireland . . . did not require this.' (ibid: 41) Generational revolt has been seen as playing an important role, with the Cork IRA taking over friendship networks and styles from local youth gangs and thus inheriting the 'sub-political' or even 'anti-political' nature of youth culture (Hart 1990:23; 1998 ch. 8). And contrary to later apologetics, clear elements of religious sectarianism and blanket anti-English sentiment have been discerned in that Republican subculture by some scholars (Leonard 1990, English 1996a, Hart 1996, 1998, Augusteijn 1996:294–9).

Johnston and Coughlan, seeking to break from this constricted legacy, argued that the Lemass economic reforms marked the abandonment of even De Valera's 'half-hearted' pursuit of independence and Ireland's full integration into a neocolonial system, with Fianna Fail's leaders in the 'ignominious role of local managers for imperialism'.[13] The transformation of Irish politics opened the prospect for British strategy too to change radically: 'the imperialist power ... [is] finding it increasingly difficult to maintain the huge profits it has been drawing from the neo-colonial exploitation of its former empire' and therefore 'Britain will be increasingly anxious to weld Ireland more tightly to her side as a secure neo-colony.' Partition was increasingly an obstacle to this wider British goal; and the British might therefore be expected soon openly to favour a united, but neo-colonial, Ireland. In this situation the main task of Republicans was no longer to fight Partition but to build a broad anti-imperialist alliance of 'workers and small farmers . . . small business and the intellectuals', north and south. Support for a civil rights movement in the north was an essential 'ground-clearing' exercise to enable such an alliance, uniting Protestant and Catholic workers, to develop—and indeed the birth of the Northern Ireland Civil Rights Association came in significant part directly from the Wolfe Tone Society and the perspective Johnston had sketched, as Bob Purdie demonstrates (1990:121–33).

As both Bob Purdie (ibid: 123–4) and Henry Patterson (1989:91–2) point out, Johnston and Coughlan's analysis was desperately flawed. Its nationalism, in the end, predominated over its Marxism; especially in pursuing the chimera of 'real' independence—a small country totally breaking its economic links with its powerful neighbour and with international capital. It refused to recognise that the Republic's 'neocolonial' post-1958 strategy, in which it could only see deepening dependence, might bring real benefits to and achieve real popularity among working-class and other voters in the south. Conversely, it failed to anticipate that Protestant workers in the north might obdurately refuse to recognise their 'real' anti-imperialist interests and hold firmly to exclusivism. In other words, it simultaneously greatly overrated the strength of Irish national-ism among southern Catholics, and even more dramatically underrated British nationalism's hold on northern Protestants.

For all these flaws the analysis—substantially that held by the Irish Com-munist and Workers parties' at least into the early 1990s—was vastly more developed than that propounded by the Provisionals. As Provisional Sinn Fein worked its way back towards a 'social Republican' outlook during the 1970s, what it came up with was no more than a cruder form of the anti-imperialist theory. Thus Gerry Adams in the fullest published expression of Sinn Fein's 1980s thought, after the obligatory quotations from Connolly and Liam Mellows and a rambling disquisition on the Republic's poverty, slums, careerism and 'contradictions . . . which stem basically from the unresolved status of the national question', confined discussion of its economy to the plaint that:

Hundreds of millions of pounds of profits are being exported every year, alongside the export of Irish people.

Since the state was established our natural and mineral resources have been used to subsidise capitalists, both foreign and domestic. At no time has there been a serious effort to use these resources for the gainful employment and benefit of the mass of Irish people. Irish interests are subordinated to the interests of transnational capital. It could hardly be any other way in a state which was established for 'the protection of British interests with an economy of British lives'. (Adams 1986:48–9)

The argument was returned to at greater length under the rubric of 'British Strategy'. It is itself symptomatic of Adams's stance that he mounted his indictment of the Republic's economic record mostly here rather than in a chapter on the state itself. He made five main claims: that the hiving off of Ireland's most industrially developed region by Partition 'doomed to failure' the Republic's hopes of building a viable economy; that '[t]he resources of the state are controlled and exploited by foreign interests and even the ruling class is not based principally on native capitalism but is an "agent" class, acting as agents for foreign capital'; that an adverse balance of trade, itself a consequence of Partition and of British strategy, stunted industrial growth and increased reliance on foreign capital; that European Community membership had intensified these processes, making Ireland now a 'powerless part of a new kind of collective imperialism' without even the formal sovereignty to initiate nationalist economic policies; and that all this had 'stunted' the growth of class and radical politics. The term 'neo-colonial' was invoked time and again, but never defined or fleshed out (Adams 1986:91–4).

The substantially revised second edition of Adams's work, retitled *Free Ireland: Towards a Lasting Peace* (1995) retains the same lines of analysis and most of the same terminology, including that of colonialism and neo-colonialism. The view of Unionism and Loyalism as entirely colonial and sectarian in character, too, remains in all essentials unaltered (esp. 110–25). It does, however, take Europeanisation more seriously (whilst viewing it entirely negatively, as 'a new kind of collective imperialism' (92)), and acknowledge more explicitly than hitherto that in certain circumstances Britain might be prepared to withdraw from Northern Ireland (96–8). Gerry Adams continues to believe, seemingly self-contradictorily, that in Ireland 'we live in a modern consumer society, but with all the characteristics of a developing society' and with 'no indigenous industry.' (Adams 1995:149) Still more oxymoronically—an oxymoron reflecting the tension between Pearsean romanticism and Connollyite neo-Marxism—Ireland is described as 'in many ways classless, but with social and economic polarisation' (150).

Thus Sinn Fein economic policy, derived from the colonial model, amounted still to little more than a call for Irish autarky and ill-evidenced arguments for the supposedly huge economic benefits that would ensue from ending Partition (Sinn Fein 1994). The basic belief was that once the British had gone everything would fall into place: every Irish problem from unemployment to drug addiction was attributed to 'imperialism' and external interference.

Very much the same view was the mainstay of the secret training handbook for IRA volunteers, the *Green Book*. It is worth quoting at some length, as one of the fullest expressions of a crude anti-imperialist analysis, and because the inclusion of such an analysis in such a document indicates its emotional power—that this is a view people will kill and die for:

The nationhood of all Ireland has been an accepted fact for more than 1,500 years ... [Irish] civilisation was a shining light throughout Europe, prior to the Norman invasion of 1169 with which there commenced more than 8 centuries of RELENTLESS AND UNREMITTING WARFARE that has lasted down to this very day.

The objective of the 800 years of oppression is economic exploitation with the unjustly partitioned 6 counties remaining Britain's directly controlled old-style colony, and the South under the continuing social, cultural and economic domination of London ...

[F]rom 1958 on, the Free State abandoned all attempts to secure an independent economy, and brought in foreign multi-national companies to create jobs instead of buying their skills and then sending them home gradually. 'Africanisation' is the word for this process elsewhere. Control of our affairs in all of Ireland lies more than ever since 1921 outside the hands of the Irish people. The logical outcome of all this was full immersion in the EEC in the 1970s. The Republican Movement opposed this North and South in 1972 and 1975 and continues to do so. It is against such political economic power blocks East and West and military alliances such as NATO and the Warsaw Pact.

It stands with our Celtic brothers and the other subject nations of Europe, and with the neutral and non-aligned peoples of the Third World; it seeks a third, socialist alternative which transcends both Western individualistic capitalism and Eastern state capitalism, which is in accordance with our best revolutionary traditions as a people. (Quoted in Coogan 1987a:683–4)[14]

Clearly, a perception of Irish Republicanism as part of a global anti-imperialist struggle came to be very widespread among IRA Volunteers. One of the few publications issued under the IRA's name (as opposed to Sinn Fein's), the 1973 pamphlet *Freedom Struggle*, refers to British 'genocide' in Northern Ireland and proclaims the resultant international embarrassment 'the worst in her long imperial history.' (Irish Republican Army nd:I) British media and propaganda slurs against the IRA 'have been used in Kenya, Palestine, Cyprus, India, in fact wherever the presence of the Saxon Oppressor was challenged.' (ibid). The anti-imperialist discourse of the international left is employed throughout, with the IRA's enemy described as 'imperialism and neo-colonialism' (ibid: 13). Several reports have suggested, however, that in this era IRA/ Sinn Fein activists' reading about international revolutionary struggles was directed more towards learning direct tactical lessons than emotional solidarity or theoretical perspectives.[15]

Some indication of the extent to which such views became generalised further down the IRA hierarchy is provided by the prison memoirs of Raymond

McLaughlin, jailed after an abortive bombing attempt in Coventry in 1974. McLaughlin, describing his prison reading, offers uncritical endorsement of Lenin's *Imperialism*—'essential reading for anyone interested in understanding the economic, political and social problems besetting this world. It is a clear and concise analysis on how the major capitalist powers use foreign investment to impoverish small underdeveloped countries. The Irish Free State is a classic example of this form of exploitation.' (McLaughlin 1987:44) He goes on to commend the work of Ngugi wa Thiong'o as ideal illumination of 'the parallels between the Free State and other neo-colonial countries.' (ibid) Such attitudes took, if we can accept McLaughlin's account, more practical forms also with political camaraderie being established between IRA prisoners, Palestinian and Libyan 'POW's (ibid: 68, 70, 83), and politicised black British inmates (55, 80).

As Sinn Fein has gradually, if largely tacitly, abandoned this line of analysis during the later 1990s, it has been retained by its breakaway, more 'fundamentalist' rival Republican Sinn Fein. The latter's main policy document, *Eire Nua*, continues to reiterate all the classic themes:

Ireland in its national experience is unique in western Europe. The country's history as a colony of England has left its mark on Irish political, social, economic and cultural life.

Though the Ireland we have inherited has all kinds of resources and great potential for national achievement, it is far from realising that potential. Ireland is marked by underdevelopment, unemployment, emigration, poverty on a large scale, and a huge national debt. These problems, serious enough in themselves, are magnified by the continuing conflict in the Six Counties, which also has its origins in Ireland's colonial history . . .

One great obstacle to changing all that is our lack of hope. Another major obstacle is the slave mentality engendered in many of our people by centuries of conquest . . .

The Rising of 1916 and the Irish War of Independence inspired whole nations, particularly in Africa and Asia, to throw off the yoke of colonial oppression. In the light of these achievements, and of the spectacular recent advances of national rights and democracy in eastern Europe, it is tragic that the shackles still binding Ireland to its colonial past have prevented us from developing our nationhood . . .

This country, with its history of colonisation and exploitation, has much in common with former European colonies in the Third World. (Republican Sinn Fein 1996).

More complex arguments for the continued centrality of British imperialism in the economies of both parts of Ireland, making some serious use of empirical evidence, did emerge from the 1970s onward, such as those of D. R. O'Connor Lysaght and Raymond Crotty. Lysaght, a veteran theoretician of Irish Trotskyist politics, rejected the claim that Britain has intervened persistently and in detail to perpetuate Irish underdevelopment. Rather, in his view:

The British ruling class's interest in suppressing Ireland has never been paramount in its overall strategy. On the contrary, it has tended to react to Ireland rather than to plan consciously for its long-term subordination . . . In general the relationship between British imperialism and Ireland is reminiscent of the theologian Paley's metaphor for God's working of the universe—the Divine Watchmaker as first cause. Britain initiated its control over Ireland, and then left the conditions thereby established to work themselves out, intervening only when matters threatened to get out of hand. (Lysaght 1980:13–14)

Lysaght had also, in his impassioned but learned little book of 1970, *The Republic of Ireland*, mounted the most detailed pro-Republican critique of the Lemass reforms as cementing the hold of neocolonialism in Ireland. Distancing himself from the polemical crudities of a view like Adams's, he not only acknowledged the relative autonomy of the Irish state but sought to trace divisions within the ruling elite between 'big bourgeois' and 'bureaucrats'. Though both fractions were seen as dependent on foreign interests, the nature of the dependence and consequently of desired economic strategies was varied (Lysaght 1970: esp. 183–90, 198–207). His conclusion was inevitably that Ireland's is a 'neocolonialism' of a very unusual sort:

There are no dictators of the obnoxiousness of Ky or Batista. Instead there is, in the Republic, a bourgeois democratic constitution equal to any, and, in Northern Ireland, a bourgeois democracy, albeit a twisted one . . . Native industry has been expanded to a greater extent than in other neo-colonies. Foreign policy gives the appearance of independence. There is no lumpen-proletariat of a scale comparable to those of the shanty suburbs of the Third World . . . In each of the Irish semi-nations the internal situation has much in common with that of a metropolitan capitalist state. (ibid: 219–20)

Since Lysaght recognised all this, his conclusion that 'the reality remains neo-colonialist' seemed more an affirmation of political faith than the logical consequence of the evidence he himself provided.

Of all the major contemporary works on Irish economic development it is Raymond Crotty's *Ireland in Crisis* (1986) which comes closest to the 'neocolonialism' model. Crotty writes under the influence of Gunder Frank and other theorists of the 'development of underdevelopment', though his conceptual framework, drawing in ideas about literally the whole range of human history and prehistory, is substantially original—not to say idiosyncratic. His work has been lauded by fellow-spirit Desmond Fennell as 'an enterprise unequalled in scope on the Irish intellectual scene since Yeats'. (Fennell 1993:258) Certainly *Ireland in Crisis* is hugely ambitious and fertile. But this polemic against post-1958 economic policies and especially against emigration and EC membership, powerful in its indictment of the fate of Irish agriculture under the Union, and imaginative in its drawing parallels with Irish experience everywhere from ancient Egypt, through precolonial African pastoralism, to modern India, degenerates into mere sloganising about an ill-defined contemporary 'heritage of colonialism' in its discussion of the more recent past. The book's purpose is perhaps best understood when it is noted that its publication coincided with

Crotty's legal campaign to have ratification of the Single European Act declared incompatible with the Irish Constitution.

Some of the flaws in Crotty's argument derive from the crudity of the general model with which he operates. It is premised on the twin claim that *no* part of Europe other than Ireland was ever a victim of 'capitalist colonialism', whilst *every* part of the world which did experience modern colonial rule (other than where the indigenes were almost entirely destroyed, as in North America and Australia) has, apparently inevitably, been the subsequent victim of underdevelopment. The experience of much of eastern and southern Europe, as we have noted, calls into question the first claim; whilst that of much of Latin America and, even more, South-East Asia undermines the second, and has done so ever more decisively since Crotty was writing in the mid-1980s.

There is a decided and disconcerting xenophobia in Crotty's work, as in his complaint that 'the emigration of Irish radicalism left the field clear for the remarkable dominance of Irish politics, from O'Connell to Cosgrave, by a polyglot collection of non-Irish persons.' (103) On the other hand he is unusual in decoupling his concerns about colonial legacies in Ireland from the issue of Partition. He sees the Ulster situation as essentially a settler-colonial one—with South Africa, one of only two such still remaining. But far from claiming, as the orthodox Republican view has done, that the separation of the north has been crucial to perpetuating underdevelopment, he sees the whole discourse of 'reunification' as a mere distraction from Ireland's real problems. Indeed he believes that in Ireland as in Africa:

Using the standard ploy of diverting public discontent from domestic failure by foreign adventurism, political leaders in black Africa and in the Irish Republic seek to distract attention from domestic affairs by stimulating discontent among their racial followers in the settler colonies. (105)

And the economic failures of the Republic make Protestant resistance to unification, in order to defend their relative privileges, all the fiercer; rendering inevitable a violent process of decolonisation: 'the situation in Northern Ireland proceeds to a denouement that has already taken place in the other capitalist colonies' (107).

Crotty's alternative vision for Ireland is premised on a repudiation of the individualism which he believes was, as an alien cultural implant, imposed on Ireland with the Tudor conquest and has been perpetuated ever since.

The proposals [which Crotty had sketched] imply the replacement of that order by one that holds that an individual's income shall be determined, in large part, by the size of the total social product and by the number of those who share that product . . . That socio-economic order would imply the reversion, in a fundamental sense, to the sort of society that existed in Ireland, as in other former capitalist colonies, before their colonization. (140)

(iii) The 1990s: Rhetorics of Modernisation

Crotty, perhaps, aside, all of the serious analyses surveyed above are closer to 'revisionist' than to traditional nationalist, Republican or Connollyite views in their emphasis on internal developments, on social class and state capacity, and in the very minor role they accord British policies, Partition or the border in explaining the Republic's economic fate. Some at least of these scholars are by almost anyone's definition Irish nationalists—for instance the most influential of them, Joseph Lee, is viscerally hostile to the ethos and record of Ulster Unionism (see the critique by Graham Walker 1992a)—but they are very far apart from the simple anticolonialist model.

It must then bluntly be said that there is no solid evidential support for the notion of the contemporary Irish Republic as economically or politically a British neo-colony. Its patterns of economic activity, so long massively dominated by trade with Britain, have been substantially transformed over the past three decades. As former Taoiseach Garret Fitzgerald notes:

During this period exports to Britain have risen about five-and-a-half times; exports to the world outside the EC over twenty times; and exports to continental EC countries almost one hundred times! As a result Irish exports to continental European countries now constitute well over two-fifths of total Irish exports, with barely one-third going to the United Kingdom. (1991:13)

Fitzgerald adds that Ireland's economic relations to the outside world have changed far more radically than have Britain's: 'This far greater change . . . is not, however, confined to the area of exports. To a striking degree Brussels has replaced London as *the* external centre towards which Ireland looks.' (ibid: 14) And there has, he believes, also been a transformation of attitudes:

Despite the deep tensions created between our two States and peoples by the situation in Northern Ireland, the multi-lateralisation of Ireland's external relationships during this period has, I believe, had beneficial effects on Irish attitudes towards Britain. It can never be healthy for any country to feel itself dominated in economic or political or cultural terms by one larger neighbour, and the anglo-centrism of Ireland in the post revolutionary period—compounded of a large dose of anglophobia and a smaller dose of anglophilia!—was clearly unhealthy. (ibid: 17)

Fitzgerald is naturally an interested witness; and the economic record is far from fully bearing out the optimism he evinces. Given the persistence of high-level structural unemployment, emigration, per capita incomes which remained low by European Union standards, and the fact that the most profitable firms by far have in recent years been foreign (mostly US) owned, it remains possible for serious analysts to argue that Ireland 'is close to a Third World pattern of growth.' (Hazelkorn and Patterson 1994:63) Such a judgement,

however, might be thought to indicate that the category of 'Third World' economic circumstances is stretched to cover so vast a range of countries that it has
become as near-meaningless as the more recently fashionable catch-all category
of 'postcolonial' political and cultural circumstances. If Ireland is to be included
under such a rubric, then surely Portugal, Greece or for that matter Scotland
and much of the English north must also be. Certainly Ireland's economic position within the European Union can accurately be characterised as one of
'peripherality' (ibid: 62), its pattern of development 'dependent' (Jacobsen
1994); but it shares these fates with much of the rest even of western Europe, let
alone the continent's east. However exaggerated some of the late-1990s rhetoric
about a 'Celtic Tiger economy' may prove to be, it is clearly perverse to continue
writing as if Ireland's economic performance were unusually, let alone
uniquely, constricted. To think that it could be otherwise, that a path of fully
'self-reliant' development could be achieved under any imaginable set of economic policies and political arrangements, is to invoke the ghost of Third
Worldist dependency theory, whose prescriptions bear little relation to the reality of contemporary global economic relations. Every complaint that could
possibly be mounted about the directions and limitations of Ireland's economic
policy in recent years, including complaints from traditional socialists and from
anti-EU nationalists, can be paralleled for a half-dozen or more other European
states' policies.[16]

Rapid economic change has, naturally, brought with it major social and cultural shifts including substantial secularisation and liberalisation of values: but
across these, some older patterns have retained their vitality.[17] Religious observance remains very high, and possibly the highest in Europe (Malta being the
only likely exception[18]). Most of the major political crises of the Republic's history have centred around questions of religious teaching and public morality,
rather than the 'national question'. It may indeed be that the near-consensual
public adherence to Catholic values, until very recently, helped ensure the
Republic's high level of stability, pre-empting for instance the political space
within which fascist-type movements might have emerged in strength. It may
also be that such values' hold has been much facilitated by mass emigration:
secularisation has been diasporic, and migration (although undoubtedly
always mainly economic in motivation) a means by which individuals escape
the hold of 'tradition' rather than directly challenge it.

The 'modernisation' or 'Europeanisation' of Ireland has thus been associated, albeit unevenly and ambiguously, with secularisation and 'detradition-
alisation'.[19] The chain of associations over-simplifies, but of the strength of many
of the individual components, not least Europeanisation, there can be little
doubt. By every indicator of public opinion, Ireland has become virtually the
most enthusiastically integrationist of all European Union member states.
Undoubtedly this owes much to the direct financial benefits EU membership

has brought, but it also reflects deeper and often more idealistic motives, a gradual but profound transformation of popular consciousness. Social and cultural aspirations, like social and cultural problems (strikingly symbolised by the urban blight, unemployment, crime and drug abuse of Northside Dublin housing projects) in Ireland today are those shared by all advanced industrial states. In this context, notions of an all-determining colonial legacy, let alone a persisting neocolonial 'Third World' status, verge on the meaningless. The matter is very different with relation to the 'colonial' status of Northern Ireland, and to the concept of cultural imperialism in Ireland, as we shall now see.

9

Northern Ireland after 1968: An Anticolonial Struggle?

Blood flows easily,
all it needs is an opening.

The blood of someone killed by accident
is not the same, on the pavement,

As the blood of someone killed for liberty,
also spilled on the pavement.

They are, each of them, ways
of being red, and of crying.

Guillevic: 'Object Lesson' (1974:57)

(i) The Six-County Colony: The Model Established

It was with the opening of the Northern Ireland 'Troubles' after 1968 that the discourse of anticolonialism became truly widespread in, and in relation to, Ireland. The descent into pervasive sectarian and anti-state violence in the north coincided with the upsurge in left-wing, largely student, radicalism in many advanced industrial countries. Among the legacies were a massively increased production of and audience for Marxist theory, and rapid growth for hitherto tiny Trotskyist and other programmatically revolutionary groups in Britain and other industrial states. Many of these came passionately to back the Republican struggle in Northern Ireland, despite the lack of support for such a stance in Marxist theory, not to mention Trotsky's own fierce anti-nationalism. Some writers even came to refer to the Catholics of the north as 'the anti-imperialist population' (De Baroid 1990:xiii).

The Ulster crisis also coincided with the high tide of Third World 'anti-imperialist' armed insurrections, headed and symbolised by the 1968 Tet Offensive in Vietnam. It was the era of widespread rural guerrilla struggle in Latin America, the start of serious armed resistance to white minority rule in Rhodesia and to Portuguese colonialism in Mozambique, Angola and Guine-Bissau, and of the emergence of the Palestine Liberation Organisation as an independent force. These were not, most of them, anticolonial struggles in the strict sense, although often described as such, but uprisings against indigenous 'Third World' regimes backed by the USA and other Western powers. Formal colonialism was, by 1968–9, largely defunct. The great European colonial empires had been almost entirely dismantled between the late 1940s and the early 1960s: usually by negotiation, as with most of Britain's tropical colonies; sometimes after extended guerrilla war, as in Algeria. In their place had emerged dozens of new states, mostly declaring themselves non-aligned, many proclaiming adherence to some form of socialism, and all the objects of enthusiasm and optimism from sympathetic observers—an optimism which the subsequent political instability or authoritarianism and economic plight of many of these states was later rapidly to erode.

All this provided the backdrop and stimulus to presenting the Northern Ireland conflict as an anticolonial one. Whereas before 1921 associating Ireland's demand for independence with the fate of Britain's overseas colonies was counterproductive both in pragmatic political terms, and in its running athwart pervasive racial beliefs, now the situation was reversed. To link the Ulster conflict with Third World anticolonial struggle was to associate it with revolutionary glamour, with movements which commanded massive sympathy amongst the young and radical in advanced capitalist states including Britain itself, with new and imaginative models of social development, perhaps above all with success. As John Whyte says, by 1970: 'To label a situation "colonial" was to imply two things: first, that it was illegitimate, and secondly, that it was unlikely to last.' (1990:178) And as Eamonn McCann observed of the early seventies, 'The more unequivocal the pledges given (of British refusal to negotiate with the IRA) the more clearly the Provos recalled Cyprus, Aden, Kenya and Ireland in the 1920s.' (1980:113)[1] As Fred Halliday has pointed out, global events 'provided a new language of legitimation and encouragement' not only in Northern Ireland, but in the two other European regions where insurrectionary violence broke out around the same time, Corsica and the Basque country (1997/8:10). Invocations of the idea of Northern Ireland as 'Britain's last colony'—last, just as Ireland had supposedly been first—became popular, and invoked a teleology by which the province must itself be destined for imminent decolonisation, the final unfinished business of the global collapse of empires.

The international legal framework had also changed. By the 1970s it had become generally accepted practice that former colonies should receive independence in accordance with the boundaries established under colonial rule—which, it could be argued, meant in this case the whole island of Ireland. National minorities within such boundaries, on the other hand, were not usually conceived under United Nations practice as having the right to self-determination. Thus if Ireland as a whole had been, and Northern Ireland now was, a British colony, it might plausibly be concluded that Partition had been illegitimate and should be undone. There were, however, three very large qualifications to this view. First, most glaringly, Ireland had not been juridically a British colony at least since the Union; and arguably had never formally been one at all. Second, international law and United Nations resolutions had, for evident reasons (maintaining international stability and, less creditably, upholding the claims to jurisdiction of existing UN members) consistently placed greater emphasis on states' territorial integrity than on demands for self-determination. Third, an alternative interpretation of the concept of majority self-determination would grant that right to the Unionist population.[2] Perhaps because of this ambivalence, the language of international law featured little in the disputes over Ulster's status after 1968. It was a potential embarrassment to both contending communities there; and also to both British and Irish governments. As Conor Gearty recently suggested:

Both London and Dublin assume that a colonial people have the right to self-determination, so that a battle over this label is also a battle over the future. Neither side wants to face the implications of a united Ireland on these terms.

If we borrow the terminology of the criminal law . . . we see that Britain might admit to being 'guilty of colonialism', without necessarily facing the punishment of 'mandatory self-determination for Ireland' . . .

1985 was the year in which the case was finally settled. The British admitted guilt, and were sentenced to the Anglo-Irish Agreement. (Gearty 1992:9–10[3])

Thus discussion of the conflict in a legal framework was rare. The most striking exception is a recent one; a book by Anthony Carty (1996) which surveys some of the relevant international law arguments—though from a somewhat partisan perspective, as evidenced by its references to 'Ulster Protestant identity as a misplaced settler-conqueror society.' (15) Carty suggests, in a fashion which might be thought at least to verge on the sectarian, that southern Irish Protestants even today constitute a powerful and 'very articulate Anglo-Irish minority' (14) which is identified in its turn with historico-political 'revisionism'. Roy Foster, for instance, 'represents an irreconcilable Anglo-Irish perspective.' (45) More substantively, Carty argues that the still dominant fact of Irish history is straightforwardly that of conquest and cultural destruction. 'There was a conquest. It was complete and devastating. What is left of Irish Ireland is an artificially constructed entity . . . a fragmented one which it hardly appears possible, at present, to piece together again.' (15) He argues moreover that the 1921 Treaty must be viewed as coerced, and 'only just' legal (165). This coercion, and the lack of full independence for the Free State until at the earliest 1932, mean that the present Irish Republic is not—or not clearly—in international law the same state as that which came into existence in 1921. The implication appears to be, as it was for De Valera and in articles 2 and 3 of the Republic's Constitution, that the modern-day state is not bound by that Treaty or by the 1925 Boundary Agreement. The Treaty 'continued the main features of the original pattern of the conquest of the island. The boundary was drawn having regard to the strategic and economic interests of the majority of Northern Ireland and with the usual coercion of a smaller community by a much more powerful one' (114). Northern Ireland, therefore, 'has no historical legitimacy' (113); though to be fair Carty does not thereby conclude that the political desires of its Unionist population are necessarily, wholly illegitimate.

The first uses of the colonial model for Northern Ireland after 1969 did not come from the Provisional IRA or its close supporters—they had, after all, just broken away from the left-wing coalition-building 'anti-imperialist' strategy of Cathal Goulding and Roy Johnston. John Whyte (1990:177) is probably correct in suggesting that the initial post-Troubles deployment of the colonial idea was by a distinguished Irish archaeologist, Liam de Paor, in his *Divided Ulster* (1970; revised edition 1971). In analysing Northern Ireland as a colonial state de Paor was not seeking, as many subsequent 'anticolonialist' writers were to do, wholly to delegitimise the Ulster Unionist case or write it out of existence. On the contrary, his main concern was to combat the then-prevalent view that religious bigotry was the sole root of the crisis; a view he thought 'unfair in particular to the Protestants of Ulster' (1971:xvii). Their preference for the British connection was, he said firmly, 'a perfectly valid political aspiration' (ibid). The point of stressing the colonial context, for de Paor, was to explain Protestant intransigence as a product of colonialism and its fear of the 'native'; and to emphasise the British Government's political responsibility for the crisis and thus its moral obligation to resolve it. He advocated a united Ireland: but his account was marked neither by insensitivity to Unionist traditions nor by endorsement of the IRA's military campaign. Thus de Paor's insistence in later writings (1986, 1990) that 'within the island of Ireland we have at least two histories, not one' (1990:4), his rejection of unification as unworkable though ideally desirable, and his cautious advocacy of an autonomous or even independent Northern Ireland, do not represent a conversion or capitulation to 'revisionism', as is sometimes suggested. De Paor's trajectory has actually been a rather consistent, and certainly a consistently thoughtful, humane, and democratic one.

The same cannot be said for some of the 'anticolonialist' analyses of the north that soon followed de Paor's. Much Republican rhetoric since the 1960s has constituted, as Irish-American historian (and former leading IRA man) Sean Cronin sadly observes 'theological not political arguments'. (1980:203) Nowhere was this more evident than in calling up the image of the anticolonial struggle. Thus so apparently independent-minded a commentator as Eamonn McCann could conclude a cool, and in fact highly critical, analysis of the IRA's ideology, with the breathtakingly *ex cathedra* pronouncement that: 'There is no such thing as an anti-imperialist who does not support the Provos and no such thing as a socialist who is not anti-imperialist.' (1980:176) End of chapter, end of book, end of argument. McCann's old comrade Michael Farrell could turn abruptly from years of engagement in the non-violent politics of civil rights— premised on the assumption that Ulster's most relevant international parallel was the US South—to argue that the Northern Ireland situation was in all its essentials identical to that of Algeria. The Protestants were *colons*, and the IRA would win by emulating the tactics of the FLN. (Michael Farrell 1974, 1977[4]) Mass Protestant belief in the Union was quite simply 'support for Protestant privilege and supremacy' (1977:73), Northern Ireland was 'essentially a counter-revolutionary creation' with 'no democratic validity whatsoever', and the Republican struggle should be 'seen within the context of anti-imperialist and anti-colonial revolutions in general.' (ibid: 71)[5]

Later Farrell produced a vastly expanded, and far more thoughtful, elaboration of the colonial model for understanding Northern Ireland's history in his *Northern Ireland:The Orange State* (1976; 2nd edn. 1980). Here the main focus shifted to an analysis of sectarianism, electoral politics and Unionist government policies within Northern Ireland itself; and as such the book was scholarly and valuable. Indeed the 'anti-imperialist', as opposed to anti-Stormont (and, some critics alleged, anti-Protestant) perspective seemed to function as little more than rhetorical window-dressing in the very first and last sentences of the book. Yet Farrell's book still stands, to date, as the nearest thing there has been to a detailed substantiation from an orthodox Republican perspective of the colonial analogy for Northern Ireland. The best-argued and best-informed subsequent argument for British withdrawal, by Bob Rowthorn and Naomi Wayne (1988) almost entirely avoids explicit reference to the colonial model.[6]

Otherwise, the simplistic sloganising has, by and large, continued. The analytical feebleness has had severely disabling political as well as intellectual consequences, even for Republicanism's own self-proclaimed project. In relation to the Unionist population, publicly expressed Sinn Fein-IRA views appeared across the years to be notably confused and confusing, insisting that this was a classically settler-colonial community, but also that it was or should be part of the Irish nation. Thus Daithi O'Conaill told Padraig O'Malley in 1981 that:

The reality is that they are a colon class. They are the settler class that arose out of the plantation. Republicans accept that fact, and the fact that they are of colonial breed. But they've been here so long that they're part and parcel of the Irish nation. (P. O'Malley 1983:298)

From this, however, O'Conaill went on to an extended invocation of the Algerian analogy, stopping only just short of drawing the conclusion that an Algerian-style mass exodus of the *colons* was the most likely or desirable solution (ibid: 299). Thus so long as perception of the conflict as a colonial one was retained, real dialogue with Protestants or even a clear recognition of their right

to be in Ireland seemed virtually impossible. Latterly, despite a widespread perception that there had been important changes in Republican thinking about
such questions, Gerry Adams's published thoughts have seemed no less
ambiguous. Unionism and Loyalism (Adams uses the terms interchangeably)
are about the sectarian defence of privilege and nothing else: 'Their political
philosophy expresses loyalty to the union with Britain precisely and solely
because that union has, to date, guaranteed them their privileges and their
ascendancy.' (Adams 1995:110) Their origins are seen solely as a colonial 'garri-
son' imported by Britain to keep down the natives (111); despite the obligatory
bow to the eighteenth-century radical Presbyterian tradition, their beliefs today
are viewed as being, almost without qualification or exception, 'bigoted and
irrational hatred of Catholics' (113). Such convictions necessarily required a
one-party state to sustain them, which Stormont provided (111, 122). Yet Republicans, with astonishing forbearance, offer them equality (121), sympathise with
the 'desperate identity crisis' which leads them to 'waste their time trying to
work out some kind of obscure notion of Ulster Protestant culture' (123) and
recognise that 'loyalists are Irish'. They too are 'victims of colonialism' (124).
Only with the removal of British overrule will they awaken from colonially
induced false consciousness and realise their Irishness. They 'need to be encouraged' into that state (124).[7]

The view of Unionists earlier expressed by another key Republican strategist,
Danny Morrison, appeared yet more discouraging: 'There is nothing we can do
to convince them and I think it is pointless to waste energy in trying . . . it is only
breaking the political will of the British to remain in Ireland that will affect the
loyalist community.' (Martin Collins ed. 1985:92) The notion that Unionists
have a distinct culture or tradition of any worth or even reality was dismissed.
In Sinn Fein's 'Republican Lecture Series' it was proclaimed that:

Orange leaders have hijacked the Protestant religion into a defence of imperialism . . .
The heritage that the loyalists think they have depends on a complete distortion of history. The vague memories of glorious battles in the distant past against the evils of the
Papists, and of the suffering that they have had to endure to preserve their freedom, is
[sic] a figment of the imagination. The notion of having different roots is part of the
present-day mythology of loyalism, which was invented to serve the purpose of justify-
ing partition as well as the sectarian divisions within the six counties. And since the loyalists have cut themselves off from the hinterland of Irish culture by denying themselves
nationhood, the culture of the Protestant people—when it tries to aspire above street-
level Orangeism—can reach nothing higher than a pathetic imitation of English traditions. (quoted in Brendan O'Brien 1995:88)

Although the ambiguities, and indeed the fundamental lack of realism, in
Republican views of Unionism have not disappeared, it cannot be doubted that
an increasingly serious recognition of the strength of Unionist loyalties has
appeared in Sinn Fein thinking during the 1990s. Sinn Fein strategists Tom

Hartley and Mitchel McLaughlin, in particular, have been marked by their apparent recognition that traditional Republican views of Ulster Protestants made them, in Hartley's words, 'a non-people robbed of their power to be a crucial component in the search for a just and lasting settlement'. Hartley went on to urge that 'In our vision of a united and independent Ireland there must be a place for those who consider themselves British and those who wish to stay British.' (quoted in Henry Patterson 1997:260) Yet as Patterson comments, even such seemingly conciliatory and pluralist language 'could not disguise the fact that Protestants were being cordially invited to participate in a journey to a destination which they had repeatedly made clear they had no wish to reach. Republican generosity was based on the assumption that the "tide of history" was flowing in an all-Ireland direction' (ibid: 262).[8]

Some commentators, such as Conor Cruise O'Brien (e.g. 1978:28–9) have been sharply scornful of any idea that ideological or theoretical pronouncements by contemporary Republicans should be taken in any way seriously— and indeed insistent that the activists of the movement itself do not take them seriously. Similarly, a Scottish historian, far more sympathetic to Celtic and anticolonial nationalisms than O'Brien, writes of Sinn Fein's 'lack of any intelligible programme' (Victor Kiernan 1993:18). This is probably mistaken: the programmatic statements are not only for external consumption, and they are of some real significance. But this only makes their intellectual poverty more striking, and more disturbing.

In any event, attitudes very similar to those we have traced among northern Republicans have also had a wider constituency. For a certain kind of Irish nationalist chronicler, the deplorable character of Ulster people presented no analytical problem or mystery at all, but was a straightforward product of their disreputable origins. Thus T. A. Jackson (who combined his very traditional brand of nationalism with becoming a leading member of the British Communist Party) suggested in 1946, apparently in all seriousness:

Few Englishmen or Scots were willing to expatriate themselves [to the Ulster plantations] unless for some reason, creditable or otherwise, they feared facing the wild Irish less than the risks of staying at home . . . Many wished to bilk their creditors or the mothers of their illegitimate children, or for other reasons to get beyond the reach of 'avenging justice'. A contemporary Scottish writer said that the settlers were 'generally the scum of both countries . . . abhorred at home.' (1946:34)

Some recent polemical writing from the Irish Republic has continued to propose simplistically colonial models for understanding Northern Irish Unionism.[9] And not all of this has come from Sinn Fein supporters. A proclaimedly democratic socialist line was taken by the then General Secretary of the Irish university lecturers' union, Daltun Ó Ceallaigh, a veteran of the civil rights campaign and of the trade union movement whose vehement dismissal of historical 'revisionism' we have already encountered. Ó Ceallaigh described himself as 'neo-nationalist' (1991:11)—though it is not wholly clear where the 'neo' part comes in. Jokingly (one hopes) suggesting that 'the last refuge of the scoundrel is complexity' (ibid: 10) he showed himself, by this standard, an honest man, for his analysis was resolutely simple. He urged that 'Ireland was culturally and socially a nation in Celtic times' (49), and suggested that this makes British control of part of it today necessarily illegitimate. That control, repeatedly described as imperialist, remains the core of the Northern Irish problem. Unionist interests:

were further played upon and their passions inflamed by the English when it suited London's purposes. And, when this manipulation was not taking place, the passive support of empire remained, whatever about distancing exercises or Pontius Pilate washing of hands. (55)

Although he admitted that Unionists have had their own agenda and have not been purely and simply puppets of London, and that British policy itself has not been homogeneous, still 'British official thinking has at best oscillated between old-style imperialism and some sort of neocolonial arrangement.' (56) The intellectual exhaustion of this vein of thought is apparent in Ó Ceallaigh's conclusion, where apparently he could propose nothing more innovative than that Irish socialists should return to the 'vision' of Connolly (87). Similarly exhausted is the final message of Irish-American academic Lawrence J. McCaffrey that the Ulster Protestant psyche 'defies reasonable explanations' except that perhaps Protestants 'receive a psychological lift in believing that they are superior to Catholics' (McCaffrey 1979:177). But, says McCaffrey, neither Irish nationalism nor British state strategies have solutions to this conundrum. 'Perhaps Northern Ireland is Britain's inferno' doomed to endless and inexplicable violence (193).[10]

Even an attempt to recuperate and celebrate alternative, radical Ulster Protestant political traditions, like the massive historical work of Flann Campbell, can be framed within a perspective of the dominant tradition as being simply colonialist: 'it is hoped that the Protestants of Northern Ireland, angry and confused as many of them are . . . appreciate that they have another heritage apart from the dying colonialism and sterile Orangeism to which so many apparently still cling.' (Campbell 1991:7) And some nationalists, like novelist Ronan Bennett, continue to assert that Ulster Protestants simply have no distinctive cultural traditions worth the name: to be a Unionist 'is to be enclosed in a world where "culture" is restricted to little more than flute bands, Orange marches and the chanting of sectarian slogans at football matches.' (1994; see also his 1998). The usually more thoughtful Liam O'Dowd believes that Unionism is as devoid of intellect as of culture: Unionist communities have unvaryingly proved themselves incapable of producing an intellectual class, or of articulating their beliefs in a modern, inclusive political idiom (1991:165).

These crude dismissals are not, however, typical of the public views of contemporary Irish nationalists on Unionism. It may well be that some nationalists privately harbour the kinds of belief usually described as those of ethnic nationalism, in which belonging to the nation derives from ancestry or even 'race': only the descendants of the 'original' inhabitants are Irish, and Protestants can never really belong. Some, too, may have held ethnicist and/or religiously exclusivist conceptions of nationhood without fully realising or acknowledging that these are their beliefs. And some may have partaken of the confusion or hypocrisy identified by a Free State Senator in 1939: 'We have had a habit, when it suited a particular case, of saying that they [the Unionists] were Irish, and when it did not suit a particular case, of saying they were British, or planters' (quoted O'Halloran 1987:31). None of these stances is often openly expressed. Insofar as the logical conclusion of claims that Ulster Protestants are *colons* is that they should be given no choices other than to assimilate to a Catholic-Irish culture or undergo forced migration, few even among extreme Republicans have explicitly drawn the bottom line: though De Valera and some other nationalists did so—see Bowman 1982:318–19, O'Halloran 1987:34–7—as have a few contemporary commentators like Kevin Kelley (1982:353).

Far more common is the claim that Ulster Protestants are a part of the Irish nation: that all who live in the island of Ireland belong to the Irish nationality. This appears to be a form of civic nationalism—that which identifies nationality according to citizenship, or political will. But it amounts to a very peculiar kind of civic nationalism, in which membership of the nation is attributed according to the choices which people supposedly *should* make, the citizenship they supposedly *should* claim, rather than those which they actually do. The mystery then is why they obdurately refuse to recognise their true nationhood—the explanation usually being in terms of manipulation by the British state and/or Unionist elites, or of relative economic advantage, or specifically religious antagonisms.[11]

(ii) Nations and Classes: The Model Criticised

Critical analysis and rebuttal of these views by other Irish radical, socialist and Marxist writers—usually labelled, like those concurrently engaged in reappraising the myths of Irish history, as 'revisionists', though they themselves often preferred the label 'post-nationalist'—began almost as soon as did use of the colonial model itself. The responses were enormously varied in form as well as in political provenance: it is far beyond the scope of the present discussion to do more than cursorily to summarise or assess them. At one extreme was the attempt to show that the notion of imperialism employed by Irish Marxist-nationalists departed from Lenin's theory. This was undertaken by Paul Bew,

Peter Gibbon and Henry Patterson (1979:19–29). It seemed a rather pious and formalistic enterprise, though it did at least allow them to make the point that for Marxists 'Struggles over the status of the north are no more automatically anti-imperialist than crimes against property are automatically anti-capitalist.' (ibid: 29) At the other extreme, perhaps, lay Conor Cruise O'Brien's polemic against the dismissal of Protestant feelings—and, he believed, thinly concealed Catholic-Gaelicist chauvinism—that characterised the Republican tradition (O'Brien 1974, and numerous subsequent writings).

Then there were proponents of the so-called 'Two Nations theory', initiated in the pamphlets of the British and Irish Communist Organisation (1971a, 1971b, 1975) and supported by Scottish Marxist-nationalist Tom Nairn (1981: esp. 230–45).[12] The claim that Ulster Protestants were a distinct nationality naturally implied rejecting Republican views of them as a mere settler-colonial implant, and thus undermined belief that unification was an anticolonialist cause.[13] As Nairn argued:

'[I]mperialism' *in the sense required* by the theory does not operate in any part of the Irish island, while 'imperialism' in the looser meaning of capitalist or metropolitan dominance . . . has no interest whatever in saving the Protestant state. (1981:232; emphasis in original)

BICO's theorists—pre-eminently the enigmatic Brendan Clifford—went further, coming to argue that insofar as 'imperialism' was a factor in Irish history and politics it was a progressive one. This view, though arguably quite consistent with Marx's own writings, aroused scandalised reactions elsewhere on the left.[14] Clifford himself, however, was not in a straightforward way a literal believer in 'two Irish nations'. Although his earlier writings had made a very strong case for Ulster's historical distinctiveness, especially in economic terms (Clifford 1992a), and although he was savagely critical of even moderate Catholic nationalists,[15] he polemicised fiercely against separatist 'Ulster nationalism', which he believed to be the failed product of a British state conspiracy (Clifford 1992b).[16] Nor could he be called without qualification a pro-imperialist, at least in his later writings: in 1991 he bitterly attacked ex-Marxist Middle East expert Fred Halliday for the latter's 'pro-Western' stance on the Iraq–Kuwait conflict. In rather familiarly insular fashion, though, Clifford was even here more concerned about Ireland than about the Middle East. Arguing implausibly that the nationalisms of the latter were less deeply imbued with religion and anti-modernism than Ireland's, he asserted that 'The Iranian people only rejected the superficial liberalism of the Shah and the coteries supporting him. The liberal culture rejected by the Irish was the genuine article—British liberalism of the 19th century and the early 20th.' (Clifford 1991:34–5)

Tom Nairn, too, is hard to fit neatly into the category of 'two nations theorist', since in fact he argued that Ulster Protestants had failed to develop the national consciousness or political nationalism which, he believed, they should 'naturally' have done. Isolated from the mainstream of British life and constantly oppressed by its sense of fragile frontier status, of threat both from Catholic nationalism and from potential British 'betrayal: 'Ulster Protestantism was unable to formulate the normal political response of threatened societies: nationalism.' (ibid: 236) A distinct Ulster 'community' or even 'nationality' clearly existed, but not yet a separate 'nation' conscious of itself as such. That, though, was in Nairn's view now emerging. The renewal of national conflict after 1969 had been 'a direct by-product' of the economic advance and modernisation which both parts of Ireland had undergone over the previous decade or so (1981:227). These had destroyed the conditions of rule of the old Unionist elite, and enabled the emergence into independent action of first, a Protestant 'lumpen bourgeoisie', but then a vigorous working-class politics. 'It was the working class which made the Ulster nation' (242) with the 1974 strike and the UDA's raising of demands for independence (demands whose significance and degree of support, it is clear in retrospect, Nairn massively overrated). He thought it 'more likely than not' that an independent, repartitioned Northern Ireland would take its seat at the United Nations before the end of the 1980s (252).

In more tentative yet visionary style, Tom Nairn has returned in the 1990s to the themes of his *Break-Up of Britain*. He continues to expect, or at least hope for, the emergence of an Ulster nationalism, and thinks there are good reasons for hope that this will be civic rather than ethnic in form, one 'which could in time easily be ranged beside those already functioning in Scotland and Wales.' (Nairn 1997:165) 'Together, European regionalism and a long overdue political restructuring of the UK's periphery could then support the consolidation of the new Ulster sub-state.' (165) He finds the voice of this emergent consciousness not only in new thinking among Unionist and Loyalist politicians, but in the 'incomparable voice of Ulster Protestantism' (162), Van Morrison, whose songlyrics Nairn uses throughout his argument to illustrate the 'parochial universalism' (166) he applauds in modern, peaceable small-country nationalisms like the Scottish one he has long supported, and the Ulster one he believes will yet still emerge.

Nairn's interpretation of Morrison may be questioned—alongside the visionary nostalgia for East Belfast childhood scenes which Nairn emphasises in Morrison's work, and for him makes the singer a distinctively proto-national Ulster voice, there have been almost equally frequent, powerful evocations of pan-Irish (*Veedon Fleece, Irish Heartbeat*), rural English (*Common One*), Scottish (Morrison's use of traditional Scots airs, and of the title 'Caledonian' for his backing bands and music publishing), and above all religiously transcendental idylls. Van Morrison sits, after all, on the editorial board of the *Irish Studies Review*, not the *Ulster Review*; and even Nairn notes the lack of 'national' resonance the singer's message has had among Ulster Protestants themselves (158). One may also doubt more broadly whether the vision of civic, non-sectarian Ulsterness which Nairn discerns is, or is likely soon to be, anything like as strong as he believes. The contemporary idea of Ulster remains in important ways, to borrow Brian Graham's phrase, 'a representation of place yet to be imagined' (Graham 1997a), despite the range of evocations from John Hewitt, through the exhibitionary structure of the Ulster Folk Museum, to Morrison's 'Orangefield' or 'Hyndford Street'.

The contributions of Nairn, of Clifford and other BICO-associated writers, therefore, were important in their time. They were among the most thoughtful and thought-provoking analyses of Northern Ireland to come from the left, and for a while almost the only serious left-wing alternatives to the often simplistic colonial analogies of pro-Republican writers. But they were very much *of* their time, polemical interventions in particular contexts—and in some cases, as with Nairn, involving predictions which were rapidly falsified. The most substantial critiques and alternatives to the colonial model took a different track, and two main forms. One was systematically to examine the Ulster situation in a comparative context; such comparative analyses are discussed separately below in Chapter 11.

The other major 'revisionist' strategy in relation to Northern Ireland has been to undertake detailed historical investigations of the nationalist and Unionist traditions—and of that crucial point of intersection, the Ulster working class. In the process it is shown beyond serious doubt that the images on which Republicanism bases its claims to be waging an anticolonial struggle, images both of itself and of its opponents, are hopelessly inadequate and misleading. Important works here include Peter Gibbon (1975), Brian Walker (1989), Michael Laffan (1983) and Alvin Jackson (1989) on the origins and early development of Ulster Unionism, Henry Patterson on Protestant workers (1980) and on the social Republican tradition (1989, 1997), Austen Morgan on 'green' and 'orange' socialisms (in Morgan and Purdie eds 1980), on Connolly's thought (1988) and on Belfast politics (1991), Bob Purdie on the origins of the civil rights movement (1990), and Frank Wright on the nineteenth-century evolution of Ulster's political divisions (1996).[17]

Perhaps the most important single area of contention and revision related to one major strand of attempts at a class-based analysis of Northern Ireland, which had effectively subordinated such analysis to nationalist perspectives. This was the 'labour aristocracy' thesis. For some socialists, and especially the more economistic kinds of Marxist-nationalist from James Connolly onwards, the adherence of the Protestant working class to Unionism was a puzzle if not a scandal. Their 'natural' allegiance, it was felt, should be to a politics of Irish self-determination held in class alliance with other Irish workers and peasants and in opposition to the British-Unionist ruling class. In seeking to explain their failure to follow that ordained course, some analysts invoked the theory of the labour aristocracy which had become Communist orthodoxy in the 1920s, building on arguments Lenin had presented in his *Imperialism* and *Left-Wing Communism: An Infantile Disorder* and, less directly, on some passing comments by Engels.[18] In the Irish context, the first use of the idea was probably, like so much else in local socialist thought, the responsibility of James Connolly; though he deployed such arguments only in brief and undeveloped form.

The theory's general assertion was that, in the era of advanced capitalism and imperialism, some privileged sections of the working class in the metropolitan—and especially the colony-owning—powers had been 'bribed' with part of the proceeds of capitalist super-profit and thus tended to compromise with or even become entirely subservient to the wishes of the ruling class. In the Irish context, it was claimed that sections of the Protestant working class had fallen victim to this bribery, especially those employed in shipbuilding and engineering. This was held by some to explain their lack of support for radical politics. There was, however, a crucial ambiguity over what *kind* of politics this bribery was supposed to have blocked: international socialism or Irish nationalism? The ambiguity was glossed over, ordinarily, by the Connollyite presumption that these were natural partners; though later non-nationalist Marxists (e.g. Gibbon 1975, Austen Morgan 1991) made it clear that for them it was the weakness of socialism, rather than of Irish nationalism, among Belfast Protestant workers which most needed to be explained and deplored.

A further ambiguity lay in the relationship between 'labour-aristocratic' political values and sectarianism. Was the 'bribe' the consequence of Northern Ireland's, and especially Belfast's, powerful position in the British imperial economic structure—so that sectarian division within the workforce, though important to the maintenance of the aristocracy because the jobs which carried the biggest imperial backhanders were largely reserved for Protestants, was a secondary and derivative phenomenon? This was the more recognisably Marxist line of explanation, seeing the imperialist world-system as primary and local sectarian divisions as epiphenomenal, part of the ideological 'superstructure'. There was no intrinsic reason, nothing in the logic of capital, why under different historical circumstances the boot need not have been on the other foot, with Catholic labour aristocrats upholding conservative and exclusionary politics against a Protestant underclass. The other alternative, however, was to see sectarian exclusions in the workplace as primary and fundamental to the formation of the labour aristocracy. The resulting differentials in income, status and job security between Protestants and Catholics were thus the *direct* cause of Protestant working-class politics: they upheld the Union and opposed all forms of Catholic assertion including nationalism because these would threaten their economic privileges.[19]

This may appear, and evidently would appear to those who see socialism and Irish nationalism as inseparably twinned, to be a distinction without a real difference. In fact, the political implications of the two lines of argument

diverge sharply. For the first, the Unionism of the labour aristocracy is derivative of and dependent on its conservatism rather than its sectarianism: it represents a failure to unite with fellow workers, rather than with fellow Irish people.
So far as it is rational, it is so because and only as long as membership of the
United Kingdom and thus of a global British Empire confers significant advantages on whoever occupies employment sectors benefiting from Britain's powerful international economic role (which might well imply that it has become
steadily less rational for several decades now). For the second, however, working-
class Unionism is directly dependent on discrimination in employment
and relatively independent of Britain's global economic fortunes: it remains
rational so long as political pressures can maintain significant wage and job-
security differentials in the local economy. But—and here the analysis hits a
political brick wall and bounces back, baffled—even if it loses this rationality,
there is no obvious reason why the 'natural' alternative is for Protestant workers
to embrace Irish nationalism, unless one regards a national identity uniting all
the island's inhabitants as natural. Thus for the first interpretation, class solidarity is the norm and any departure from it requires a special explanation,
while for the second, national unity (with the nation seen as encompassing all
who inhabit Ireland) is natural and it is departures from *this* which require
explanation. In the Northern Irish context, the labour aristocracy theory has
thus been invoked to do two incompatible political tasks—both of which
depend on unsustainable historical assumptions.

Irish Marxist revisionism has been—more than a little reductively—
summed up by one hostile critic as a compound of 'an Althusserian theoretical
heritage, a traditional historical methodology, and a virulently anti-nationalist
politics.' (Munck 1992:105[20]) In fact the Althusserian (actually more Poulantz-
ian) influence is present only in the very earliest works of Bew, Gibbon and
Patterson, effectively disappearing by the early 1980s. Subsequently, the 'heritage'
of Althusserian or other 1970s Marxist state theories is at most marginal to their
writings; whilst other major 'Marxist revisionists' like Morgan and Purdie were
never Althusserians. Indeed it is by no means clear which, if any, of these
authors would still describe themselves as Marxists. The 'traditional historical
methodology' has also become steadily less apparent, as the influence of various
kinds of 'history from below' has increased; and 'virulent anti-nationalism' is
naturally very much in the eye of the beholder.

(iii) 'Anglo Pigs and Scotties': The Model Globalised—and Feminised

So far as some writers and politicians outside Ireland are concerned, apparently, none of the historians and critics mentioned above need have bothered
putting finger to keyboard. The most egregious excesses of 'anti-imperialist'

polemic have usually come from non-Irish sympathisers with Republicanism; most copiously from the alleged imperial metropole itself. One could multiply *ad nauseam* the invocations by British left-wingers of Northern Ireland as a colony and the Republican movement as anticolonial. This writing has proved largely impervious to argument and evidence. And there has been rather little variation in the nature of the claims made. Even while bitterly denouncing one another for incorrect analyses and insufficient enthusiasm for Sinn Fein's cause, far-left groups have constantly replicated identical positions. Ordinarily the medium has been agitational rather than reflective: speeches, articles in left-wing journals, pamphlets; occasionally television programmes like Kenneth Griffith's *Hang up Your Brightest Colours* and Jim Allen's aborted *The Rising*, or rock songs like John Lennon's 'Sunday Bloody Sunday' and Paul McCartney's 'Give Ireland Back to the Irish'. Many of the songs and media treatments ran into recurrent problems of censorship by British broadcasting organisations.[21] Some, though, just sunk under the weight of their own absurdity—or worse. The Irish material on Lennon's *Some Time in New York City* LP was the nadir both of the ex-Beatle's own career and of British 'anti-imperialist' commentary on Northern Ireland, as Robin Denselow rightly complains:

'If you had the luck of the Irish . . . you'd wish you was English instead' seemed down-right insulting, while the suggestions at the end of 'Sunday Bloody Sunday' that the problem be solved by shipping back to Britain the Protestants who had lived in Ulster for over 300 years was [sic] scandalous, naive and even racist. Lines like 'You anglo pigs and scotties sent to colonize the North', 'Repatriate to Britain all of you who call it home' or (worst of all) 'Internment is no answer, it's those mothers' turn to burn' simply weren't worthy of Lennon, especially with his concern with racial problems, and his earlier avowed pacifism (Denselow 1989:115).

It was left, later, to Irish performers like U2, the Pogues, That Petrol Emotion and Christy Moore—some of them staunch Republicans, but people whose political seriousness, thoughtfulness and non-sectarianism are beyond doubt—to restore some dignity to popular music's treatment of the Ulster crisis.

Extended analyses of the conflict as a colonial one were far rarer. Among the most thoughtful early attempts was Bob Purdie's Trotskyist tract *Ireland Unfree* (1972), produced for the International Marxist Group. Perhaps symptomatically, Purdie—who unlike most writers in this vein had the advantages both of substantial historical knowledge and of long residence in Belfast—later revised his views of Northern Ireland through virtually 180 degrees, from fierce pro-Republicanism to substantial sympathy for 'civic Unionist' positions. Later versions of the colonial argument made at substantial length included a short book produced by the Revolutionary Communist Party's Irish Freedom Movement (1983), and a long one by David Reed for the unrelated (well, a relative but no friend) Revolutionary Communist *Group*. (1984)

Given the nearly interchangeable nature of the arguments deployed, their character can be indicated by quotation from a fairly small selection.[22] Veteran British left-wing journalist Paul Foot, in a 1989 pamphlet, reasoned as follows:

Ireland is Britain's oldest colony. From earliest times it was a rich source of plunder for English kings and nobles.

Although Ireland was often invaded in earlier times, it wasn't finally conquered for England until the sixteenth century.

The method of conquest was to plant English and Scottish people in Ireland, and grant them special privileges and rights over the land and native people there . . .

Famine was an extremely useful way of keeping the natives in order . . .

To support three centuries of land seizure and enforced famine, the British devised the theory that the Irish were an inferior people . . .

The Conservative Party . . . sought therefore a means to hamstring Home Rule without defeating it. The means they chose was to play the Orange Card: to divide Ireland in two, securing part of the Protestant North for Britain, while allowing the South a measure of independence . . . What was in fact a defence of property and dividends was cloaked in the language of religion. (Paul Foot 1989:3–9)

Today, Foot believes, the economic and strategic reasons for Britain retaining her presence have largely eroded. He recognises that Northern Ireland is a financial drain, not an asset, for London. The reason for hanging on, he suggests, is simply fear of being seen to be defeated, a fear which 'is nothing more nor less than political paralysis.' (ibid: 69) This is not perhaps implausible; but Foot's historical account condenses almost every conceivable myth about Ireland's past as well as perpetrating numerous very basic factual errors. Quite obviously he—like many external 'friends of Irish freedom'—has not even second-hand awareness of any modern writing about the country's history.

More fundamentalist Leninists, by contrast, claimed that there are still vital British interests at stake in the north. The attempt to show that these interests are directly economic has been generally abandoned as implausible. The usual contemporary argument is instead that the very survival of the British state is at issue:

Withdrawal from Ireland now would be tantamount to dismantling a part of the British state itself. No significant section of the British ruling class could ever countenance this because it would represent a major blow to the capitalist system . . . This is the *revolutionary significance* of the 'Irish Question'. Defeat in Ireland would weaken the British capitalist class to such an extent that it would fundamentally alter class relations in Britain. (Irish Freedom Movement 1983:8–9; emphasis in original)

David Reed of the RCG, conversely, still believed economic exploitation to be the essence of the British game:

Imperialism will never voluntarily relinquish political control over an oppressed nation because such control enormously strengthens its ability to economically exploit that nation. Any movement by British imperialism to make concessions to the Irish people has, therefore, only been brought about by revolutionary force. (Reed 1984:372)

The rhetoric of such tiny far-left groups would hardly be worth reproducing, if it were not that on this issue—perhaps more than any other—it was only a more strident version of views held far outside their ranks. It is not too much to say that, in the 1970s and 1980s, the 'anti-imperialist' analysis of the Northern Ireland conflict became the common sense not only of the Marxist but of the Labour left in Britain. The published views of Ken Livingstone, at least in the 1980s, seemed to differ little in substance from those of Paul Foot or the RCP.[23] More muted echoes of such attitudes—though without the apologias for paramilitary violence—could also be found in the statements of Tony Benn, or of Kevin McNamara, Labour's Northern Ireland spokesperson from 1987 to 1994 (e.g. McNamara *et al.* 1993: a pamphlet which was, apparently, in fact largely drafted by Dr Brendan O'Leary of the LSE). Especially in the early 1980s, in the aftermath of the IRA hunger strikes and at the high tide of 'Bennite' left-wing insurgency within British Labour, such views became for a time seemingly hegemonic. Labour's 1981 conference voted in favour of a united Ireland; and although motions calling for an immediate British withdrawal were defeated a majority of constituency parties apparently supported the milder of them (Geoffrey Bell 1982:147–9; Craig ed. 1982:426–8). Groupings on the Labour left, such as that around the journal *London Labour Briefing* which was for a time effectively dominant in London Labour, espoused a passionate pro-Republicanism which was associated with renewed interest in Irish ethnic identity—a part of the 'Rainbow Coalition' or 'Beyond the Fragments' politics which Ken Livingstone's Greater London Council pursued. It was by no means clear that this association, or even identification, of pro-Republicanism with Irishness, and of both with 'anti-anti-Irish racism' was favoured by a majority of people of Irish descent in London, or in Labour's ranks.

And even the 'soft' or 'strategic' Labour left (as those who abandoned Bennism for a more centrist position called themselves) of the 1980s continued to reproduce this stance: perhaps largely because the particular London Labour social networks its architects inhabited included few Irish people other than romantic pro-Republicans. To pluck out one example from a myriad: immediately after Labour's crushing 1987 election defeat *Chartist*, magazine of the Labour Coordinating Committee, reviewed Constance Markievicz's prison letters with references to Irish Protestants as a 'colonial class', to the IRA as 'the world's first guerilla army', and to the 'right wing colonial government of the Free State'; with the conclusion that 'Ireland is still suffering from what went wrong in those days, the cause of Ireland is still the cause of Labour' (Joyce Neary 1987). 'Ireland', here as so often in this rhetorical mode, means Northern

Ireland: for much of the British and international left, the Republic does not seem to exist. This tendency to read all Irish history from the perspective of the north is reproduced in one of the few extended 1990s attempts to perpetuate the old perspective, Liz Curtis's *The Cause of Ireland* (1994)[24]; and as we have seen some critics have argued that it pervades such modern expressions of cultural nationalism as the Field Day project. During the 1990s, changes in the political culture and alignments both of Ireland and of the British left greatly weakened the pro-Republican camp, especially within the British Labour party—but even near the end of the decade some prominent left-wing journalistic voices, such as Roy Greenslade and Mark Steel in the *Guardian*, continued to relay stereotypical nationalist stances and to portray Unionists as unrelievedly bigoted and supremacist.[25]

Apart from British left-wingers, the other main source of such writing was the United States: especially, but certainly not only, works by Irish-American publicists.[26] Leftist groups elsewhere also, for a considerable time, generally adopted the colonial model to describe Northern Ireland. For instance Maurice Goldring (1990) remarks the near ubiquity of such an understanding on the French left: though this was, he underlines, *not* necessarily accompanied by sympathy for the IRA's methods. The usual stance of French Socialists and Communists in relation to the IRA was that: 'The cause is right but the war is wrong.' (1990:111)

A great deal of such writing did, however, espouse or imply the belief that the pursuit of violence in Northern Ireland, or at least of the political ends to which Republican violence had been directed, would somehow advance the cause of socialism there, throughout Ireland, and indeed in Britain too. Such a belief could only be held on the basis of adopting an unqualified colonial model of Irish history, seeing Ulster Protestants as *colons* and refusing any understanding of or empathy with their fears, and accepting unquestioningly militant Republicans' self-images including their (often honest) blindness to the fact that their actions *are* often sectarian. It has been standard, indeed virtually unquestioned, procedure in such 'anti-imperialist' circles to assert that there is an absolute distinction between Loyalist and Republican paramilitaries, with the former profoundly sectarian and the latter wholly free of such a taint.

Loyalists themselves justify their privileged position in apartheid Northern Ireland on the basis of their cultural peculiarities and their claimed superiority to Catholics . . . The difference between the Loyalist and republican traditions could not be more striking . . . The Loyalist 'armed struggle' turns out to be sectarian murder pure and simple, where any Catholic will do. In contrast, the republican tradition is not to fight for Catholic privilege, but for equal rights for all in a secular state. The politics of ethnic identity are alien to Irish anti-imperialism. (Alex Farrell 1993:11)

The falseness of this claim, expressed in these terms, is evident. Both sides' paramilitaries have engaged in sectarian killings; equally, both have usually convinced themselves that their choice of targets has had a morally legitimate rationale. To go beyond that simple negative point is to enter extremely murky waters. It can certainly be said that by some indicators, sectarianism appears more overt among Loyalists than Republicans, and that unequivocally sectarian murder has more often been committed by Loyalist than by Republican para-militaries. These, however, are differences of degree rather than of kind, and may at least partly be explained by Republicanism's ability to 'sublimate' poten-tially sectarian feelings by directing both rhetoric and armed violence against the state and its personnel rather than (at least overtly) against Protestants as such. The facts that the IRA is a more tightly disciplined organisation, and one more alert to its international image, than the Loyalist paramilitaries, may also be relevant. Despite all this, almost no Republican will privately deny that many IRA and INLA killings, especially in the 1970s, were purely sectarian in charac-ter. So far as wider publics are concerned, attitude surveys have offered widely variant judgements on whether sectarian hostility is more prevalent in one community than the other, with two major studies finding Catholics more prejudiced than Protestants, three others reversing the verdict, and several arguing for approximate equivalence.[27]

The assimilation of international socialism to armed Republicanism also leads such commentators to ignore or scorn the honourable record of anti-sectarian socialist, social-democratic and trade union politics in Northern Ireland across the decades. From the 'anti-imperialist' perspective, the whole history of the Northern Ireland Labour Party, the trade union movement in the north, and the various smaller secular, leftish groupings of Ulster's modern past is either an irrelevance, or a story of 'partitionist' collusion with Unionist hegemony. For that matter, the self-proclaimed socialism of some Unionists, including leading members of what are usually called 'the fringe Loyalist parties' (those closely linked to the Protestant paramilitary groups) can only be dismissed out of hand. Thus prominent Sinn Fein member and IRA veteran Tommy Gorman can scorn the socialist convictions of Loyalist Billy Hutchin-son—whom he claims to respect on a personal level—thus: 'Billy would claim to be a socialist. To me, you can't be a socialist in an imperial context, you can't be a socialist and a colonialist.' (quoted in Stevenson 1996:178)

This is both an unfair and a simplistic view: those who have looked closely at the contemporary history of the labour and trade union movement have shown it to have displayed not only a conscientious, but often a highly sophisticated, engagement with the issues of sectarianism, clashing identities, and rival national loyalties.[28] There is a serious case for attempts to reappraise and re-habilitate the historical reputation of earlier Northern Irish Labour leaders. Bob Purdie (1994, 1998) has argued with strength that the pioneer Belfast socialist William Walker—so often viewed merely as a feeble foil for his more famous opponent in controversy, James Connolly, as a dull 'gas and water' municipal labourist, or even a crude sectarian bigot—deserves to be treated with far more respect. His belief that 'the interests of the working class of Ireland were best served within the United Kingdom' (Purdie 1994:116) was neither poorly argued, nor grounded in religious prejudice (which, with the brief and deplorable exception of his rhetoric during a Belfast by-election in 1905, Walker eschewed) nor in imperialist chauvinism (for Walker shared the general, if often ambiguous, anticolonialism of his socialist and radical generation). Walker's insoluble dilemma was that he adhered to a tradition of socialist thought, shared by both Fabians and the ILP in the United Kingdom as well as by most early continental Marxists, which simply had no coherent body of ideas about nationality or ethnicity. The founding presumption was that the clash of Nationalism and Unionism was rapidly being made irrelevant by the advance of socialism. But Walker and other early Labourists were seeking to operate in a political milieu where such issues were increasingly ubiquitous, were becoming more, not less, central to political debate.[29] In related vein Graham Walker (1985) has produced a detailed study of the slightly later Northern Ireland Labour Party leader Harry Midgley. He sees Midgley as the most important in a series of figures, through Paddy Devlin and Gerry Fitt to even Glen Barr, who have tried to use social-democratic or labourist appeals to break the sectarian structures of Northern Ireland politics: 'Each has paid the price to trying to break tribal politics: each has suffered at the hands of his own "tribe", and each has been reduced to a position of marginal influence.' (216) Midgley was thus at least 'the most interesting failure in an area where no-one has yet succeeded.' (221)

Elective affinities have also been proclaimed, not only between Irish Republicanism and socialism, but between Republicanism and feminism. Women's movements in Ireland, north and south, have engaged for many years and with increasing success in campaigns for civic, political, social and reproductive rights. Challenging the entrenched and allied hierarchies of state and churches, they have arguably been, especially in the Republic, the most important of all forces for change, the cutting edge of social progress. Yet a significant body of feminist opinion outside Ireland, and once again not least in Britain, has virtually ignored all these campaigns and instead acted as cheerleaders for armed Republicanism, bizarrely identifying its cause with that of women's liberation.

An extreme example can be found in a co-authored 1984 work by three women writers, only one of them Irish, which purports to present 'the truth about women's experiences in the Six Counties of Northern Ireland.' (Fairweather *et al.* 1984:vii) In fact *Only the Rivers Run Free* was almost exclusively devoted to presenting the views of women active in the Republican movement, three of its six chapters being about and mostly in the words of women IRA members, women imprisoned for Republican terrorist offences, and women campaigning on behalf of male Republican prisoners. A fourth and fifth dealt with life in Belfast nationalist 'ghettoes' and attitudes to the Catholic Church and sexual-familial structures. Neither presented the views of anyone who was not from a Catholic family, and hardly a single interviewee was not a Republican activist. The single chapter ostensibly concerned with Belfast Protestant women, organised round notions of Protestant 'fundamentalism', 'extremism', and patriarchal violence, gave its last and longest word to Suzanne Bunting, a woman of Protestant background who became a Republican activist and member of the Irish Republican Socialist Party.[30] Throughout the book, the Republican version of events, and of history, is either assumed or stridently propounded. It is asserted amidst much else, without evidence, that 'Sectarian hatred is stronger among Loyalists than it is among Republicans. Of course not every Protestant is a Loyalist or extremist, but the bottom line of sectarianism runs very deep.' (287) One can well believe the principal author's confession that 'I had tried to read history books and analytical articles about Ireland but always found them difficult.' (viii) Escaping such difficulty seems to be the *raison d'être* of the book. It is less easily achieved by those women more closely involved in Irish politics.

Self-proclaimedly feminist groups have continued to work within or in association with the Republican movement in both parts of Ireland, though more particularly the north. They have been unable to resolve or avoid the continuing dilemmas of subordination to the politics of 'national liberation' and to what is still a strongly masculinist movement and culture (see e.g. Clara Connolly 1995, Hackett 1995). In recent years Sinn Fein has had women in the posts of general secretary and publicity director, and about a quarter of its national executive has been female (Linder 1995). Few observers believe, however, that these women have a central role in the key political decisions: and it appears, unsurprisingly, that there has never been a female member of the IRA Army Council.

In a more academic register, the four Galway-based editors of an important collection of essays on 'Gender and Colonialism' (three of them, incidentally, male) proclaim categorically that for feminists not to be pro-Republicans is for them to be imperialists:

[T]here are certain historical conjunctures in which feminism and imperialism can be regarded as unequivocally aligned. Indeed such alignments are as evident today, in the disassociation of many contemporary feminist writers from the politics of republicanism in Northern Ireland, as they were in Emmeline and Christabel Pankhurst's strong support for British participation in the First World War. (Foley *et al.* eds 1995:9)

And a contributor to that collection, Laura Lyons, typing the Republican movement as the only true representatives of both anticolonial and feminist resistance, asserts of Sinn Fein's female activists that: 'As colonized women they are forced to exist outside of public discourse.' (Laura Lyons 1995:183) All and any writing about women in Northern Ireland which fails to endorse IRA violence is viewed as colluding in this exclusion, and is condemned by Lyons. Only the passionately pro-Republican playwright Margaretta D'Arcy appears to be excepted from such strictures.

Yet more tendentious is the work of Harvard University anthropologist Begona Aretxaga, whose ill-informed book *Shattering Silence* (1997) celebrates the 'resistance' against British 'imperialism' and against patriarchy of nationalist women in Belfast. Aretxaga's lack of familiarity with her subject is evident on many levels, from her inability to spell Irish names (we are treated to 'Maud Gone', 'Bernardette Devlin', 'Michael Gauhgam' for Gaughan, and both 'Nuget' and 'Nugget' for Nugent), through her references to a game called 'hurlic' (60, 178) and the Irish Famine 'of 1854' (181), to her repeated citations of a journal called *The English Times*. For Aretxaga as for some others writing in this vein, 'women in Ireland' are a rather small and homogeneous group: they are in fact Republican women on the Falls Road. The stance, the style, and the theoretical pretension can best be conveyed just by sampling a few sentences, a page apart: '"The troubles" materialized Northern Ireland as phantasmic and negated "other" of Britain and Ireland and constituted it as a place out of place on which the hegemonic nationalist order of Britain and Ireland hinged and by which violent excess it was threatened.' (15) It is hard to discern here which verbs correspond to which nouns, let alone how one can materialise something as phantasmic. Just a bit further on, we are told, in a manner both ponderous and sectarian, that:

Women in Northern Ireland would occupy a variety of positions. Catholic women could be colonized and Western; their Protestant counterparts could be colonizer and Western. But the status of this Protestant colonizer-Western woman in Northern Ireland would be different from the status of the Western woman in England who would undoubtedly form part of the metropolitan colonizer. In its turn, the status of the colonized woman in Northern Ireland would not be the same as that of the Irish woman of preindependence Ireland . . . (16)

Such partisan presentations underpin an unargued assimilation of feminism to Republicanism, and effective dismissal of the former in favour of the latter, present not only in works such as these but in such formations as 'Women Against Imperialism' and in the editorial policy of *Spare Rib* through the later years of its existence (see for instance its 'Irish' special issue of August 1989).[31]

A romantic nationalist leftism, recognisably derivative of the Connollyite legacy but sometimes now given a feminist twist, may thus still be encountered. It finds expression in claims that any conservative, patriarchal, inegalitarian or undemocratic features of Irish life are British legacies and impositions, pure and simple. 'True' Irish national traditions, by contrast, are not only participatory and egalitarian but at least proto-feminist. As Carol Coulter put it: 'British and patriarchal, centralised, bureaucratic concepts of politics were not . . . seriously shrugged off at all by the nationalist movement which sought the overthrow of British rule in this country. Instead, it was a concept that would allow for the domination of the male elite.' (quoted Clara Connolly 1995:121) In Coulter's writings, Ireland is both unique and part of an undifferentiated 'colonial situation'. Feminism there is entirely different 'from that of women in the imperialist countries because of the space created by the existence of mass nationalist movements, the widespread rejection of existing political institutions and culture, and the different family relationships which existed in colonial countries'—the latter being, supposedly, more egalitarian (Coulter 1993:3, 11–14). Only from the 'oppressively masculine' colonial state did gender inequality come: the idea that Irish society, colonial or precolonial, might have harboured any kind of patriarchy or sexism 'from below' is just 'the modern propaganda of the Irish state' (19). That state's own patriarchy derives from its being 'modelled in every significant way on its colonial predecessor' (23). 'Ireland's new rulers, aping their imperialist masters in this as in so many things' excluded women from government (27).

This pseudo-traditionalism involves Coulter and others in hostility to the contemporary women's movement as, allegedly, defined by 'middle-class, highly educated urban women influenced by Anglo-American radical feminism' and wholly out of touch with rural and working-class women (40–1). The preference is for 'Tradition in the Service of Resistance' (41–8), as exampled by both Islamicist movements (Coulter seemingly approves even of the return of veiling! (44–6)) and militant Republicanism in the north, which oxymoronically 'appears as a unifying ideology of all those involved and therefore is subversive of all authority and plays a decentralizing role' (54).[32] The presumption or implication is that feminist objectives were integral to earlier phases of militant nationalism but were betrayed by the Free State, only to be revived in contemporary Republicanism. Historically, this claim is largely without basis. Cumann na Mban, the Republican women's organisation, was in 1917–23 entirely subordinate and auxiliary to the male body, and espoused no specifically feminist aims at all, whilst more generally the militarist orientation of the movement entirely marginalised women's concerns and roles.[33]

Few observers would doubt that important sections of the international and especially British left have exhibited notable political and analytical failures in dealing with Northern Irish affairs. Naturally, how such weaknesses are characterised and explained will depend heavily on personal viewpoint. The present analysis has seen a central flaw as being an ill-informed, simplistic and romantic pro-Republicanism. Others, inevitably, take an almost exactly opposite view, seeing *lack* of pro-Republican stances as the great British socialist error. This is the argument presented, in a recent version of an old polemic, by Sam Porter and Denis O'Hearn (1995) in assailing *New Left Review*'s Irish coverage (or lack of it). Ostensibly their main complaint is at the near absence, from 1970 to 1994, of articles on Ireland in the *Review*. Actually, their gripe is against the lack of pro-Republican articles on *Northern* Ireland, and the great bulk of their polemic is directed against the 'anti-Republican stance' and 'Podsnappery' of an analysis of the Republic's political economy by Ellen Hazelkorn and Henry Patterson (1994). In classic and by now clichéd style, Porter and O'Hearn identify 'revisionism', Unionism, conservatism, apologetics for British policy and non-endorsement of Sinn Fein's programme as a single, undifferentiated target—and appear (as Hazelkorn and Patterson's scornful response rightly suggested) to believe that any discussion of the Irish Republic which does *not* focus on an anti-imperialist analysis of the north but instead investigates the Republic itself is inherently reactionary.[34] Despite the vast waves of change that have swept over both Northern Ireland and the Republic in recent years, despite the mass of modern historical research calling old assumptions into question, and even despite the global crisis of socialist thought itself (a crisis to which socialism's interaction with various nationalisms has evidently been central), the timeworn notion of an Irish nationalist-socialist synthesis centred on militant Republicanism appears to have an inexhaustible capacity to renew itself.

10

Ulster Unionism—A Colonial Culture?

(i) Nation, Colony, Ethnicity, Religion . . . Unionist Kaleidoscopes

Many critics have noted the virtual silence of Irish nationalist intellectuals, from Pearse and Connolly to most contemporary cultural theorists, about the history, culture and politics of Ulster Unionism. Yet assumptions about the latter necessarily play a crucial role in assessment of Ireland's past and future, including questions about how far and in what ways the Irish situation may be described as colonial or postcolonial.

Judgements on that score have time and again been made without serious investigation. Successive generations of cultural nationalists, in particular, have had a gaping blind spot in relation to the real politics of Unionism. What Conor Cruise O'Brien said of the generation of the Revival is little less true of their counterparts among contemporary cultural critics: that 'the Ireland they loved had an enormous West Coast and no Northeast corner.' (1965:94)[1] Republicans and their sympathisers, as we have seen, tended to view northern Protestants very simply as a settler-colonialist bloc; though more recently some rethinking of that stance has become apparent. Wider circles of southern Irish political and public opinion frequently either ignored the north, or felt a certain disdain for it. In the first decades of the Free State's existence, far from agitating persistently for unification, much public opinion and many official statements in the south viewed Northern Ireland as an alien place apart, stereotyping its inhabitants— even its Catholics—in hostile, uncomprehending, at best condescending ways (as traced in O'Halloran 1987). Such perceptions have evidently been renewed and intensified by the Northern violence since 1969. As Harvey Cox suggests, opinion polls in the Republic indicate that:

The northern Irish are not greatly liked; most ominous for northern Irish Catholics, they are regarded by a majority, according to one survey, as having more in common with northern Irish Protestants than with their southern co-religionists. In particular 55 per cent in the south attributed to both sides in the north the epithet 'extreme and unreasonable'. (Cox 1985:38)

Mainstream academic historiography has also had notable lacunae: Ulster Unionism has been less studied than that of the South, the major Unionist parties and politicians have attracted less attention than the paramilitary fringes. As Alvin Jackson laments 'Unionism, suburban and constitutional' seems less enticing to writers than 'the ganglands stalked by Lennie Murphy.' (1996a:131)[2] We turn now to attempt a balance-sheet of the literature which *has* significantly addressed such issues, and an assessment of whether or how far Ulster Unionist and Loyalist ideologies can adequately be analysed via colonial categories.[3]

Multiple lines of explanation invoking concepts of nationality, ethnicity, religion, imperialism, and regionalism have been proposed. None on its own is satisfactory. Negotiating the maze, we need waste no time on the notion that Northern Irish Protestants and Unionists constitute a 'race', for that is a concept whose social and political uses have been arbitrary where they are not malevolent.[4] Have they, however, seen themselves as a nation? Uncertainty and insecurity have been evident here too, and have been reflected in the vigorous but inconclusive debate about identity conducted among Unionists since the 1980s.[5] Ulster Unionist Party leader David Trimble lamented that the 'loyalist's sense of identity is usually instinctive, it is rarely carefully thought out and may sometimes may [sic] be poorly articulated'—but, he protests, he has no doubt who he is! (Ulster Society 1986:3) Yet Trimble himself seemed to partake of the unclarity he lamented, for his championing of what he calls 'the Ulster British nation' (ibid: 4) failed to say whether this is thought of as a distinctive nationality, or merely a fragment of a wider British nation. Dr Peter Brooke, in the same collection of essays, appeared more definite: there *is* a separate Ulster nationality, based above all on distinctive churches but (in a seeming paradox if not oxymoron) also characteristically liberal and secular in ethos, and certainly not anti-Catholic. (ibid: 8–11) John Braidwood concurred in identifying a distinct Ulster 'people', with its peculiar dialect the main marker of distinctiveness (ibid). Anthony Alcock, for his part, believed that the 'Ulster-British amalgam' is not a nation but may be in the process of becoming one; though alternatively, it might turn into one of a hundred regions of a federal Europe (ibid).[6] Another senior Unionist politician, John Taylor, made the claim for distinctiveness with a crudity which is, perhaps, increasingly rare: 'I'm an Ulsterman, not an Irishman—I don't jig at crossroads or play Gaelic football. We've got two races on this island; of course, a Protestant can be an Irishman, but most Protestants are Ulstermen.' (Hall ed. 1995:39–40)

A stronger case for separate Ulster nationality is made by the Rev. Brett Ingram, who believes it to be founded on a series of historical memories from the Tain legends, through the Boyne and the Relief of Derry, to the 1912 Covenant and the Somme (Ingram 1989:141). The crucial era of its (re)creation, however, was 1886–1914, when 'Ulster was emerging as a nation apart from the rest of Ireland, due to the rest of Ireland wanting to leave the United Kingdom. Ulster was regaining its identity after seven centuries.' (ibid: 23) Confusingly, however, Ingram punctuated his insistences of a separate Ulster nationhood with the apparently incompatible claim that the United Kingdom was 'One Undivided Nation' (ibid: 33).

A further theme in recent Unionist literature has been a new, or renewed, emphasis on the specifically Scottish roots of much of Northern Ireland's Protestant population and culture. However this has not, on the whole, taken any directly political form, with few commentators of any kind seeking to link argument over Scotland's political future with that over Northern Ireland. That is partly, no doubt, because Scottish nationalists and Labour or Liberal Democrat devolutionists in Scotland have largely eschewed any engagement with Northern Irish affairs; and this may in its turn be connected to fears of awakening what some see as the sleeping dragon of religious divisions in Scottish society itself.[7] From the Irish side, Ulster Unionist politicians seem unsurprisingly to have found recent Scottish political developments notably unhelpful to their case, and have therefore remained silent about them; while Northern Irish political debate in general has evinced a remarkable lack of informed interest in actual or potential Scottish parallels.

These recent debates have not, apparently, significantly challenged the long-dominant if always uneasy Ulster Unionist association of its sense of self with Britishness. James Loughlin points to the late-nineteenth-century stress in Unionist and Ulster rhetoric on the 'Englishness' of Ulster Protestants (Loughlin 1995: e.g. 23, 26, 27). This was in line with Victorian racial thought on 'Anglo-Saxon' versus 'Celtic' characteristics. In the 1910–14 Home Rule crisis, paranoid ideas even circulated in some English and Ulster Unionist circles of a 'pan-Celtic' conspiracy against the Anglo-Saxons, one in which Irish, Scottish and Welsh Liberals and Home Rulers combined (ibid: 55–7).[8] But the emerging Victorian language of Ulster identity also reflected beliefs in an Irish north-south divide resembling the stereotypical English one: the north was urban, industrial, puritanical, hardworking; the south rural and agrarian, leisured or indolent. Thus problems emerged for Ulster Unionist self-images as, from the 1880s, England's own 'northern' images came to be less culturally valued than its 'southern' ones (27). The classic interwar expressions of Britishness as subsumed within a southern English ruralist myth, those of Conservative Prime Minister Stanley Baldwin, effectively excluded Ulster from the British nation, contrary to the overt Tory statements of support for Ulster between the wars (ibid: 98–9).

In its early years the Stormont regime's efforts to 'sell' itself, especially to London political opinion, including contested efforts to present Ulster history sympathetically, focused overwhelmingly on the theme of shared British identity. The Northern Ireland government's attempts to present itself as integrally British, however, were repeatedly undermined by the sectarian utterances of Stormont politicians (see e.g. Loughlin 1995:103–10, 116–17). Wartime propaganda efforts, including the officially sponsored pamphlet *Ulster: The British Bridgehead* (1943), urged the same message—but London propaganda, film and newsreels of the war years underlined the relative failure of this, since Northern Ireland was not usually integrated into their picture of an embattled, united Britain (ibid: 120–34). On the contrary, British officials and politicians frequently suspected or suggested that Ulster's allegedly hidebound patrician rulers, inefficient economic managers and fractious workers were failing to 'pull their weight' in the war effort (Bardon 1992:561–86). Such mutterings were muted in the chorus of official praise for Ulster's wartime loyalty—especially after the Luftwaffe's devastating 1941 attacks on Belfast, and even more especially as compared against the Dublin government's neutrality, which extended even to official condolences on Hitler's death—but the experience of war probably did far less to integrate Northern Ireland into the British imagined community than Unionists believed at the time, and less than it did further to separate Belfast from Dublin.

The efforts to present a favourable, and essentially British, image of Ulster continued into the postwar era, as with the magazine *Ulster Commentary* founded by Stormont in 1945. W. R. Rodgers's pamphlet, published by the British Council, *The Ulstermen and Their Country* (1947), sought to project Ulster's regional distinctiveness, though also suggesting that the Ulster character had been formed by gradual interaction of the different traditions' Irish, Scots and English 'racial' qualities. The 'modernising' views of the 1960s, as again expressed in an officially commissioned book, Robin Bryans, *Ulster: A Journey through the Six Counties* (1964), tried to suggest that sectarianism, and such institutions as the Orange Order, were gradually dying out. Ulster was depicted as becoming ever more like 'mainland' Britain. The idea of an entirely separate Ulster nationality, then, continued to be rejected by almost all shades of Unionism, while the publications of the Ulster Society, founded in 1986, explicitly counter it, presenting instead an Ulster British culture and heritage, a distinctive regional cultural variant within a shared Britishness.

It does not necessarily follow, however, from the weakness of explicit support for a conception of Ulsterness as a separate nationality, that Unionism should not be conceived of as a form of nationalism. As Fred Halliday has argued, it clearly has many of the attributes that, on any broad comparative view, would mark it as nationalist:

Unionist discourse itself talks of a Protestant nation, and it is evident to all that the Britishness proclaimed by unionists concerns an identity, and community, distinct from the population of the rest of the UK—as not only the English but also the Scots will insist. To deny unionism the quality of nationalism is no more valid than to say that Catholic nationalism is not nationalism because it is mixed up with an international value system tied to Rome.

Unionism defines a distinct community. It chose to exercise its right to self-determination not by demanding independence but by choosing to adhere to the UK. There is nothing peculiar about this, as plenty of nationalist movements . . . made the same choice. (Halliday 1997/8:9)

If conceptions of nationality have been uncertain, perhaps the notion of a distinct ethnicity has more mileage in it. Attempts explicitly to theorise the Northern Ireland conflict in terms of ethnicity have nonetheless been few, and have seemed either to be rather formalistic (e.g. Fulton 1995), to invoke ethnicity sketchily as only one explanatory category amongst many (B. O'Leary and McGarry 1993:3–4, 56–62, 307–8, McGarry and O'Leary 1995:152), or to use it without defining it, merely as a synonym for Unionist identity-formation (Bruce 1994⁹). Indeed it is not clear what, if anything, is gained by using the 'ethnic' label as opposed to speaking of 'communities', 'identities', 'cultures' or even 'nationalities' in Northern Ireland. John Fulton's claim that 'thinking ethnic' might help move public discourse to 'the post nation-state level' and 'avoid the traumas of the past 25 years happening all over again' (1995:354) thus seems over-ambitious. Less problematic perhaps, if somewhat baroque, is Ruane and Todd's attempt to argue for ethnicity—with religion, nationality, colonial relationships, and an imagined differentiation between the civilised and barbaric or progressive and backward—as one of five major 'dimensions of difference' which overlap and interrelate in Northern Ireland (Ruane and Todd 1996:10–11, 24–5). This view takes its place, in their major book, in what is certainly one of the most analytically sophisticated attempts to map the conflict, even if one might suspect that the stress on complexity results in indeterminacy, resolved only by their hope for an 'emancipatory' solution which seems more attractive than it is either clear or imminently realisable.

None of these authors offers a clear definition of what they mean by ethnicity, but it appears usually to mean something roughly synonymous with 'cultural tradition'. This only pushes the problem a stage further back, for there is no agreement and little clarity as to what Ulster identity is in these terms either, or on what if anything culturally unites what one study calls the 'Protestant mosaic' or 'majority of minorities' in Northern Ireland (Boal, Campbell and Livingstone 1991). Events such as the October 1994 conference on the Shankill Road, tellingly entitled 'Beyond the Fife and Drum' (Hall ed. 1995) have been shot through with self-doubt, self-questioning, even self-pity. Even as some participants, such as Ian Paisley Jr., lauded the Ulster Protestant tradition as having 'inspired a rich tapestry of ideas: individualism intertwined with community; political beliefs with cultural identity; and a respect for the past that does not preclude a preparedness to move into the future' (3) most others appeared full of uncertainty about what kind of common identity, if any, might indeed lie 'beyond the fife and drum'. Speakers questioned what meaning a common Protestantism had in the contexts of both denominational fragmentation and secularisation, what space there might be for a 'secular Protestant' identity, what relation it might have to Irishness, and most angrily what benefits Unionism had brought to Belfast's Protestant poor and working class.

Some contemporary authors have pushed on from this to argue that Unionist

senses of historical identity are not only more insecure and less solidly historically based than Nationalist ones, but somehow less *real*. This is, naturally, the
guiding assumption of much Irish nationalist thought past and present, especially in its Republican variants, but more detached commentators have also
echoed it. Thus Lucy Bryson and Clem McCartney's study of the use of national
symbolism in Northern Ireland (1994) claims that Unionists rely more heavily
on such symbols than Nationalists because their identity—apparently unlike
that of Nationalists—has no secure existence outside such expression.

The insularity of such representations has often been stressed. Maurice
Goldring, the prominent French analyst of Irish affairs, underlines one significant and otherwise entirely unanalysed facet of this: the virtual international
invisibility of northern Protestants. In an era where not only has the Irish
Republic embraced a European destiny perhaps more whole-heartedly than
any other EU member state, but an Irish diaspora and its cultural representations are more evident and, often, more affluent than ever before in continental
Europe, Ulster Protestants have no recognised presence:

The Irish in Paris are seen, and make themselves seen, as a community because they
meet sympathy when they do so. Nobody knows how many (Irish) Protestants live in
Paris. They might have their own network, but no public meeting-places, no pubs, no
papers that I know of. They are invisible. I can imagine that a Loyalist living in Paris
might have tried several times to state the case for Unionism, even in a moderate fashion, and would have given rise to polite misunderstanding or, at worst, direct hostility.
(Goldring 1994:28)

A sense of decline as well as the older one of siege, a sense of an increasingly
defensive, unselfconfident ensemble of ideologies, especially since the 1985
Anglo-Irish Agreement, seems to mark debates on Unionist identity. Exploring
this decline and its likely consequences, Steve Bruce (1994) focuses on two specific groups: the Loyalist paramilitaries with their urban, working-class reser-
voir of support, and the largely rural evangelical religious circles who form the
bedrock of 'Paisleyism'.[10] The evangelicals in particular, Bruce emphasises, are
an often underrated component of the Northern Ireland political scene. Radical Protestantism is a crucial element in ethnic identity, even if not more than
15 per cent of the population actually adhere to its theological tenets (Bruce
1994:22, 25–31). It is in that sense that the Northern Ireland conflict is a religious
one.[11] Failure to appreciate the strength of religious identification as a source of
ethnic bonding helps perpetuate a widespread tendency of which Bruce, with
some justice, complains:

much Irish nationalist and left-wing thinking about Ireland . . . takes it for granted that
one form of ethnicity and nationalism—Irishness—is natural and inevitable but makes
the competing form of Protestant unionism accidental and temporary . . . Protestant
ethnicity is described as merely a product of British imperial manipulation.

As the British government has apparently increasingly distanced itself from support for the Union, the ideology of Britishness among Protestants has been thrown into crisis:

For many Protestants in Northern Ireland, Ulster loyalism has displaced the Ulster Britishness which was common prior to the present conflict ... Ulster Protestants have had to contemplate the possibility of a future on their own, and the result of that contemplation has not been the one desired by Irish nationalists: recognizing that they are really Irish. Instead Protestants have come increasingly to see themselves as 'Ulster' people. Though independence remains the preferred option of only a small minority, it is the second best of almost every unionist. (Bruce 1994:30)[12]

Where Bruce is most clearly accurate is in emphasising the centrality of religion to most varieties of Ulster Protestant identity. If senses of nationality and ethnicity are loosely articulated and shifting, religious identification appears more clear-cut as a basis for identity in Northern Ireland. As the Opsahl Commissioners agreed, 'For many Protestants, religion is a far more important element in defining their identity than their "unionism" or "Britishness". Their attitudes to the Republic of Ireland are explained almost entirely in religious terms: Catholicism is seen not just as a religion, but as a threatening political system with international dimensions.' (Pollak ed. 1993:96; see also Morrow 1997) Certainly Northern Ireland stands high in the European league table of religious observance—though in fact church attendance and other indicators of active faith are considerably higher among Catholics than Protestants (McGarry and O'Leary 1995:173–5 summarise the data). Bruce's contention that evangelical Protestantism—which he identifies in its turn closely with 'Paisleyism'—represents a (if not the) core element of Unionist political identity, has however been much criticised (e.g. Colin Coulter 1994:6–8). Even if it were true, naturally it would not necessarily follow that religious belief as such can meaningfully be said to be the cause of conflict in Ireland.

(ii) Gateway, Bastion or Ruin? Colonial Rhetorics and Their Decline

> for we have rights drawn from the soil and sky;
> the use, the pace, the patient years of labour,
> the rain against the lips, the changing light,
> the heavy clay-sucked stride, have altered us;
> we would be strangers in the Capitol;
> this is our country also, nowhere else;
> and we shall not be outcast on the world.
>
> John Hewitt: 'The Colony' (1991:79)

How far, if at all, has Unionist popular consciousness seen itself as colonial, identified with the British Empire or with 'settler' populations elsewhere? The questions remain both controversial and clouded, with clear answers made elusive both by the dearth of serious research, and by the conceptual vagueness of much of what has been written on the subject. Recent Unionist self-presentations—and to a degree the activities of official bodies such as the Northern Ireland Tourist Board—have emphasised the role of Ulster people in building American democracy, and conversely made very little if any reference to their part in expanding and maintaining the British Empire.[13] Affirmative invocations of an Imperial past, and even laments at Empire's passing, may indeed occasionally still be found in Unionist publications—mainly those of the more Conservative organisations such as the UUP and the Orange Order—but little differentiates these from similar intermittent panegyrics in, for instance, the London *Daily Telegraph*. And when the *Orange Standard*, reacting to the *Satanic Verses* controversy, commented with apparent surprise that: 'To learn that there are one million Muslims in Britain is very revealing, if not frightening' the racist-sounding remark was immediately followed by clear acknowledgement of Muslims' positive contribution to British life ('Comment' (unsigned), March 1989).

Colonial imagery or analogies have rarely featured in modern Unionist litera-ture. Even when the Queen's University Unionist Association produced a pamph-let resoundingly entitled *Ulster—the Internal Colony* the authors (including David Trimble) made no historical or comparative argument. Rather, the aim of the 'colonial' label was simply to highlight the lack of democracy involved in Direct Rule as the basis for demanding a revived Stormont-style Northern Ire-land government. (Gavin Adams *et al.* 1989) Some other Unionist writers have also described Northern Ireland's status as 'colonial' (see Clayton 1996:123–4, 160–91), and expressed mounting bitterness at the diminution of status and autonomy which Direct Rule imposed on them. The usual response, however, has not been to explore further the possible parallels with 'colonial' rule elsewhere, but simply, indignantly to insist on its unacceptability to Ulster Unionists.

The most extended Unionist examination of colonial analogies was Hugh Roberts's polemic against comparing Northern Ireland with France's war of decolonisation in Algeria (Roberts 1986). Roberts's main target and the stimu-lus for his intervention was a seemingly rather ephemeral one: a brief, journal-istic *New Society* article by R. W. Johnson (reprinted in Johnson 1985). Johnson, an academic specialist successively in the affairs of Francophone West Africa, of France and of South Africa—but not Ireland—had essayed the Algerian ana-logy (he was hardly the first to do so: cf. Michael Farrell 1974, among others) by way of urging the need for British statesmen to show the knot-cutting 'courage' of De Gaulle and announce British withdrawal from Northern Ireland. Nat-urally, this outraged Roberts, who brought a disproportionately massive weight of historical and theoretical artillery to bear in sinking Johnson's frail little craft.

Elsewhere and more recently, some Unionist writers have begun to employ the rhetoric of opposition to 'cultural imperialism' to dramatise their fears of being taken over by a Catholic Republic. Thus Arthur Aughey deplores what he describes as Irish nationalism's 'pervasive notion of general cultural superiority' and charges that for such northern nationalist figures as novelist Ronan Bennett and artist Robert Ballagh 'culture' as such is simply equated with cultural nationalism and indeed with a monolithic, blinkered nativism (Aughey 1995b:7, 13).

In comparison with settler-colonial politics elsewhere, Irish Protestant ideologies have been marked by the absence or weakness of themes which in such contexts as southern Africa and North America have been central to settler self-perceptions. There is no fully articulated racial ideology: the discourse of race, although it gained a certain presence in the late nineteenth century (at a time when it was becoming ubiquitous in the Anglophone world) failed to sustain itself, and it is not clear that it was ever more salient in Irish Unionist discourses than it was either in metropolitan British or in Irish nationalist ones. Even weaker, perhaps, was a specific frontier ideology: it is questionable whether one can speak at any stage in Irish history of a definable 'frontier of colonial settlement' on the north American or southern African model (neither the borders of the early-modern Pale nor those of the Ulster plantations really fit the bill).[14] Certainly no 'frontier tradition' of historiography can be discerned in Ireland comparable to that famously proposed by Frederick Jackson Turner for the USA and adapted for Africa by Martin Legassick (1980) and others.

Unionists in the late nineteenth and early twentieth centuries were clearly keen to celebrate the Empire, and as Alvin Jackson notes were 'bombarded at every stage in their lives and in every sphere of their activity with the image of Empire' (1996b:143). The 1899 Anglo-Boer War was, it seems, a watershed in Unionist political consciousness, just as we have seen it to have been for many Nationalists: but with very different results. The war, in which generals of Ulster Protestant origin played many prominent roles, brought Protestants' British and Imperial patriotism into sharper focus, in Jackson's view. (ibid: 131–5)[15] James Loughlin too emphasises a turn-of-the-century picture of Unionist politicians' and Ulster local newspapers' pro-imperialism, their bitter attacks on Liberals' less bellicose foreign policy, their anti-alienism (and some anti-semitism), and fervent support for the Boer War (1995:30–3). He disagrees, however, with Alvin Jackson's view (e.g. his 1989:120) that Ulster Unionists' pro-imperialism was largely tactical or parochial.

It is not clear, however, whether this propaganda bombardment and popular responses to it were more intense among Ulster Unionists than in England or Scotland during what was, quite generally, a period of intense pro-imperial public expression. Among Unionist politicians, in Jackson's view, fervent expressions of faith in the Imperial mission were not matched by action; they 'frequently demonstrated that their true political priorities had little to do with the future security of the Empire.' (ibid: 124) As we have seen, subsequent Unionist self-presentations and images of history, from the publications of the Orange Order to those of the Northern Ireland Tourist Board, have made very little reference to specifically imperial themes. Graham Walker suggests that, far from pro-imperial rhetoric having an especially powerful appeal in Ulster, it was on the whole weaker and more 'passive' there than in Scotland. For many Scots, participation in British empire-building was an important source of pride on many levels from military prowess to missionary endeavour. Theirs was an 'active and crusading' conception of empire: whereas in Ulster it was a fixed part of one's inheritance.[16] Ulster Unionist politicians played very little part in wider debates on the future of empire (Graham Walker 1994:104). Scottish identification with the Empire was expansive, while Ulster's was defensive. It must be added, however, that Walker offers very little documentary evidence in support of this interpretation.

Donal Lowry has sought to trace the degree to which Ulster Unionists have drawn parallels between their situation and that of British-descended settlers elsewhere, especially those involved in conflict with local anticolonial nationalists or with the British government itself. He finds that expressions of solidarity, identification of shared situations and values between Ulster Protestants and South African Anglophone whites, Rhodesian and Kenyan settlers were common—and manifested in both directions—from the 1900s to the inter-war years (Lowry 1996a:192–201). More recently he, like Clayton, discerns substantial support among Unionists for the Rhodesian settlers' 1960s revolt and Unilateral Declaration of Independence, as well as identifying strong similarities in the position of the two groups. The Unionist admirers of Ian Smith whom he cites, however, are predominantly from the more extreme Loyalist currents— statements by William Craig's shortlived Vanguard and by figures like Roy Bradford, articles from the Paisleyite *Protestant Telegraph*—rather than the mainstream of Unionism (ibid: 205–8). Lowry's arguments should, in addition, be viewed in the light of his general assessment of Ulster Unionist beliefs: 'Set in an imperial rather than a domestic context the paradoxes of Ulster's loyalist rebellions seem typical rather than strange. Ulster's Britishness was and remains primarily an imperial, not a metropolitan variety of Britishness.' (ibid: 208–9) He sees strong affinities and links also between Loyalism and South African racial supremacism. This is, naturally, a highly contentious judgement whose terms few other analysts of Unionism seem to support.

Pamela Clayton (1996) has produced the most extended argument that Unionism is, and frequently knows itself to be, a settler-colonial ideology. Her evidence, however, comes almost entirely from a selective survey of published readers' letters in various Northern Ireland newspapers—hardly a clear or systematic indicator of general popular opinion—whilst the quotations which most strongly support her case come mainly from a very small number of habitual correspondents. Dividing Unionist attitudes crudely between two categories of 'ultras' and 'moderates', she asserts repeatedly that the former are in fact the majority: an odd procedure, since both her specific source for this division, the work of Richard Rose (1971), and the normal usage of such terminology, takes the category of the 'ultra' to be by definition a minority stance.

The comparative and theoretical framework on which Clayton relies, too, is both sketchy and schematic; she takes no account of much of the most important relevant work, never for instance referring to Frank Wright's major comparative study. Asserting that Ireland has been neglected in literature on settler colonialism—and vice versa—and even calling this an 'apparent conspiracy of silence' (24) she merely reveals the limitations of her own knowledge, failing to note the writings of Nicholas Canny, Toby Barnard, Sean Connolly, Aidan Clarke and many others. Her own claims are peremptory and categorical: 'It would be an extraordinary perversion [!] to deny that Ireland's history has been colonial at least since the time of Elizabeth I.' (25) But they also sometimes betray a peculiar ambivalence. The central thrust of her argument is that Protestants *are* a settler-colonial enclave, but in places she says instead that they are *like* one in some major respects (e.g. 82–3). Protestant attitudes to Catholics are unproblematically assimilated to the concept of racism (50–83), though she acknowledges that there has latterly been a muting in the overt expression of such attitudes. She emphasises the sympathy some Unionists expressed with white minorities in Rhodesia and South Africa, though again without any indication of how widely shared were the views she cites (40–3, 45–6).[17] Although recognising change over time, her conclusions one-sidedly emphasise the alleged 'ideological fixity', and 'persistence' of settler beliefs (232). In Northern Ireland, as in Algeria or Rhodesia, 'the settler mentality has displayed greater durability than the empire which spawned it.' (227)

A very different model of Unionist political culture, and the most influential of all among subsequent analysts, is that proposed by David W. Miller (1978). Unionism is, he argues, not best understood in terms of nationality—or ethnicity, religion, or empire—at all. Rather, Ulster Protestants adhere to a pre-nationalist—and in British contexts pre-imperial—contractarian ideology, involving allegiance to a sovereign who repays by offering physical protection against enemies, rather than to the symbolism and discourse of nationhood. Such an analysis, if true, would certainly explain the ambivalent and shifting historical coexistence among Unionists of 'British' and 'Irish' identities—since this community did not primarily conceive of itself in national terms—as well as the propensity of loyalists in recent years to rebel against the very government to which they proclaim loyalty. This phenomenon, which has so puzzled journalistic observers of loyalist protests from the 1912 armed mobilisation, through the 1974 Ulster Workers' Council strikes, to anger over the 1993 Downing Street

Declaration, is readily explicable in terms of contractarian ideology's insistence on the right of subjects to rebel if the sovereign breaks its side of the contract by failing fully to protect them. Broadly, this view is supported by Alvin Jackson (1989); though as we have seen Jackson has also come to emphasise the poverty of historical imagination on which he believes loyalist ideology has been based. Miller's view that this lack of a clear-cut sense of nationality made it an anachronism or aberration in the modern world was, however, naturally contested by Unionist intellectuals: contractual or conditional loyalty, they pointed out, was a far more widespread phenomenon in the modern world than Miller seemed to claim. Indeed the apparent presumption that *un*conditional loyalty to the state was more normal, modern and rational was highly contestable; while it might also be suggested both that conditional loyalty was a sensible pragmatic response to Ireland's and later Northern Ireland's precarious status within the United Kingdom, and more generally that contractarianism may be the typical *form* of Unionist beliefs, but focus on it tells us nothing about their ideological *substance*.[18]

James Loughlin, by contrast, attacks both Miller's ideas of conditional/contractarian loyalty (in his view these syndromes certainly existed, but were not central to Ulster Unionist discourse (Loughlin 1995:33–7; see also his 1986:154–8)) and Alvin Jackson's claim that a separate 'Ulster patriotism' was forged early—or at all. Loughlin asserts that while it could be argued that Ulster Unionists 'can be defined as an ethnic *group*' (1995:33; his emphasis; see also the further criticisms of Jackson in ibid: 61–2), they clearly were not an 'ethnic nationality', and did not define themselves as such. There was very little collective sentiment on these lines: 'Certainly there is nothing either in the loyalist speeches against Home Rule in this period, or in their pamphlet literature, to suggest an alienation from British identity.' (1995:35) The localism of much Ulster political language in the era proves nothing, in Loughlin's view, for, as many studies of pre-1914 British politics show, local and regional distinctiveness was ubiquitous in English Scottish and Welsh debates too.

Rather there was for Ulster Unionists, so Loughlin believes, a very close relationship between national identity and constitutionalism: 'for Ulster Unionists, the Act of Union was their cornerstone of the British constitution, one that guaranteed, not only freedom from oppression by Catholic Nationalists, but the means by which they could legitimately identify themselves as British—the terms "British" and "English" being virtually interchangeable in this period.' (1995:26–7)[19] Again, the link with any specifically colonial belief-system is tenuous. Constitutionalism of this type was not a strong feature of the political beliefs of British settler communities anywhere in the overseas Empire, whether in Canada, Australia, and New Zealand where they were majorities, nor in South Africa, Rhodesia or Kenya where they were increasingly embattled minorities (see, for instance, Dane Kennedy 1987, Trainor 1994).

Social contract theory in general has been usually, though by no means exclusively, linked to the emergence of liberalism; and undoubtedly perceptions of themselves as upholding liberal values, as opposed to the supposed authoritarianism of Catholic culture, have been important to Ulster Protestants' self-image. The claim that Protestant preference for the Union had its origin in ideas of defending individual liberty and notions of progress is emphasised in the Field Day pamphlets of Marianne Elliott (1985: also in Field Day 1991:III) and, more sceptically, of Terence Brown (1985b). The more contentious notion that this liberal and progressive ethos remains central to Unionism today is upheld by writers like Arthur Aughey (1989, 1991, 1995a), John Wilson Foster (ed. 1995), and in part by Steve Bruce (1986). Some brought up in the Unionist tradition may even regard the very invocation of such ideas as 'Protestant privilege', let alone 'Protestant supremacy' as 'inaccurate or inappropriate and, moreover, decidedly unhelpful in negotiating a way through the political impasse.' (Graham Walker 1992a:65) Aughey urges that, by contrast, Unionists should be conceptualised not as a dominant majority in Northern Ireland but as a threatened one within the whole United Kingdom, and suggests with tongue only partly in cheek that from such a perspective: 'They might even become politically correct.' (1995a:15)

Identification with contemporary liberalism, and even multicultural theory, has grown in Unionist self-presentations.[20] The increasingly influential argument is that Unionism is a doctrine more appropriate to the end of the twentieth century than is Irish nationalism, even if not an intrinsically superior one irrespective of context (though evidently many Unionists proclaim or believe the latter too). This is because it is—supposedly—in essence a secular, modernist creed, and one which relates to citizenship and statehood rather than nationality. As Aughey puts it: 'Unionism is a very pure political doctrine in the sense that it is concerned, almost exclusively, with issues of rights and citizenship.' This differentiates it sharply from Irish nationalism which is allegedly 'fully exercised by the issue of identity, with degrees of nationhood defined in cultural rather than political terms.' (1991:15) Unionism's identification with the United Kingdom does not, therefore, involve—or *necessarily* involve—a claim about nationhood, but one about what kind of state one prefers to live under. The United Kingdom is seen as multinational, multicultural, secular, whereas the Irish Republic allegedly remains tied to backward-looking, ethnically, culturally and/or religiously exclusivist doctrines—it is essentially a monocultural state and society. Unionism, therefore, is a more generously inclusive ideology than Irish nationalism; whatever the traits of sectarianism or triumphalism which, so most liberal Unionists will admit, have marred it in the past. It is also a more genuinely democratic ideology—for as Alan Finlayson notes, however much non-Unionists have doubted its democratic credentials, Unionist discourse itself, in all its varieties, constantly invokes appeals to democratic values (Finlayson 1997b:84–7).

There is much to doubt in this version of Unionism. Its view of the United Kingdom verges on the utopian; and idealised images of particular contemporary state forms may carry dangers analogous to those involved in idealising national pasts. The UK is not, in fact, a fully secular state: it still has an established Church, whose role in constitutional, educational and other affairs is more than purely vestigial. It can only be called fully multicultural by ignoring the clearly documented facts of continued racial inequality and discrimination. And its multinationality has not, to say the least, been given full institutional expression, since there has been no democratic form of Scottish, Welsh or regional self-government. It is, indeed, the most heavily centralised state of its size in the democratic world: a position only now, at the time of writing in 1999, being altered by the devolutionary reforms of the Blair government. Conversely, the Unionist view of the Irish Republic is clearly in important respects unfair and outdated. Although it is 'monocultural' in the sense of being religiously and 'racially' far less diverse than the UK, and although the Catholic Church still has an entrenched role in its constitution, its protection of individual and minority rights is in some clear ways stronger than the UK's, and religious minorities have played probably a larger proportional public role in Ireland than in Britain. For instance, it remains constitutionally impossible for the UK's Head of State to be a Catholic or other non-Anglican, whereas the Republic's first Head of State was a Protestant. It must also be said that some manifestations of liberal 'New Unionism' in the 1990s have not, in fact, appeared very liberal: anti-Catholic sentiments and crude scorn for the Irish Republic are not far beneath the surface even of Robert McCartney's rhetoric, while the self-proclaimed modernisation of the UUP under David Trimble has appeared to leave a substratum of deeply prejudiced attitudes unchanged.[21] If such an avowedly non-nationalist reinterpretation of the past is to have the benign political consequences claimed for it, it requires much harder thinking about what citizenship means than has yet been in evidence—though Norman Porter's *Rethinking Unionism* (1996) offers important steps in that direction, with its prescription for a 'civic unionism' that is both more theoretically sophisticated and more determinedly inclusive than is apparent anywhere else in this literature.

For some more traditional kinds of Unionist, by contrast, it is precisely the most archaic and undemocratic features of the UK state which are the object of their loyalty. The Rev. Robert Dickinson, in a submission to the Opsahl Commission, presents this stance very clearly:

Unionists owe allegiance not to a particular shade of political government but to the monarch as head of the state. Moreover, they see the monarch under the British Constitution not only as the supreme ruler by whose decree and under whose authority all others govern, but also as being charged with the preservation of the Protestant succession to the throne. (Pollak ed. 1993:196)

An explicit and aggressive rejection of liberal pluralism can naturally be found in some such circles. Thus during the bicentennial of the 1688 'Glorious Revolution' Orange Order Grand Master the Rev. Martin Smyth MP could be encountered charging that liberals and secularists had entirely mistaken the meaning of that struggle:

Others captivated by the mythology of secular humanism and the supporters of a so-called pluralistic society would accuse those who re-emphasise our Nation's Protestant heritage of bigotry.

If they stopped to think, they would realise that the toleration William brought to the nation stemmed from the ideals of Biblical Protestantism. And a nation cannot be bound together by the chimera of pluralism. That which united a nation was the mortar of Protestantism. (*Orange Standard* February 1988).

As the Rev. Dickinson's remarks suggest, a special regard for the institution of Monarchy, and for the British royal family, has often been seen as especially central to Unionist beliefs, especially in such conservative and middle-class circles (see Hennessey 1996, Loughlin 1995:40–5, 65–6, 89–90, 11–15, 136–8, 149–52, 163–7, 205–7, 222–4). Liam de Paor has even suggested that the most significant barrier to Irish unification might yet prove to be the division between royalist and republican worldviews—republican in the international sense of being opposed to the principle of hereditary rule, that is, rather than the special Irish meaning of the term (1990:158–9). It is less clear, however, whether Ulster monarchism has been historically more intense than, or significantly different in character from, that of Britain—except perhaps in the sense that Unionist politicians have been able to make tactical use of it, proclaiming their loyalty to the Crown as something transcending the less abiding claims to legitimacy of other features of the United Kingdom's constitution, such as the principle of the parliamentary majority. Intriguingly, most of Feargal Cochrane's interviewees (1997) insisted that their Unionism or Loyalism would not be shaken if the UK ceased to be a formally Protestant state or even became a republic. Once again, there seems no reason to interpret Unionist monarchism as having particular imperial or colonial features. Although the British monarchy was quite consciously 'imperialised'—and conversely, imperial imagery 'royalised'—in the last decades of the nineteenth century, and although this clearly had an impact in Ireland as elsewhere (this was, for instance, apparently the point at which specifically imperial images of royalty began to appear on Orange banners), that structure of representations was equally deliberately dismantled after the 1950s and a new, domesticated monarchy depicted instead. There seems little basis for supposing that the transformation was differently presented or received in Northern Ireland from the way it was in England: Ulster, after all, received largely the same TV and tabloid press images of royalty as did the rest of the UK. It would also be hard to argue that in recent decades (or, perhaps, at any time) a specifically settler-colonial set of attitudes to monarchy arose in British colonies and former colonies. 'Loyalty to the Crown' played no major part in the rhetorics of revolt against Westminster deployed by white settlers in Rhodesia or Kenya. Nor does it seem plausible to suggest—though close comparative investigation is as yet lacking—that enthusiasm for royalty has remained generally greater among overseas settlers of British descent than it has within Britain: that monarchism has remained central to the political beliefs, for instance, of British-descended South Africans or Canadians. If anything, surely, the reverse would seem to be the case, as the strength of popular republicanism in Australia and New Zealand suggests.

Undoubtedly, northern Protestant self-images have involved expressions of a 'superiority complex' *vis-à-vis* Catholics and southerners. Qualities of industriousness, independence of spirit, rationality, civic-mindedness and so on, supposedly held dear by Unionists, have frequently been contrasted to alleged Irish Catholic deficiency in these virtues. Such perceptions have a long history, and have by no means always only been expressed from within the community thus praised. There could be no more striking, or extreme, version of it than the writings, around the turn of the century, of the then-celebrated southern Catholic anticlerical campaigner Michael McCarthy, who in a series of lectures contrasted the 'characters' of north and south to the systematic discredit of the latter (M. McCarthy 1904 esp. chs 4–7). McCarthy's purpose, to be sure, was not so much to flatter his northern audiences (though evidently he won wide applause among them for so doing) as to use an idealised image of their qualities as a stick with which to beat the Catholic hierarchy and uphold the secularist, rationalist values with which he exaggeratedly associated Irish Protestantism. For him the 'universal cause of the superiority of North over South in Ireland' (ibid: 144) was to be found in the weaker hold theocracy held over the former.[22] Despite uneven but often genuine liberalisation and modernisation, such attitudes have by no means disappeared: many northern Protestants still seemingly conceive of their community as especially strongly imbued with the work ethic, and see southerners and/or Catholics as lacking it.

Some Ulster writers, however, challenged such stereotypes head on. St John Ervine (1883–1971), brought up in Belfast though resident for much of his adult life in London, was an intriguing instance.[23] Ervine, who as a young man was a socialist and a Home Ruler but after 1918 became increasingly sympathetic to Ulster Unionism and wrote, among numerous other works, a semi-official biography of Lord Craigavon, insisted still in his 1915 book *Sir Edward Carson and the Ulster Movement* that he, and the Ulster people, are unhyphenatedly Irish: 'There appears to me, who am a member of an Ulster Protestant family, as great a difference between a Manchester Dissenter and a Tunbridge Wells Anglican as there is between a Belfast Protestant and a Cork Catholic. There is certainly as much bitter feeling: in some instances, there is more . . . I doubt whether Catholics and Protestants in Ireland, generally speaking, feel as antagonistic towards each other as Low Churchmen feel towards High Churchmen, or vice versa, in England.' (Ervine 1915:13–14) Ervine was an early protestor against 'two nations' theories: 'The first of the many illusions held about Ireland by English people which must be dispelled is that there are two nations in Ireland'. (ibid: 16) He was especially concerned to dispel the myth of a clear division in character types, between sober, practical, industrious Ulster folk and feckless southerners or Catholics. Strikingly, however, three decades later in his biography of Craigavon Ervine was to reproduce the very same stereotypes and the same perception of a fundamental psychological and cultural division between north and south, against which he had earlier protested. Indeed he did so with such intemperate zeal that, apparently, even Lady Craigavon was upset by it. (Maume 1996:75)

All such arguments over a putative Ulster discourse not only of distinctiveness but of superiority, whether mounted by Unionists themselves or critical scholars, may be accused of a certain one-dimensionality. Another influential analysis, that of Jennifer Todd, proposes that such questions as whether Unionist culture is supremacist cannot be answered in a simple 'either/or' fashion. This is because Northern Irish Protestants have adhered to two distinct ideologies, which Todd calls Ulster loyalist and Ulster British. The first, heavily influenced by radical, evangelical Presbyterianism, tends strongly towards exclusion and intolerance (Todd 1987:5). It is also distinctly and indigenously northern Irish: such close relatives as it may have had within Britain have (with the marginal exception of a few declining sectarian enclaves, especially in western Scotland) long since lost their political force. This is the ideology sometimes described as 'Paisleyism', and certainly Ian Paisley and the DUP have often exhibited the characteristics Todd describes. The other ideology, the Ulster British, is more liberal and tolerant, at least in its self-image. It stresses attachment to traditionally 'British values', including democracy, hard work, fair play, freedom of conscience, and progress. It may be anti-Catholic insofar as Catholics are stereotyped as lacking such values and even threatening their preservation amongst Protestants—but it is not inherently incompatible with self-identification as Irish (ibid: 16), and it is at least rhetorically hostile to sectarianism (19).

Steve Bruce, in the most detailed investigation of Paisleyite ideology (Bruce 1986) broadly concurs with Todd's view, and also strongly emphasises the specifically religious roots and the sense of embattled identity of this tradition. He has further suggested (1994:70–1) that to a considerable and perhaps increasing degree the distinction between the two ideologies corresponds to class differentials. Middle-class people have a more 'British', and even European, perspective, not least because they tend to have transferable skills and often overseas educational or work experience.

But the working classes, the small farmers, the small business men, they have nowhere else to go. Their identity and their sense of self-worth are firmly located in the history and geography of Northern Ireland. If they move to England or Scotland to work, as many do, far from carrying their high status as loyal diligent citizens of the power house of the British Empire, they are seen as humourless bigots, or worse, they are taken for 'Paddies' (Bruce 1994:70–1).

As Brendan O'Leary and John McGarry argue, drawing on Todd's ideas—in a work whose basic assumptions are in fact very hostile to the Unionist case—it is thus at best simplistic and misleading to see Ulster Protestant political culture as being entirely formed by a colonialist ideology premised on the necessity of domination:

[T]here is not just one homogeneous Ulster Protestant identity based on colonial domination of Catholics. There are at least two traditions . . . One of these, Ulster loyalist ideology, is a settler-ideology, but the other, Ulster British ideology, professes liberal political values which *prima facie* refute it. A purely colonial reading of unionist political culture requires us to discount Ulster Protestants' expressed fears in favour of external, reductionist, and imputed conceptions of their core identity. The . . . development and sustenance of the fears of Ulster Protestants is comprehensible without recourse to a historicist and essentialist conception of their identity. (1993:141)

It might still be, though, that a more properly historical analysis, seeking to trace the ways in which Northern Irish society and the roots of conflict have been shaped by legacies of a settler-colonial past, has major explanatory force. This is the approach taken by a number of modern scholars, but most powerfully and in most detail by the late Frank Wright.

Among the merits of Wright's analysis is that, in place of the simple affirmation or dismissal of settler-colonial models which we have been seeing, it puts the colonial features of Ulster's past in their proper historical setting, showing both the importance of those features for understanding the present, and their explanatory limits. As he argued in an early essay: 'If Northern Ireland were a settler colony and the ethnic division characterised by an absolute opposition of economic interests, it would have to be admitted that drastic solutions, such as the removal of settlers, would be the only possible ones. But Northern Ireland, although having some of the features of a settler colony, is not one, and most of the moral and political ambiguities that flaw everything which passes for "solutions" arise from the existence of these limited features in the absence of the settler colonial substance.' (Wright 1981:154)

Wright's central argument is that from the seventeenth century the Catholic population, rather than being segregated and subordinated within a settler economy, became largely marginalised. It was possible, he suggests, for Ulster employers to practise sectarian exclusivism in recruiting their workforces precisely *because* there was little if any difference in expectations about wage-rates or conditions of employment between the communities. Thus there was little incentive for them to resist 'populist' Protestant demands for preference in employment. Catholics—unlike, for instance, blacks in South Africa—were not a distinctive low-wage labour pool subject to special legal restrictions, and had not been so at least since the abolition of the Penal Laws (1981:165). As Wright argues:

the most important feature of any settler colonial structure which has maintained its integrity is the separation of status between the settler and the native, which permits the subordination of the native to a special labour code and creates areas of economic life which are reserved to the settler and within which he [sic] is free from low wage competition from native labour . . . On this definition Ulster has not been a settler colony for at least the last century and a half. But having evolved out of a structure that has had some of these features the marks of that past have remained deeply ingrained. (Wright 1981:161)

The decay of the settlement colonial structures, already far advanced by the early nineteenth century, and the gradual extension of the franchise which made relative Catholic-Protestant numbers ever more important, opened the way to two contradictory possibilities. On the one hand was 'an opportunity for workplace solidarity between workers of all denominations on a basis of equal pay for equal work' which would lead to a fading of antagonism. Or 'it might mean that conflict over places and spaces simply became more reciprocal and equal. In this case the decay of the economic substance of colonization might leave behind a more unlimited battle between two sectarian blocs which were actually becoming more and more alike.' (1996:11)[24] The first possibility was never entirely foreclosed. It was strenuously fought for by successive generations of liberals, labourists and socialists. At various points they—and their subsequent, sympathetic chroniclers—believed they could win. But in the long run, clearly enough, it was the second alternative, of reciprocal, ambient conflict, which prevailed.

In his last work before his tragically early death, Wright traced the political history of Ulster from the United Irishmen's rebellion to the onset of the Home Rule crisis in the 1880s. Embedded in the detailed historical narrative was a more general interpretive argument, of an important and provocative kind. He suggested that previous writers on the North of Ireland's nineteenth-century evolution had neglected or underrated inter-communal relations in the region itself: they had tended either to focus on the conflict between London and southern Irish nationalism, or to study Ulster's Unionist or (less often) Nationalist politics in a virtual vacuum. Even where the local politics of northern Ireland had been closely studied, the 'relationships of different sectarian groups to state power and to each other' (1996:2) had been neglected—sometimes because, as with the early work of Peter Gibbon (1975), sectarian divisions were wrongly dissolved into ones of social class. In other cases, as with A. T. Q. Stewart and David W. Miller, Protestant perceptions were looked at in abstraction from the actual relationships with the Catholic community.

Economic differences were—and are—'on their own quite insufficient to explain the primacy of the sectarian relationship', Wright believed (1996:3). The central fact in accounting for the continuity over time of northern Irish conflict is, with deceptive simplicity, *fear*. It has been embodied in a persisting but shifting 'deterrence relationship' between communities.[25] Sectarian, non-state violence from one's 'own' side came to be seen as a guarantor of one's security; that from the other side as an existential threat. People living in more 'normal' societies, ones which are not national or ethnic frontiers, says Wright, often find the consequences difficult to understand—'unless they themselves have experienced fascism in the metropolis.' (510) Most of us live in circumstances of 'bourgeois order', where acts of violence are almost always seen as being the behaviour of an individual against another, and where the culprit is socially and morally isolated. On an ethnic frontier, conversely, the perpetrator of violence is liable to be seen as representative of their community, as is the victim: 'people tend to judge "them" by their worst representatives. This is not just bigotry; it is sometimes pessimistic common sense.' (7) The motto of Northern Irish politics thus becomes: Tell me who and what you fear, and I will tell you who you are.

Thus for Wright, attitudes and social structures inherited from Ulster's settlement colonial era remained important, but it is misleading to attribute the character of the conflict to them. The colonial structures had rested on pillars not only of economic inequality but of legal control—the Penal Laws. Removal of the control system was gradual and uneasy. Protestants could only feel comfortable with it so long as they themselves could 'control the process of decontrol.' (17) During most of the eighteenth century, and in some respects still in the 1830s, this was broadly the case. It was mostly Protestant sympathisers with Catholic grievances—the Patriots, the Volunteers, the first incarnation of the United Irishmen, and later Whig politicians in London—who directed the campaigns for abolition of the Penal Laws, for Catholic political rights and self-government, not Catholics themselves. Indeed the viability of the process was dependent on Catholic elites (above all the Church hierarchy) abstaining from political activism which would involve Catholics publicly defining their own goals. That condition too eroded as the nineteenth century progressed. With the extension of democracy and the rise of pan-Catholic nationalist assertion in the rest of Ireland—the crucial turning point being O'Connell's movement—northern Protestant liberalism was increasingly embattled. Given the inherited, if sometimes latent, structure of fear and communal deterrence, the actions of even small minorities of anti-Catholic extremists could then precipitate a spiral of breakdown. And the longer the delay in grasping the nettle of structural reform, of constructing a 'compact' between communities, the greater were these dangers of breakdown. If Protestant radicals succumbed to their fears of Catholic self-organisation rather than allying with it then, ironically, the more time passed the more substance those fears would acquire. Wolfe Tone in the 1790s was, in Wright's view, almost unique in grasping this point and seeking to act on it (1996:18, 42–6).

Thus extremely localised groups of sectarian rioters, or bigoted preachers like Hugh Hanna, could have a disproportionate and disastrous wider impact. Decay of the settlement structures here, as elsewhere, did not generate solidarity between descendants of natives and of settlers (to view the United Irishmen as a full-fledged moment of such solidarity is simplistic if not utopian, even if it was indeed the most hopeful and even noble effort toward it in Ulster's modern history) but rather a paternalistic relationship between dominant classes—above all landlords—and natives. Such a relationship was always open to two threats: from populist or plebeian mobilisation within the Protestant communities, and from Catholic assertion. Faced with such destabilising dual threats, the least dangerous option for the rulers is liable to be that of rebuilding their relationship with lower-class Protestants, even if this means jettisoning that with Catholics and playing along with militant and even violent pan-Protestant elements. Broadly, this is what happened in Ulster in recurrent and intensifying moments of crisis.

Ulster Protestant liberalism was not, however, dead: in Wright's view, its 'climax' came at the start of the 1880s, when it was mainly successful in preventing the issue of agrarian reform becoming a sectarian one (1996:432–75). It could still be argued that decisive polarisation into clearly defined national-religious blocs took place only with the mid-1880s Home Rule crisis and the general elections of 1885 and 1886 (as suggested by Brian Walker 1989), but in important ways the dividing lines had already been 'nationalised'. In Ireland as elsewhere in western Europe, the decades following the French Revolution witnessed a vital shift in the understanding of nationhood, from geographical to politico-cultural—what many historians have seen as the birth of modern political nationalism as such. As Wright argues:

In 1798, being Irish had meant living in the place called Ireland. It was a fact about which institutional jurisdiction you lived under . . . The rise of culture-based (which is to say education system-based) nationalisms changed the meaning of nationality into something like the belonging together of a people with the same educational culture. (1996:49)

The bitterness of conflict in Ulster over education itself was the clearest local instance of this, with the growing gulf between liberal Protestants and Catholics evident in the former's opposition to denominational education: a stance which was inevitably perceived as anti-Catholic, even in Wright's words 'the intellectual equivalent of an Orange arch.' (474) Ulster, then, was different from most

ethnic frontier regions in that religion rather than language became the main
marker of national division: but as in other such regions, control over education
became the crucial early battleground.

But there was an ironic twist to this. Wright suggests that whereas Catholics
increasingly thought in these culturalist terms, to the point of seeing Catholicism and Irishness as synonyms, most Protestants did not make the change.
They 'continued to think of themselves as Irish, because for them it remained a
geographical association and not a cultural badge.' (1996:50) On this view, it
might be thought that the rather rapid abandonment of the designation 'Irish'
as a self-description among northern Protestants in the late twentieth century
was a belated coming into line with shifts that had happened elsewhere, including among Irish Catholics, up to 150 years earlier. It would also imply that
analysts like David W. Miller, in viewing Unionist beliefs as falling outside
the categories of modern nationalism, have caught an important reality but
misdescribed it. Unionist ideas about identity are not best seen as belonging
to a contractarian ideology quite distinct from beliefs about nationhood:
rather, they are the debris of an older, pre-French Revolution, conception of
nationality.

It was also one in which religious identity retained a centrality to ideas of
nationhood which it was losing elsewhere—the association declining with particular rapidity in mainland Britain itself. Thus while, in the course of the nineteenth century, the north of Ireland became ever more like Britain (and in some
regards more unlike the rest of Ireland) economically, cultural patterns were
diverging rather than converging.

Once upon a time Protestant cultural values had been norms throughout the UK. But as
the modern state became the centre of authority, the role of the Churches declined.
When the cultural values of Church-centred living were losing their importance in the
metropolis altogether, these same values were being transformed into the (British)
national ideology on the frontier. (Wright 1966:512)[26]

Well into the nineteenth century, indeed, aggressive anti-Catholicism remained
a normal part of those cultural values in England and Scotland, as in North
America. In those contexts, though, it did not become—or fairly soon ceased to
be—intertwined with relations of communal deterrence and the attitudes to
non-state violence which these engendered. Moreover, in Scotland, Wales and
(especially) England, levels of religious observance became low even by the
standards of industrialised European societies. Even more telling is that religious background became a poorer predictor of political choice than almost
anywhere else. Thus there coexisted within the same United Kingdom structure
of political sovereignty, societies at virtually opposite extremes in the global
spectrum of religion's political significance.

The violence always latent in structures of communal deterrence reached its apotheosis in 1919–23. The pattern of violence in Ulster during those years was sharply distinct from that elsewhere in Ireland. The IRA was relatively ineffectual in the province during the 'Black and Tan War', and it saw very little of the near conventional warfare that characterised Cork or Kerry, with their extended firefights involving dozens of armed men on each side. Far more characteristic of Ulster, and especially Belfast, was sectarian rioting and assassination, some of it carried out by uniformed bodies, and accounting for the great bulk of the (probably) 752 deaths between 1919 and the July 1921 Truce. More people were killed in Ulster than in the rest of Ireland put together in that period—though in the subsequent months it largely escaped the ravages of the South's Civil War—and roughly two-thirds of them were Catholics (Austen Morgan 1991:301–3).[27] Thereafter the deterrence relationship re-stabilised, at a far lower level of violence, until 1969. Its drastic re-intensification then instituted a new spiral which has not ended, and which did not alleviate—if anything, the reverse—during the 1995–6 IRA ceasefire or, as the tensions of July 1998 showed, after the 'Good Friday' agreement. Wright's analysis thus offers few reasons for optimism about the future, at least for those who cannot share his religious faith with its belief in the redemptive possibilities of individual witness.

Whatever the varieties of analysis of Unionist political culture—whether it is seen as deriving from a British national identity, a specifically Ulster one, a primarily religious tradition or a largely secularised 'mosaic', or from a social contract rather than a nationalist ideology; and whether its consolidation as a pan-class bloc is viewed as near-inevitable or as highly contingent—there is virtual consensus in modern scholarship as to what it is *not*. It is not a mere creature of manipulation by the British state, nor is it premised exclusively (or, many historians suggest, even mainly) on maintenance of material and other privileges *vis-à-vis* Catholics. Furthermore, it is near-universally agreed that the Northern Ireland conflict is in some strong sense *structural*, not merely a result of distorted cultures or manipulated attitudes. As Ruane and Todd, with many others, emphasise, it is wrong to see individuals in Northern Ireland as uniquely, or even mainly, intolerant in their views (Ruane and Todd 1991[28]). The two pillars of the colonial model, which have sometimes stood separately, sometimes been mutually supporting—that seeing the Northern Ireland conflict as the product of British imperialist interests, and that explaining it by way of an Ulster settler-colonial ensemble—have both fallen. What is increasingly taking their place, and is most fully exemplified in the work of Frank Wright on the one hand, of Todd and Ruane on the other, is a multidimensional and properly historical analysis, recognising the imperial and settler-colonial influences on the evolution of modern conflicts and belief systems, but recognising also the inadequacy of believing that these were the only important influences, or the dominant ones today. The final message, perhaps, is that Unionist ideology, and Northern Ireland itself, cannot be understood without reference to settler-colonial origins, but equally are inexplicable without reference to those original structures' long erosion. As Wright, especially, has shown, it is precisely their disappearance which dictated the nature of nineteenth- and twentieth-century communal conflict.

11

Comparative Perspectives

At various points in this book so far, allusions have been made to different kinds of comparison between Irish and other histories and societies; some with other parts of the British Empire, some with other European countries. As has been suggested, a great deal of contention both academic and political has been framed by questions as to which comparative points of reference are most appropriate and enlightening for Ireland: for instance, whether colonial parallels, or continental European ones, are more useful. We shall return to offer some general judgements on this issue in the concluding chapter; but before doing so, it is necessary to attempt a more systematic appraisal of existing comparative models.

Truly comparative, international study of Irish development under and after the Union, and of Northern Ireland since Partition, has begun to flower only quite recently. Very little serious work precedes the early 1980s. Some research which proclaims itself as comparative, such as John Darby and his co-editors' 1990 collection on political violence, actually includes no explicit or systematic comparisons at all, instead merely juxtaposing articles on facets of the Northern Ireland problem with quite separate discussions of conflicts elsewhere. There may even, it seems, be those in Ireland who actively dislike comparative analysis or interchange, as in the astonishing xenophobe outburst of Robbie McVeigh (1995) against non-Irish (especially British) scholars working in Ireland—whom he calls 'colonial academics' (112) imbued with anti-Irish racism (115), pursuing 'teaching and research that is actively racist, sexist and sectarian' (117). McVeigh also disapproves of people living in Ireland studying 'what is going on across the water or in the US or in Europe, or anywhere other than Ireland.' (116)

Yet comparative work has already taken many variant forms, and sought to serve a wide range of purposes. Sometimes the ostensibly—or indeed covertly—comparative method does little more than forge a chain of associations whose effect is merely to reinforce presumed truths about one or other of the situations compared. Thus for instance Conor Cruise O'Brien's substantial body of writing about the Arab–Israeli conflict functions, up to a point, as an extended metaphor for Ireland.[1] The Israeli national security state is necessary just as—or *because?*—the Northern Ireland one is. Israel cannot risk concessions to Arafat just as—or because?—Britain cannot do so to Gerry Adams. In less nakedly polemical vein but still with evident axes to grind, Christopher Hewitt has used comparative material on economic inequalities in Northern Ireland and various other divided societies including New Brunswick, Quebec, the Basque country, Cyprus and the USA to assert that the eruption of ethnic conflict in Ulster cannot be attributed to such inequalities or to discrimination against Catholics, since sharper differentials elsewhere have not led to such violence. Rather, it can best be explained by Irish nationalist indoctrination and foreign interference (Hewitt 1991).

Some comparative work has introduced the Northern Ireland case largely to make a negative point; simply to emphasise its *lack* of resemblance to the main cases analysed. Thus Leo Kuper's discussion of Northern Ireland in a comparative treatment of *Genocide* (1981) stressed mainly the absence of similarity between political violence in Ulster and genuinely genocidal conflicts (195–6, 204–6) and in a broader structural context insisted on difference rather than resemblance between social segregation in Ireland and settler-colonial or South African apartheid policies (191–209).

Other academic comparative studies forfeit much of their usefulness through egregious empirical or methodological shortcomings. Such is all too evidently the case with Katherine O'Sullivan See's *First World Nationalisms* (1986), which seeks to compare the valencies of ethnic politics in Northern Ireland with those in Quebec. The framework adopted is a 'resource competition model', premised on an economic reductionism actually far more marked than is to be found in almost any Marxist account of Northern Ireland, despite See's ostensible critical distance from the latter. Considerable emphasis is given to colonial backgrounds in explaining the evolution of, and differences between, the two societies, but neither 'straight' colonial nor internal colonialism models are judged adequate to account for twentieth-century developments. The major, and crippling, weakness of the work, however, is the shakiness of its empirical grasp. Virtually every sentence of the Ulster historical sections contains factual errors, often of a very basic kind: some attributable to reliance on a restricted and outdated range of sources, some apparently to sheer carelessness.

Another Irish-Canadian comparative analysis, Edmund Aunger's work on Northern Irish and New Brunswick politics, is empirically far more substantial. Aunger's problematic was to enquire why New Brunswick, a society strongly divided between Francophone and Anglophone, Catholic and Protestant, communities, has remained politically stable and peaceable as against Northern Ireland's endemic violence. He believes that the answer may be found in New Brunswick's having substantial 'cross-pressures': religious, ethnic and class divisions cross-cut one another, so that a number of different lines of group conflict emerge, each limited rather than ambient, and thus manageable. In Northern Ireland, by contrast, the different social divisions largely coincide, and reinforce one another. (Aunger 1981)[2]

Some comparisons, perhaps especially in recent times those made between Northern Ireland and the South African democratisation process, have had more limited, pragmatic and policy-oriented aims, in thinking about what kinds of constitutional arrangements, or what forms of policing and monitoring, may be best suited to peace and reconciliation in Northern Ireland. These may from a practical point of view be the most valuable of all forms of comparative analysis.[3]

Possibly the least enlightening, by contrast, have been the small clutch of 'applications' of political science models—most influentially, the consociational model originated by Arend Lijphart—to Northern Irish experience. These have tended to be highly abstracted and entirely ahistorical in approach: and may as Frank Wright suggests lead to the depressed conclusion that Northern Ireland, like Lebanon, shows that consociationalism only works where it isn't really necessary (Wright 1987:274).[4] Others again have had very specific focuses and little if any wider conceptual or theoretical bite, as with Tom Bowden's study of policing and security policy in Ireland during 1916–21 and British Mandatory Palestine in 1936–39 (Bowden 1977).

Limited in a different, more productive sense have been those few studies seeking to analyse not Northern Ireland as a whole, but particular places—usually the city of Belfast—in comparative frames. A. C. Hepburn has sought to compare Belfast's historical experience as a religiously and ethnically divided city with other urban centres which shared some similar features, especially Trieste whose Italian–Slovene division offers parallels with Belfast's Protestant–Catholic one. Both cities were of roughly the same size, and both were products of strikingly rapid late-nineteenth-century industrial growth—in which migrants from the surrounding countryside played a crucial role, and which led to the establishment of residentially and occupationally segregated minority communities of similar proportions. The local politics of both cities were vital to the political fates of their regions: arguably, Ireland would never have been partitioned but for Belfast, and at the same time (1918–21) Istria would have belonged to Yugoslavia rather than Italy but for Trieste (Hepburn and Cattaruza 1996).

Such work underlines that in a wider urban-comparative frame, Belfast is not at all unusual in its communal divisions. Brussels and Montreal, Beirut and Sarajevo, offered comparable ethnic profiles (Hepburn 1996:22). The fact that ethnic rivalry in the former pair has been largely peaceable, while in the latter it led to violence on a vastly greater scale than Belfast's, owes far more to broader political contexts than to the character of the cities or local community relations themselves. The processes by which religious difference became a marker of nation-state identity or aspiration found in nineteenth-century Belfast can be closely paralleled in several other divided cities, though in places such as Prague or Brussels the divisions were increasingly secularised. The degree of residential segregation in Belfast, which has intensified rather than diluted in recent years, is extremely unusual by European standards even among ethnically divided cities—but it is not dissimilar, to take a different point of comparison, to the levels of black–white segregation in many US conurbations. The combination of separateness and interaction, of objectively very minor but subjectively important differences in cultural life and everyday behaviour, found in Northern Irish Catholic–Protestant relations by researchers like Rosemary Harris (1972) and Anthony Buckley (1982) can be closely paralleled in other, bloodier sites of communal division like Bosnia, as suggested by Tone Bringa's 1995 study of a rural Muslim community and its relationships with Christian neighbours.

What is perhaps most distinctive about Belfast is the very persistence of its divisions. In some other cases, peaceful demographic change led to the withering away of previously salient ethnic rivalries: between the mid-nineteenth and the early twentieth centuries, Budapest changed without violence from a German-majority to a Magyar-speaking city; Helsinki from Swedish to Finnish (Hepburn 1996:28). Probably more common, though, have been traumatic 'solutions' to urban ethnic division. In the 1940s the large Jewish minorities (in some cases majorities) of numerous central-eastern European cities disappeared through genocide, and the German populations of places like Danzig, Königsberg and Potsdam were forced into flight, the changed ethnic character of their former homes symbolised by changes of name. In 1962 Algiers changed almost overnight from a French-majority to an Arab city. In the 1990s murder and expulsion have homogenised numerous previously mixed Balkan centres. And in a few cases, partition between different sovereignties—whether *de jure* as in Jerusalem until 1967 or Nicosia more recently, or *de facto* as in Beirut and Sarajevo (or Jerusalem since 1967)—has been an imposed solution to urban ethnic division, though rarely a durable one. In Belfast neither benign nor malign resolutions have taken place. Demographic change has been slow-paced: a Catholic majority for the city, let alone for the greater Belfast area, is not in sight. 'Ethnic cleansing' has led mostly to very short-distance population movements within the city, not wholesale flight from it by one or other community. Violence, however endemic, has been far short of genocidal. And even those who believe that repartition (transferring areas like South Armagh, Fermanagh and Tyrone to the Republic) might be a solution to Northern Ireland's problems have usually baulked at the prospect of dealing with Belfast in this way.

More wide-ranging comparative analyses have also taken a variety of forms. In one version, they have attempted to trace Ireland's and Ulster's similarities with and divergences from a range of other conflicts both colonial and non-colonial: Bohemia, Moravia, Prussian Poland, French Algeria, the US South, Cyprus and the Lebanon. This was the route taken by Frank Wright (1981, 1987); and the conclusion was that Ulster displayed sharp divergences from the 'classic' model of the settler colony and could more enlighteningly be compared with 'ethnic frontiers' where two distinct ethnic groups, at least one of them linked to a metropolitan power, are in contention. Ulster Protestants evidently do not, on the whole, think of England or Scotland as 'home', as did the classic *colon* communities. They are not on average wealthier than the population of the metropole, nor is there a vast economic gap between them and the 'natives'. Their political culture has few, if any significant similarities with those of settler-colonialist enclaves outside Europe (cf. also Nelson 1984; Todd 1987; Brian Walker 1992). To see Northern Ireland as a frontier site of national conflict is far more illuminating:

The only difference between the North of Ireland and most other national conflicts was that the settler-native division ran between peoples of different religions rather than of different language groups. But such a peculiarity alters only the details, not the essential ground rules of national conflict. Similar things happened in the land of the South Slavs, where the military frontier of Austro-Hungarian Croatia contained Serb settlers. Serbs (Orthodox), Croats (Catholics) and Bosnian Moslems shared the same language, but were of separate nations. (Wright 1996:515)

Adrian Guelke's work (1988) is in a sense complementary to Wright's: tracing the interaction of internal and extraneous determinants of the conflict, he accords primacy to the former. International involvement has, however, made the dispute more intractable: the widespread international support for the idea of a united Ireland, involving most external commentators and many governments in a near-consensus that British rule in Ulster is illegitimate, has increased Unionist insecurity and Nationalist maximalism.[5] By supporting the Republican analysis that theirs is an anticolonial struggle, international public opinion has strengthened Sinn Fein/IRA's unwillingness to moderate their demands or seek accommodation with Unionists. This is, then, far from being a case of Britain doggedly hanging on against Irish wishes, as the colonial model suggests. In fact Westminster's explicit acknowledgement of Northern Ireland's right of secession is in international terms very unusual; and Guelke finds no reason to think that Protestant resistance to Irish unity is egged on or shored up by Britain—rather the reverse.

Other comparative analyses reached conclusions more compatible with the colonial model. Another major effort, Donald Harman Akenson's *God's Peoples* (1992) focuses on religious traditions as its explanatory key. Akenson sees South African Afrikaners, Israeli Jews and Ulster Protestants as all sharing a powerfully determining, religiously based worldview, centred on the idea of a covenant between 'chosen people' and God. The covenant includes, crucially, belief in divine entitlement to the land occupied or claimed by the people in question. Akenson's view, which as will be seen has a certain congruence with that of his hero Conor Cruise O'Brien, is by no means wholly hostile to the groups he analyses. He says they 'Share something—concreteness of outlook and directness of expression—that makes me trust them' (5). '[A]lthough covenantal cultures make hard enemies, they also make superb allies. Their emphasis on the long term, on loyalty, and on corporate identity means that they are much more trustworthy than are more conventional allies.' (355)

The main problem with a model such as Akenson's, with its stress on the role of an inherited, rigid and essentially unchanging religio-political ideology, is that it is ill-equipped to explain patterns of change. Akenson's predictions, published in 1992, were that whereas the covenantal ideology remained important in all three cases, only in Israel was it likely to become more, not less, intransigent in its stance. Israel would continue to move 'more and more into the classical covenantal template, as set down by the ancient Hebrews . . . fit that template more and more closely by the late 1990s' (345). In South Africa, although important Afrikaner groups 'effectively declare that the covenant was dead' (308), there remained powerful beliefs in 'the ancient imperative that the body, the family, the "seed" must be protected from admixture with the impure and the profane.' (310) In Northern Ireland, too, he believed the covenantal ideology had frayed, only 'holy fragments of Ulster's once-united covenantal culture' remain. (293) Nonetheless these are still 'red-hot and volatile. It will take more than a single generation for them to cool down and during the waiting period, a miscue by British, Irish or European authorities could make them coalesce once again. If that happens, an implosion of fierce proportions could occur, as in the process of nuclear fusion.' (293–4)

Arguably, developments in all three cases since Akenson wrote call his essentialist picture into question. In face of peace negotiations and, in the South African instance especially, dramatic political transformation, all three cultures have apparently been more secularly pragmatic in their responses than he predicted. In particular, the Israeli religious right appeared weaker, and less hegemonic in the culture as a whole, than he suggested—and his model could not account for the growing, often bitter rift between the religiously Orthodox and the secular majority in Israel. Somewhat similarly, it can make little sense of the political divisions between a primarily rural Presbyterian Ulster culture and the largely irreligious, urban working-class communities who provided the mainstay of support for Loyalist paramilitaries but also some encouraging signs of political flexibility in face of Sinn Fein's shifts.

Three major attempts at analysing Unionist politics and culture within the conceptual framework of settler colonialism stand out in the literature; those of Ian Lustick, Michael MacDonald, and Ronald Weitzer. All of these analyses are distinct from those identifying British imperialism as the direct root of conflict in Ireland, in that they see the 'settlers' as having become substantially independent from the colonial power, and often acting in contradiction to its interests.

Lustick's comparative analysis of British Ireland and French Algeria (1985) was, intriguingly, prompted not by an original research interest in either case as such, but in a third, Israeli occupation of the West Bank and Gaza Strip. Israel, after 1967, seemed to be pursuing an attempted incorporation of the conquered territories; and Lustick, politically hostile to this effort, wished to discover why earlier attempts at incorporating colonised territory by Britain and France had failed. Neither cultural difference between rulers and ruled, nor physical distance between colony and metropole, would suffice as an explanation, in his view. His basic answer was that:

one particular mechanism of expansion and territorial control used in Ireland and Algeria—i.e., large nonmilitary settler populations . . . standing in a privileged relationship to the central authorities but in numerically weak relation to the native population—explains the failure. (Lustick 1985:5)

The presence of settlers, then, blocked any possibility of transforming the loyalties of the natives and winning legitimacy for British and French overrule. Britain never clarified the purpose of settlement itself: 'no clear and systematic rationale for plantation as a means to consolidate British rule over the natives of Ireland was adhered to or even articulated, by successive governments.' (7) Such early Stuart administrators as Sir John Davies and Sir Francis Bacon had argued for conciliatory policies, respecting local institutions and customs and integrating Irish elites into the British system (22–4). But, said Lustick, the settlers themselves 'scuttled' this (25); and the subsequent behaviour of Cromwell's 'ideologically driven, fanatically anti-Catholic' army only made the failure more certain (30). The final straw was delay in achieving Catholic Emancipation until well after the Union. Thereafter Irish Catholics were driven 'into a political posture from which the loosening of ties with Britain was consistently viewed as the solution to their problems.' (38)

How, though, did Protestant settlers first in Ireland as a whole, latterly in Ulster, succeed thereafter in wrecking British hopes for incorporation? Lustick suggested four factors:

i) by their being the main conduit for information on Ireland to London, spreading negative views and stereotypes there about Irish Catholics;
ii) through their forming the main recruitment pool for staffing the administration, security forces, and judiciary;
iii) the intensity of their concern with the issue, which was a secondary one to most other interest groups potentially concerned, made them a highly effective and cohesive single-issue lobby;
iv) the flexibility and instrumentalism of their leaders' strategies.

Lustick is not primarily an expert on Irish history and politics, and there are evident empirical shortcomings in his account. He did not distinguish at all clearly between *Irish* Unionism before 1922 and *Ulster* Unionism thereafter, or note

either the very different social bases of each or the internal divisions both manifested. Many would doubt whether 'flexibility' has really been a distinguishing
characteristic of Unionist stances. Indeed in a later and more substantial work,
Unsettled States, Disputed Lands (1993), again comparing the three cases of Ireland, Algeria and Israel's Occupied Territories, Lustick shifted substantially
away from this stress on the role of settler minorities. Instead he developed an
elaborate model of the 'punctuated equilibrium' of state formation, within
which the formation and breakdown of hegemonic conceptions of state boundaries was the crucial point of analysis. He now argued that such a conception in
relation to Ireland—in which separation was unthinkable to the British political mainstream—broke down during the second half of the nineteenth century.
In the 1840s and 1850s, despite O'Connell's campaigns for Repeal, the breakup
of the Union was barely considered as an option except to be dismissed out of
hand. By the 1880s it was a subject for vigorous and vehement debate, but in the
context of widespread beliefs that Irish self-rule would entail severe regime
crisis in Britain. By 1916–21 a further threshold had been crossed, after which it
could safely be assumed 'that payoffs and repercussions associated with
attempts to disengage from Ireland would be calculated solely in terms of partisan advantage within presumptively stable state institutions.' (Lustick 1993:238)
His silent abandonment of the earlier explanatory emphasis on settler colonialism tells its own story.

Weitzer's (1990) point of comparison, Zimbabwe, is quite different and has
been far less widely invoked in Ireland itself than has Lustick's Algeria.[6] It is
arguably a less enlightening analogue, on several grounds. Algeria was and
Northern Ireland is politically integrated to the metropole, whereas in what was
then Rhodesia such integration was never pursued, and a minority settler
regime broke away and declared unilateral independence in 1965. It is a distinction the author himself recognises as significant (Weitzer 1990:32). *Colon* politics in Algeria were diverse, ranging from Communists to fascists, reflecting a
highly developed civil society. So, despite decades of single-party domination at
Stormont, were Northern Ireland Protestant politics. Rhodesian white political
debate, by contrast, took place within very narrow bounds, within a relatively
newly established, small and homogeneous population with few and rudimen-
tary institutions of civil society. And white-ruled Zimbabwe was *minority* rule
(by a very small minority), which denied all rights of political participation to
the majority, was based on rigid 'colour bars', massive income inequalities, and
very sharp labour market differentiation between whites and blacks. None of
these features was shared by Northern Ireland: which is as much as to say that
Rhodesia was a settler colony *par excellence* while Northern Ireland is a far more
questionable case. The main shortcoming of Weitzer's work is that he more or
less simply assumes that the six counties belong to that analytical category.[7] The
book relies on a brief outline sketch of the history of seventeenth-century

settlement and British overrule, and then posits a basic continuity thereafter. In particular, Weitzer makes no close examination of Unionist ideology, taking it for granted that it was and remained what he takes to be a 'typically' settler collective psychology dependent on colonial privileges and inherently committed to hegemonic control.

So far as Northern Ireland itself is concerned, if Lustick's main purpose is to explain the failure of integration, Weitzer's is to account for the breakdown of 'settler' control. He argues that such control depends in a settler regime on three preconditions. These are 'to achieve autonomy from the metropole in the exercise of political authority and coercive power', to consolidate control over the native population, and to 'maintain the settlers' caste solidarity and the state's cohesion' (Weitzer: 26–8). After 1969, he says, all three of these preconditions ceased to be met, resulting inevitably in the collapse of the regime. And this too exposes the inappropriateness of the comparison Weitzer has chosen to make, for the 'breakdown' involved in the abolition of Stormont and imposition of direct rule, accompanied by continued guerrilla and sectarian war, has little in common with the 'breakdown' of the Smith regime, which was replaced only very briefly and formally by restored British sovereignty, and substantively by independence and majority rule under former guerrilla leaders. If it is appropriate to regard modern Northern Ireland as a settler colony in the first place— which Weitzer has not established—then it would seem to follow that essential elements of that dispensation have persisted after 1972, especially if one drops the dubious assumption made by Weitzer that desire for political autonomy from the metropole is inherent to settler desires.

The third of these works, that by Michael MacDonald, takes Northern Ireland as its primary focus rather than, like Lustick and Weitzer, as one pole in a comparative argument whose main concerns are at least as much elsewhere. MacDonald's comparative passages, relating Ulster to South Africa (1986:134–47) are relatively perfunctory; even he calls them 'tentative' (xii). His is also the only one of these books to espouse serious interest in Unionist ideology and political psychology. Yet this is far the weakest of the three analyses; essentially because it is driven by strong ideological predispositions dictating an unrelentingly hostile view of the Protestant community.

MacDonald's central claim is that 'the imperative to exclude and antagonise the native population is rooted in the structure of settler colonialism.' (xii) More, it has become rooted in the Unionist (or Protestant: MacDonald, unlike some pro-Republican writers, uses the terms interchangeably) psyche. The very meaning of being a Protestant in Northern Ireland is constructed on being superior to, ruling over, and excluding Catholics. Thus they have never actually *wanted* legitimacy, or for the Catholic community to accept the Union, because for that to happen would undermine their own sense of identity, which is premised on irreducible difference, superiority, and embattledness. 'Protestant "loyalty" is meaningful only in contradistinction to the "disloyalty" of Catholics. Thus Protestants, especially the more marginal ones, have developed an enduring stake in sustaining the disloyalty of Catholics, even at the cost of chronic instability and violence.' (8)

Thus religion as such is not a significant independent variable, but merely the 'badge' distinguishing settlers from colonised. This was, as we have seen, also the view of De Paor and others, though it is open to contestation on the ground that very probably had it not been for the confessional divide, intermarriage would long since have been sufficiently widespread as to blur if not wholly remove the communal boundaries. This distinction, albeit a counterfactual one, may be thought to be one of the major factors differentiating Northern Ireland from classic settler colonies like Algeria or Zimbabwe, where the differences between colonist and native have been thought very clearly in 'racial' terms.

MacDonald's analysis of the conflict also downgrades British policy as an explanatory variable. It is always the 'settlers' who have sought to drive and manipulate Whitehall and Westminster, not vice versa. Recent British government motivation is summarised, rather glibly, as 'avoiding the whole mess' (161) if it can. It is this emphasis which most clearly distinguishes *Children of Wrath* from classical Republican views, which it otherwise closely resembles. The claims MacDonald makes about Unionist ideology and psychology are not grounded in substantial empirical analysis. Hardly a single quotation from any Ulster Protestant is adduced in support of the opinions he says they hold. Still less is there any social survey or poll data which do so. Much of the book consists of an outline sketch of Irish history—more detailed, but more partisan, than those of Lustick or Weitzer. It relies heavily on such outdated sources as W. E. H. Lecky's *History of Ireland* and, for the more recent past, such intensely *parti pris* ones as Michael Farrell's *The Orange State* and McCann's *War and an Irish Town*. MacDonald sometimes refers to Protestants hanging on only to the 'vestiges' of colonial privileges; but in general assumes, without offering statistical support for the view, that such privileges remain economically substantial. This, though, is something of a side-issue, since Protestant supremacism is seen as resting not so much on any material advantage as on inherent psychic predisposition. The implication is evidently that Northern Ireland Protestants simply have no basis for an identity except this purely negative one.

The assumption on which MacDonald's case rests is not unique to him, though few others have tried to construct a theory on its shaky foundations. Joseph Lee proposed something similar in suggesting, rather jocularly, that:

There is a wonderful reassurance about the zero-sum game when you are always on the winning side. The winnings may not amount to much materially or objectively. That is not the point. The feeling of winning is itself the most important of the winnings. If

Protestants were to be deprived of this pleasure, could an increase in their per capita income really compensate for the consequent decline in their quality of life? (Lee 1989:425)

MacDonald ignores all evidence contradicting his thesis. All the ideological crosscurrents of Irish and Ulster history, including Protestant Nationalists from Tone onwards, Catholic Unionists, and the different varieties of socialist or labourist politics, are bypassed or dismissed, the last through a hasty despatching of Bew, Gibbon and Patterson's work (15–17). He does not consider the possibility that Northern Irish Protestant identity was substantially formed, not so much through triumphalism as through perceptions of past underprivilege, threat, and betrayal (see, for such suggestions, Buckley 1987; Longley 1991). Recognition of the extent to which this was so would not, by any means, necessarily imply accepting the validity of Unionist political claims. After all, Afrikaner identity in South Africa too was substantially shaped by discourses about suffering at the hands of Zulu impis and British armies, the concentration camps of the 1899 war and subsequent disadvantage in an economy dominated by English-speaking whites (cf. Hofmeyr 1987; O'Meara 1983). Few would think that this fact legitimised apartheid.

One sphere in which serious comparative work with a central Irish or Northern Ireland dimension has been almost entirely absent has been the relationship of politics to religion.[8] Here too, even a cursory survey of the general patterns of European political development across at least the first half of this century disposes of the idea that Ireland was exceptional. It was, rather, Britain that was exceptional in having low correlations between religious affiliation and voting patterns. It was the norm, not the exception, for party systems and indeed labour movements substantially to follow confessional lines—especially but not only in Catholic countries (for a summary of the international evidence see Mann 1995). Even after 1945, religious non-observance or 'rare church attendance' was a better predictor of left-wing voting habits than manual occupation or (where data were available) trade union membership, in Belgium, France, West Germany, Greece, Italy, the Netherlands and Spain (ibid: 46: Table 3). And even if the main impact of religious allegiance on political choice has thus come to be a division between the observant and the secular rather than one between denominations, the latter too retains salience in several western European states, as in Switzerland and the Netherlands. Malta, the 'other' European ex-British colony and (with Poland) the state most closely matching Ireland in homogeneity and intensity of Catholic observance, had its political alignments long and intensely drawn on clerical–anticlerical lines—though by the 1980s and 1990s such conflicts had lost much of their salience. In Poland, by contrast, it appears increasingly that such divisions will be one of the key determinants of maturing post-Communist politics.

So far as international law and practice in relation to decolonisation are concerned, there are many twentieth-century controversies which parallel *some* part of the situation in Ireland. For instance, there have been very many secessions or attempts at them, during or (more often) after the process of colonial withdrawal, from political units which had been ruled as unitary possessions by the colonialists.[9] On the whole, both the departing colonial powers and international opinion as expressed at the United Nations, have been hostile to such secession efforts, viewing them as illegitimate—a notable exception was Bangladesh's successful breakaway from Pakistan; a partial and temporary exception Biafra's attempted exit from the Nigerian federation, which won some international support for a mixture of idealistic and *realpolitik* reasons. However, none of these is at all a close parallel with the Irish case. Ireland had been legislatively and in other important formal respects integrated with Great Britain, so that from many points of view the only 'secession' involved was that of twenty-six counties of Ireland from the UK, not of six counties from Ireland.[10] The closest legal parallel found by Michael Gallagher in his study of possible comparisons (1990) is a tiny and relatively unknown one: the island of Mayotte in the Comoros, whose inhabitants voted in 1975 to remain French when those of the Comoros' three other main islands opted for independence. Apart from size, distance from the 'mother-country', the happy non-violence of the Comoros dispute, and crucially, timing (1970s rather than 1920s), the similarities to Northern Ireland's position in 1921 are striking.[11] It is therefore intriguing that voting at the United Nations has over the years near-unanimously backed the Comoros' claim to sovereignty over Mayotte. On the other hand, as Gallagher also notes, in cases which are more different from that of Northern Ireland than Mayotte's in juridical terms, but more similar in the size of populations involved, or geographical contiguity to those claiming sovereignty, international opinion has been more resistant to attempts at incorporation. Thus Moroccan claims over Mauritania and Western Sahara, let alone Iraqi ones over Kuwait, did not gain general acceptance.

12

Conclusions

Colonialism and imperialism, in several of the meanings of those complex, contested words, have indisputably been important shaping forces in Irish history. An Anglo-Norman aristocracy and monarchy, establishing themselves as rulers of a conquest state in England after 1066, soon attempted to create spheres of domination in Ireland as they did also in Wales, Scotland and France. Success was slow and uneven, as were the accompanying processes of seeking to turn domination into fully sovereign rule and to incorporate Ireland's inhabitants into English political, legal, religious and cultural structures. From the mid-sixteenth to the late seventeenth centuries, these efforts became more concerted and centrally directed by first the English, then after 1602 the new British, states. They also became associated both with post-Reformation religious rivalries and with English (and to a lesser extent Scots) colonisation projects in the Americas. Ireland came to be seen by some as part of an 'Atlantic Empire'— though the term Empire was still neither widely nor unambiguously used in English, and although colonising activities in Ireland may in some respects have hampered rather than furthered those further west. In some ways, though always complex and ambiguous ones, British views of the Irish became 'racialised' and denigratory, as did those of native Americans, Indians and Africans: but as schemata of racial hierarchy emerged in European thought, the Irish had the advantage of being (at least in most eyes) 'white'.

A new factor in the situation from the early seventeenth century was a rapid influx of Scottish and English migrants, some of it state-sponsored through planned 'Plantations'. Alongside the ambiguously colonial or 'imperialised' political status of Ireland as a whole, there thus came into existence a distinct phenomenon—far more distinct and independent, indeed, than Irish nationalists later tended to believe—of 'settler colonialism', concentrated in the north. Although the peculiarly settler-colonial features of the north of Ireland, such as legalised segregation of the labour market, gradually decayed, that decay did not end the clash of rival politico-religious identifications in the region but merely changed its form. It persists to the present.

Meanwhile after failed attempts, first by the Patriots to achieve legislative self-government, then by the United Irishmen to gain full independence, and under threat of French intervention, legislative Union was pushed through.

Incorporation into the structures of the United Kingdom, and thus also into those of a rapidly expanding global Empire (a term whose use to describe overseas territorial possessions was now taking hold), seemed complete.

That incorporation had been, in many of its phases, extremely violent and always had an element of coercion. But it also involved ever-varying, but always significant, elements of consent and cooperation, of seemingly willing Irish assimilation to what were originally English, then in some measure syncretically British, institutions and cultural patterns. The coercive element was longer-lasting, and in the aggregate certainly bloodier, than that which was exercised in Scotland or Wales—though there were periods, like the first half of the eighteenth century, when English domination over Scotland seemed more precarious, and was maintained by harsher repression, than that over Ireland. Conversely, the ratio of coercion to consent was (insofar as such things can be measured) nearly always lower than in most of Britain's more distant possessions. This was most apparent in the last stages of political domination. For instance, at the same time as the Irish 'War of Independence' in 1919–21, British troops were also engaged in suppressing 'tribal' revolts in Iraq. The affair has been almost entirely forgotten: it barely features in histories of the British Empire, let alone of Britain itself or of Ireland. Yet although there are (symptomatically enough) no reliable estimates on casualties, it is clear that the death-toll was many times the Irish total. The RAF bombed numerous Iraqi villages to force the rebels' submission: such acts would have been quite unimaginable— that is, entirely politically intolerable—in Ireland. In Northern Ireland since 1970, British and local security forces have killed just over 300 people, both insurgents and civilians. During the Kenyan 'Mau Mau' revolt a few decades earlier, they had killed at least thirty times as many: despite suffering far fewer casualties themselves. On the other hand, across these postwar decades, at most half a dozen people in Britain itself have died at the hands of the police in circumstances of riot or civil strife, and with serious suspicion of deliberate intent. Which should one view as the more appropriate reference point for Ireland?

State coercion and violence, then, were integral to colonial rule everywhere. Ireland was not unusual in this: rather, insofar as British domination there was conceived of as colonial, what stood out was the extent of political integration and cultural assimilation extended to the 'natives', including by the early nineteenth century a system of electoral representation that gave them proportionately at least as strong a parliamentary voice as it did the English or Scots. Even those who agitated for reform or abolition of Ireland's political link with Britain, from Wolfe Tone, through O'Connell, Parnell and Redmond to the leaders of Sinn Fein in the early twentieth century, tended in different ways to share in these patterns of integration. Almost all were strongly shaped by English-model educational and cultural systems. Many, such as O'Connell and Arthur Griffith, were monarchists. Hardly any were 'anti-colonialists' in some generalised or principled sense: some might attack Britain's colonial record in Africa or Asia, but this was often just a way of drawing attention to Irish grievances, and others were eager to dissociate Ireland's cause from that of any 'non-white' people. Some militant nationalists, like James Connolly and legendary IRA leader Tom Barry—and like hundreds of thousands of other Irish people—had been enthusiastic participants in Britain's global imperial ventures, as soldiers, administrators or settlers.

But although this integration and representation were unique in the British imperial system, it remains true that almost everywhere—everywhere, that is, where indigenous populations were not physically eliminated, as they were in parts of Australasia and the Americas—colonial rule rested also, and many historians would argue more essentially, on collaborative alliances with elements of the colonised population. We cannot use the relationship between coercion and consent, repression and reform, as a means of distinguishing colonial situations from others. Throughout the history of English/British domination over Ireland, rival perceptions of Ireland jostled and overlapped: sister-kingdom and colony, integral part of the polity and alien, inferior, incomprehensible 'place apart', victim of and partner in the expansion and consolidation of British global imperium.[1]

In some ways, on some levels, the continuing impact of that historical relationship is absolutely all-embracing, involving minute details of everyday life. Had Ireland never been part of England's, then Britain's, expansionary outreach across the centuries, never incorporated into the Kingdom or the Empire, then people in Ireland would presumably drive on the other side of the road, measuring their journey in kilometers and looking forward to a half-litre rather than a pint at the end of it. No doubt association football would be just as popular—it's the one English-originated game whose distribution now bears no relation to the limits of Empire—but fewer Irish people might support Manchester United. Perhaps 'Gaelic' games, lacking the stimulus of late-Victorian reaction against Britishness, would be less widely played, or even would not exist at all. Probably most people would still speak English, but far fewer would read London-based newspapers—and perhaps, conversely, important sections of the London press would not be Irish-owned. There would probably not be a million people in Ireland who, for some purposes at least, call themselves British, nor an even larger number in Britain who call themselves Irish—though there would surely still have been significant groups of both, whatever the islands' political history.

Perhaps if there had been no English/British conquest, crowds would be braving the rain today in the bullring of Kinsale, the national capital, to watch Ernesto Kelly, Ireland's leading toreador, do his stuff. Or perhaps a leading article in *Le Monde Irlandais* would be asking, provocatively, whether now—fifty years after the country had ceased to be a Department of 'La France l'Outre-Mere'—it was not time to reinstate Bastille Day as a public holiday, and offer financial compensation to the former settlers (or 'pieds verts') who had fled Ireland in the 1940s. A cascade of readers' letters would follow, denouncing this outrageous piece of 'revisionist' coat-trailing and blaming anti-national historians (such as Professor Foster of the Sorbonne) for it.

One could extend the speculative list almost indefinitely: which only indicates the impossibility of trying the assess Ireland's imperial legacies in that way. As we have seen, even where quantification of the British impact, and thus informed estimates of how Ireland would have done without that impact, have seemed possible, historians have failed to get anywhere near agreement on such estimates. For example, did the Union retard Irish economic development? Historians have mostly concurred that it simply made much less of a difference, for good or ill, than most nineteenth-century commentators claimed—but beyond that rather minimal, negative consensus there lies only dispute. Ireland was profoundly reshaped by many forces that operated independently of the British connection, though naturally their Irish form was also inflected by that connection: Renaissance and Reformation, the American and French Revolutions, industrialisation, urbanisation and population growth (it is worth recalling Eric Hobsbawm's contention (1994) that on any long-term view, the most important factor in modern history, *everywhere* in the world, has been the population explosion), Cold War and communist collapse, globalisation and European integration.

A colonial past, then, yes; though one that took unique hybrid forms, involving extensive integration and consensual partnership as well as exploitation and coercion. And only as part, and not on all levels the dominant part, of an extremely complex and unusual set of historical legacies shaping the Irish present. It certainly does not mark out Ireland as having a peculiarly 'postcolonial' destiny distinguishing it from the rest of Europe. If the Irish Republic is to be defined as postcolonial because it attained independence from alien rule early this century, then it shares the status with at least ten other European states. Albania, Czechoslovakia, Estonia, Finland, Iceland, Latvia, Hungary, Lithuania, Norway and Poland all achieved statehood in 1905–21—the first six being wholly new creations in terms of sovereignty, the latter four revived sovereign entities. Indeed if we take a slightly longer time-scale, Ireland's position as product of secession, of the breakup of a multinational or imperial system, makes it one of the *majority* of present (1999) European states.[2] To pose of Ireland the question 'postcolonial or modern European' is a radically false antithesis. Most of Europe is 'postcolonial'; and most historically salient features of British-Irish relations have evident affiliations to both European and 'Third World' experience. Divisions between Catholics and Protestants across the past four centuries can be seen as like the religious conflicts of many European societies, and also as like the native–settler antagonisms of many colonies. British stereotypes of inferior or degenerate 'Irish' characteristics were like those visited on Bengalis or Ghanaians, but also very similar to those developed by Germans about Poles, northern Italians about Sicilians, Serbs about Albanians, and so on. Ideologies of a 'civilising mission' operated with great if uneven strength in all these cases.

As has been suggested throughout this work, it was always misleading to think of Irish national questions primarily or only in the context of European colonialist expansion over non-European peoples. Such perceptions may have gained their currency in large part because the issue of Irish self-determination coalesced in its modern form in the last decades of the nineteenth century, the high tide of European imperialism—what some historians, misleadingly, call *the* age of imperialism. And the contemporary Northern Ireland conflict erupted at another point of high water, this time that of 1960s–70s 'Third World' anti-imperialism. The more important ideologically as well as materially deter-mining contexts of each, though, were quite different from those suggested by analogies with African or Asian struggles. In the nineteenth century they were the chain-reaction of nationalist movements across Europe from Italy's Risorgi-mento through Poland's long battle for independence to the emergence of Balkan nation-states. Often, as we have noted, these were assertions of national consciousness in regions which had between the twelfth and the seventeenth centuries been subjected to processes of incorporation by major neighbouring dynastic states, or had become 'marches' and frontiers between contending powers, much as Ireland's fate had been at English hands. And now in the late 1990s, we can perhaps see the conflict in Northern Ireland not so much as a belated anticolonialist struggle on the Afro-Asian model, but rather as a pre-cursor of the renewed battles over identity and sovereignty which have since 1989 disfigured more and more of Europe's south-east and east. Ireland is, hap-pily, distinguished from these by the fact that the deathtoll from its civil wars has been far lower than theirs: a little over three thousand dead in Northern Ireland since 1969 as against a Bosnia where (as of 1999) the very lowest responsible esti-mates suggest over 100,000 slain. But comparing Northern Ireland with the various battlegrounds of the former Yugoslavia and Soviet Union, instead of with Algeria or Vietnam, underlines that these are issues which are simply and bloodily impossible to solve in terms of the politics of nationalism, or of appeals to the past.

The central trope of 'postcolonial' Irish writing is, as we have seen, a claim that there are significant similarities, past and present, between Irish experience and that of African, Asian and other formerly colonised territories. We have shown at length how poorly the colonial and postcolonial models fit modern Irish experience itself. Yet in fact much of the invocation of Afro-Asian parallels for contemporary Irish developments is as misleading also about the former as about the latter. It typically involves a grossly exaggerated perception of the capacity of colonialism wholly to remodel or even destroy indigenous societies, including their cultural and artistic production. In some contemporary Irish 'postcolonial' writing, thirty-year-old strictures from Chinua Achebe, and twenty-five-year-old ones from Ngugi wa Thiong'o, about cultures and education systems dominated by the former colonialists are related both as if they referred to the present and as if they could simply be transposed to the Irish situation. In fact colonial administrators as often as not were concerned only to maintain political 'order' and ensure that profit continued to be extracted (or at least that the Treasury at home wasn't running a loss on the colony-owning business). They neither knew nor cared what the natives were writing, singing and so on. When they were interested at all, it was often by way of an Orientalist fascination with 'exotic' native cultural production rather than a desire to destroy the colonised's cultures.

Analogies between Irish and Afro-Asian cultural nationalisms have often been equally misplaced. Utterly diverse movements such as negritude and Pan-Africanism (the latter hugely internally disparate as well as quite distinct from negritude) are lumped together quite indiscriminately. A handful of prominent, supposedly exemplary 'Third World' cultural figures—above all Fanon, but also Rushdie, Ngugi, Cesaire or Cabral—are plucked from their contexts and suggested to provide parallels or inspirations for Ireland. Certainly one can find some similarities, but they are hardly the ones most cultural nationalists or postcolonial theorists would wish to highlight. One might explore parallels, for instance, between the culturalist chauvinism of negritude and that of a Pearse or Moran, or between the erstwhile socio-economic theories of some African one-party states such as Tanzania and that of Sinn Fein. Pearse's thought, and that of much later Republicanism, should be seen (as Bob Purdie and others have argued) not as 'socialist' but as a species of social contract ideology, anti-capitalist because it is anti-modernisation, hostile to notions of class conflict because they disrupt the imagined national unity, but in no way hostile to private property rights, and entirely consistent with traditional Catholic social thought. These features indeed bring it close to the organicist, neo-traditionalist and in practice highly authoritarian doctrines of certain African and Asian 'socialisms'.

Within many Irish literary-critical circles, even where they adhere to a postmodernist-poststructuralist theoretical stance which in other contexts is often perceived as allied to a postnationalist politics, a highly traditional conception of cultural nationalism has gained a new lease of life. Sometimes deliberately, sometimes unwittingly or reluctantly, it finds itself aligned with the most unreconstructed (or un*de*constructed), and even violent, manifestations of the separatist nationalism which flourished before 1922 and can now retain only an enfeebled and anachronistic afterlife. The premodern and the postmodern form uneasy solidarities against the claims of modernity, setting themselves against not only prospects of European or wider transnationality but also against universalist conceptions of democracy, citizenship, human rights and equality. Ironically, much that defines 'republicanism' in its usual international meanings is repudiated by such currents of Irish Republicanism and its friends.

The most disconcerting current feature of this ensemble is perhaps that anti-colonialist rhetoric, with all its exclusions and historical inadequacies, is reproduced and even (as in some contemporary literary theory) renewed in such diverse circles: among erudite cultural nationalists, sophisticated poststructuralist theorists, sincere democrats, liberals, socialists and radicals as well as among unreconstructed Belfast Republicans. And external observers, sympathisers, analysts and political tourists, especially but by no means only in the dwindling band of the international Marxist left, share the same syndrome. The rigidities of cultural nationalism, ever more often dressed up in the gaudy robes of postmodernist theory, are not just an Irish problem. Still less are they, as some have suggested, the peculiar pathology of Irish emigres in Camden or Boston.[3]

Much of this writing, in its more academic and theoreticist forms, also slips into a glib antihumanist rhetoric, the now-standard postmodernist/postcolonial identification of humanist and universalist values with colonialism. It forgets, as so much contemporary theorising does, that the intellectual roots of this kind of antihumanism lie not in liberationist politics, nor yet in the ex-colonial world, but in the thought of the Nazi sympathiser Martin Heidegger. The widely proposed idea of liberationist thought needing historical consciousness only as a source for symbolic patterns from which utopian moments are to be extracted—history, that is, as useful myth—is equally dubious. What guarantee can there be that the choice of such patterns and moments is not wholly arbitrary or, worse, made by demagogues and authoritarians?[4]

On other levels the postcolonial comparisons immediately collapse: partly because of Ireland's relative wealth, but in part precisely because the authoritarianism of romantic nationalist thought did *not* come to dominate independent Ireland's politics. Many of the postcolonial states with which Ireland is routinely compared have witnessed massive primary poverty, famine, recurrent military or civilian dictatorship, and civil war. Leftists, dissidents and creative artists are widely persecuted, forced into silence or exile. Meanwhile Ireland, despite its small size, its economic dependence first on Britain, then the EU, its relative poverty by European standards, and the presence of a small but nasty war on its doorstep (deliberately begging the question whether the doorstep is really part of the house or not!) has retained stable democratic politics, cultural pluralism, and strong protection for civil liberties. So far as I am aware, not one Irish writer or artist since 1922 has been executed, imprisoned, tortured, or exiled for their writings or their beliefs—the voluntary emigration of a Joyce or

Beckett is a quite different matter.[5] Such comparisons merely underline the use-lessness of a generalised 'postcolonial' model for understanding Ireland. Or, perhaps, anywhere else.

It is constantly implied, by those radical cultural critics who bemoan the con-servatism, clericalism and supposedly neocolonial dependence of the Irish state which emerged after 1921, that there was a readily available and far more attract-ive alternative. This has recently often been posed as the possibility of what is called, following Fanon, a 'liberationist' as opposed to merely nationalist out-come to the struggles of 1916–22. For some, that alternative would have emerged simply if Partition could have been avoided (how this was to have been done is never specified), or if the 'right' side had won the Civil War. For others, a dwindling band, it would have come from following the vision of Connolly or of Lenin. For others still, more vaguely, it should have emerged from the aspirations of a handful of imaginative artists, aspirations the politicians betrayed.[6]

Yet it is surely more realistic to see the most probable alternative outcome to what actually surfaced from the years of violence as being, not some more liber-atory scenario, but a species of militaristic dictatorship or at best populist authoritarianism. These were, after all, the most common heirs both of the other revolutions of the era—the Russian, the Mexican, the Turkish, the Hun-garian—and of many decolonisations after 1945. The emergence of Irish democracy, conservative, mediocre and quasi-theocratic though it may have been, was as Tom Garvin points out 'rather a close-run thing.' (1993a:9) Distrust of parliamentarism and electoral politics was strong. The tradition of the all-male secret society, the militant band, was an old one in Ireland, 'older than the tradition of popular parliamentary politics.' (Garvin 1993a:13) The Irish Repub-lican Brotherhood and the IRA were its heirs, and figures such as De Valera wavered between the traditions.[7] Yet in the event Irish civil society triumphed, not least because of the revulsion of a myriad local communities against 'uncontrollable, self-appointed bands of armed men contemptuous of the elect-oral process.' (Garvin 1993a:22–3)

Having escaped the very real dangers of postcolonial military dictatorship, there may be good reason for endorsing Joseph Lee's apparently paradoxical claim that modern Ireland 'has been one of the luckiest countries in the world.' As Lee points out, Irish nationalism has 'invested a good deal of emotional and even intellectual effort in nurturing a self-image that presents the Irish as a peculiarly persecuted people.' It's a view, he thinks, which involves 'an impres-sive capacity for self-deception.' (Lee in Regan and Sinclair eds 1986:22) Such a syndrome has been hard to shake, Lee believes, because it *does* have 'just suffi-cient historical truth to make it plausible . . . to coin a Hibernicism, half the lies are true.' (ibid: 22) There certainly was a colonial relationship between Britain and Ireland, and some of its legacies linger. Yet:

The Irish colonial legacy was a unique one. She was much more advanced, economically and politically, absolutely and relatively, than virtually any other new state of the nineteenth or twentieth century, with the possible exception of Czechoslovakia. (ibid: 23)

Even if we confine our comparisons to Europe, Ireland's fate seems relatively very fortunate.[8] War and civil war have, during the present century, clearly taken a terrible toll in Ireland. But it is a toll which pales into virtual insignificance when set against those of the Russian or Spanish Civil Wars, the 1914–18 and 1939–45 conflicts, the genocides against Europe's Jews and Armenians, the 1990s wars in the former Yugoslavia, or indeed such half-forgotten conflicts as Greece's 1940s civil war, the battles for Cyprus, or the Russo-Finnish war. Almost certainly the greatest loss to Ireland's population through violent death in modern times was among Irish soldiers in the British army in 1914–18: about 27,000 deaths as against perhaps 6,500 in the cycle of violence from the Easter Rising to the end of civil war in 1923[9] and rather over 3,000 in the 'Troubles' since 1969. However, even in the 1914–18 conflict Ireland—where conscription was never introduced—suffered a proportionate loss less than a sixth that of France, less than a quarter that of Germany, Italy or Austria-Hungary, less than a third that of Britain.

Comparing such experiences of conflict, secession and redrawing of boundaries across Europe and beyond, the main lesson for modern Ireland may be the need, in searching for solutions, simply to dismiss arguments purporting to derive from historical origins and settlement patterns, ancestries and ancestral claims. This is for three good reasons. One, a moral/political reason: that in contexts of rival claims to particular territorial rights—unless, perhaps, the claims relate entirely to disputes within living memory[10]—any argument between clearly defined and antagonistic groups must be resolved with reference only to the rights and desires of the living. Simply, dead people don't have votes (whatever about a time-honoured and trans-communal West Belfast practice!). Two, a historical/empirical reason: such historical disputes cannot, in most cases, be resolved by available evidence—not even resolved in ways that would satisfy professional historians, let alone ones that would satisfy the contending parties or their organic intellectuals.[11] Three, a pragmatic reason: any attempt to settle scores in accordance with such criteria will almost certainly leave more people feeling dissatisfied or aggrieved than it will make content with some notion of historical justice. By these criteria, I would argue, even claims that, say, some particular farm ownership in Armagh derives from seventeenth-century dispossession—let alone that 1990s patterns of political preference must be referred back to centuries-old migration or settlement for their democratic legitimacy—have no valid entailments for the living.

That, in part, is why seeking settlement on the basis of ascribed or self-ascribed group identities and their ideas of tradition, offers little hope. The communalist or communitarian approach to Northern Ireland, and the notion of such an approach as a route toward solutions of the conflict, was first articulated by SDLP politicians from the 1970s onward. It has gained ever greater strength after the Anglo-Irish Agreement, substantially prodded and funded by the Northern Ireland Office.[12] It has also attracted sharp criticism, especially from Unionists who allege an inherent pro-Nationalist bias in the whole paradigm (e.g. English 1994b); though there have been attacks from pro-Republican writers too. Thus Bill Rolston accuses the 'cultural traditions' paradigm of seeking to create a 'chimera of symmetry' which is 'highly political in intent . . . an exercise in depoliticising a cultural movement. It is multiculturalism as counterinsurgency.' (1998a:32) Desmond Bell (1998), focusing on the way in which, he believes, this approach has shaped the presentation of such historical exhibitions as Derry's Tower Museum, is similarly scornful of an allegedly sanitised and depoliticised thrust, which he associates also with postmodernist theories.

Critics from both sides, then, attack the 'chimera of symmetry'. For English, it is both politically dangerous and indeed 'fundamentally incoherent' to 'accord equal legitimacy on the one hand to a tradition whose instinct and drive is to support and maintain the state and, on the other, to a tradition aiming at some form of dismemberment of the state' (1994b:99). For Rolston, conversely, there can be no true symmetry because Irish (nationalist) culture is authentic, dynamic and progressive whilst Unionist culture was merely a sterile echo of official British state traditions—'predictable, formal, conservative—restrictive rather than expansive'—and Loyalist cultural expression confined to marching bands and pictures of King Billy. No wonder that 'those artists who came from loyalist working-class areas usually ended up denying their origins in one way or another.' (Rolston 1998a:27, 29).

The central (and in my view more apt) objection to an approach based on 'cultural traditions' and 'parity of esteem', however, is that it freezes—potentially, in perpetuity—the perception of there being two fixed, opposed blocs in Northern Ireland. Each of these is treated as an ensemble of culture, tradition, and political allegiance, with far more internal homogeneity and less permeable borders than is in fact the case. At best, such an approach restricts choice (often apparently assuming that everyone is a member from birth of one or other 'tradition' and will remain so), and may militate against the further development of an open, fully plural civil society. At worst, it may perpetuate or even deepen the sectarianism it is intended to overcome. It is probably incompatible with moves in such directions as towards a more integrated education system in Northern Ireland, which many commentators have viewed as crucial to long-term social peace.

Conferences devoted to the approach seem too often to have been dialogues of the wilfully deaf. At one such, Edna Longley (1992) tried another revival of the John Hewitt regionalist vision, setting this antagonistically against Field

Day's nationalism. Seamus Deane (1992) responded in hyperdrive, viewing Longley as a kind of literary arm of the RUC, 'always preternaturally alert to the next step in the Field Day conspiracy' (32). For his part: 'I assume, as part of my own enterprise, that Irish culture has for a very long time been a colonial culture, and that Irish literature is essentially a colonial literature.' (27) The concept of pluralism as espoused by the 'cultural traditions—equal esteem' paradigm was 'not an answer to anything . . . scandalously unintelligent.' (32)

Thus one can readily understand why Mark Ryan (1994:110–11, 138–40), for instance, argues quite simply that pluralism is a negation of democracy and a recipe for yet further fragmentation, sectarianism and authoritarianism. Shane O'Neill (1994), in a more measured argument, believes that pluralist and communitarian conceptions of justice—for which he takes Michael Walzer's work (1983) as the paradigm case—are actively unhelpful to the Northern Ireland case, where many of the preconditions which even Walzer himself recognises as necessary to the functioning of such an approach are absent (agreement on the boundaries and legitimacy of the relevant political unit, habits of compromise between community aspirations, and so on). Approaches premised on the prior existence of community identities offer little in situations where those identities are sharply antagonistic and tend to deny legitimacy to one another. Frameworks urging critical interrogation of one's group identity, as in Jürgen Habermas's discourse ethics (1990, 1993), offer far more hope, in O'Neill's view.[13] Their political counterpart is the Habermasian notion of constitutional patriotism (Habermas 1989 esp. pp. 207–67). It will be apparent that this is a stance for which I have much sympathy, though it is slightly disconcerting that in O'Neill's application it is seen as offering 'the basis for a critique of the liberal Unionist case' (1994:376) without similarly considering its implications for Nationalist views. It might indeed be argued that there are close elective affinities between Habermas's post-conventional identity and Norman Porter's (1996) civic Unionism—even if Porter himself draws his theoretical resources from the rather different traditions of communitarianism and hermeneutics.

A somewhat different cause for disquiet lies in the perception that underlying most arguments about identity, rights and justice in Northern Ireland is a definition of those concepts which conceives of these as appertaining to communities rather than individuals. There are, in my view, strong grounds for scepticism about such views on justice and rights. Equally, however, it is either naive or disingenuous of liberal Unionists to appeal to the liberal individualist theory of justice and rights as if it were not just something to be aspired to, but an achieved state of affairs within the United Kingdom, to be protected against an allegedly collectivist and repressive Catholic-nationalist ethos.[14] Quite simply, the constitutional structures of the United Kingdom do not fulfil those ideals.

New conceptions of national identity, and arguments for Irish places in new postnationalist and transnationalist alignments, have been widely and vari-ously proposed among Irish thinkers—some of them have been noted in these pages, and the list could be much further extended. It may, though, be appro-priate to note the possible relevance for Ireland and especially for the north of the new thinking since the 1970s in other autonomist movements of Europe's northwest fringes: above all in Scotland and in Wales. There has, it is true, been some intellectual interchange between the different nationalisms of the 'Celtic fringe'—not only Irish, Welsh and Scottish but Cornish, Breton and so on. But such interchange has too often been between the most narrowly culturalist and even obscurantist currents within such movements. A transfusion and inter-mingling, instead, of ideas drawn from the imaginative and socially radical wings of these formations—thought whose most fertile development has per-haps come from Welsh nationalism, despite its electoral weakness—is poten-tially crucial for the future. What Emyr Wyn Williams of Plaid Cymru's 'National Left' said of the tradition of 'fossilised Liberal Nonconformist Welsh nationalism' is equally true of its Irish Catholic-Gaelicist (and indeed Marxist-Republican and postcolonialist-poststructuralist) counterparts: that its 'fixed concept of Welsh identity is incapable of contributing' to the process of forging a politics appropriate to the twenty-first century. (Williams 1988:9)

One way forward for understanding, and seeking to transform, the politics of the north Atlantic archipelago and its constituent parts may then be the daunt-ing one of trying to configure simultaneously the *multiple* interrelationships of national, racial, regional and other imaginings—as some Welsh and Scottish nationalist thinkers have sought to do. It means not merely recognising, as George Boyce does, that 'Irishness and Englishness constituted utopias: forever beckoning, but forever retreating, and, paradoxically, utterly necessary for each other's survival.' (Boyce 1986:249) That perception, acute as it is, remains too fixated upon a bilateral relationship. We need to think Irishness and English-ness also in their relation to Welshness and Scottishness, Yorkshireness and Kerryness, as well as all the multiple, non-territorial other social identifications in which individuals engage, the compound identities developing beyond nation-alism, and forming sites of resistance to exclusivist nationalism's current global revival. As the authors—many of them prominent figures in Loyalist paramili-tary politics—of the Shankill Think Tank's 1995 report, *A New Beginning*, urged:

we challenge Loyalists and Republicans to acknowledge that over the centuries each community has imbued many of the other's attributes, to the extent that the heritage of both traditions has increasingly become a shared one. We challenge Loyalists to acknowledge the 'Irish' component of their heritage, and Nationalists to acknowledge the 'British' component of theirs. (1995:24)

Thus hope may lie primarily not in seeking yet again to achieve a fair polit-ical compromise between opposed identities and views, but in attempting to transcend—if one prefers, to 'deconstruct'—the identities concerned. As Alan Finlayson—drawing on a very different theoretical tradition and idiom—puts it:

[W]e must *not* seek to establish a middle ground, find commonality between communities or push for parity of esteem. Rather the task is one of deconstruction. Firstly it is to deconstruct the traditions in question. By deconstruction I mean precisely showing that each is dependent on that which it excludes and that each is dependent on a contradictory and empty logic. Rather than think of each 'tradition' as equally legitimate we should demonstrate that each is equally illegitimate. (1998:121; emphasis in original)

And, Finlayson adds, we must go further, by 'deconstructing' also the very conception of the political in Northern Ireland, opening it to many more voices, different desires and experiences, multiple expressions of what 'politics' should be about—'to drown out the monotony with as much shouting as possible' in recognition that the local conflict cannot be 'solved' but can be 'transcended' by rethinking the idea of the political.

Here is the aspect of transnational colonial and postcolonial theory which might be most genuinely valuable for the Irish case: that which posits the necessity for moving on from a 'nationalist' to an 'emancipatory' mode, as suggested by Fanon and repeated (however ambiguously) by Said and others. The teleology implied in some of these accounts—and echoed by some of their Irish epigones, as by Declan Kiberd—may be questionable, but the aim is worth sustaining.[15]

Yet in insisting, as we must, on the impossibility of resolving conflict by reference to ancestral claims of right, we should not slip into the trap of thinking that, simply by demonstrating the 'artificiality' of identity-claims, their status as—in the two great current clichés of Anglophone historiography—'imagined communities' based on 'invented traditions', we have thereby defused their appeal and effectiveness. J. G. A. Pocock, the great New Zealand-born historian who has perhaps done more to stimulate rethinking about identity and political theory in the Anglophone world than any other postwar writer—and who has lamented the way in which, with entry to the European Community, Britain unilaterally severed his native country from both Britishness and Europeanness (1995:297) has this to say:

It is disturbingly easy for the critical intellectual (in this case including the historian) to point out how every identity has been constructed, with the implication that it is for the critic to say how and when it is to be deconstructed.

And he applies that thought to the fate of

the last of the historic nations formed in the past in this archipelago: the Protestant people of Northern Ireland, now asserting that they are 'British' whether or not the other 'British' peoples want them to be, and justly suspicious of a conspiracy to classify them as 'Irish' without their consent. I do not endorse the brutality of their extremists' methods when I say that I know what they are about. (1995:300–1)

Alongside the recognition of multiple, perhaps fragmentary and often highly individualised identities, then, we cannot ignore the continued strength of more totalising, overarching ones. We cannot hope to supplant them only through a 'postmodernist' kind of celebration of diversity and plurality; nor (in Finlayson's style) by a poststructuralist faith in the political potentialities of deconstructing identity.[16] As Arthur Aughey responded to Finlayson's argument, unity for its own sake might not be a very attractive political model, but there is little merit in advocating pluralist dissent for its own sake either (Aughey 1998:125). We must also seek kinds of societal bonding with an encompassing range and universalising intent which enable them effectively to rival the appeal of national, religious, 'ethnic' or 'racial' claims. They must, that is, be *political* identities (in the classical republican sense of that term), appealing both to shared interests and to universalist moral codes.

Towards the end of the twentieth century, the historic failures of statist social-ism and its model of inter-nationalism have been miserably apparent and much rehearsed. Equally widely criticised have been the somewhat similar failures of liberalism and its 'Enlightenment' ideas of universal rights and reason. Those failures have included apparent helplessness before, or in some notable instances deep complicity in, savage national and ethnic conflict. Yet the verdict on socialist—or liberal—internationalism in such situations of conflict should not perhaps be so harsh as it has tended recently to be. Surveying the efforts of socialists to combat and overcome national antagonisms in Bohemia and Northern Ireland, Frank Wright points out that however limited its practical effectiveness:

Working-class solidarity was both a constructive instrument of class power and a way of bringing out the grisly fact that national conflict was both an unpleasant evil (rather than a righteous cause) and something that could suck everything worthwhile down into the gutter . . . The history of these societies is apt to bury efforts of this kind and in so doing to bury their most redemptive moments; the greatest achievement of socialism in ethnic frontiers was to erect barriers of restraint against real possibilities of mad-ness . . . These barriers erected by socialist internationalism were nowhere near absolute, but they were a lot stronger than anything else available; and their failure is a tragic state-ment about these societies, not a condemnation of themselves. (1987:84–5)

The west European countries where social democrats have crucially shaped postwar destiny all come at the top of world league tables in every measure of democratic accountability, social welfare provision, and human rights obser-vance. They educate more of their people, execute and imprison fewer, and keep more of the newborn and the elderly alive for longer, than almost any-where else on the globe, including very rich societies like the USA or Japan. The local tragedy of Northern Ireland is not so much the failure there either of revolutionary socialism or insurrectionary nationalism, as that no social democratic party ever managed to take off—for such parties, despite everything and sometimes despite themselves, have played the major role in creating some of the least awful societies ever to have existed on earth. The strongest rational hopes for the future must lie in the belief that a vibrant social-democratic movement, or its close historical ally, a strong liberalism imbued with concern for social citizenship, may yet take root in Northern Ireland. Neither the Unionist nor the Republican traditions as such will have much to contribute to it, though the social and economic concerns of many who have identified with each tradition will certainly do so. It will prove, in the long view, quite unimportant whether it flourishes under the formal sovereignty of the United Kingdom, the Irish Republic, both, or neither.

NOTES

CHAPTER 1

1. 'Northern Ireland' (rather than 'Ulster', 'the six counties', etc.) is the nearest thing to a neutral available term in this notorious terminological minefield, and will be my normal usage. I use 'Ulster' where the reference is to the pre-partition nine-county region, or to Unionist discourses which themselves ordinarily employ that name for the modern six-county unit. As to the other most routinely contested issues of nomenclature: I refer to the city of Derry in County Londonderry, on the simple basis of following the official titles chosen by those entities' democratically elected local authorities; to the 'Irish Republic' for the 26-county state established in 1922 (though of course its title has changed more than once, and it only formally proclaimed itself a Republic in 1949). I use the inelegant but handy compound 'English/British' where I am referring to policies and trends which operated in Ireland both before and after the Unions of the Crowns and later the Parliaments of England and Scotland.

2. It is certainly not only the advocates of contending national or sectarian forces who have contributed to the rhetorical ferocity. As Terry Eagleton wryly comments 'even Irish liberal pluralists can be a bitterly partisan bunch, excoriating traditional prejudices with a virulence so unremitting as to involve them in a kind of performative contradiction.' (1995b:130)

3. As we shall see, however, almost all these theorists draw on a very narrow range of materials and ideas about colonialism, showing little knowledge of colonial histories elsewhere, and certainly taking no account of the growing body of criticism which has appeared identifying the shortcomings of the 'colonial discourse analysis' and 'postcolonial theory' which they utilise. Such critical accounts would include Ahmad 1992, Chrisman 1991, Dirlik 1994, MacKenzie 1995, Parry 1987, Robbins 1992, Thomas 1994—and see my 1998b and forthcoming 2000c *passim*.

4. Unless simply the Latin 'colonia'—a place of settlement. See Finley 1976 for a sketch of the etymology of the term 'colony'.

5. This claim also sits oddly with the extended efforts Ellis has elsewhere made—including elsewhere in the very same article—to debate Irish history's place in various comparative typologies of colonialism.

6. Though I am *not*, if it should need saying, attempting another contribution to the vast literature proposing 'solutions' to the Northern Irish conflict. For those who wish to pursue that theme more directly, major recent contributions include Anderson and Goodman eds 1998, Barton and Roche eds 1991, Boyle and Hadden 1994, Guelke ed. 1994, Keogh and Haltzel eds 1993, O'Leary 1999, Pollack ed. 1993, Norman Porter 1996. Perhaps the best succinct analysis of contemporary Northern Ireland's politics and political economy is Bew, Gibbon and Patterson 1994.

CHAPTER 2

1. The main features of nationalist historiography, as it coalesced into a dominant discourse, may thus roughly be summarised in what one of the founding 'revisionists',

T. W. Moody (1978/1994), identified as a series of guiding myths of Irish nationalist thought. I have drawn on his categorisation here.

2. The notion of a classless, or at least exceptionally egalitarian, Gaelic Ireland has also been a recurringly important theme in nationalist interpretations. It has, however, sometimes been somewhat uneasily mixed with a desire to emphasise the dynamism of an expanding, mercantile proto-capitalist economy: a dynamism which English conquest subverted. One finds this dual track already in the work of Alice Stopford Green, who rather contradictorily lauded both egalitarianism and acquisitive entrepreneurship in her *Making of Ireland and its Undoing* (Green 1909).

3. Or sometimes as a label for the ideology of expansion, so that in some usages 'imperialism' is the theory or aspiration of which 'colonialism' is the practice. Numerous other arguments over definition have been fought out—I analyse some of these, in mainly British contexts, in my 1993.

4. This was not entirely novel for English monarchs: tenth-century kings of Wessex had, with more than a touch of hubris, occasionally styled themselves emperors (Davies 1990:4).

5. Both 'revisionists' and their opponents tend to accuse the other camp of Anglo- or Brito-centric readings of Irish history. For nationalist historiography, both archipelago models and those sceptical about nationalism's historical claims involve denying or undercutting Irish distinctiveness—this is, for instance, Brendan Bradshaw's central complaint against Steven Ellis, on which see below p. 93. For writers such as Roy Foster, conversely, it is the nationalist interpretation which fails to accord Ireland's history sufficient autonomy, seeing it always through the spectacles of conflict with England. Yet as J. G. A. Pocock says, even on the nationalist assumption that such a conflict should be the determining interpretive theme: ' "Irish history" is not part of "British history", for the very good reason that it is largely the history of a largely successful resistance to being included in it; yet it is part of "British history", for exactly the same reason.' (1995:295)

6. A pioneering popular version of this approach is Hugh Kearney 1989. The essays in Bradshaw and Morrill eds 1996, Connolly ed. 1999, Ellis and Barber eds 1995, and Grant and Stringer eds 1995 provide overviews of the state of debate. Pocock's terminological shift—like the more widely used, less cumbersome, if absurdly woolly 'these islands'—has of course been taken up in part to assuage Irish sensitivities over the perceived chauvinism of the term 'British Isles'. Steven Ellis has argued, however, that the political sensitivity is misplaced, since the phrase 'British Isles' for the whole island group was widely used well before there was a British state or a United Kingdom (Ellis 1996a:15–16).

7. For the multiple anachronisms involved in unwary uses even of the term 'Ireland' itself for earlier periods, see S. Ellis 1996a:3–5.

8. See *inter alia* Davies 1990, 1993; Gillingham 1992, 1995; and for the wider claim about unusually if not uniquely early emergence of an English national identity, Greenfeld 1992, A. D. Smith 1986, Hastings 1997. For a powerful argument that French nationalism too can be shown to have developed already in the later Middle Ages, see Beaune 1991; and for 'colonial' models in medieval English history, West 1999.

9. The view of an early emergence of ethnic stereotyping, even senses of racial superiority, by the English over the Irish is endorsed also in Jane Ohlmeyer's synthesis of recent research (1998 esp. 130–3). Other medieval historians have, however, been more sceptical about how clearly senses of 'ethnic' or 'national' identity can be discerned so early. For a

sense of how limited were the Irish manifestations of any putatively distinctive conceptions of English power, see several of the contributions to Barry, Frame and Simms 1995. Ironically, some research appears to support one of the medieval stereotypes: apparently organised political violence *was* more endemic in medieval Irish society than in English (Charles-Edwards 1996, Frame 1996), even if full-scale conventional warfare was rare (Charles-Edwards:26). This is not to say that other kinds of brutality and oppression may not have been at least as pervasive under English rule.

10. The question echoes, of course, the title of Gwyn A. Williams's great investigation (1985) into the mutations of Welsh national identity. For some Scottish parallels, see William Ferguson's recent imaginative reconstruction of historiographical argument on *The Identity of the Scottish Nation* (1998).

11. England's economic lead may also have done so: it appears that already in the early Norman period, England was very much the dominant partner in Anglo-Irish trade, and it may even be possible to speak of Irish economic 'dependence' on England (Davies 1993:7).

12. See Greenfeld 1992 ch. 1. I am sceptical about some of this author's wider claims on the early coalescence of English nationalism, but her arguments concerning early-modern political language are powerful.

CHAPTER 3

1. See, as sources for these arguments, Perceval-Maxwell 1991, Bradshaw 1979, Brady 1991, Lennon 1994, Morrill 1995, and essays by Brady, Ford, Lennon and Cunningham in Brady and Gillespie 1986. Anthony Carty 1996 traces, in somewhat idiosyncratic style, the contemporary legal arguments about conquest and sovereignty.

2. For the African experience of colonial military conquest, see the judicious synthesising work of Vandervort 1998.

3. See Canny 1995 for a recent comparative analysis of religious, linguistic and political change across the kingdoms.

4. See also, on sixteenth- and seventeenth-century English ideologies and practices of colonisation, W. K. Andrews *et al.* eds 1978, Armitage 1992, Bradshaw *et al.* eds 1993, Canny ed. 1994, Canny and Pagden eds 1987, Carlin 1985, 1987, Durston 1986, Hirst 1994, Quinn 1940, Treadwell 1998. For the general picture of early-modern English expansion, still the best overview is Angus Calder's neglected classic, 1981, supplemented now by the contributions to Canny ed. 1998. Canny's forthcoming *Ireland in the English Colonial System* will be a summation of all his work in the area.

5. Tristan Marshall 1998 makes a similar argument, in seeking to demonstrate that *The Tempest* was not and could not have been the 'colonialist' play, relating to the Americas or to Ireland, that it has so often been analysed as being. Marshall insists that: 'Theatrical events located or concentrating on Ireland were in fact extremely rare in the early Jacobean period' (378).

6. See *inter alia* Armitage 1992, Canny 1973, 1988, Pagden 1995, 1998.

7. The felt need to elaborate moral and historical justifications for English conquest in Ireland was already evident among medieval writers. As R. R. Davies comments, the sheer variety and number of such justifications which Gerald of Wales put forward, for instance, suggests that Gerald felt a certain discomfort about the strength of his own case (Davies 1990:109–10).

8. Although Nicholas Canny, among others, has several times underlined the fact that some early English colonists in North America also sought to co-opt and assimilate native elites (e.g. Canny 1998c:158–64), no one disputes that this was a comparatively shortlived and unsuccessful endeavour, soon to be replaced by far more hostile, exclusionary and even exterminatory attitudes among the settlers.

9. Lennon 1994 gives a lucid overview of England's 'incomplete conquest' during the sixteenth century.

10. For classic expressions of this 'peripheral' approach to empire-building, see Fieldhouse 1961, 1981, Ronald Robinson and J. A. Gallagher 1961.

11. The Reformation was, for Bradshaw, the root cause of Ireland's—and Britain's—'British problem' (see also Bradshaw 1996); and, implicitly, a general 'return' to Catholic values is the solution. For more explicit formulations of that argument, see Patrick O'Farrell 1971 and, from a Welsh Catholic historian's perspective, Edwin Jones 1998.

12. This does not prevent another less careful analyst—predictably, one writing from a literary-critical rather than historical background—proclaiming unequivocally that Davies' writing 'seeks to bury the struggles and conflicts of history, to erase the story of colonial opposition, and to defend the injustices of colonial rule.' (Fogarty 1995:32)

13. On this theme, see also Canny 1991. Lennon 1994 is now the best available synthesis of research on the topic.

14. Morgan notes, however, that there is little hard evidence for O'Neill having been educated in England, as opposed to among the English in Ireland.

15. As Colm Lennon suggests, the process of reworking O'Neill into the leader of a 'Catholic crusade' began even in his lifetime, conducted by Counter-Reformation apologists. Already, among contemporaries, 'the elements of an ideology of Irish Catholic nationalism which emerged in the seventeenth century were being put into place' (1994:324).

16. It may also, so Steven Ellis believes, have involved Irish 'rebels' being treated with greater brutality than was visited on contemporary risings against the Crown within England, or on French and other continental opponents (Ellis 1996b:130–1).

17. Cf. also S. Ellis 1985, 1986, and the Ulster-Bohemia comparison drawn, apparently quite independently, for more recent times in Wright 1987.

18. See Brian Fitzpatrick 1988, J. M. Hill 1993, Philip Robinson 1984; while Treadwell 1998 is now the most detailed account of English 'patronage and plantation' policies in the early seventeenth century. As several historians of Ulster have pointed out, however, these divisions too were less clear-cut than often thought. Some of the Scottish migrants to northern Ireland were Gaelic-speaking, and many were Catholic.

19. Amidst a vast literature see e.g. Brian Fitzpatrick 1988, Russell 1991, Morrill 1995.

20. On Unionist senses of history see below pp. 95–106; cf. also A. T. Q. Stewart 1977, Barnard 1991, Buckley 1987, Richard Davis 1994, Alvin Jackson 1992, 1994, 1996a, McBride 1997, Brian Walker 1992. For the latest on the old controversy about the scale and agency of the 1641 killings, Mac Cuarta 1993, Perceval-Maxwell 1994.

21. See Richard Doherty 1998 (the best modern narrative of the 'Williamite war'), Brian Fitzpatrick 1988, Ohlmeyer 1996; and for an unequalled evocation of Aughrim—by some margin, the bloodiest day in all of Irish history—and its historico-mythic legacies, see Richard Murphy's long poem 'The Battle of Aughrim' in Murphy 1989.

22. Ohlmeyer 1996:185 thinks it likely that Petty's 'inspired guesses' on the total loss of life were too high, but historians 350 years later can still do little more than guess.

23. See Hayes-McCoy 1964:106–7, noting *inter alia* that muster rolls for the nominally

English army in Ireland in 1598 show only 2,300 of the 6,500 soldiers were born in England; 1,700 were from the Pale and 2,500 were Gaelic Irishmen; also Hayes-McCoy 1969, Ellis 1996b, Ohlmeyer 1996.

24. The literature on emergent cultural patterns is vast: for a selection and overview, see Field Day 1991, I:274–1010, and for a recent assessment Ross 1998. It is arguable, however, that the manichean opposition of Englishness to Irishness was itself in some sense the creation of mid-seventeenth-century discourses about ethnicity and religion. Kathleen Noonan (1998) makes such an argument in some historical detail, centring on the impact of John Temple's 1646 tract *The Irish Rebellion*. Wider, more sweeping claims about the reciprocal constructedness of English and Irish identities have become a common currency of recent Irish cultural theory, as in the work of Declan Kiberd: see below pp. 121–5.

25. Roy Foster (1988:162–3; 177–8), for instance, describes the colonial aspect of Ireland's situation in almost exclusively psychological terms. Perhaps the most detailed argument for the existence—continuing into the present—of a profound colonial impact on 'the Irish psyche' is Moane 1994; though as we shall see, this has also been a frequently reiterated theme in recent Irish literary and cultural criticism.

26. Indeed 'a great variety of forms of cultural cross-fertilisation' can be observed from at least the fifteenth century onward, as Colm Lennon notes (1994:11).

27. There are evident parallels and connections with the view of eighteenth- and early-nineteenth-century England too as a classic 'ancien regime': cf. Clark 1985.

28. Hechter 1975:81–95 presents the classic 'underdevelopment' case in comparative perspective. L. M. Cullen 1972 and 1981 are the major founding statements of the 'optimistic' or 'revisionist' view. R. F. Foster 1988:196–206 attempts a synthesis, tending more to the optimists' side. It is sometimes suggested (e.g. Ruane and Todd 1996: 26–8) that already the stronger economic growth of Protestant-dominated sectors helped fuse the religious division with perceptions of a gulf between the civilised or enterprising and the backward: this may however be a shade anachronistic.

29. McCracken 1986. Canny, however, argues that the Irish 'settler' elites, like those of the West Indies but *un*like those of mainland North America, were accepted as social equals in England. This, plus their consciousness of minority status, explains why the former did not rebel outright when the latter did. (Canny 1988:131–3) Marshall 1995 offers suggestive lines of thought on the attempts to create a global Britishness in what was becoming 'a nation defined by Empire' in the middle third of the eighteenth century, but emphasises how these were blocked by 'that deep-rooted plant that was British parochialism' (222) as well as by emergent colonial nationalism. This 'British parochialism' was indeed essentially English, experiencing difficulty in accepting either Scots or Irish as part of the imagined community. On this, see also Colley 1992; though as Nancy Curtin rightly complains Colley's widely praised work has little to say on the relation of Irishness to the formation of Britishness (Curtin 1996:213–14). Colley's is indeed at bottom, as Raphael Samuel also noted, 'a unionist history' (1998:28, 31). Perhaps the fullest modern accounts of Irish 'Patriot' politics are McDowell 1979 and Gerard O'Brien 1987.

30. Gough and Dickson eds 1990, Kelly 1992, Philpin ed. 1987, McDowell 1979, Jim Smyth 1992.

31. As Nancy Curtin (1996) points out, this wholesale revision of views on Ireland's eighteenth century has taken place with very little of the bitter political controversy which has accompanied 'revisionism' in other fields of Irish history.

32. Curtin 1994, James Quinn 1998, Jim Smyth 1992, Kevin Whelan 1996a, 1998, and several of the contributors to Dickson *et al.* 1993 and to Bartlett *et al.* 1999.

33. A. T. Q. Stewart 1995 emphasises the fragility of the links between the Defenders and the mainly Presbyterian United Irish organisation in Ulster, and the former's feeble contribution to the rising. Kevin Whelan 1996a sees the alliance as stronger and the contribution as greater, but does not appear wholly consistent on these points, referring in one place to the Orange Order inserting 'an implacable barrier to the linking of the United Irishmen and Defender territories' (124). There has been a tendency to see the Defenders, by contrast with the United Irishmen, as an essentially apolitical as well as sectarian peasant movement. Jim Smyth 1992, however, highlights the Defenders' social radicalism, though noting also the strains between the two movements imposed by religious antagonism, both that of the Defenders themselves, and that mobilised by Loyalists.

34. Pakenham 1969, Elliott 1982, Cullen and Bartlett in Corish 1985, Thomas Bartlett 1996, Keogh and Furlong eds 1996—and for what is now the most detailed modern narrative history of the Wexford rebellion, Gahan 1995. Both Gahan and, more sharply, Kevin Whelan (1996a:174, 1996b:30) argue that the most widely read modern account, Pakenham's, exaggerates the sectarianism of the Wexford rebels and strips the movement of its politics. The bicentenary of the revolt has produced an outpouring of new work: notable contributions include Chambers 1998, Mary Cullen ed. 1998, Hill, Turner and Dawson eds 1998, Keogh and Furlong eds 1996, McBride 1998, Maguire ed. 1998, O'Donnell 1998, Whelan 1998 and above all Bartlett, Dickson, Keogh and Whelan eds forthcoming 2000. I discuss this writing, and its place in the historiography of 1798, in more detail in my 1999a.

35. On late-Victorian Catholic clerical appropriations of the legacy of 1798, see also Kinsela 1996, Kevin Whelan 1996b.

36. Liam Kennedy and Johnson 1996 is a clear, succinct overview of these recurring debates. The great majority of contemporary economic historians have tended towards the view that the Union was *not* crucially significant either for good or for ill: economic change was relatively independent of political shifts. See among others L. M. Cullen ed. 1969, Liam Kennedy 1996, Mokyr 1983, Ó Grada 1994, Eoin O'Malley 1981, 1989, Ó Tuathaigh 1972. I discuss modern political uses of these arguments below.

37. After a long era of relative neglect, the historiography of the Famine has grown dramatically in recent years, in part boosted by the sesquicentennial commemorations from 1995 onward. Ó Grada 1996 surveys the literature produced around the commemoration period. Other major interventions include Goldstrom 1981; Mokyr 1985; Ó Grada 1989; Peter Gray 1994, 1998; Kinealy 1994; Kelleher 1997, Crawford ed. 1997, contributions to Vaughan ed. 1989 and Hill and Ó Grada eds 1993 (especially those of James Donnelly and Austin Bourke), and the overviews in Daly 1996, F. S. L. Lyons 1973:34–46, and R. F. Foster 1988:318–44. For more popular accounts—and thus of course ones probably more influential on public perceptions of history—see Woodham-Smith 1962 and Thomas Gallagher 1982. The 'Great Famine' was certainly not the first major demographic disaster to strike Ireland under British rule: failed harvests and epidemic disease in 1741 may have claimed as many as 300,000 lives.

38. A striking contrast may still however be noted, for instance, between the insistence (or perhaps rather assumption) in one fine study of famine and emigration (Scally 1995: e.g. 8, 202–3, 231–4) that colonialism and resistance to it are crucial categories for understanding the experience, and the total absence of reference to such ideas in another, near-simultaneously published and equally scholarly such study (Fitzpatrick 1994).

39. The less extreme case that official British responses were marked and conditioned by anti-Irish racism has, rightly, more contemporary support. See for instance the historiographically naive but powerful polemic of Hazel Waters (1995), and the more nuanced arguments on this point of Peter Gray (1994, 1998), Christine Kinealy (1995) or James Donnelly (1993).

40. For the interaction of nationalist and agrarian questions in the later nineteenth century, see above all Bew 1978, 1987.

41. Wright 1996:400–1 notes that reading Ulster newspapers of the Victorian era, one is left with the impression that whenever Portadown is mentioned, it means bad news. That same impression is likely to remain with the newspaper readers of the 1990s. Wright's book—especially chs 9, 11, and 12—is probably the best account of the evolution of nineteenth-century sectarian conflicts, though for Belfast see also Boyd 1969, Budge and C. O'Leary 1973, Hepburn 1996.

42. See for instance Bulpitt 1983, Birch 1989, Samuel ed. 1989, and the whole 1990s explosion of 'four nations' or 'archipelagic' history discussed above.

43. Perhaps the most incisive recent overview on these questions, including the rehabilitation of Redmond, is Bew 1994. On the distinctiveness and strength of Ulster (as against Irish) Unionism even before the turn of the century, see especially Alvin Jackson 1989.

CHAPTER 4

1. For an excellent recent analysis of Griffith's political thought, emphasising its highly conservative and anti-democratic character and supplementing Richard Davis's intellectual biography, see Maume 1995. Clare O'Halloran notes that, whereas Irish nationalists rejected comparisons with non-white colonial subjects before the Treaty, thereafter it rapidly became rather popular for them to present the position of northern Nationalists in such terms. This indicates, in O'Halloran's view, the widespread Free State presumption that northerners were inferior beings (O'Halloran 1987:61–3).

2. Thomas Dixon's famous racist novel *The Clansman* specifically attributes white Southern resistance against Reconstruction to the 'Scotch-Irish' nonconforming spirit (Dixon 1905: e.g. 187–8, 342). His heroic Klansmen, executing summary justice on carpetbaggers and uppity blacks, are based in 'Ulster County', South Carolina. Latterly, it is reported that when, in October 1995, the Irish-American Unity Conference compared Ulster Unionist leader David Trimble to US white supremacist and former Klansman David Duke, Trimble naturally complained—but so did Duke, who resented being thus linked with a man who fought against fellow white Christians! (Stevenson 1996:214–15)

3. The subject remains little researched; but see Brasted 1980, 1985, Cumpston 1961, Fraser 1996. Gopal 1975:22 and Nehru 1953:99 treat Nehru's early Irish links, Devi 1992 discusses the literary associations between India and Ireland, and several contributors to M. and D. Holmes eds 1997 cover other aspects of Irish-Indian relations. Forthcoming work by Tony Ballantyne, Elleke Boehmer, Lynn Innes, Joseph Lennon and Gauri Viswanathan, among others (much of it presented at the Third Galway Conference on Colonialism, June 1999) explores further literary and historical interconnections.

4. Though elsewhere, inconsistently, Crummell lauded the tenacity of Irish desires for freedom, linking this to an exaggerated perception of Irish anti-slavery sentiment (Crummell 1891:240–2).

5. I have, however, not been able to see a copy of R. P. Davis: 'India in Irish Revolutionary Propaganda, 1905–22' *Journal of the Asiatic Society of Bangladesh* 22, 1 (1977), which may show more extensive influences than I have suggested.

6. See for instance L. P. Curtis 1968, 1971, Gibbons 1991, Lebow 1976; and on more popular, agitational level Liz Curtis 1984b.

7. Scally suggests, far more emphatically than most historians of the subject would do, that to the Victorian English the Irish 'were a paradigm of the barbarian . . . "Paddy" stood beside the Fedayeen [sic] or Aborigene, just above the apes on the "monkey chart".' (1995:8) 'Fedayeen' is Arabic, roughly, for 'freedom fighters' (more literally, self-sacrificers) and is very much a late-twentieth-century term: possibly Scally means 'fellaheen' (or 'peasants').

8. For a sample of British perceptions of the Irish from the mid-sixteenth to the mid-nineteenth centuries—unsurprisingly indicating very mixed and by no means entirely hostile attitudes—see Hadfield and McVeagh eds 1994. Roy Foster's case for a more nuanced—or in his critics' eyes Panglossian—view of Anglo-Irish 'racial' attitudes is set out in several of the essays of his 1993.

9. There is a vast and rapidly expanding literature on ethnic and religious attitudes and conflicts in relation to Irish migrants in both Britain and North America. For Britain, see *inter alia* L. P. Curtis 1968, Graham Davis 1991a, Devine 1991, Fielding 1993, Finnegan 1982, David Fitzpatrick 1989, Gilley and Swift 1985, Colin Holmes 1988, J. A. Jackson 1963, Lees 1978, Lennon *et al.* 1988, McFarland 1990, O'Day 1994, Waller 1981; for the USA (a briefer selection from an even larger literature) Drudy 1985, Erie 1988, Horsman 1981, Knobel 1986, Kerby Miller 1985.

10. See especially Roediger's admirable dissection of these crosscurrents in his 1991 ch. 7; also Roediger 1993, Emmons 1989, Erie 1988, Theodore Allen 1994 and a more popularly oriented work, notably ill-informed about Irish and even Irish-American history, which nonetheless suggests a story more subtle than its manichean political stance or its eye-catching title, *How the Irish Became White*, would suggest: Ignatiev 1995. Some other commentators have, like Ignatiev, wished to argue that the Irish were by no means necessarily viewed as 'white' in various nineteenth-century contexts: see e.g. Liz Curtis 1984, Lebow 1976, Lloyd 1991. All are highly polemical, and somewhat thin on specific historical evidence, but such claims have tended to be accepted unproblematically in some non-specialist literature: see for instance Dyer 1997:51–3.

11. See e.g. Bhreatnach 1998, Moore 1981, Mac Laughlin 1995, McVeigh 1996 and, for a range of views on ethnic minorities and prejudice in contemporary Northern Ireland, Hainsworth ed. 1998.

12. For the USA, though one recent work argues that eventually reliance on the urban public sector has proved a barrier to further mobility, trapping many Irish in declining occupations (Erie 1988), several other studies have shown that Irish Americans are the second most successful white ethnic group in the USA (after American Jews) in income and educational levels. For Irish Australia, see Patrick O'Farrell 1987, 1990, Cieran Kiernan 1986; and for a range of Irish-Australian cultural responses Wannan 1965. Romantic emphasis on Irish-Australian rebelliousness and 'social banditry' *à la* Ned Kelly may have obscured the steady upward mobility of the community as a whole. The many bushrangers and other supposed romantic rebels or social bandits who were of Irish origin are often noted; the fact that a large majority of the police who hunted them were Irish-born (82 per cent in Victoria in 1874, 67 per cent in New South Wales in 1865) less often (Akenson 1996:145).

13. For the best available summary of the global evidence and its implications, including sharp critique of the common, usually unargued-for presumption that 'Irish diaspora' means 'Irish Catholic diaspora', see Akenson 1996. It is striking to note that in the USA, while Catholic Irish-Americans are as previously noted the nation's second most successful ethnic group economically and educationally, US Protestants of Irish descent (to a significant degree a Southern, rural population) are probably the *least* successful major white group (ibid: 243–4, 251–2).

14. For a useful overview of arguments associating racism more with European state-making than with colonialism, see Miles 1993.

15. And in fairness it should perhaps be noted that Stewart, a historian of Northern Irish Protestant background, appears to include his own community in this negative stereotyping.

16. Cf. Jones and Stallybrass 1992, Innes 1993, 1994, Watson 1991, Catherine Nash 1993, Hamer 1989, Cairns and Richards 1988:48–50.

17. See Cullingford 1990, Innes 1993, MacCana 1980, MacCurtain 1980, Wills 1993:52–60, Longley 1994 esp. ch. 7, many passages in Kiberd 1995; and for a psychoanalytical interpretation centred on an overblown reading of the 1907 'Playboy' riots, Tifft 1992.

18. See, amidst a huge literature on these questions, Garvin 1987; Hutchinson 1987; Field Day II:950–1020.

19. See especially 'The Irish Mind' and 'The Shirt of Nessus' in C. C. O'Brien 1988a, and O'Brien 1994. The long-awaited autobiography, O'Brien 1998, unfortunately adds little to the Cruiser's previously published thoughts on these themes. It was, after all, produced when the author was over eighty years old, and had suffered both a stroke, and a tragic bereavement in the sudden, premature death of his daughter Kate.

20. Though see Jeffery ed. 1996, especially the contributions by Bairner, Fraser, Ollerenshaw and Jeffery himself; plus H. Morgan 1993b, and the forthcoming work, especially on Irish-South African connections, of Donal Lowry: see his 1996b.

21. In the 1830s over 40 per cent of the British army was Irish-born, while at peak the Irish 'share' of entrants into the British Indian civil service was over 24 per cent (Akenson 1996:142–6, Cook 1987).

22. Already the Atlantic plantation societies of the sixteenth and early seventeenth centuries were, as Canny comments, 'dominated by the English, who tolerated a sequence of sub-communities where either Scots or Irish predominated, and which were expected to fulfil special functions for the benefit of the wider plantation effort.' (1998b:14) Two centuries later and a world away, settlement in New Zealand told a rather similar story. Despite substantial Irish representation—and significant Scottish *over*-representation —among migrants there, the English always remained the largest single group, in the formative earlier stages of migration the absolute majority, and throughout the colonial period the politically and culturally dominant element (Belich 1996:313–37).

23. For the inter-war Dublin battles over Armistice and Remembrance Days, which pitted Republicans against ex-servicemen (especially Protestants) and Trinity College students, see Leonard 1996.

24. The most detailed account of these activities is the very hostile survey in English 1994a.

25. The actual historical evidence on resisting or rebellious alliances between Africans and Irish in Britain's slave colonies is fragmentary, though several historians have indeed suggested that Irish indentured labourers were more likely to form such alliances than were other poor whites—e.g. Beckles 1989; Philip Morgan 1991:196–7.

26. For expressions of such sympathy, see also Richard Davis 1994:275–89. As he notes, there has been little if any evidence of practical cooperation, at any stage, between ANC and IRA despite the assiduous efforts of rightwing 'counter-insurgency experts' to establish it. The IRA has had a great deal to gain, in terms of prestige, from association with the ANC and has fought hard for this; but without notable success. Nelson Mandela, in 1990, called for Sinn Fein to be included in peace talks and thus aroused some British and Unionist anger, but has never expressed any reliably recorded sympathy for the IRA. At Sinn Fein's 1998 conference, ANC Deputy General Secretary Thenjiwe Mtintso—himself a former officer in the ANC's military wing—addressed parallels between the situations in detail. On the one hand, he appeared to be strongly identifying with the Republican position, and suggesting that in Ireland as in South Africa the enemy must be forced, rather than persuaded, to submit. On the other hand, he was clearly urging the IRA to fall in behind the Sinn Fein leadership's strategy of negotiation and compromise (*An Phoblacht/Republican News* 23 April 1998).

27. See Richard Davis 1974 for a detailed examination of Griffith's Listian economic nationalism, and the often wild claims about Irish natural resources on which it was based. This was despite the fact that List himself had argued that his prescriptions applied only to large states, and that Ireland's best prospects lay with further integration into the British economic system: ibid: 130.

28. Esp. G. O'Brien 1921; see also Johnson and Kennedy's discussion of O'Brien, in their 1991. Such thinking, with its founding presumption that political independence was the cure for all economic ills, and consequent neglect of practical, immediate suggestions for economic development, was already subject to substantial critique in the decades before 1921. James Connolly's Marxist criticism is the best-known instance, but other strands worth more retrospective consideration than they have yet received included the ideas of the Irish Co-operative movement and of George William Russell. See for instance Catherine Nash 1998: which also makes the important point that such circles carried on a more sophisticated and forward-looking conversation about gender than did mainstream nationalism.

29. See above all Elliott 1989 for the reality—and the myths—of Tone's political ideas; while J. Quinn 1998 surveys the evidence for United Irish views on social and economic justice.

30. On the myriad posthumous ideological uses and abuses of Connolly, see *inter alia* W. K. Anderson 1994, English 1994a, Austen Morgan 1988, Henry Patterson 1989.

31. Gibbons's co-thinker David Lloyd, almost as fancifully, claims close congruence between Connolly's thought and that of Gramsci (Lloyd 1996:264, 277).

32. See, *inter alia*, C. C. O'Brien 1974:88–98, Austen Morgan 1988, Henry Patterson 1989:7–12. Amongst a huge literature still retaining the illusion that Connolly *did* resolve the problems of combining nationalism and socialism, see for instance W. K. Anderson 1994, Minnerup 1979.

33. On the social conservatism of the dominant rural forces in the 1919–21 war, see David Fitzpatrick 1977, Garvin 1996, Michael Laffan 1985, Arthur Mitchell 1995. Peter Hart (1997) has recently demonstrated that the geography of IRA violence in 1917–23 does not correlate strongly with any indicator of social structure, levels of poverty etc.; while his subsequent book (1998) emphasises the essentially conservative ethos of 'respectability' and community binding together IRA volunteers in Cork—with one of the consequences being the ostracism, persecution and not infrequently murder inflicted on

people defined as outside that conception of community, whether they were vagrants, alleged sexual deviants, or Protestants.

CHAPTER 5

1. Turner's is a very heavily footnoted article; but these sweeping statements are referenced not to any work of research but solely to an offensive 'Irish joke' supposed to have been told by Lord John Russell.
2. See, as a selection only from a very large literature, Bew 1978, 1987, 1994, Boyce 1988, Buckland 1973, Gailey 1987, Harvie 1976, Jalland 1980, Kendle 1989, 1997, Loughlin 1986, 1995, Lubenow 1988 and for a comparative perspective Lustick 1993.
3. Jeffery 1996a:4–14 surveys some of the arguments, offering rather non-committal conclusions.
4. Thus Richard Hawkins (1991) argues that Irish influence on British colonial policing was minimal—or at least that no historian has yet demonstrated such influence—while Keith Jeffery (1996a:10–12) asserts that it was substantial.
5. For overviews, in roughly chronological order of period dealt with, see Boyce 1972 and 1988, Gailey 1987, Jalland 1980, Townshend 1975, Canning 1985, Harkness 1969, McMahon 1984, Fisk 1983, Bew and Patterson 1985, Guelke 1988, Arthur and S. Evans 1998, Jeffery 1988.
6. As was argued, for instance, in a *New Statesman* editorial at the time, ('Heart of the Union' 3 August 1990, written by the present author). James Loughlin, quoting the editorial, believes this judgement 'exaggerated only slightly' (1995:213).
7. See amidst a substantial—but usually more polemical than analytical—recent literature O'Dowd 1994, Sinn Fein 1994, Mike Tomlinson 1994, 1995. More detailed and nuanced accounts from broadly similar perspectives include Munck 1993, O'Hearn 1989, 1998a, b.
8. For instance Birnie 1995, Cadogan Group 1992, 1994, Gudgin 1995, Roche and Birnie 1995: a literature little if any less crude and polemical than that on the other side.
9. A pioneering work was Paul Bew and Henry Patterson's *The British State and the Ulster Crisis* (1985), considering the era from the outbreak of the 'Troubles' to the early 1980s. Subsequently, there has been no substantial monographic discussion devoted specifically to British policies in Northern Ireland; though sections in such general surveys of the problem as Bew, Gibbon and Patterson 1995, McGarry and B. O'Leary 1995 and Ruane and Todd 1996 have been of value. Catterall and McDougall eds 1996 has some important contributions, while Ruane and Todd 1996 ch. 8 is a succinct and level-headed summary. Anthony McIntyre (1995) has discussed the ways in which the British state has sought—in his view successfully—to dictate the political agenda of its sworn foes, the Republican movement. McIntyre is himself a former IRA activist, and brings a certain disillusioned insider's perspective to bear: though also an overly conspiratorial view of state strategies. Thinking about British aims in pro-Republican circles has, however, generally seemed to remain on a considerably cruder level than this.
10. Major modern discussions of Marx and Engels on Ireland include Strauss 1951, Bew, Gibbon and Patterson 1979 ch. 1; Horace B. Davis 1967; Cummins 1980 esp. ch. 5; Nigel Harris 1990 ch. 3.
11. For examination of this tradition of writing and action, see Gupta 1975 and Howe 1993.

CHAPTER 6

1. See Ruane 1992 for an attempted categorisation of a wide range of modern scholars according to their acceptance or rejection of colonial models for Ireland. I have learned much from Ruane's work, though he does not consider literary or cultural studies, and I find his pigeonholing of particular writers sometimes misleading. More important, the extreme agnosticism of his conclusions seems unwarranted. Ruane believes that the existing literature 'points to the questions that are outstanding and have to be answered, but it does not let us answer them. At the current stage of research in Irish historical studies, the questions of whether, for what period, or in what sense Ireland should be viewed in colonial terms are unanswerable.' (319) I hope, naturally, that the present book at least substantially qualifies that judgement. Brief, polemical repudiations of the aptness of colonial models for Ireland include Liam Kennedy 1993, 1996, Brian Walker 1990. Neither discusses any substantial range of the literature adopting the colonial model. Kennedy, though rightly identifying cultural theorists as its main contemporary exponents, mentions only Fredric Jameson and Edward Said among these, ignoring all the contributions from Ireland itself. A more substantial discussion, focusing on literary politics and directing its critique mainly against the Field Day collective, is the long 'Introduction' to Longley 1994.

2. Thus David Miller (of Stirling University; not to be confused with David W. Miller) argues at length (1998) that the failure of many scholars to adopt colonial models is a quite direct result of political censorship or self-censorship, of a pro-Unionist or 'British Establishment' kind. Similar claims are made by Robbie McVeigh (1998a) and Pamela Clayton (1998), among others.

3. Invention or popularisation of this metaphorical use of 'Dublin 4' (in reality a postal district which contains some areas that might be thought to fit the stereotype, and some poorer ones which clearly do not) has been attributed both to Fennell and to the late John Healy.

4. Other important work stressing the power of geographical analysis for understanding Irish history includes Heslinga's pioneering study (1979) of the Irish border as a cultural divide—one which, he argues, precedes rather than deriving from the political divisions—A. T. Q. Stewart 1977, Estyn Evans 1981, and the essays in Brian Graham ed. 1997 and M. Anderson and E. Bort eds 1999. Heslinga's book, which sees the border between Northern Ireland and the Republic as corresponding, culturally, to that between Scotland and England, has been rather tendentiously pressed into service recently in support of Unionist claims: see Arthur Green's contribution to J. W. Foster ed. 1995.

5. Poole 1990 begins the task of exploring the local variations of political violence in Northern Ireland. Even virtually contiguous working-class districts within the narrow confines of Catholic West Belfast have had radically divergent experiences of the contemporary conflict: see, for a sample of accounts of particular enclaves, Frank Burton 1978 on the Ardoyne (thinly disguised as 'Anro'), Conroy 1988 on Clonard, and De Baroid 1990 on Ballymurphy.

6. No doubt this was heavily influenced by reaction to an English/British historiography which has, until quite recently, had few global rivals in its tendency to proclaim or assume national uniqueness. Similarly, the failure of much Irish history-writing to register the full complexity of relations with the 'other island' is at least matched by what Victor Treadwell rightly castigates as the difficulty of locating Ireland on the mental map of most English historians (1998:15).

7. Not only journalistic writers like Toolis, but almost all professional historians, have to some degree fallen into this trap. There is depressingly little awareness of—often directly parallel—debates about the 'pathologies of national identity' elsewhere. To take just one of these, the running argument among Arab intellectuals about the burden of the past and the problems of nationalism, see *inter alia* Ajami 1981, al-'Azm 1984, al-Khalil 1993, Barakat 1993, Sharabi 1988. There are some notable similarities with analogous Irish discussions; but so far as I have seen, no cross-referencing whatever.

8. In both of these, moreover, there is rather little overt *national*, as opposed to religious, prejudice. The myriad failings that Macaulay, in particular, discerns among the Irish are almost all held to be attributable to their Catholicism. One later historian, however, has suggested that Macaulay had a massive influence on Ulster Unionist historical images and self-images (Loughlin 1995:24–6; 1999:110–12).

9. On the bardic response to conquest see Caball 1998, Canny 1982b, Anthony Carty 1996 ch. 3, Dunne 1980, Leerssen 1988, O Riordan 1990, as well as the bilingual selection from the poetry in Ó Tuama and Kinsella eds 1981.

10. Donoghue is clear about the extent to which the messages of his education remain with him—his dislike of historical 'revisionism' (159–62, 166–72), his acceptance of strongly stereotyped views of Protestants (e.g. 46–7, 53–4), even such bizarrities as his being unable to say the word 'chorister' because he associates it with Protestant worship (125)!

11. See the comments on her early historical education, familial and formal, in her 1969 autobiography *The Price of My Soul*. There, she appears ambivalent and sometimes caustic about the romantic nationalist conception of history she imbibed as a child. The subsequent career of Bernadette McAliskey might suggest to some that nonetheless she learned its lessons all too well. Augusteijn 1996:13 notes the influence of nationalist accounts of Irish history, learned especially in Christian Brothers schools, on many otherwise fairly unideological IRA Volunteers in 1916–22.

12. A formulation which rather begs the question of what had formed the popular opinion itself. One answer might be sought, as I have suggested above, in the striking degree to which cultural nationalism already dominated popular and school-level historiography under the Union: see also Tierney 1919, and for a wider view of such themes, O'Mahony and Delanty 1998.

13. For overviews of post-1920s Irish historiographical development, see Lee 1989:587–97, Fanning 1986/1994, R. F. Foster 1993b, McCartney 1994, Gabriel Doherty 1996, O'Mahony and Delanty 1998, and above all the contributions to Brady 1994, and to Boyce and O'Day 1996, among which the articles by Boyce 1996b and Ó Tuathaigh 1994 may be especially singled out.

14. For Deane, the historians' besetting sin is their naive belief in their own capacity for objectivity, for 'telling it as it really was'. This is not the place to pursue that argument, beyond noting how caricatured is Deane's picture—little modified when he returned to the attack in his 1997—of historians' practice. For an important survey of how the historical profession of another country, the USA, has dealt with these issues over the decades, see Novick 1988.

15. And the 'linguistic turn' in historical studies, under the influence of Foucault, so widespread in Anglophone historical studies in the 1990s, appeared even in the later 1990s to have had very little influence on Irish history.

16. Though see Coakley 1994 on the post-1950s transformation of the treatment of contemporary history in the Republic's school textbooks.

17. For instance in the Field Day anthology, or O Snodaigh 1991.

18. E.g. Dalton 1974, Coakley 1983. For a more balanced and well-documented, though still sharply negative, view of Pearse see Edwards 1977. All these writers see a romantic, even apocalyptic kind of Gaelicist nationalism, imbued with ideas of blood sacrifice and redemptive violence, at the heart not only of Pearse's thought but of the Republican tradition in general. The most recent major study of Pearse, by Sean Farrell Moran (1994) broadly concurs but offers three major qualifications: a) that in Moran's opinion, writers imbued with a secularist worldview, like Edwards, will inevitably not only be hostile to Pearse but will necessarily fail to understand him; b) that Pearse's irrationalism and sacrificial ideology were not peculiar to him or to Ireland but part of a general, Europe-wide revolt against reason in the years before the First World War; c) that Pearse's ideas triumphed in the end: the 'lasting nature of his vision has vindicated him despite the excesses it has since inspired.' (202) The veteran socialist-nationalist Desmond Greaves more sweepingly rejects the idea that 'blood sacrifice' was central to the beliefs of the 1916 rebels in his 1991, while Boyce 1996a surveys some of the disputes over the Easter Rising in would-be dispassionate fashion. As David Fitzpatrick points out (1996:379) vainglorious militarism was certainly not confined to Irish Nationalists, but was a 'common rhetoric' of almost all varieties of early-twentieth-century politics in Ireland and Britain and indeed much of Europe. Compare, for instance, the late writings of Charles Peguy.

19. Pursewarden in *Balthazar* (Durrell 1968:283).

20. For some recent instances of just this being done, in the sphere of feminist history, see Holmes and Urquhart eds 1994, Luddy 1995, O'Dowd and Wicher eds 1995.

21. Visceral hostility to 'revisionism' and especially to O'Brien also marks even the work of the highly respected political scientists Brendan O'Leary and John McGarry, based in London and Ontario respectively: see their remarkably ill-tempered comments in 1995:426 n. 13.

22. The same comparison has several times been made (in conference presentations at which I was present, though not I think in print) by Brendan Bradshaw. The obvious response to such claims is to suggest that the most meaningful parallel is that between Irish nationalist (ab)uses of history and instrumentalist Israeli-Zionist deployments of ideas about historic Jewish suffering. On this analogy, Ulster Protestants would—in ways few of them would like—be cast in the role of Palestinians! Bradshaw's other main point in this connection, that historians of Ireland, like those of the Shoah, require special sensitivities to deal with the 'catastrophic dimension' of history, might have more merit. I attempt a preliminary comparative analysis of Irish and Israeli 'revisionist' historiographies in my 2000a. On the methodological and moral problems involved, in the case of the Shoah, see Friedlander ed. 1992.

23. A similar attack, regarding Irish 'revisionism' as, quite simply, politically motivated Unionist apologetics—though seeking to distinguish this from 'genuine' historical revision—is mounted in Berresford Ellis 1989.

24. Odder connections were also sometimes made—ones for all their oddity, symptomatic of unreconstructed cultural nationalism. Thus a Professor of English (!) at University College Galway, P. L. Henry, linked Cruise O'Brien's historical revisionism, his supposed hostility to the Irish language, and his support for allowing Irish television owners to receive BBC broadcasts. The last was 'tantamount to reconquest'; the three together 'treasonable' (quoted Akenson 1995:412).

25. A related complaint is made in Canny 1995, where he insists that the proper approach to relations among the histories of England, Ireland, and Scotland is *comparative* rather than the currently influential *integrative* one; though in urging this 'I would prefer to be labelled with the modern-sounding tag of "Brito-sceptic" rather than with the tired nineteenth-century label of "Nationalist Historian".' (1996:147) It might be said that insofar as Canny is directing his critique against 'four nations' or 'archipelagic' historiography, it is misplaced; though in relation to some influential histories of 'Britishness' (like that of Linda Colley) it has more force.

26. Elsewhere Bradshaw has been yet more explicit about the pieties which govern his view of history, as in attacking Ruth Dudley Edwards's study of Pearse as a 'condescending and mean-spirited biography of that heroic figure' (1994:37). See the angry responses to Bradshaw by Hugh Kearney 1991, Ellis 1991, and Dunne 1992.

27. See for instance the way in which Tomas MacSiomoin insists on a *deliberate*, planned English destruction of the Irish language, and his apparent view that anyone who doubts the conscious malevolence of the scheme is an apologist for oppression (1994).

28. See for instance Bhabha 1992, 1994, Chakrabarty 1992, Fabian 1983, Robert Young 1991. I discuss these themes in some detail in my 2000c.

29. And certainly they were not created, as some southern Irish writers have suggested with tongue in cheek, to keep the wild, barbarous Ulster folk fenced off from their more civilised neighbours!

30. These arguments have been subject to surprisingly little critical analysis, though see H. J. Morgan 1993, Richard Davis 1994:104 ff., Berresford Ellis 1989 (which, in a remarkably insensitive coupling, likens the Cruthin theory first to Zionist beliefs, then to Nazi race theory!). Some commentators have appeared uncritically to accept their historical truth, though not on the basis of any visible knowledge of ancient history: e.g. Bruce 1992:234; Stevenson 1996:153.

31. The Ulster-Scottish association, and particularly that between Ulster and Galloway (southwest Scotland) are constantly stressed in this writing. On some levels—if not necessarily those of ancient history as Adamson and Hall proclaim—this is experientially accurate. Anyone who has spent much time in, say, both Kirkudbrightshire and North Antrim will know in how many ways they are strikingly similar places, on levels from architecture and town planning, through accent and dialect or patterns of socialisation, to historical memory.

32. James Loughlin too urges the lack of wider popular appeal for such ideas, and for the notion of an independent Ulster which they were widely taken to underpin—since most Unionists could not accept that their Britishness or their UK membership was under imminent threat (1995:202–3).

33. On the complex and contested symbolism of parades, banners and murals in Northern Ireland, see also—as recent contributions to a rapidly swelling literature—Buckley ed. 1998, Jarman and Bryan 1998.

34. The passionate identification of Ulster First World War military experience with specifically *Protestant* experience may however also have been a relatively late flowering, not least in its more sectarian dimensions. It is striking that the semi-official history (Falls 1922) of the Ulster Division, which was largely recruited from the ranks of the UVF and which suffered so severely at the Somme, makes no reference at all to its being an almost exclusively Protestant force. The book, which was published under Lord Carson's patronage and which obtained a revered status in many an otherwise almost bookless

working-class Ulster home, made not a single allusion to the Division's religious composition; and even in discussing its origins and recruitment, where political allusions were unavoidable, made them in an extremely reticent, almost coded manner. James Loughlin however suggests (without citing much evidence) that there was in 1914–18 a greater strength—or at least a more overt presence—of patriotism among Ulster soldiers, and even on the Ulster home front, than elsewhere in the islands (Loughlin 1995:78–80). The mythology of the Ulster Division, he believes, begun during the war itself, not only in retrospect (ibid: 82–4).

35. Though as Brian Walker argues (1992:57–8) there are good reasons for scepticism as to whether this reflects a 'deep-seated historical memory' as opposed to more recently created myth. Such 'memory', where not fabricated, is of course highly selective. As Walker also notes, probably more east Antrim Protestants were killed by Crown forces in the 1798 rebellion than by Catholics in 1641—but the former deaths are forgotten, the latter 'remembered' (ibid: 58).

36. And as Belinda Loftus notes, tracing the history of images of William III in Loyalist iconography, the standard trope of William at the Boyne on his white horse owes less to the portraits of William's own lifetime than to a tradition founded by Benjamin West's 1780 painting of the Boyne, while the tradition of mural painting appears to date only from the first years of this century: Victorian photographs of Belfast show no murals (Loftus 1990:31).

37. There has been a vigorous debate among American historians—well summarised in M. A. Jones 1991—over whether or how far the 'Scotch-Irish' in the New World should be thought of as a culturally distinct group (let alone Fitzpatrick's separate 'race'), or as subsumable within wider Scottish, Irish and/or even 'Celtic' identities. This debate has, however, made little reference to modern writing on identity-formation in Ireland itself—or apparently, vice versa—despite its evident resonances especially for Ulster history and politics. For a moving personal evocation of 'Ulster-Scots' family history and memory in the USA, see Dunbar-Ortiz 1997, esp. pp. 43–8.

38. The following content analysis of the *Orange Standard*'s historical material intends to treat it as symptomatic, rather than necessarily in itself influential—for it would appear that, despite the Orange Order's large membership, the journal is not very widely read.

39. For a wider and more detailed study of the significance of the siege in popular Protestant historical consciousness, see McBride 1997.

40. Some Orange publications, however, have suggested a more positive attitude to the Antrim and Down rebels of 1798, including commemoration of 'heroes' of the revolt: see for instance *The Orange Standard* March 1988; though the same journal also, rather earlier, had reprinted anti-revolutionary rhetoric from 1798 including a contemporary song proclaiming that the true 'Liberty Tree' was the Orange one (*Orange Standard* April 1975). At an Orange Order commemorative dinner for the 1798 bicentenary, Brian Walker suggested that though the United Irishmen's proclaimed ideals were laudable, their faith in revolutionary France was very like that of many 1930s intellectuals in Stalin's USSR—Loyalists were more realistic. (*Irish Times* 13 June 1998).

41. Perhaps the best concise regional overviews are in Wright 1996 and Bardon 1993. The essays in Kinealy and Parkhill eds 1997 offer a county-by-county survey, of uneven quality, while Mac Atasney 1997 gives a detailed analysis of Lurgan/ Portadown, where official neglect and incompetence led to a horrifying deathtoll in the workhouse even of a comparatively prosperous (and mainly Protestant) district. John Killen's edited collection of

contemporary accounts (1995), though including material from all of Ireland, concentrates particularly on the northeast. Recent work on imaginative and literary representations of the Famine—e.g. Morash 1995, 1997, Morash and Hayes eds 1996—still largely ignores Ulster.

CHAPTER 7

1. See also, apart from works discussed separately below, the monographs analysing various individual Irish writers through colonial or postcolonial lenses—for instance Vincent Cheng (1995), Emer Nolan (1995), and Joseph Valente (1996), all on Joyce—and numerous contributions to such collections as Massoud ed. 1996 and Furomoto *et al.* eds 1996, notably Grene 1996 (on Shaw), Smythe 1996 (on the Gregorys), and Hashem 1996 (again on Joyce). The passing assertions of other literary critics about Ireland's colonial, postcolonial or neocolonial condition, and/or about Northern Ireland today as 'essentially colonial' (Matthews 1997:230 n. 5) could be cited almost *ad infinitum*. In such journals as the *Irish Studies Review*, for instance, such invocations are the repetitively expressed orthodoxy of many contributors. A more supple and sophisticated recent application of postcolonial theory to selected eighteenth-century Irish writers is McLoughlin 1999.

2. See for instance, on Spenser and Ireland, Brady 1986, Hadfield 1997, Maley 1997, the contributions to Patricia Coughlan ed. 1989, and Tracey Hill 1993. There have been numerous briefer and often more polemical discussions, some of them well fitting the bill of Maley's complaint that recent writers have been 'only too eager' to make Spenser a 'scapegoat' for English actions in Ireland, often doing so in 'hackneyed, stereotyped, or dogmatic' ways (Maley 1997:3). On Milton as anti-Irish colonialist, see Maley 1994: though the most detailed attempt to argue that *Paradise Lost* is a colonialist text, J. M. Evans 1996, finds (or forces) its colonial images and applications to be in the Americas—not Ireland, which Evans barely mentions. Some more historically attuned critics have, conversely, seen Milton's poetry as consciously and powerfully anti-imperial: see Armitage 1995. The massive earlier attempts by Christopher Hill (esp. 1977, 1984) to reinstate Milton as thoroughgoing radical included frustratingly little discussion of his views about England's overseas ventures, while Milton's views on Ireland clearly cause Hill some embarrassment (e.g. 1977:155).

3. Whether Eagleton should be counted an insider or an outsider to these debates is (for those who think such things matter) a difficult question. Lancashire-born, he has often highlighted his Irish descent, but also called himself a 'semi-outsider' to Irish culture (1995a:ix); while David Lloyd, in a rather ungenerous polemic, labels him an outsider *pur sang*, a colonialist 'panther-sahib' wishing to master and profit from the work of Irish scholars (1997:89): 'his perspective remains the familiar one of a British leftism all too beholden to metropolitan liberalism' whose attitudes betray 'a disregard of Irish modes of theorisation'(ibid: 90). I have not here engaged in close discussion of Eagleton's major recent works on Irish literary history, *Heathcliff and the Great Hunger* (1995a) and *Crazy John and the Bishop* (1998a), if only because they are so heterogenous, and their discussions of particular writers mainly so detached from the avowed main themes, that little in them connects closely with the issues debated here. In numerous rhetorical flourishes, Eagleton aligns himself with colonial models for understanding Irish cultural history, excoriates 'revisionists', and so on—but the richness of his more local insights is quite at

odds with an interpretive frame which he seems to discard almost as soon as it has been announced.

4. The claims made in the next few paragraphs are much expanded, and I hope substantiated, in my 1998b (from which they are partly taken) and forthcoming 2000b and 2000c, as well as numerous reviews and review essays on works of postcolonial theory.

5. The Friel and Deane quotations are taken from a December 1988 BBC2 documentary profile of the group, quoted in Stephen Regan's valuable (if in my view insufficiently critical) analysis of its development: Regan 1992:27, 26, 36. The phrase 'Fifth Province' apparently first appeared in the inaugural issue of *The Crane Bag*, coined by Richard Kearney and Mark Hederman. See also Kearney's essay 'The Fifth Province' in his 1997, and John Waters's chapter of the same title in his 1995b: a book ostensibly about the rock band U2 which actually ranges much more widely across Irish cultural debate. The very juxtaposition of the names of Deane, Friel, Kearney and Waters already suggests how the idea may have widely divergent political connotations. An audio-visual exhibition in Derry city also entitled 'The Fifth Province' has been, at the time of writing, always-just-about-to open for over three years. Its designers seem to have another conception again of what the phrase means, for it is described as being about 'the history and culture of the Celts—a race of people who thundered against every empire in Europe for a thousand years yet never created an empire of their own.' (Derry City Council *Visitor's Guide* 1996).

6. It should be added, however, that this play *was* later included in the Field Day Anthology.

7. This passage has been quoted and requoted numerous times by historians and critics of Irish cultures in recent years. None seems to have noticed that it is, let us say, somewhat unoriginal. The same sentiment is expressed in almost the same words by George Steiner: *In Bluebeard's Castle* (1971:13). It has also been pointed out that the Irish Ordnance Survey cannot readily be pressed into the 'colonialist' mould as Friel does: far from suppressing Irish history and folk-memory through the process of map-making, its architects had a genuine devotion to uncovering that history and memory (J. H. Andrews 1975).

8. See for instance Hayden White 1983, 1987; later, in his contribution to Friedlander ed. 1992, White repudiated or withdrew from this position, apparently disturbed at its potential applications to the literature of Holocaust denial.

9. Eagleton returns to this association of historical revisionism and postmodernism, to similar effect though with a characteristically ironic edge, in his 1997. He writes of the study of Irish history having been 'ensnared' by the 'potent mythologies' of 'liberal humanism, postmodern pluralism, Eurocentrism, Anglophilia, multinational cosmopolitanism, ideologies of progressivism, modernisation and the like.' (1997:5) He appears to object both to these supposed traits and to most of their Irish critics, since all sides neglect issues of class and capitalism. A related argument, though this time directing its fire more against the concept of the postcolonial—both generally and in its Irish applications—may be found in Eagleton 1998b.

10. Deane's later work repeats this valorisation of mythic discourse over rationalism, urging that myth has an 'important, and acknowledged, alliance' with nationalism (1997:182).

11. On Hewitt and regionalism, see Dawe and Foster eds 1991; McDonald 1992. There has been a recent attempt to analyse Hewitt's thought from what purports to be a specifically 'postcolonial perspective'—that is, somewhat sketchy comparisons with locations ranging from Australia to Guyana (Olinder 1996). This, however, fails to advance beyond

vague and portentous invocations of Hewitt's 'ambivalence' and 'the tensions between native and alien, between colonized and colonizer, between dominated and dominating . . . ' which are said to be 'of existential weight'. (ibid: 309) We are told nothing about where Hewitt stood amidst these 'tensions', or what a 'postcolonial perspective' adds to understanding Hewitt or vice versa. Matthews 1997: esp. 45–73 includes a more substantial discussion of political themes in Hewitt's poetry. On MacDiarmid's political thought, see the important forthcoming study by Bob Purdie.

12. As of the middle of 1999—over six years on—there is no imminent sign of this appearing; while all authors so far in Field Day's 'Critical Conditions' series have been male.

13. A similar complaint at Field Day's Derrycentricity is mounted by Edna Longley, in her 1994:39–40.

14. Although in fact the teleology, invoked here, of progression from a 'nationalist' to a 'liberationist' phase of decolonisation is arguably not consistently proposed either by Fanon himself or by his most influential latterday interpreter on this point, Edward Said.

15. Kiberd 1995:380–94 reformulated this argument in less strident (and less frankly sexist) terms, though still making sweeping and unargued-for assertions about gender roles.

16. Colin Graham (1996b) also criticises Kiberd for using only a relatively restricted and mainly older range of texts from the body of postcolonial theory; and relates this to a complaint that Kiberd uses such theoretical work to justify, rather than amend, a rather traditional conception of Irish culture.

17. Kiberd's—and others'—tendency to attribute a vast range of Irish phenomena (especially, of course, dysfunctional ones) to colonialism and its legacies, without at all clarifying why they should be seen as specifically colonial, is sharply criticised also in Bruce Stewart 1998. This is a besetting sin of much colonial discourse and postcolonial theory in non-Irish contexts too: discussed in some detail in Howe 1998b and 2000c.

18. For an indication of the range and kinds of work on gender and colonialism which should be considered in relation to unevidenced claims like Kiberd's, see for instance Ballhatchet 1980, Bleys 1996, Antoinette Burton 1994, Lane 1995, McClintock 1995, Melman 1992, Midgley ed. 1998, Rajan 1993, Sinha 1995, Stoler 1995.

19. So far as one can discern a rationale for this complaint, it would seem to lie not in the novels of Bolger, Roddy Doyle *et al.*, but perhaps in some of the contributions to the pamphlet series 'Letters from the New Island', collected in Bolger ed. 1991. In less skilled and knowledgeable hands than Kiberd's, such charges can be turned, for instance, into an extended accusation that neither Doyle's novel *The Commitments* nor the film based on it blame modern Dublin poverty sufficiently clearly on 'the results of seven hundred years of colonialism' (T. D. Taylor 1998:297).

20. Bruce Stewart (1998) launches a somewhat similar but less *ad hominem* critique of Kiberd, suggesting that the book indeed mounts a substantial critique of the cultural nationalist tradition, and strong arguments for pluralising and problematising it; but that the critique and the arguments remain entirely immanent, mounted from within the tradition itself.

21. For instance, 'Irredentism' is erroneously defined, in a politically interested way, on III:578; there is a mistaken 'application' of Gramsci's concept of hegemony to Northern Ireland on III:585; *parti pris* is mistranslated as 'having preconceived views' on III:586; at III:596 it is quite wrongly suggested that Scullabogue was the only massacre of Protestants in the Wexford fighting of 1798; the Stuarts are misdescribed as a 'Catholic dynasty'

on III:625; the description of Bloody Sunday at III:644 is at least questionable; and 'atavism' is bizarrely glossed as 'tribal or collective memory' on III:649.

22. This and subsequently cited essays of Gibbons's are reprinted in his 1996. They are there almost entirely unrevised, so I have retained quotations from their original appearances.

23. Ryder 1995 makes a similar (indeed rather Lloyd-derivative) argument about the rhetoric of Young Ireland, highlighting especially its use of gendered imagery.

24. US cultural theorist Anne McClintock repeats Lloyd's ill-evidenced claims uncritically (1995:52–3), while elsewhere asserting that 'for the inhabitants of British-occupied Northern Ireland . . . there may be nothing "post" about colonialism at all.' (1992:87) She appears, like so many others, to be under the impression that Northern Ireland contains only a Nationalist population.

25. In another, remarkably unwary, formulation Lloyd claims that the 'authority' of both nationalist and revisionist historians is quite simply 'derive(d) from their service to the state.' (1997:87)

26. Typically of this literary-theoretical genre, Lloyd seems to think the fact that such rural violence escaped 'capture' by the realist novel of the time at least as important as its supposed evasion of the hegemonies of colonial state and bourgeois nationalism.

27. The predictability of Graham's procedures here is perhaps surprising, since elsewhere (Graham 1994) a more critical stance had seemed in evidence from this writer. The connecting argument (though not very explicitly formulated) appears to be that whereas some Irish applications of postcolonial theory, taking their cue primarily from Said, have tended to reinforce or reproduce familiar nationalist positions, other local uses—drawing on ideas of ambivalence, hybridity and mimicry, mainly from Bhabha—have more productive and innovatory potential. For another attempt to apply Bhabha's thought to a 'postcolonial' Irish literary text, see Schneider 1998 on Glenn Patterson's novel *Burning Your Own*.

28. Instances of this postcolonial painting-by-numbers could be multiplied *ad nauseam*. To take the examples of just two major recent conferences, the 1995 and 1999 second and third Galway Culture and Colonialism gatherings, no fewer than sixty-one papers presented on Irish-related topics seemed to me to be (where I heard or read them) or to be likely to be (judging by the abstracts distributed to participants) in this vein. This is not to say that the work concerned does not exhibit some internal variety, originality, learnedness and other virtues: but nonetheless we are evidently here in the presence of a fully elaborated discourse in the strong Foucauldian sense, with relatively homogeneous and repetitive rhetorics and protocols. More mundanely, we are in the presence of an academic fashion involving rather rigid dress codes and strategies of self-presentation.

29. See also Lloyd 1995, where such claims are pursued via a somewhat undiscriminating critique of the supposed 'anti-nationalist prejudice' of major theorists of nationalism like Benedict Anderson, Ernest Gellner and Eric Hobsbawm (none of whom have, in fact, dismissed nationalism quite so sweepingly as Lloyd himself had earlier done!), a somewhat simple differentiation between virtuous and progressive 'insurgent' nationalisms (clearly intended to include, as an exemplary instance, the IRA) and undesirable 'hegemonic' ones, and an extended, forced parallel between Irish and Philippine nationalist movements. Much of the same argument is repeated in Lloyd 1996.

30. And even though the operating assumption is that these were peculiarly colonial agrarian movements, there is disconcertingly little reference to historical writing about peasant protest anywhere in the colonised world, with the exception of the *Subaltern Studies*

school. Even in Lloyd's own contribution to *Subaltern Studies* (Lloyd 1996) there is little direct engagement with Indian history as such. He refers only to essays in the single-volume *Selected Subaltern Studies*, not to any of the original texts or to other Indian historical writing. Clearly this cannot be attributed to ignorance, for Lloyd's historical awareness is evidently far broader than that of many postcolonial theorists. Rather, it reflects a mode of abstracted argumentation typical of this genre: instead of seeking to demonstrate particular parallels or interconnections, Lloyd asserts that Irish and Indian histories of revolt can be associated through what he calls a 'subalternity effect' (ibid: 263); a notably ahistorical notion.

31. For a careful re-examination of Yeats's relationship to nationalism, inducing renewed scepticism about such claims, see Regan 1995. Joseph Chadwick, sharply criticising Said's account, pushes the poet firmly into the opposite camp, seeing in Yeats's work a 're-sidual colonialism' and an 'attempt to situate itself in the position of a colonial ruling class'. Yeats was, in Chadwick's view 'largely caught up with the contradictory situation of the colonizer—rather than the colonized—in a society in the process of decoloniza-tion.' (Chadwick 1996:114) Given Yeats's lifelong, passionate nationalism, this is a more self-evidently misleading view than the one it criticises: the disagreement mainly under-lines the ahistoricality of typing Yeats's position as 'colonial' in the first place. In the same collection as Chadwick's essay, Devy 1996 and Yamasaki 1996 offer brief but helpful bio-graphical discussions of Yeats's attitudes to 'Orientalism' and to Asian cultures.

32. See the extended discussion of Said's career and work in my 2000b.

33. For a wide-ranging critique of the kinds of geocultural thinking that produce, among many other conceptual confusions, this sort of muddle about the idea of 'Europe', see Lewis and Wigen's excellent *The Myth of Continents* (1997).

34. Gerry Adams, similarly, proclaims that the Irish language 'is a badge of a civilisation whose values were vastly different from the one which seeks to subjugate us . . . The Gaelic social system in Ireland was communal . . . the Irish language is the reconquest of Ireland and the reconquest of Ireland is the Irish language.' (1995:138, 148)

35. He refers rather helplessly to Bhabha's 'complex (often obscure)' and 'enabling, if con-fusing' thought; while his account of Spivak's work relies entirely on Robert Young's (1990) paraphrase. The political consequence of their ideas 'remains unclear'—though that does not prevent him from later making very bold claims for it: Smyth 1998:20–4.

36. This last is an emphasis which one might expect to grow in future, as and if Unionist fears of gradual absorption by the Republic intensify. One straw in the wind is Arthur Aughey's fierce denunciation of an alleged Irish Catholic 'cultural imperialism' (1995b).

37. Naturally Clara Connolly's is a particular view of a particular event. David Lloyd's, Bar-bara Harlow's and Carol Coulter's contributions to the volume of essays emerging from the conference (Foley *et al.* eds 1995) do not include sentiments as strident as those cited by Connolly—which is however not to say that their spoken presentations did not do so, prior to revision for publication. Others to whom the author has spoken, who attended the Galway conference, had more positive impressions; and the second and third, still larger Galway conferences on the same themes and organised under the same auspices, which this writer attended, were certainly more intellectually ecumenical. The present author has, however, encountered anti-humanist rhetorics similar to those described from some of the same figures at other events.

CHAPTER 8

1. Given his background, O'Brien's is perhaps the most interesting of these recyclings. He proclaims the Union 'an act of international banditry' (167), believes that in 1993 'discrimination on religious grounds is as deeply entrenched in the six counties as ever' (175), and sees IRA figures such as Bobby Sands and Mairead Farrell as martyrs within a direct apostolic nationalist succession (180–1).

2. On the relationship between economic strategies and beliefs about Irish national identity in the 1920s and 1930s, see Daly 1992, 1999.

3. For overviews see Breen *et al.* 1990, Lee 1989, Kieran Kennedy *et al.* 1988; more polemical views include the pro-nationalist Crotty 1986 (discussed further below), and the anti-nationalist Peter Neary 1984.

4. For surveys see Anthony Brewer 1990, Larrain 1989, Ramirez-Faria 1991. David Fieldhouse attempts a global balance-sheet of the colonial and postcolonial economic record, from a more conservative perspective, in his 1999.

5. As we shall see below, this is quite untrue.

6. Brendan Clifford gives the same argument an intriguing twist, by associating the Irish Civil War's role as midwife for a multiparty system with that of the seventeenth-century English Civil War in establishing England's subsequent partisan alignments (Clifford 1993).

7. Garvin 1996 presents a more nuanced account of these conflicts as they crystallised at the birth of the Free State.

8. Patterson (1999) has more recently rethought and re-emphasised the connection, seeing Lemass's combination of rapprochement with the North and continued antipartitionist rhetoric as driven essentially by internal developments within the Republic, especially economic ones.

9. See for instance Cahery *et al.* eds 1992, and the publications of the Belfast-based Centre for Research and Documentation. For a far more careful and nuanced discussion of links and parallels between Ireland and one particular 'Third World' state, India, see Michael and Denis Holmes eds 1997.

10. Cronin 1980:186–91; Henry Patterson 1989:84–112; Coogan 1987a:419–22, 428–30; Bishop and Mallie 1987:33–42. Both Johnston and Coughlan remained politically active in the 1990s, but in very different milieux. Roy Johnston became a leading member of the Irish Green Party, and continued to propose innovative ideas on Northern Ireland's future, now based on radical decentralisation under EU auspices—see his submission to the Opsahl Inquiry, Pollak ed. 1993:241–2. Coughlan, lecturing at Trinity College Dublin, stayed closer to the original Republican-Marxist stance—see for instance his 1994.

11. For the earlier history of Irish socialist Republican thought, see Henry Patterson 1989 (revised edn 1997), English 1994a. Both judge its theoretical achievements harshly—English particularly so, with his repeated references to its 'self-deluding myths', 'intellectual inadequacy', 'solipsistic zealotry', 'deficiency' and so on. English appears throughout implicitly to be measuring his subjects' failings, not against their real historical circumstances, but against some ideal standard of political rationality, or against the supposedly superior rationality of the Unionist tradition.

12. On the political ideas of rebel leaders in 1916–23, see Tom Barry 1962, Bowman 1982, Dan Breen 1981, Coakley 1983, Cronin 1980, Deasy 1973, 1982, Edwards 1977, English 1996a, 1998, Mac Eoin 1980, Arthur Mitchell 1995, Moran 1994, Ernie O'Malley 1936, Meda Ryan 1982. For the rank and file, apart from the works cited below, see Eoghan Davis 1990, David Fitzpatrick 1977, Sheehan 1990.

13. This and subsequent quotations are from Patterson's excellent, detailed discussion of Johnston and Coughlan's ideas, in his 1989:88–92; see also Milotte 1984, Roulston 1991 on the Communist Party's role in the evolution of 'social Republicanism'. The tiny Irish Communist Party fairly consistently, through the years after 1969, combined a continued adherence to traditional Republican beliefs with a repudiation of the IRA's campaign of violence.

14. There is no apparent reason to doubt the authenticity of Coogan's reproduction of the document, though in some places it is not wholly clear where he is reprinting it verbatim, and where he is paraphrasing it. The version of parts of the 'Green Book' reproduced in Dillon 1990 includes no such politico-historical passages, being a far more matter-of-fact statement of the IRA's constitution and disciplinary procedures: but what Dillon prints is evidently only a very partial text, although he implies otherwise. Brendan O'Brien (1995, Appendix 1) reproduces extracts from what appears to be yet another different version or edition of the 'Green Book'.

15. See Gerry Adams 1996:115 for the influence of Che Guevara on guerrilla tactics, Richard Davis 1994:70, 218–9 for IRA enthusiasm about Richard Tauber's classic *The War of the Flea*, ibid: 216–17, 223–5, 229 for the popularity of Carlos Marighela's Brazilian handbook of guerrilla war.

16. See Hazelkorn and Patterson 1994 for a summary of many of these complaints. A more wide-ranging jeremiad, lamenting supposed Irish failure in intellectual, cultural, political and scientific as well as economic innovation, occupies the final pages of Lee 1989. Liam Kennedy 1989 offers a more optimistic assessment as, from a very different (neo-Marxist and dependency) position, does O'Hearn 1998a, b. At the time of writing (mid-1999) Ireland's booming recent economic figures appear to strengthen the optimists' hand.

17. On changing value orientations in contemporary Ireland, see above all the survey data and commentary in C. T. Whelan ed. 1994 and Heath *et al.* eds. 1999. The polemical literature around such changes is very substantial: for eloquent presentations of the negative view on most of them, see Fennell 1993, Waters 1991, 1995, and for a strong, indeed near-triumphalist statement of the 'modernising' case in its affirmative version, by a former senior politician and feminist, Hussey 1995.

18. Changing Maltese social and value orientations are surveyed in Abela 1991. They reveal a profile clearly more conservative than Ireland's, despite the author's determined efforts to put a 'modernising' and 'Europeanising' spin on them.

19. Though this notably capacious and ill-defined concept is of questionable validity for Irish as for other circumstances. For one recent attempt to apply it, drawing heavily on the ideas of Anthony Giddens, see the first report of the Belfast-based think-tank Democratic Dialogue (1995). In the Northern Ireland context even such seemingly innocuous and woolly ideas can be interpreted as somehow complicit in violence and domination: as instanced in Eoin O'Broin's ferocious assault on Giddens and Democratic Dialogue as supposedly underpinning a liberal-democratic regime of inequality which 'cannot be less violent than other forms of social organisation, its violence will simply be more efficient.' (O'Broin 1996:16) O'Broin's half-hidden message is that all this modernising, democratic, liberal dialogic language is at bottom a Unionist plot.

CHAPTER 9

1. Such comparisons, especially with Cyprus, were occasionally made by British politicians too: Ronald Weitzer (1990:132) quotes James Callaghan and Peter Brooke to that effect.

2. Cf. Michael Gallagher 1990; Hannum 1990 esp. ch. 11; Margalit and Raz 1990. Gallagher's is among the fullest discussions, and his pragmatic conclusion is that the notion of an absolute right to self-determination is 'chimerical' in relation to both Nationalist and Unionist communities. Both, as he points out 'can quote current norms and interpretations of "self-determination" in support of their case' (1990:16).

3. Some would suggest, as do McGarry and O'Leary, that Britain tacitly 'admitted guilt' well before this, indicating a colonial attitude to Northern Ireland in such things as the conditional nature of the claim to sovereignty, the use of exclusion orders under the Prevention of Terrorism Act, and the refusal of major British political parties to organise in Ulster (1995:312).

4. Contrast Farrell's previous repudiation of the simple colonial model in *New Left Review* 1969:19. Although Algeria was the most favoured point of comparison—at least before its descent into a maelstrom of violence in the 1990s—pro-Republican writers also invoked Vietnam (e.g. McGuire 1973:103–4 and a book by the Italian leftist group Lotta Continua, *Un Vietnam in Europa*, to which Tom Nairn refers (1981:232) but which I have not seen), South Africa (e.g. Gerry Adams 1986) and other cases.

5. Occasionally, anti-Unionist struggles (and, conversely, anti-Irish Nationalist ones too) have even rhetorically been presented as anti-fascist. These scurrilous excesses, seeking to equate either Unionism or Irish Nationalism with fascism or Nazism, are not worth serious examination. Tiny fringe elements of both Republican and Loyalist groups have flirted with fascism at various times—the former especially in the 1930s, the latter (among a few Ulster Defence Association and Ulster Vanguard members) by way of dalliance with Britain's National Front in the 1970s. In the latter case, what the different currents had in common was a conspiracy theory—but for the NF, the conspiracy which threatened Britishness was Jewish, for fringe Unionists it was of course Catholic (e.g. Loughlin 1995:196–7). Steve Bruce (1992:150–3) points to the tenuousness of their contacts, and that a National Front attempt to field a local council electoral candidate in Northern Ireland yielded the grand total of twenty-seven votes. Certainly some proponents of both Republicanism and Loyalism share traits with fascism: authoritarianism, organicism, blind worship of leaders, fondness for flags and uniforms, and indeed racism. But by such lax criteria, *some* advocates of *every* political ideology in the modern world, and of every nationalist movement, could be called fascist.

6. Though see ibid: 18–19, 24, where brief and passing comparisons are made between the position and behaviour of Ulster Protestant 'settlers' and Algerian *colons*.

7. Sinn Fein leaders have generally avoided public assertions that Unionists, if they are not prepared to accept a united Ireland, should be expelled by force; though their sympathisers have sometimes made such suggestions. The present author's experience is that 'off the record' or spontaneously, such desires are more commonly (though certainly not typically) expressed—as indeed are their converse, Loyalist dreams of a land without Catholics. On the latter, see Rolston 1999.

8. In the evolving political thinking of Sinn Fein, see also *inter alia* B. O'Brien 1995, O'Doherty 1998.

9. Insofar as such analyses depict Ulster Unionism as a particular case in a general model of settler colonialism, they are stymied by the surprising paucity of serious theoretical

writing on the concept of settler colonialism as such. Among the relatively few major works which do address this theme, see Denoon 1983, Emmanuel 1972, Huttenback 1976, Dane Kennedy 1987, Lamar and Thompson eds 1981.

10. Other accounts tending to view Ulster Protestant ideology as purely and simply supremacist include Geoffrey Bell 1976, Liz Curtis 1994, O'Dowd *et al.* eds 1980, and with qualifications Clayton 1996. The recent work of an Australian academic, Cash 1996, though less partisan and far more theoretically elaborate (indeed devoted as much to elaborating a general theory of ideology as to specific discussion of Unionist beliefs), tends in the same direction. Whilst Cash distinguishes between 'exclusivist' and 'inclusivist' brands of unionist ideology, he clearly regards the former as the dominant and normative strain; and his work is similarly weakened by reliance on a narrow and mostly old range of sources for interpreting Unionist beliefs.

11. McGarry and B. O'Leary 1995:14–25 present a typology of ethnic and civic nationalisms in the Irish case, but greatly underestimate the extent to which individuals and political formations blur or straddle the distinction. How, for instance, should one characterise the views of SDLP leader John Hume? At different times he has sounded like an ethnic nationalist imbued with 'traditional' Catholic-Gaelicist values, a civic nationalist of the peculiar sort identified above, a more conventional kind of civic nationalist who accepts Unionism for what it is and seeks to accommodate it, and a pan-European 'postnationalist'.

12. For a brief, Marxist-inflected critique of these views from the perspective of historical geography, see James Anderson 1980. Most other 'Green Marxists' (to adopt Austen Morgan's term: Morgan 1980) have also, inevitably, treated 'two nations' theories ('Orange Marxism', in Morgan's apt designation) with dismissive hostility: see e.g. Anthony Coughlan 1994, Martin 1982. Less readily understandable is the vehemence of O'Leary and McGarry (1995:148–51). They repeatedly describe the views of BICO and associated writers as 'sectarian'; a label they do not see fit to apply to nationalist or Republican polemics, Marxist or otherwise. Their view that it is evidence of Protestant sectarian bias to see Oliver Cromwell as 'a bourgeois revolutionary (rather than a genocidal maniac)' (458, n. 85) is perhaps more revealing about their own attitudes than anything else. McGarry and O'Leary are, it should be added, only a little less hostile to those brands of Marxism which they do not smear as religiously sectarian. They wheel out a series of at best overgeneralised objections to Marxist interpretation as necessarily involving economic reductionism, blindness to the strength of nationalism and ethnicity, wild optimism about the prospects for class struggle, and so on (ibid: 151–67).

13. Such a view had, naturally, some earlier precursors. Although the notion of Ulster Protestants as a separate nation found little resonance in the anti-Home Rule agitation of the early twentieth century, it had some unexpected advocates such as the nationalist intellectual Arthur Clery—whose ideas have recently been analysed by Patrick Maume (1998). Clery was, admittedly, an idiosyncratic figure, not only in his early support for a 'two nations' approach, but in his later anti-democratic radicalism, which sought to synthesise Mussolini and Lenin.

14. BICO 1975; and see Warren 1980, an enormously influential and controversial book by a BICO member making the same argument in global terms.

15. See for instance his 1986, a ferocious attack on John Hume whose political ideas are claimed to be 'more in accordance with the divine right of kings than with Parliamentary government.' (11)

16. An earlier version of this text, issued anonymously, had directed its fire mainly against Tom Nairn's arguments for an independent Ulster.

17. It is outside the present work's scope even to summarise the literature on the origins and development of Northern Ireland. For the original Plantations and Protestant migration see J. M. Hill 1993, Philip Robinson 1984. On the establishment of the Stormont regime Follis 1995, Mansergh 1991. On Northern Catholic politics before, during and after Partition, Mary Harris 1993, Phoenix 1994, Lynn 1997. Changing attitudes to the Free State and Republic are traced in Dennis Kennedy 1988. On the Scots-Irish link Graham Walker 1995 and Wood ed. 1994, especially the contributions by Bob Purdie (1994), and Graham Walker (1994). A major pro-Unionist history is Tom Wilson 1989, a broader and more balanced account Bardon 1992. Whyte 1990 and McGarry and B. O'Leary 1995 are major syntheses of research; the latter more up-to-date, the former in my view doing better at the difficult task of maintaining neutrality. Perhaps the most even-handed and analytically sophisticated single-volume overview, however, is Ruane and Todd 1996.

18. On the history of the theory, see Hobsbawm 1973, McLennan 1981. Howe 1993:42–3, 57–9, 163–4 discusses its role in British Marxist thought on imperialism.

19. Most invocations of the labour aristocracy thesis in Irish, as opposed to metropolitan British, contexts have fallen into the second of these camps. Instances include Gerry Adams 1986, 1995, Geoffrey Bell 1976, Michael Farrell 1980, O'Dowd *et al.* 1980. The most substantial criticisms and alternatives have tended to come from 'revisionist' Marxists, such as Gibbon 1975, Bew, Gibbon and Patterson 1979, 1994, Austen Morgan 1991.

20. A more extended and thoughtful critique of Bew, Gibbon and Patterson, though also proceeding from 'Connollyite' premises, is Paul Stewart 1991.

21. The story of, and controversies over, media coverage of the Northern Irish conflict and the various attempts at censorship or manipulation of the media are beyond the scope of our present discussion. There is now a substantial literature on these questions—including notably Liz Curtis 1984a, David Miller 1994, Rolston and Miller eds 1996—though this has been heavily weighted towards Nationalist or Republican viewpoints, and includes sometimes over-sweeping allegations of bias against such viewpoints. Alan F. Parkinson (1998), conversely, argues at great length that there has been persisting misunderstanding and lack of sympathy in the British newsmedia for Unionist positions—though he concedes that this is partly attributable to Unionists' own past ineptitude at media self-presentation. Somewhat more nuanced investigations, with specific reference to media coverage of the 1981 hunger strikes, are presented in Howard Smith 1996 and Tangen Page 1996.

22. Apart from those discussed here, other examples of the *genre* include Bambery 1987, Geoffrey Bell 1984, Martin Collins ed. 1985, Kelley 1982, and a mass of pamphlet and periodical literature.

23. Cf. Livingstone 1989: ch. 6, whose outline sketch of Irish history is an unusually pure distillation of nationalist mythography; and several of the Terence MacSwiney Memorial Lectures organised by the Livingstone-led GLC (Greater London Council 1986). Interviewed by *Guardian* reporter John Carvel, Livingstone claimed astonishingly that Britain's treatment of the Irish was worse than the Nazis' of the Jews or the fate of the Kurds, that anti-Irish racism was 'much deeper' than that against blacks, and that his views were based on an extensive reading of Irish history. (Carvel 1984:161–5)

24. Curtis, similarly, believes in Britain's 'desire at all costs to hang onto' Northern Ireland (Liz Curtis 1994:viii). Her Ireland expands and contracts quite alarmingly: on the one

hand it seems explicitly to be shrunk into the island's northeast corner (viii), on the other to be so vast as to have commanded the sealanes 'for Africa, India, the Far East and South Pacific' (13).

25. See Parkinson 1998 for sharp criticism of the *Guardian*'s Irish coverage from a pro-Unionist standpoint.

26. A particularly strident and ill-informed recent example is Kate Millett's *Politics of Cruelty* (1994 esp. 97–116), where the IRA are repeatedly described as 'colonial dissidents'. Irish-descended and other US authors have naturally produced material from very varied viewpoints, including also (if more rarely) ones sympathetic to Unionism: for one of the quirkier productions see Fitzsimmons 1993—an argument for Northern Ireland to become an independent state, originally published in 1985, from an American Catholic lawyer who had lived in Belfast for a year. John McCarthy 1993—mostly articles reprinted from the *Boston Irish News*—attacks standard nationalist perceptions and promotes 'revisionist' views, selfconsciously swimming against the main Irish-American tide. Galliher and DeGregory 1985, despite its weak historical material, is one of the few North American academic works on Northern Ireland to present Protestant perspectives at length and with sympathy.

27. The earlier surveys' findings are deftly summarised in Whyte 1990:94–7. The most detailed study of anti-Catholicism in Northern Ireland is now Brewer and Higgins 1998—which, however, despite its fairly elaborate typology of different types of prejudice, may be thought somewhat to underrate the significance both of change over time and of variation in intensity of prejudice.

28. For a typical dismissal of the trade union movement's record, see Rolston 1980, and for a detailed historical account generally scornful of the Labour tradition, Michael Farrell 1980. McGarry and O'Leary, too, quite falsely claim that trade unions in Northern Ireland never discussed issues of nationality or religious discrimination (1995:157). Correctives to such dismissal include Terry Cradden's splendid history of the labour movement's struggles against sectarianism in the 1940s and 1950s (Cradden 1993), Austen Morgan's reconstruction of the world of the 'rotten Prods' who tried to build working-class unity in the first decades of the century (Morgan 1991), Paddy Devlin's moving account of interwar anti-poverty campaigns (1981), and Graham Walker's study of Harry Midgley and the NILP (1985). For the left-wing Protestant intelligentsia, see Edna Longley's 'Progressive Bookmen' in her 1994, and Gerald Dawe and John Wilson Foster's edited collection on John Hewitt and his times (1991). Purdie 1995 gives some indication of the often violent opposition which socialist pioneers in Belfast had to face in the 1890s. A century later, their successors sometimes risked more lethal dislike from sectarian paramilitaries on both sides.

29. See also Purdie 1998, linking reconsideration of Walker's significance with a wider discussion of 'revisionism' in Irish labour history.

30. In which one of the book's co-authors was then also active: a fact which is nowhere acknowledged in the text.

31. The syndrome has persisted, if in slightly more muted form. During 1995 both *Feminist Review* and *Race and Class* produced special 'Irish issues' (nos 50 and 37, 1 respectively). Neither included any contributions from or about Protestant, Unionist or Loyalist perspectives (in fact, to be blunt, just one contributor appears to be of Protestant background, and he is someone who has 'converted' to Republicanism). For both, in familiar style, 'Ireland' continued to mean almost exclusively Northern Ireland.

32. Her 1995 repeats similar arguments in only slightly more nuanced form, and proclaims that it is the liberals who are the real bigots: 'proponents of the Enlightenment values of individual freedom and Western democracy grow ever more strident in their intolerance.' (1995:202) The evidence for this categorical claim amounts only to a couple of polemical, ephemeral writings by Conor Cruise O'Brien and novelist Fay Weldon. Coulter's 1998, however, appears to edge towards a somewhat more sceptical position.

33. For sharp presentations of this view, see Sheehan 1990, Benton 1995. Other recent feminist historical scholarship has probed the complexities and conflicts between nationalism and feminism in late-nineteenth- and early-twentieth-century Ireland: see for example Louise Ryan 1995, 1997, Margaret Ward 1998 (which adopts a more pro-nationalist position), and for a fascinating instance of how intricate, and how resistant to simple categorisation, individual subject positions could be, Heloise Brown's 1998 study of Isabella Todd (1836–96)—who was simultaneously a feminist, pacifist, internationalist, anti-sectarian, an Ulster Unionist, and a believer in a British imperial 'civilising mission'.

34. Hazelkorn and Patterson 1995. *New Left Review* editor Robin Blackburn's reply to Porter and O'Hearn (1995) seemed, by contrast, unduly apologetic, appearing to accept many of the presuppositions of the critics' view about the 'anti-imperialist' nature of the Republican struggle. Porter and O'Hearn's other main target of attack was Eric Hobsbawm, whose scanty and passing references to Irish affairs they interpret oddly as constituting a defence of British 'civility' against Irish 'barbarism' (Porter and O'Hearn:140–7).

CHAPTER 10

1. For some recent deployments of the romantic image of Ireland's west coast, including its appropriation by German and other European 'New Age' visionaries, see several of the contributions to Kockel ed. 1995.

2. Lenny Murphy was leader of the notorious sectarian murder squad, the 'Shankill Butchers'. In fact, though, the world of Loyalist paramilitarism too remains under-researched, by comparison with its Republican counterpart: exceptions include Bruce 1992, Dillon 1989, Cusack and McDonald 1997, and Peter Taylor 1999; while Stevenson 1996 has perhaps the fullest journalistic discussion of Loyalist ex-paramilitaries' political rethinking yet published. Richard Davis 1994, in its focus on similarities between the beliefs of Republican and Loyalist gunmen, arguably fails to illuminate what is distinctive about either. There are major, albeit dryly institutional, studies of the old Ulster Unionist Party in its earlier phases—notably Buckland 1973, Harbinson 1973—but still very little of substance on the more recent past of the (Official) Unionists: the most important exception is now Feargal Cochrane's fine book (1997). A less critical and probing account than Cochrane's is David Hume's largely narrative history of the UUP in 1972–92 (1996). For a vivid if somewhat flattering portrait of the Orange Order, see Edwards 1999.

3. I do not attempt here to discuss all of the large body of writing which in different ways casts light on Ulster Protestant senses of identity. Apart from the invaluable literary sources, there is a large body of enlightening ethnographic and/or journalistic work: see among others Akenson 1979, Alcock 1994, Beattie 1993, Rosemary Harris 1972, McAuley 1994. The best narrative overview is Bardon 1992, which also repeatedly if ephemerally invokes the comparisons with events in continental European history which, so I am arguing, are the most helpful points of comparability for Northern Ireland.

4. This peremptory statement is, I hope, more fully substantiated in my 1998a; see also Hannaford 1996, Malik 1996.

5. Northern Protestant self-descriptions in terms of nationality have indeed seemed notably unstable and have undergone rapid change. Between 1968 and 1990 the proportion describing themselves as Irish dwindled from 20 per cent to 4 per cent, that preferring the 'Ulster' label from 32 per cent to 10 per cent, while those choosing 'British' rose from 39 per cent in 1968, to 77 per cent in 1984, falling again (in the wake of the Anglo-Irish Agreement?) to 66 per cent in 1990 (McGarry and O'Leary 110–11). It may in this context also be noted that, as Whyte comments, there seems to have been a substantial if not total transformation in southern Protestant attitudes to the Irish state since 1922. 'All authorities agree . . . that most southern Protestants see themselves as unhyphenated Irish, without hankerings after the British connection.' (1990:158) Even if he adds that there is some evidence that nonetheless 'Protestants still do not see the State as theirs in quite the same way as Catholics' (ibid: 158–9), time has apparently disclosed their attachment to a British national identity as shallowly rooted or at the least pragmatically adjustable. On this point, see also Bowen 1983.

6. For other views of the possible future significance of European integration for Northern Ireland, from very diverse political perspectives, see for instance James Anderson 1998a, b, Richard Kearney 1997 ch. 5.

7. On political and cultural connections between Scotland and Northern Ireland across the years, see Graham Walker 1995, Wood ed. 1994. Graham McFarlane (nd), in his analysis of senses of identity in a rural Ulster Protestant community makes no reference to perceptions of nationality at all other than noting that many of his informants 'link their way of life to their Scottish ancestry' (29), concentrating on religion, which he rather surprisingly claims has been neglected because 'The dominant paradigm in the study of Northern Ireland has been a Marxist one.' (25) Publications by Loyalist organisations themselves have often—it seems, increasingly often—emphasised Scots-Ulster links; see e.g. Shankill Think Tank 1995:6–9. On the Irish in Scotland, and the association of sectarianism with anti-Irish prejudice there, see *inter alia* Connell 1997, Devine ed. 1991, Tom Gallagher 1985, 1987a, b, McCready 1998, William Marshall 1996, Graham Walker 1992c. In the context of literary and cultural history, both Willy Maley (1997) and Richard English (1997) have—with very different political intentions—emphasised how attention to the Scottish dimension challenges the crude polarities of much recent writing on Ireland, not least that which adopts simple colonial models.

8. See also John Ellis 1998, on pre-1914 efforts to 'reconcile the Celt' to a loyal imperial Britishness from which an increasing number of Scots and Welsh, as well as Irish, were feared to be disaffected. It may here be noted that Loughlin's stress on Ulster Unionists' attachment to a British identity over the past century contrasts with Alvin Jackson's and David W. Miller's emphasis on a more distinctive and separate local political identity. In drawing here on the work of all three scholars, despite their quite sharp disagreements with one another, I am of course implying a view that each captures different parts of a complex historical truth.

9. A somewhat fuller elucidation is given in an article co-authored by Bruce: Wallis *et al.* 1986. Noting as others have done, that senses of nationality among Ulster Protestants are weak and ambiguous—in sharp contrast to Catholics with their strong Irish national identification—the authors see Unionists as possessing a fairly clear ethnicity based overwhelmingly on religion. It is mainly religious because 'there is nowhere else to go.'

No identity beyond one founded in evangelical Protestantism is secure' (7). This applies even to those who are not churchgoers. Paisleyism derives its strength from its appeal to and links with these evangelical Presbyterian traditions (16–22).

10. It should perhaps here be underlined that Paisley, like all senior Unionist political figures with the notable exception of former Stormont minister William Craig in the 1970s, has always publicly condemned Loyalist violence. As Bruce's analysis stresses, we are dealing here with two quite distinct groups (though see, *inter alia* Peter Taylor 1999 on the frequency of Paisley's alleged or apparent flirtation with paramilitarism).

11. And although Bruce stresses the relative lack of religiosity among Loyalist paramilitaries and their supporters, this may be less true in rural and smalltown Ulster than in Belfast. Certainly there is no reason to doubt the sincerity of adherence to fundamentalist Protestantism proclaimed by figures like the notorious, late Portadown UVF (and then LVF) leader Billy Wright, responsible for numerous sectarian murders. See the anonymously authored profile in *Fortnight* October 1996, and Martin Dillon's interview with him: Dillon 1997:56–80.

12. As we have noted, however, such hard data as are available do not support Bruce's claim: identification with the 'Ulster' identity has in fact diminished in recent years, that as 'British' has grown. As Colin Coulter shows, such a British identification has been much intensified, especially among the middle classes, under Direct Rule. The numbers dependent on the British state for employment, those pursuing or having gained higher education in Britain, regularly reading London-based newspapers, etc. have grown steadily since the 1970s (Colin Coulter 1997). On the other hand, as Brian Walker suggests, emphasis on a British identity, and gradual dwindling of identification with Irishness, can be traced in the public culture of Protestant Northern Ireland from the time of partition. Not only in the pronouncements of Unionist politicians, but in such spheres as the policies of the BBC in the region, self-description as Irish was on a steady downward curve after 1918 (Walker 1996 ch. 6). Clayton 1996 ch. 4, in more polemical vein, traces similar shifts in the language of local newspaper editorialists and correspondents. The 'second choice', according to most polls, is not independence (which comes third) but full integration with Britain; revival of a devolved assembly coming first.

13. The flow of recent popular books and pamphlets produced in Northern Ireland on US 'founding fathers' and other prominent Americans of Ulster origin is substantial: it is often pointed out that twelve US Presidents including Andrew Jackson, Ulysses S. Grant, Woodrow Wilson and Richard Nixon were of Northern Irish Protestant ancestry. The Northern Ireland Tourist Board's publications direct visitors towards sites associated with the families of Presidents Jackson, Grant, Wilson and Chester Arthur as well as frontiersman Davy Crockett and Declaration of Independence printer John Dunlap, but no identifiably British Empire historical figures. (Nor, as yet, does a 'Richard Nixon ancestral home' feature in the brochures: clearly, his rehabilitation still has some way to go.)

14. The notion of the internal frontier was first systematically applied to British history in Hechter 1975. The application is problematic for reasons well summarised in Ohlmeyer 1998 124–7: internal British and Irish 'frontier zones' were considerably more fluctuating and less homogeneous than those in the Americas or southern Africa, while unlike in the latter, political, cultural and linguistic 'frontiers' rarely coincided.

15. It may perhaps be here that one finds the formative moment of a specific Ulster British military tradition, whose most celebrated moment lies in commemoration of the Ulster

Division's sufferings on the Somme, but includes also for instance the sharp contrast between strong popular memories of the Korean War in Northern Ireland and that conflict's almost entirely forgotten status in mainland Britain. The Royal Ulster Rifles fought heroically and twice suffered massive casualties in that war: at the battles of 'Happy Valley' and the Imjin River. Ballads relating to Korea may still occasionally be heard in Loyalist bars and clubs.

16. On Scottish popular sentiment towards the Empire, see Finlay 1997, MacKenzie 1993, 1998.

17. A briefer but less partisan exploration of some Ulster Protestant circles' sympathies for South African and Rhodesian whites is Richard Davis 1994: esp. 270–5, 290. In more polemical vein, Liam O'Dowd (1990), in a long new introduction to Albert Memmi's classic analysis of settler mentalities in Algeria, has sought to apply that analysis to the collective psychology of Ulster Loyalism.

18. See the critiques of Miller in Aughey 1991:5–9 and Colin Coulter 1994:2–5. On the complexities of Protestant self-identification see also Brian Graham 1997a, Hennessey 1993, Wright 1972.

19. Compare Arthur Aughey's view of the more recent past and present, in which he believes one can discern and distinguish rival Unionist images of 'the constitutional people' (identified especially with the UUP) and 'the sovereign people' (associated with Paisley's DUP): Aughey 1997b.

20. Most of the contributors to J. W. Foster ed. 1995 put forward variants of this argument, as do Aughey 1989, his 1991, 1995a, 1997a, b, Roche 1994, and the publications of the Cadogan Group (1992, 1994). In the conventional political arena, it was probably best represented by Robert McCartney's United Kingdom Unionist Party, at least in that party's earlier manifestations. There is substantial but rather scornful discussion of such currents in Cochrane 1997 and O'Dowd 1998, and a more sympathetic appraisal in Colin Coulter 1994; while the closest and most conceptually sophisticated interrogation is Norman Porter 1996. Liberal pluralism, accompanied by a clear strain of democratic socialist rhetoric, has been yet more evident in the recent rethinking undertaken by some spokespeople for the small Progressive Unionist and Ulster Democratic Parties, closely linked with Loyalist paramilitary groups: see for instance the 1995 report of the 'Shankill Think Tank', which includes such prominent former paramilitary figures as Billy Hutchinson, Gusty Spence and John White.

21. See for instance the contributions of McCartney and others to John Wilson Foster ed. 1995, and for UUP attitudes, the *Ulster Review passim*. A single recent issue, for instance, includes a piece of ferocious invective against Irish nationalism—e.g. 'it is quite easy to show that Irish nationalism is devoid of intellectual credibility' (Roche and Birnie 1996:14)—five separate and nuanceless attacks on the 'so-called peace process', one on the 'cant about "parity of esteem"' (Bradford 1996:18), two denying claims about anti-Catholic job discrimination, and even a bitter denunciation of the spread of Irish-themed pubs and beer in England. Norman Porter 1996 includes a particularly careful dissection of the shortcomings of 'liberal Unionism', from a critical 'civic Unionist' standpoint. For a more polemical view ('If this is new Unionism, I want my old sash back') see 'Bob Jordan' (pseud.) 1996. James Loughlin argues that the 'liberal unionist' stance is simply incoherent, since it underrates the instability and changeableness of Britishness, and does not seem able to let go of an association between Britishness and Protestantism, despite the claims of analysts such as Aughey (Loughlin 1995:218–22).

The fullest and most detailed study of discrimination and inequality since the abolition of Stormont is Smith and Chambers 1991, which found that sectarian discrimination in jobs and housing had remained pervasive, if diminished, through the seventies and eighties.

22. In fact there seems to be little if any hard evidential support for the notion that the Catholic Church stymied economic development in Ireland, either institutionally or via its cultural ethos: see Liam Kennedy 1996 ch. 4.

23. There is a brief but illuminating discussion of Ervine's life and ideas in Maume 1996.

24. Another consequence of the trend towards equalisation in economic status and political strength between Catholics and Protestants was, as Wright points out, that the behaviour of violent minorities on each side became more alike. It seems clear that in the earlier outbreaks of sectarian rioting during the nineteenth century, the aggressors were usually Protestant. As time went by the dishonours became ever more even, and the riots themselves ever more lethal.

25. For the fullest elaboration of this concept, in comparative perspective linking Northern Irish history with that of Algeria and the US South, see Wright 1987 ch. 6.

26. James Loughlin concurs in pointing to the declining significance of shared histories—for instance the 'meaning' of 1688 in Britain came increasingly to be defined above all in terms of its peacefulness, whereas Ulster Unionists in celebrating it were lauding their ancestors' violent struggle (1995:38–9).

27. Townshend 1983 attempts to place the major episodes of violence in Ulster within a broader context of conflict since the 1840s.

28. One must, however, add the caveat that, notoriously, respondents to opinion polls tend to present themselves as more liberal than they 'really' are. If one took the poll data on face value, there would almost literally be no such thing as a religious bigot in Northern Ireland! There is of course a massive literature on the extent and nature of sectarian attitudes. See McGarry and B. O'Leary 1995 esp. ch. 5, Whyte 1990 chs 2 and 5 for overviews of the data and rival interpretations. Sugden and Bairner 1993, Finn 1994, and Bairner 1997 study sectarianism in sport.

CHAPTER 11

1. See especially his 1986; also, from amidst a vast outpouring of journalistic comment, his 1985 and numerous—extremely repetitive—articles in the London *Times* and *Independent*, the *Irish Independent* and elsewhere during the 1990s.

2. The original, classic application of this approach is Rose 1971, which however includes only very brief comparative allusions. Budge and O'Leary 1973, comparing Belfast with Glasgow, somewhat similarly argues that Glasgow's 'normal', peaceful politics can be attributed largely to the fact that other lines of division—above all of social class—crosscut and predominate over the religious and ethnic ones.

3. See for instance Ad Hoc Group on South Africa 1995, Guelke 1994, Wright 1994, and some of the contributions to Giliomee and Gagiano eds 1990. McGarry 1998, by contrast, tends to emphasise crucial differences rather than possible similarities between the two cases.

4. For a sample, see Alcock 1992, R. K. Carty 1993, Lijphart 1975, 1977, Schmitt 1994, Rupert Taylor 1994, and (a more extensive and thoroughly grounded work than the above) Prager 1986.

5. Thus, as Guelke re-emphasised in a more recent comparative discussion, the loss of legitimacy by the political *status quo ante* in the eyes of much international opinion helped
precipitate crisis and the search for change, in Northern Ireland as in Israel/Palestine and
South Africa. Unlike the latter two cases, however, that international delegitimisation
has not produced powerful pressures towards a lasting political solution in Ireland:
though the reasons for that failure are internal, not international. (Guelke 1994) See also
Democratic Dialogue 1998.

6. His later work on policing in Northern Ireland, Weitzer 1995, also includes some international references but is not primarily a comparative study.

7. The same objections apply to another attempt at the same Ulster–Zimbabwe comparison, that by Barry Schutz and Douglas Scott (1974), which is also a considerably weaker
piece of research than Weitzer's in that it relies on scantier reading and largely on dated
and/or highly partisan historical sources. To be fair, at that time historical work on
Zimbabwe was very much in its infancy.

8. One exception is Brian Walker 'Religion and Politics: Irish problems and European
comparisons' in his 1996, though this is a somewhat superficial, broad-brush survey.

9. The relatively few breaches of the general rule that colonial entities emerged as independent states with their colonial boundaries unaltered almost all took place *in*, not after, the
process of decolonisation: where the departing colonial power was constrained to agree
to partition, as between India and Pakistan, or where local political forces near-
unanimously prevented the creation of a 'state-in-waiting' envisaged by international
agreements, as with the non-emergence of a Palestinian state alongside Israel in 1948. See
Fraser 1984.

10. Nor was *either* juridically a full secession at any time between 1914 and (according to
political taste) 1933, 1936, 1937, or 1948–9—the successive stages in transition from Irish
Free State within the British Commonwealth to Irish Republic outside it.

11. Some might add, in the vein of seeing 'map-images' as crucial to political destiny
(cf. Bowman 1982) that Mayotte as an island is a more natural political unit than the six
counties of north-east Ireland. A counter-claim would emphasise Northern Ireland's
greater economic viability, or perhaps its greater cultural distinctiveness (Mayotte, so far
as I can gather, is religiously and 'ethnically' undifferentiated from the other islands of
the Comoros).

CHAPTER 12

1. David Miller has suggested (1998:3–4) that the failure of scholars to specify or agree on a
clear date when Ireland was, or ceased to be, a British colony indicates a pervasive intellectual and political debility on the literature, stemming from refusal to recognise that
(as he himself believes) a colonial situation has been the all-determining reality up to the
present. That dissensus is, as I have argued, more aptly seen as reflecting the actual
complexity and ambiguity of Ireland's historical position.

2. Twenty-two presently (1999) sovereign European states are fairly clearly the product of
such processes: Albania, Austria, Belorussia, Bosnia, the Czech Republic, Croatia, Estonia, Finland, Georgia, Hungary, Iceland, Ireland, Latvia, Lithuania, Macedonia, Malta,
Norway, Poland, Serbia (which still, with Montenegro, calls itself the Federal Republic of
Yugoslavia) Slovakia, Slovenia, Ukraine. Sixteen states, by contrast, do not result from
twentieth-century secession or 'decolonisation': Belgium, Bulgaria, Denmark, France,

Germany, Greece, Italy, the Netherlands, Portugal, Romania, Spain, Sweden, Switzerland and (an ambiguous case) the United Kingdom, plus the microstates of Andorra and Monaco. Even several of these are, of course, the result of somewhat earlier breakups of multinational entities, or are—like France, Spain and the United Kingdom—faced with conflict over territory and ethnic nationalism. Thus a declaration like that by Luke Gibbons (echoing sentiments voiced by many others) that Ireland's status as 'a colony *within* Europe' was a 'paradoxical position' (1998/9:27) rests on quite unwarranted assumptions about Irish exceptionalism.

3. See e.g. R. F. Foster, in Field Day 1991, III:583–6); Hugh Kearney 1991; Dunne 1992. It may, though, still be the case that archaic, romantic nationalist views of Irish history powerfully helped to shape the attitudes of Irish-American and other diaspora communities to contemporary events. Certainly a recurrent theme in Irish-American responses to the Northern Ireland crisis since 1969 has been a traditionalist, idealist kind of nationalism, seemingly deaf to the appeal of other intellectual frameworks and indeed often hostile to the modernist, leftish and secular currents in modern Irish politics including those of the Civil Rights movement and later red-tinged Belfast Republicanism. See Holland 1989, O Dochartaigh 1995 and (the best, fullest account so far) Andrew Wilson 1995 for these interchanges. On the other hand, one London-based academic has attacked historical 'revisionism' precisely because it is irrelevant to the supposed needs of Irish diaspora communities, who require and demand a more orthodox nationalist narrative (Moore 1988).

4. See for instance Patrick Taylor's powerful *The Narrative of Liberation* (1989) for Caribbean appropriations of such myths of tradition to legitimise dictatorship, by 'Papa Doc' Duvalier and others. I discuss these themes in detail in my 2000c.

5. For the far less drastic but still vexing problems of literary censorship in Ireland, see Michael Adams 1968, Carlson ed. 1990.

6. This last is the central contention of Kiberd 1995.

7. See also Garvin 1991, 1996, Macmillan 1993. Garvin 1996 and Arthur Mitchell 1995 analyse the unstable mixture of legalism and militarism which marked Dail Eireann's 'underground' government in 1919–22, while Alan Ward 1994, Eunan O'Halpin 1999, and Charles Townshend 1998 show the length and strength of the countervailing constitutionalist tradition within Irish nationalism.

8. For a general argument on these lines see Liam Kennedy 1996 ch. 8: perhaps an overly didactic attempt to correct what Kennedy calls the 'MOPE (most oppressed people ever) syndrome' by arguing—more wholeheartedly than does Lee—that, to the contrary, Ireland has in fact been almost uniquely fortunate in everything from climate to religious toleration.

9. Exact figures are not agreed in relation to any phase of these conflicts. They cluster around the deathtolls of 500 in the 1916 Rising, 1,500 in the 'Black and Tan war', 500–700 in the 1920–2 sectarian strife in the north, and—the area of greatest uncertainty—between 800 and 4,000 in the South's 1922–3 Civil War. Some of the estimates are summarised in O'Leary and McGarry 1993:21.

10. Even then, only 'perhaps': in the Israeli–Palestinian conflict, for instance, quite apart from the rival claims about ancient history involved, entirely incompatible versions of the contemporary (post-1930, say) history of particular patches of land may be encountered from and sincerely believed by different protagonists. I have had several personal experiences of hearing completely variant accounts of the history of individual houses or

apartments, in such cities as Jaffa, Jerusalem and Hebron, from their present and former inhabitants and from local chroniclers. In almost all these cases, I had no doubt about the honesty of those relating the accounts—but equally, the intent to claim not only personal but 'national/ethnic' right to the properties was usually evident. Thus when Gerry Adams of Sinn Fein asserts that in many parts of rural Northern Ireland Catholics can 'show you the land that was taken off their family three or four hundred years ago and they will name the families that took it' (1986:27), it certainly cannot be presumed that such folk-memories are historically accurate.

11. Thus, it is extremely likely (so far as one can judge on the patchy available evidence) that, for instance, a very high proportion of Catholic Nationalists in Northern Ireland today can trace their ancestry partly to Scots or English 'planters', whilst at least as many Protestant Unionists have some 'Gaelic Irish' ancestry; and that—to go further back— there is a grain of probable truth in Ian Adamson's claims that many of the seventeenth-century Lowland Scots migrants to Ulster had distant Irish family origins. Within the next decade, the Human Genome Diversity Project may shed some new light on these questions—but one may safely predict that it will not offer much support to anyone's nationalist claims.

12. The 'cultural traditions' approach is generating a growing literature, mainly proceedings of conferences sponsored by such bodies as the Community Relations Council and the International Fund for Ireland: see Brown 1992, 1993, Crozier ed. 1989, 1990, 1991, Hughes ed. 1991, Kerr comp. 1996, Lundy and Mac Poilin eds 1992, Mackey ed. 1994, Ó Drisceoil ed. 1993, Robb 1992. At least indirectly, the founding text of this school is F. S. L. Lyons 1979.

13. Another, wider-ranging Irish application of Habermas—this time relating primarily to the evolution of national identity in the Irish Republic and its relationship to European integration—is O'Mahony and Delanty 1998.

14. For an important critique along these lines, see Porter 1996.

15. For a sketch of an 'emancipatory' framework's basic features as it might be applied to Northern Ireland, see Todd 1995, Ruane and Todd 1996 ch. 11. Finlayson 1997a, b provides additional critiques of identity politics in Northern Ireland, albeit ones over-burdened with a theoreticist jargon largely borrowed from Ernesto Laclau. Finlayson's argument also suffers from apparent uncertainty as to whether it is based on a 'hard' or a 'soft' version of the claim that political identities are invariably discursively constructed. There is a large gap between the modest suggestion that 'identity claims are a key part of political discourse but it is important not to accept them at face value' (1997b:72) and the far bolder claim that: 'Chains of equivalence are constructed that lock subjects into a sec-tarian, particularistic universe. Within these chains of equivalence the discourses are *entirely* self-referential and self-supporting.' (ibid: 75; my emphasis). On shifting social identities in Northern Ireland, see also McCall 1999.

16. It must be added that thus far, at least, attempts to 'operationalise' such theoretical frameworks in close analysis of particular political conjunctures—let alone practical interventions—have been extremely thin on the ground. Writers like Finlayson on Northern Ireland, or Aletta Norval (1996) on South Africa, have tended to produce extensive 'declarations of intent' setting agendas for such work, rather than actually doing it (though parts of Finlayson 1997b are an exception here).

BIBLIOGRAPHY

Abela, Anthony M. (1991): *Transmitting Values in European Malta* (Malta and Rome).

Adams, Gavin *et al.* (1989): *Ulster—The Internal Colony* (Belfast, Queen's University Unionist Association pamphlet).

Adams, Gerry (1986): *The Politics of Irish Freedom* (Dingle).

——(1995): *Free Ireland: Towards a Lasting Peace* (Dingle).

——(1996): *Before the Dawn: An Autobiography* (London).

Adams, Hazard (1991): 'Yeats and Antithetical Nationalism' in Vincent Newey and Ann Thompson (eds): *Literature and Nationalism* (Liverpool).

Adams, Michael (1968): *Censorship: The Irish Experience* (Dublin).

Adamson, Ian (1974): *The Cruthin* (Belfast).

——(1979): *Bangor—Light of the World* (Belfast).

——(1982): *The Identity of Ulster* (Belfast).

——(1991): *The Ulster People: Ancient, Medieval and Modern* (Bangor).

——(1994): 'The Ulster-Scottish Connection' in Wood (ed.).

Ad Hoc Group on South Africa (1995): *The South African Experience—Lessons for Northern Ireland?* (Belfast).

Ahmad, Aijaz (1992): *In Theory. Classes, Nations, Literatures* (London).

Ajami, Fouad (1981): *The Arab Predicament* (Cambridge).

Akenson, Donald Harman (1979): *Between Two Revolutions: Islandmagee, County Antrim 1798–1920* (Dublin).

——(1988): *Small Differences: Irish Catholics and Irish Protestants 1815–1922. An International Perspective* (Kingston, Montreal and Dublin).

——(1992): *God's Peoples: Covenant and Land in South Africa, Israel, and Ulster* (Ithaca and London).

——(1995): *Conor. A Biography of Conor Cruise O'Brien* (Montreal and Kingston).

——(1996): *The Irish Diaspora: A Primer* (Streetsville, Ontario and Belfast).

——(1997): *If the Irish Ran the World: Montserrat, 1630–1730* (Liverpool).

al-'Azm, Sadiq Jalal (1984): 'Orientalism and Orientalism in Reverse' in Khamsin: *Forbidden Agendas* (London).

Alcock, Anthony (1992): 'Northern Ireland: Some European Comparisons' in Brian Hadfield (ed.): *Northern Ireland Politics and the Constitution* (Buckingham).

——(1994): *Understanding Ulster* (Lurgan).

al-Khalil, Samir [Kanan Makiya] (1993): *Cruelty and Silence: War, Tyranny, Uprising and the Arab World* (London).

Allen, Kieran (1990): *Is Southern Ireland a Neo-Colony?* (Dublin).

Allen, Theodore W. (1994): *The Invention of the White Race*, Vol. 1, *Racial Oppression and Social Control* (London).

Amin, Samir (1990a): *Delinking: Towards a Polycentric World* (London).

——(1990b): *Maldevelopment: Anatomy of a Global Failure* (London).

Anderson, James (1980): 'Regions and Religions in Ireland: A Short Critique of the "Two Nations" Theory', *Antipode*, 12, 2.

Anderson, James (1998a): 'Integrating Europe, Integrating Ireland: The Socio-Economic Dynamics' in Anderson and Goodman (eds).

—— (1998b): 'Rethinking National Problems in a Transnational Context' in Miller (ed.).

Anderson, James and Goodman, James (eds, 1998): *Dis/Agreeing Ireland: Contexts, Obstacles, Hopes* (London).

Anderson, Malcolm, and Bort, Eberhard (eds, 1999): *The Irish Border: History, Politics, Culture* (Liverpool).

Anderson, W. K. (1994): *James Connolly and the Irish Left* (Blackrock, Co. Dublin).

Andrews, J. H. (1975): *A Paper Landscape: The Ordnance Survey in Nineteenth-Century Ireland* (Oxford).

Andrews, K. R., Canny, N. P. and Hair, P. E. (eds, 1978): *The Westward Enterprise: English Activities in Ireland, the Atlantic and America, 1480–1650* (Liverpool).

Arden, John (1977): *To Present the Pretence: Essays on the Theatre and its Public* (London).

Aretxaga, Begona (1997): *Shattering Silence: Women, Nationalism, and Political Subjectivity in Northern Ireland* (Princeton, NJ).

Armitage, David (1992): 'The Cromwellian Protectorate and the Languages of Empire', *Historical Journal*, 35, 3.

—— (1995): 'John Milton: Poet Against Empire' in Armitage *et al.* (eds.): *Milton and Republicanism* (Cambridge).

—— (1997): 'Making the Empire British: Scotland in the Atlantic World 1542–1707', *Past and Present*, 155.

—— (1998): 'Literature and Empire' in Canny (ed.).

Arneil, Barbara (1992): 'John Locke, Natural Law and Colonialism', *Journal of the History of Political Thought*, 13.

—— (1994): 'Trade, Plantations and Property: John Locke and the Economic Defence of Colonialism', *Journal of the History of Ideas*, 55, 4.

—— (1996): *John Locke and America: The Defence of English Colonialism* (Oxford).

Arthur, Paul and Jeffery, Keith (1988): *Northern Ireland since 1968* (London).

Asch, Ronald G. (ed., 1993): *Three Nations—A Common History? England, Scotland, Ireland and British History, c.1600–1920* (Bochum).

Aughey, Arthur (1989): *Under Siege: Ulster Unionism and the Anglo-Irish Agreement* (Belfast).

—— (1991): 'Unionism and Self-Determination' in Barton and Roche (eds).

—— (1995a): *The Union: Two Conflicting Interpretations* (London; Friends of the Union pamphlet).

—— (1995b): *Irish Kulturkampf: A Critique of Irish Cultural Imperialism* (Belfast; Ulster Young Unionist Council pamphlet).

—— (1997a): 'A State of Exception: The Concept of the Political in Northern Ireland', *Irish Political Studies*, 12.

—— (1997b): 'The Character of Ulster Unionism' in Shirlow and McGovern (eds).

—— (1998): 'Reconceptualising the Political in Northern Ireland: Reply to Finlayson', *Irish Political Studies*, 13.

Augusteijn, Joost (1990): 'The Importance of Being Irish: Ideas and the Volunteers in Mayo and Tipperary' in David Fitzpatrick (ed.).

—— (1996): *From Public Defiance to Guerrilla Warfare: The Experience of Ordinary Volunteers in the Irish War of Independence 1916–1921* (Blackrock, Co. Dublin).

Aunger, Edmund (1981): *In Search of Political Stability: A Comparative Study of New Brunswick and Northern Ireland* (Montreal).

Bailyn, Bernard and Morgan, Philip D. (eds, 1991): *Strangers Within the Realm: Cultural Margins of the First British Empire* (Chapel Hill, NC and London).

Bairner, Alan (1996): 'Ireland, Sport and Empire' in Jeffery (ed.).

——(1997): '"Up to Their Knees"? Football, sectarianism, masculinity and Protestant working-class identity' in Shirlow and McGovern (eds).

Ballhatchet, Kenneth (1980): *Race, Sex and Class under the Raj: Imperial Attitudes and Policies and their Critics, 1793–1905* (London).

Bambery, Chris (1987): *Ireland's Permanent Revolution* (London).

Barakat, Halim (1993): *The Arab World: Society, Culture, and State* (Berkeley).

Bardon, Jonathan (1992): *A History of Ulster* (Belfast).

Barnard, T. C. (1990): 'Crises of Identity among Irish Protestants, 1641–1685', *Past and Present*, 127.

——(1991): 'The Uses of 23 October 1641 and Irish Protestant Celebrations', *English Historical Review*, cvi.

——(1998): 'New Opportunities for British Settlement: Ireland, 1650–1700' in Canny (ed.).

Barry, Kevin (1996): 'Critical Notes on Post-Colonial Aesthetics', *Irish Studies Review*, 14.

Barry, T. B., Frame, Robin and Simms, Katherine (eds, 1995): *Colony and Frontier in Medieval Ireland: Essays Presented to J. F. Lydon* (London and Rio Grande).

Barry, Tom (1962): *Guerilla Days in Ireland* (Tralee: orig. pub. Dublin, 1949).

Bartlett, Robert (1993): *The Making of Europe: Conquest, Colonization and Cultural Change 950–1350* (London).

Bartlett, Thomas (1985): 'Indiscipline and Disaffection in the Armed Forces in Ireland in the 1790s', in Corish (ed.).

——(1987): 'An End to Moral Economy: The Irish Militia Disturbances of 1793' in Philpin (ed.).

——(1990): '"A People Made Rather for Copies than Originals": The Anglo-Irish 1760–1800', *International History Review*, XII, 1.

——(1992): *The Fall and Rise of the Irish Nation: The Catholic Question 1690–1830* (Dublin).

——(1996): 'Defence, Counter-Insurgency and Rebellion: Ireland, 1793–1803' in Bartlett and Jeffery (eds).

——(1998): '"This Famous Island Set in a Virginian Sea": Ireland in the British Empire, 1690–1801' in Marshall (ed.).

Bartlett, Thomas, Dickson, David, Keogh, Daire and Whelan, Kevin (eds, 2000): *The Irish Rebellion of 1798: A Bicentennial Perspective* (Dublin, forthcoming).

Bartlett, Thomas and Jeffery, Keith (eds, 1996): *A Military History of Ireland* (Cambridge).

Barton, Brian (1996): 'The Impact of World War II on Northern Ireland and on Belfast–London Relations' in Catterall and McDougall (eds).

Barton, Brian and Roche, Patrick J. (eds, 1991): *The Northern Ireland Question: Myth and Reality* (Aldershot).

Baumgart, Winfried (1982): *Imperialism: The Idea and Reality of British and French Colonial Expansion, 1880–1914* (Oxford).

Bayly, C. A. (1989): *Imperial Meridian: The British Empire and the World, 1780–1830* (London).

Beattie, Geoffrey (1993): *We Are the People: Journeys Through the Heart of Protestant Ulster* (London).

Beaune, Colette (1991): *The Birth of an Ideology: Myths and Symbols in Late-Medieval France* (Berkeley, CA).

Beckles, Hilary McD. (1989): *White Servitude and Black Slavery in Barbados, 1627–1715* (Knoxville, Tenn.).

Belchem, John (1992): 'Britain, United States and Australia: Some Comparative Reflections', *Labour History Review*, 57, 3.

Belfrage, Sally (1988): *The Crack: A Belfast Year* (London).

Belich, James (1996): *Making Peoples: A History of the New Zealanders From Polynesian Settlement to the End of the Nineteenth Century* (Auckland and London).

Bell, Desmond (1990): *Acts of Union: Youth Culture and Sectarianism in Northern Ireland* (London).

——(1998): 'Modernising History: The *Real politik* of Heritage and Cultural Tradition in Northern Ireland' in Miller (ed.).

Bell, Geoffrey (1976): *The Protestants of Ulster* (London).

——(1982): *Troublesome Business: The Labour Party and the Irish Question* (London).

——(1984): *The British in Ireland: A Suitable Case for Withdrawal* (London).

Bell, J. Bowyer (1996): *Back to the Future: The Protestants and a United Ireland* (Dublin).

Benjamin, Andrew (ed., 1992): *Judging Lyotard* (London).

Bennett, Ronan (1994): 'An Irish Answer', *Guardian* 16 July.

——(1998): 'Don't Mention the War: Culture in Northern Ireland' in Miller (ed.).

Benton, Sarah (1995): 'Women Disarmed: The Militarization of Politics in Ireland 1913–23', *Feminist Review*, 50.

Berresford Ellis, Peter (1988): *Hell or Connaught! The Cromwellian Colonisation of Ireland, 1652–1660* (Belfast).

——(1989): 'Revisionism in Irish Historical Writing: The New Anti-Nationalist School of Historians' (Desmond Greaves Memorial Lecture, Conway Hall, London, 31 October).

Bew, Paul (1978): *Land and the National Question in Ireland, 1858–1882* (Dublin).

——(1987): *Conflict and Conciliation in Ireland, 1890–1910: Parnellites and Radical Agrarians* (Oxford).

——(1994): *Ideology and the Irish Question: Ulster Unionism and Irish Nationalism 1912–1916* (Oxford).

Bew, Paul, Gibbon, Peter and Patterson, Henry (1979): *The State in Northern Ireland* (Manchester).

——(1994): *Northern Ireland 1921–1994: Political Forces and Social Classes* (London).

Bew, Paul, Hazelkorn, Ellen and Patterson, Henry (1989): *The Dynamics of Irish Politics* (London).

Bew, Paul and Patterson, Henry (1982): *Sean Lemass and the Making of Modern Ireland, 1945–1966* (Dublin).

——(1985): *The British State and the Ulster Crisis: From Wilson to Thatcher* (London).

Bew, Paul and Wright, Frank (1983): 'The Agrarian Opposition in Ulster Politics, 1848–87' in Clark and Donnelly (eds).

Bhabha, Homi K. (1992): 'Postcolonial Authority and Postcolonial Guilt' in Lawrence Grossberg *et al.* (eds): *Cultural Studies* (London).

——(1994): *The Location of Culture* (London).

Bhreatnach, Aoife (1998): 'Travellers and the Print Media: Words and Irish Identity', *Irish Studies Review*, 6, 3.

Birch, Anthony H. (1989): *Nationalism and National Integration* (London).

Birnie, Esmond (1995): 'Economic Unification: The Economic Consequences of the Peace' in J. W. Foster (ed.).

Bishop, Patrick and Mallie, Eamonn (1987): *The Provisional IRA* (London).

Blackburn, Robin (1995): 'Ireland and the NLR', *New Left Review*, 212.

Bleys, Rudi C. (1996): *The Geography of Perversion: Male-to-Male Sexual Behaviour outside the West and the Ethnographic Imagination 1750–1918* (London).

Boal, Fred, Campbell, John A. and Livingstone, David N. (1991): 'The Protestant Mosaic: A Majority of Minorities' in Barton and Roche (eds).

Boehmer, Elleke (1995): *Colonial and Postcolonial Literature* (Oxford).

Bolger, Dermot (ed., 1991): *Letters from the New Island* (Dublin).

Bottigheimer, Karl (1978): 'Kingdom and Colony: Ireland in the Westward Enterprise, 1536–1660' in Andrews, Canny and Hair (eds).

Bowden, Tom (1977): *The Breakdown of Public Security: The Case of Ireland 1916–1921 and Palestine 1936–1939* (London).

Bowen, Kurt (1983): *Protestants in a Catholic State: Ireland's Privileged Minority* (Kingston, Ontario).

Bowman, John (1982): *De Valera and the Ulster Question 1917–1973* (Oxford).

Boyce, George (1972): *Englishmen and Irish Troubles: British Public Opinion and the Making of Irish Policy, 1918–1922* (London).

——(1986): 'The Marginal Britons: The Irish' in Robert Colls and Philip Dodd (eds): *Englishness: Culture and Politics 1880–1920* (Beckenham).

——(1988): *The Irish Question and British Politics, 1868–1986* (Basingstoke).

——(1991a): 'Northern Ireland: A Place Apart?' in Hughes (ed.).

——(1991b): 'Federalism and the Irish Question' in Andrea Bosco (ed.): *The Federal Idea*, Vol. 1, *The History of Federalism from the Enlightenment to 1945* (London).

——(1995): *Nationalism in Ireland* (3rd edn, London).

——(1996a): '1916, Interpreting the Rising' in Boyce and O'Day (eds).

——(1996b): 'Past and Present: Revisionism and the Northern Ireland troubles' in Boyce and O'Day (eds).

Boyce, George and O'Day, Alan (eds, 1996): *The Making of Modern Irish History: Revisionism and the Revisionist Controversy* (London).

Boyd, Andrew (1969): *Holy War in Belfast* (Tralee).

Boylan, Thomas A. and Foley, Timothy P. (1992): *Political Economy and Colonial Ireland: The Propagation and Ideological Function of Economic Discourse in the Nineteenth Century* (London).

Boyle, J. W. (1962–63): 'The Belfast Protestant Association and the Independent Orange Order, 1901–10', *Irish Historical Studies*, XIII, 1.

Boyle, Kevin and Hadden, Tom (1994): *Northern Ireland: The Choice* (Harmondsworth).

Bradford, Roy (1996): 'Undermining the Greenprint', *Ulster Review*, 20, Summer.

Bradshaw, Brendan (1978): 'Sword, Word and Strategy in the Reformation of Ireland', *Historical Journal*, xxi.

——(1979): *The Irish Constitutional Revolution of the Sixteenth Century* (Cambridge).

——(1989): 'Nationalism and Historical Scholarship in Modern Ireland', *Irish Historical Studies*, XXVI, 104. Reprinted in Brady (ed.), 1994.

——(1994): 'Revising Irish History' in Ó Ceallaigh (ed.).

——(1996): 'The Tudor Revolution and Reformation in Wales and Ireland: The Origins of the British Problem' in Bradshaw and Morrill (eds).

Bradshaw, Brendan, Hadfield, Andrew and Maley, Willy (eds, 1993): *Representing Ireland: Literature and the Origins of Conflict, 1534–1660* (Cambridge).

Bradshaw, Brendan and Morrill, John (eds, 1996): *The British Problem, c.1534–1707: State Formation in the Atlantic Archipelago* (Basingstoke).

Brady, Ciaran (1986): 'Spenser's Irish Crisis: Humanism and Experience in the 1590s', *Past and Present*, 111.

——(1991): 'The Decline of the Irish Kingdom' in Mark Greengrass (ed.): *Conquest and Coalescence: The Shaping of the State in Early Modern Europe* (London).

——(1994): *The Chief Governors: The Rise and Fall of Reform Government in Tudor Ireland, 1536–1588* (Cambridge).

——(ed., 1994): *Interpreting Irish History: The Debate on Historical Revisionism* (Dublin).

Brady, Ciaran and Gillespie, Raymond (eds, 1986): *Natives and Newcomers: The Making of Irish Colonial Society 1534–1641* (Dublin).

Brailsford, H. N. (1915): *The War of Steel and Gold* (3rd edn, London).

Brasted, H. V. (1980): 'Indian Nationalist Development and the Influence of Irish Home Rule, 1870–1886', *Modern Asian Studies*, 14, 1.

——(1983): 'Irish Nationalism and the British Empire in the Late 19th Century' in Oliver MacDonagh, W. F. Mandle and Pauric Travers (eds): *Irish Culture and Nationalism, 1750–1950* (Dublin).

——(1985): 'Irish Models and the Indian National Congress 1870–1922', *South Asia*, VIII, 1–2.

Breen, Dan (1981): *My Fight for Irish Freedom* (orig. pub. 1921; citations from 1981 Dublin edn).

Breen, Richard, Hannan, D. F., Rottman, D. B., and Whelan, C. T. (1990): *Understanding Contemporary Ireland* (Dublin).

Brewer, Anthony (1990): *Marxist Theories of Imperialism: A Critical Survey* (2nd edn, London).

Brewer, John D. and Magee, Kathleen (1991): *Inside the RUC: Routine Policing in a Divided Society* (Oxford).

——and Higgins, Gareth (1998): *Anti-Catholicism in Northern Ireland 1600–1998* (Basingstoke).

Bringa, Tone (1995): *Being Muslim the Bosnian Way: Identity and Community in a Central Bosnian Village* (Princeton, NJ).

British and Irish Communist Organisation (1971a): *On the Democratic Validity of the Northern Ireland State* (Belfast).

——(1971b): *The Two Irish Nations* (Belfast).

——(1975): *Imperialism* (Belfast).

Brown, Heloise (1998): 'An Alternative Imperialism: Isabella Tod, Internationalist and "Good Liberal Unionist"', *Gender and History*, 10, 3.

Brown, Terence (1985a): *Ireland: A Social and Cultural History 1922–1985* (London).

——(1985b): *The Whole Protestant Community: The Making of a Historical Myth* (Derry, Field Day pamphlet).

——(1992): 'Identities in Ireland: The Historical Perspective' in Lundy and Mac Poilin (eds).

——(1993): 'The Cultural Issue in Northern Ireland, 1965–1991' in Keogh and Haltzel (eds).

Bruce, Steve (1986): *God Save Ulster! The Religion and Politics of Paisleyism* (Oxford).

——(1992): *The Red Hand: Protestant Paramilitaries in Northern Ireland* (Oxford).

——(1994): *The Edge of the Union: The Ulster Loyalist Political Vision* (Oxford).

Bryan, Dominic, Fraser, T. G. and Dunn, Seamus (1995): *Political Rituals: Loyalist Parades in Portadown* (Coleraine).

Bryans, Robin (1964): *Ulster: A Journey through the Six Counties* (Belfast).

Bryson, Lucy and McCartney, Clem (1994): *Clashing Symbols: A Report on the Use of Flags, Anthems and other National Symbols in Northern Ireland* (Belfast).

Buckland, Patrick (1973): *Irish Unionism*, Vol. II, *Ulster Unionism and the Origins of Northern Ireland, 1886–1922* (Dublin).

Buckley, Anthony D. (1982): *A Gentle People: A Study of a Peaceful Community in Ulster* (Cultra, Co. Down).

——(1985–86): 'The Chosen Few: Biblical Texts in the Regalia of an Ulster Secret Society', *Folklife*, 24, 1.

——(1987): 'God's Chosen People', *Irish Review*, 2.

——(ed., 1998): *Symbols in Northern Ireland* (Belfast).

Budge, Ian and O'Leary, Cornelius (1973): *Belfast: Approach to Crisis* (London).

Bukharin, Nikolai (1918): *Imperialism and World Economy* (Moscow; cited from 1973 NY edn).

Bulpitt, Jim (1983): *Territory and Power in the United Kingdom* (Manchester).

Burchell, R. A. (1982): 'The Historiography of the American-Irish', *Immigrants and Minorities*, 1, 3.

Burnett, Mark Thornton and Wray, Ramona (eds, 1997): *Shakespeare and Ireland: History, Politics, Culture* (Basingstoke).

Burton, Antoinette (1994): *Burdens of History: British Feminists, Indian Women and Imperial Culture, 1865–1915* (Durham, NC).

Burton, Frank (1978): *The Politics of Legitimacy: Struggles in a Belfast Community* (London).

Butt, Isaac (1874): *Irish Federalism: Its Meaning, Its Objects and Its Hopes* (4th edn, Dublin).

Cabal, Mark (1998): *Poets and Politics: Reaction and Continuity in Irish Poetry, 1558–1625* (Cork).

Cadogan Group, The (1992): *Northern Limits: Boundaries of the Attainable in Northern Ireland Politics* (Belfast).

——(1994): *Blurred Vision: Joint Authority and the Northern Ireland Problem* (Belfast).

Cahery, Therese *et al.* (eds, 1992): *Is Ireland a Third World Country?* (Belfast).

Cain, P. J. and Hopkins, A. G. (1993): *British Imperialism*, Vol. I, *Innovation and Expansion 1688–1914* (London); Vol. II, *Crisis and Deconstruction 1914–1990* (London).

Cairns, David and Richards, Shaun (1988): *Writing Ireland: Colonialism, Nationalism and Culture* (London).

Calder, Angus (1981): *Revolutionary Empire: The Rise of the English Speaking Empires from the Fifteenth Century to the 1780s* (London).

Campbell, Flann (1991): *The Dissenting Voice: Protestant Democracy in Ulster from Plantation to Partition* (Belfast).

Candy, Catherine (1994): 'Relating Feminisms, Nationalisms and Imperialisms: Ireland, India and Margaret Cousins's Sexual Politics', *Women's History Review*, 3, 4.

Canning, Paul (1985): *British Policy Towards Ireland, 1921–1941* (Oxford).

Canny, Nicholas (1973): 'The Ideology of English Colonisation: From Ireland to America', *William and Mary Quarterly*, xxx.

——(1978): 'Dominant Minorities: English Settlers in Ireland and Virginia 1550–1650' in A. C. Hepburn (ed.): *Minorities in History, Historical Studies*, XII (London).

——(1982a): *The Upstart Earl: A Study of the Social and Mental World of Richard Boyle, First Earl of Cork* (Cambridge).

——(1982b): 'The Formation of the Irish Mind: Religion, Politics and Gaelic Irish Literature 1580–1750', *Past and Present*, 95.

Canny, Nicholas (1986): 'Protestants, Planters and Apartheid in Early Modern Ireland', *Irish Historical Studies*, xxv, 98.

—— (1987): 'Identity Formation in Ireland: The Emergence of the Anglo-Irish' in Canny and Pagden (eds).

—— (1988): *Kingdom and Colony: Ireland in the Atlantic World, 1560–1800* (Baltimore).

—— (1991): 'The Marginal Kingdom: Ireland as a Problem in the First British Empire' in Bailyn and Morgan (eds).

—— (1994): 'Irish Resistance to Empire? 1641, 1690 and 1798' in Lawrence Stone (ed.): *An Imperial State at War: Britain from 1689 to 1815* (London).

—— (1995): 'Irish, Scottish and Welsh Responses to Centralisation, *c.*1530–*c.*1640: A Comparative Perspective' in Grant and Stringer (eds).

—— (1996): 'Review Article: Revising the Revisionist', *Irish Historical Studies*, 30, 118.

—— (1998a): 'Westward Enterprise' (interview with Hiram Morgan), *History Ireland*, 6, 1; Spring.

—— (1998b): 'The Origins of Empire: An Introduction' in Canny (ed.).

—— (1998c): 'England's New World and the Old, 1480s–1630s' in Canny (ed.).

—— (ed., 1994): *Europeans on the Move: Studies in European Migration, 1500–1800* (Oxford).

—— (ed., 1998): *The Oxford History of the British Empire*, Vol. 1, *The Origins of Empire. British Overseas Enterprise to the Close of the Seventeenth Century* (Oxford).

Canny, Nicholas and Pagden, Anthony (eds, 1987): *Colonial Identity in the Atlantic World, 1500–1800* (Princeton, NJ).

Carlin, Norah (1985): 'Ireland and Natural Man in 1649' in Francis Barker *et al.* (eds) *Europe and Its Others* (Colchester), vol. 2.

—— (1987): 'The Levellers and the Conquest of Ireland in 1649', *The Historical Journal*, xxx, 2.

Carlson, Julia (ed., 1990): *Banned in Ireland: Censorship and the Irish Writer* (London).

Carty, Anthony (1996): *Was Ireland Conquered? International Law and the Irish Question* (London).

Carty, James (1932): *A Junior History of Ireland* (2 vols, London).

Carty, R. K. (1993): 'From Tradition to Modernity and Back Again: Party-building in Ireland' in Hill and Marsh (eds).

Carvel, John (1984): *Citizen Ken* (London).

Cash, John Daniel (1996): *Identity, Ideology and Conflict: The Structuration of Politics in Northern Ireland* (Cambridge).

Catterall, Peter and McDougall, Sean (eds, 1996): *The Northern Ireland Question in British Politics* (London).

Chadwick, Joseph (1996): 'Yeats: Colonialism and Responsibility' in Furomoto *et al.* (eds).

Chakrabarty, Dipesh (1992): 'Postcoloniality and the Artifice of History: Who Speaks for "Indian" Pasts?', *Representations*, 37.

Chambers, Liam (1998): *Rebellion in Kildare, 1790–1803* (Dublin).

Charles-Edwards, T[homas] M. (1996): 'Irish Warfare Before 1100' in Bartlett and Jeffery (eds).

Chatterjee, Partha (1986): *Nationalist Thought and the Colonial World: A Derivative Discourse?* (London).

Cheng, Vincent J. (1995): *Joyce, Race, and Empire* (Cambridge).

Cheyfitz, Eric (1991): *The Poetics of Imperialism: Translation and Colonization from The Tempest to Tarzan* (New York).

Childs, Peter and Williams, Patrick (1997): *An Introduction to Post-Colonial Theory* (London).

Chrisman, Laura (1991): 'The Imperial Unconscious? Representations of Imperial Discourse', *Critical Quarterly*, 32, 3.

Chubb, Basil (1982): *The Government and Politics of Ireland* (Dublin; 2nd edn).

Clark, J. C. D. (1985): *English Society 1688–1832: Ideology, Social Structure and Political Practice during the Ancien Regime* (Cambridge).

——(1994): *The Language of Liberty 1660–1832* (Cambridge).

Clark, Samuel and Donnelly, James S. (eds, 1983): *Irish Peasants: Violence and Political Unrest 1780–1914* (Manchester).

Clarke, Aidan (1978): 'Colonial Identity in Early 17th-century Ireland' in T. W. Moody (ed.): *Nationality and the Pursuit of National Independence, Historical Studies*, XI (Belfast).

Clarke, Peter (1978): *Liberals and Social Democrats* (Cambridge).

Clayton, Pamela (1996): *Enemies and Passing Friends: Settler Ideologies in Twentieth Century Ulster* (London).

——(1998): 'Religion, Ethnicity and Colonialism as Explanations of the Northern Ireland Conflict' in Miller (ed.).

Clifford, Brendan (1986): *Parliamentary Despotism: John Hume's Aspiration* (Belfast, Athol Books pamphlet).

——(1991): *The New Left Imperialist: A Comment on the Imperialist Apologetics of Professor Fred Halliday of the LSE* (London, Bevin Society pamphlet).

——(1992a): *The Economics of Partition: A Historical Survey of Ireland in Terms of Political Economy* (Belfast: reprint of 1972 4th edn).

——(1992b): *Against Ulster Nationalism* (3rd edn, Belfast).

——(1993): *The Irish Civil War: The Conflict that Formed the State* (Aubane, Co. Cork).

Coakley, John (1983): 'Conflict and Violence: Patrick Pearse and the Noble Lie of Irish Nationalism', *Studies*, lxxii.

——(1986): 'Political Succession and Regime Change in New States in Interwar Europe: Ireland, Finland, Czechoslovakia and the Baltic Republics', *European Journal of Political Research*, 14.

——(1987): 'Political Succession during the Transition to Independence: Evidence from Europe' in Peter Calvert (ed.): *The Process of Political Succession* (London).

——(1994): 'The Northern Conflict in Southern Irish Textbooks' in Guelke (ed.).

Cochrane, Feargal (1994): 'Any Takers? The Isolation of Northern Ireland', *Political Studies*, 42, 3.

——(1997): *Unionist Politics and the Politics of Unionism since the Anglo-Irish Agreement* (Cork).

Coldrey, Barry (1988): *Faith and Fatherland: The Christian Brothers and the Development of Irish Nationalism, 1838–1921* (Dublin).

Colley, Linda (1992): *Britons: Forging the Nation 1707–1837* (New Haven).

Collins, Eamon with McGovern, Mick (1997): *Killing Rage* (London).

Collins, Kevin (1990): *The Cultural Conquest of Ireland* (Cork).

Collins, Martin (ed., 1985): *Ireland After Britain* (London).

Commission for Racial Equality (1997): *Discrimination and the Irish Community in Britain* (London).

Communist Party of Great Britain (1927): *Is India Different?* (London, CPGB pamphlet).

Connell, Liam (1997): 'Irish Immigration and the Construction of Scottish Identity' paper for BAIS conference, Salford, 5–7 September.

Connolly, Clara (1993): 'Culture or Citizenship? Notes on the "Gender and Colonialism" Conference, Galway, Ireland, May 1992', *Feminist Review*, 44.

—— (1995): 'Ourselves Alone? Clar na Mban conference report', *Feminist Review*, 50.

Connolly, James (1917): *Labour in Ireland* (reprint of *Labour in Irish History* (1910) and *The Reconquest of Ireland* (1915)) (Dublin).

Connolly, S[ean]. J. (1992): *Religion, Law and Power: The Making of Protestant Ireland* (Oxford).

—— (1995): 'Varieties of Britishness: Ireland, Scotland and Wales in the Hanoverian State' in Grant and Stringer (eds).

—— (1996): 'Eighteenth-Century Ireland' in Boyce and O'Day (eds).

—— (1997): 'Cultural Identity and Tradition: Changing Definitions of Irishness' in Graham (ed.).

—— (ed., 1999): *Kingdoms United? Great Britain and Ireland since 1500: Integration and Diversity* (Dublin).

Conroy, John (1988): *War As a Way of Life: A Belfast Diary* (London).

Coogan, Tim Pat (1966): *Ireland Since the Rising* (Dublin).

—— (1987a): *The IRA* (London: 3rd edn).

—— (1987b): *Disillusioned Decades: Ireland 1966–1987* (Dublin).

—— (1990): *Michael Collins* (London).

Cook, Scott B. (1987): 'The Irish Raj: Social Origins and Careers of Irishmen in the Indian Civil Service, 1855–1919', *Journal of Social History*, 20, 3.

—— (1993): *Imperial Affinities: Nineteenth Century Analogies and Exchanges between India and Ireland* (New Delhi).

Corish, Patrick J. (ed., 1985): *Radicals, Rebels and Establishments, Historical Studies*, XV (Belfast).

Corkery, Daniel (1925): *The Hidden Ireland: A Study of Gaelic Munster in the 18th Century* (Dublin).

Coughlan, Anthony (1994): 'Ireland's Marxist Historians' in Brady (ed.).

Coughlan, Patricia (ed., 1989): *Spenser and Ireland: An Interdisciplinary Perspective* (Cork).

Coulter, Carol (1990): *Ireland: Between the First and the Third Worlds* (Dublin).

—— (1993): *The Hidden Tradition: Feminism, Women and Nationalism in Ireland* (Cork).

—— (1995): 'Feminism, Nationalism and the Heritage of the Enlightenment' in Foley *et al.* (eds).

—— (1998): 'Feminism and Nationalism in Ireland' in Miller (ed.).

Coulter, Colin (1994): 'The Character of Unionism', *Irish Political Studies*, 9.

—— (1997): 'The Culture of Contentment: The Political Beliefs and Practice of the Unionist Middle Classes' in Shirlow and McGovern (eds).

Cox, W. Harvey (1985): 'Who Wants a United Ireland?', *Government and Opposition*, 20.

Cradden, Terry (1993): *Trade Unionism, Socialism and Partition: The Labour Movement in Northern Ireland 1939–1953* (Belfast).

—— (1996): 'Labour in Britain and the Northern Ireland Labour Party, 1900–70' in Catterall and McDougall (eds).

Craig, F. S. W. (ed., 1982): *Conservative and Labour Conference Decisions 1945–1981* (London).

Crawford, E. Margaret (ed., 1997): *The Hungry Stream: Essays on Emigration and Famine* (Belfast).

Cronin, Sean (1980): *Irish Nationalism* (Dublin).

Crossman, Virginia and McLoughlin, Dymphna (1994): 'A Peculiar Eclipse: E. Estyn Evans and Irish Studies', *Irish Review*, 15.

Crotty, Raymond (1986): *Ireland in Crisis: A Study of Capitalist Colonial Underdevelopment* (Dingle).

Crozier, Maurna (ed., 1989): *Cultural Traditions in Northern Ireland: Varieties of Irishness*, Proceedings of the Cultural Traditions Group Conference (Belfast).

——(ed., 1990): *Cultural Traditions in Northern Ireland: Varieties of Britishness* (Belfast).

——(ed., 1991): *Cultural Traditions in Northern Ireland: All Europeans Now?* (Belfast).

Crummell, Alexander (1891): *Africa and America: Addresses and Discourses* (Springfield, Mass.).

Cullen, L[ouis] M. (1972): *An Economic History of Ireland since 1600* (London).

——(1981): *The Emergence of Modern Ireland 1600–1900* (London).

——(1985): 'The 1798 Rebellion in its Eighteenth-Century Context' in Corish (ed.).

——(1994): 'The Irish Diaspora of the Seventeenth and Eighteenth Centuries' in Canny (ed.).

——(1996): 'The United Irishmen in Wexford' in Keogh and Furlong (eds).

Cullen, L[ouis] M. (ed., 1969): *Formation of the Irish Economy* (Cork).

Cullen, Mary (ed., 1998): *1798: 200 Years of Resonance* (Dublin).

Cullingford, Elizabeth Butler (1981): *Yeats, Ireland and Fascism* (London).

——(1990): ' "Thinking of her . . . as . . . Ireland": Yeats, Pearse and Heaney', *Textual Practice*, 4, 1.

Cummins, Ian (1980): *Marx, Engels and National Movements* (London).

Cumpston, Mary (1961): 'Some Early Indian Nationalists and Their Allies in the British Parliament', *English Historical Review*, lxxvi.

Cunningham, Michael (1997): 'The Political Language of John Hume', *Irish Political Studies*, 12.

Curtin, Nancy (1994): *The United Irishmen: Popular Politics in Ulster and Dublin 1791–1798* (Oxford).

——(1996): ' "Varieties of Irishness": Historical Revisionism, Irish Style', *Journal of British Studies*, 35, 2.

Curtis, L[ewis] P[erry]. (1968): *Anglo-Saxons and Celts: A Study of Anti-Irish Prejudice in Victorian England* (Bridgeport, Ct.).

——(1971): *Apes and Angels: The Irishman in Victorian Caricature* (Newton Abbot).

——(1994): 'The Greening of Irish History', *Eire/Ireland*, xxix, 2.

Curtis, Liz (1984a): *Ireland. The Propaganda War* (London).

——(1984b): *Nothing But the Same Old Story: The Roots of Anti-Irish Racism* (London).

——(1994): *The Cause of Ireland: From the United Irishmen to Partition* (Belfast).

Cusack, Jim and McDonald, Henry (1997): *UVF* (Dublin).

Dalton, G. F. (1974): 'The Tradition of Blood Sacrifice to the Goddess Eire', *Studies*, lxii.

Daly, Mary (1992): *Industrial Development and Irish National Identity, 1922–1939* (Dublin).

——(1996): 'Revisionism and Irish History: The Great Famine' in Boyce and O'Day (eds).

——(1999): 'Integration or Diversity? Anglo-Irish Economic Relations, 1922–39' in S. J. Connolly (ed.).

Darby, John, Dodge, Nicholas and Hepburn, A. C. (eds, 1990): *Political Violence: Ireland in Comparative Perspective* (Belfast).

Davies, Rees [R. R.] (1990): *Domination and Conquest: The Experience of Ireland, Scotland and Wales 1100–1300* (Cambridge).

Davies, Rees [R. R.] (1993): 'The English State and the "Celtic" Peoples 1100–1400', *Journal of Historical Sociology*, 6, 1.

——(1994): 'The Peoples of Britain and Ireland 1100–1400 I: Identities' *Transactions of the Royal Historical Society* (London).

Davis, Eoghan (1990): 'The Guerrilla Mind' in David Fitzpatrick (ed.).

Davis, Graham (1991a): *The Irish in Britain, 1815–1914* (Dublin).

——(1991b): 'Making History: John Mitchel and the Great Famine' in Paul Hyland and Neil Sammels (eds): *Irish Writing: Exile and Subversion* (London).

Davis, Horace B. (1967): *Nationalism and Socialism: Marxist and Labor Theories of Nationalism* (New York).

Davis, Richard (1974): *Arthur Griffith and Non-Violent Sinn Fein* (Dublin).

——(1980): 'The Shamrock and the Tiki: Irish Nationalists and Maori Resistance in the 19th Century', *Journal of Intercultural Studies*, 1, 3.

——(1994): *Mirror Hate: The Convergent Ideology of Northern Ireland Paramilitaries, 1966–92* (Aldershot).

Davitt, Michael (1902): *The Boer Fight for Freedom* (New York and London).

Dawe, Gerald and Foster, John Wilson (eds, 1991): *The Poet's Place. Ulster Literature and Society: Essays in Honour of John Hewitt 1907–1987* (Belfast).

Deane, Seamus (1983): *History Lessons* (Dublin).

——(1985a): *Celtic Revivals* (London).

——(1985b): 'Heroic Styles: The Tradition of an Idea' in Field Day: *Ireland's Field Day* (London).

——(1990): 'Introduction' to Field Day: *Nationalism, Colonialism and Literature* (Minneapolis).

——(1991a): 'Wherever Green is Read' in Dhonnchadha and Dorgan (eds), reprinted in Brady (ed.) 1994.

——(1991b): 'General Introduction' in Field Day Anthology, Vol. I.

——(1992): 'Canon Fodder: Literary Mythologies in Ireland' in Lundy and Mac Poilin (eds).

——(1996): *Reading In the Dark* (London).

——(1997): *Strange Country: Modernity and Nationhood in Irish Writing Since 1790* (Oxford).

Deasy, Liam (1973): *Towards Ireland Free* (Cork and Dublin).

——(1982): *Brother Against Brother* (Cork and Dublin).

De Baroid, Ciaran (1990): *Ballymurphy and the Irish War* (London).

Delanty, Gerard (1996): 'Habermas and Post-National Identity: Theoretical Perspectives on the Conflict in Northern Ireland', *Irish Political Studies*, 11.

Democratic Dialogue (1995): *New Thinking for New Times* (Belfast).

——(1998): *New Order: International Models of Peace and Reconciliation* (Belfast).

De Nie, Michael (1998): 'The Famine, Irish Identity, and the British Press', *Irish Studies Review*, 6, 1.

Denoon, Donald (1983): *Settler Capitalism: The Dynamics of Dependent Development in the Southern Hemisphere* (Oxford).

Denselow, Robin (1989): *When the Music's Over: The Story of Political Pop* (London).

Devine, T. M. (ed., 1991): *Irish Immigrants and Scottish Society in the Nineteenth and Twentieth Centuries* (Edinburgh).

Devlin, Bernadette (1969): *The Price of My Soul* (London).

Devlin, Paddy (1981): *Yes, We Have No Bananas* (Belfast).

Devy, Ganesh N. (1992): 'India and Ireland: Literary Relations' in Joseph McMinn (ed.): *The Internationalism of Irish Literature and Drama* (Gerrards Cross).

Devy, Ganesh N. (1996): 'The Indian Yeats' in Furomoto *et al.* (eds).

Dhonnchadha, Mairin Ni and Dorgan, Theo (eds, 1991): *Revising the Rising* (Derry).

Dickson, David, Keogh, Daire and Whelan, Kevin (eds, 1993): *The United Irishmen: Republicanism, Radicalism and Rebellion* (Dublin).

Dickson, R. J. (1966): *Ulster Emigration to Colonial America, 1717–1775* (London).

Dilke, Charles (1868): *Greater Britain* (London).

—— (1890): *Problems of Greater Britain* (2 vols, London).

Dillon, Martin (1989): *The Shankill Butchers: A Case Study of Mass Murder* (London).

—— (1990): *The Dirty War* (London).

—— (1997): *God and the Gun: The Church and Irish Terrorism* (London).

Dirlik, Arif (1994): 'The Postcolonial Aura: Third World Criticism in the Age of Global Capitalism', *Critical Inquiry*, 20.

Dixon, Paul (1995): 'Internationalization and Unionist Isolation: A Response to Feargal Cochrane', *Political Studies*, 43, 3.

Dixon, Thomas (1905): *The Clansman: An Historical Romance of the Ku Klux Klan* (New York).

Doherty, Gabriel (1996): 'National Identity and the Study of Irish History', *English Historical Review*, cxi.

Doherty, Richard (1998): *The Williamite War in Ireland, 1688–1691* (Dublin).

Donnelly, James P. (1993): 'The Great Famine: Its Interpreters Old and New', *History Ireland*, Autumn.

Donoghue, Denis (1990): *Warrenpoint* (New York).

Doyle, Michael W. (1986): *Empires* (Ithaca, New York).

Drolet, Michael (1994): 'The Wild and the Sublime: Lyotard's Post-Modern Politics', *Political Studies*, xlii.

Drudy, P. J. (ed., 1985): *The Irish in America: Emigration, Assimilation and Impact* (Cambridge, Irish Studies No. 4).

—— (ed., 1986): *Ireland and Britain since 1922* (Cambridge, Irish Studies no. 5).

Dunbar-Ortiz, Roxanne (1997): *Red Dirt: Growing Up Okie* (London and New York).

Dunlop, John (1995): *A Precarious Belonging: Presbyterians and the Conflict in Ireland* (Belfast).

Dunn, Seamus and Morgan, Valerie (1994): *Protestant Alienation in Northern Ireland, A Preliminary Survey* (Coleraine).

Dunne, Tom (1980): 'The Gaelic Response to Conquest and Colonisation: The Evidence of the Poetry', *Studia Hibernica*, 20.

—— (1992): 'New Histories: Beyond "Revisionism"', *Irish Review*, 12.

Durrell, Lawrence (1968): *The Alexandria Quartet: Justine. Balthazar. Mountolive. Clea* (London; *Justine* 1st pub. 1957, *Balthazar* 1958, *Mountolive* 1958, *Clea* 1960).

Durston, Chris (1986): '"Let Ireland be Quiet": Opposition in England to the Cromwellian Conquest of Ireland', *History Workshop Journal*, xxi.

Dyer, Richard (1997): *White* (London).

Eagleton, Terry (1988): *Nationalism, Irony and Commitment* (Derry; Field Day pamphlet).

—— (1989): *Saint Oscar* (Derry).

—— (1990): *The Ideology of the Aesthetic* (London).

—— (1992): 'The Crisis of Contemporary Culture', *New Left Review*, 196.

—— (1994): 'A Postmodern Punch', *Irish Studies Review*, 6.

—— (1995a): *Heathcliff and the Great Hunger: Studies in Irish Culture* (London).

Eagleton, Terry (1995b): 'Ireland's Obdurate Nationalisms', *New Left Review*, 213.
—— (1997): 'The Ideology of Irish Studies', *Bullan*, 3, 1.
—— (1998a): *Crazy John and the Bishop, and Other Essays in Irish Culture* (Cork).
—— (1998b): 'Postcolonialism: The Case of Ireland' in David Bennett (ed.): *Multicultural States: Rethinking Difference and Identity* (London).
Edwards, Ruth Dudley (1977): *Patrick Pearse: The Triumph of Failure* (London).
—— (1999): *The Faithful Tribe: An Intimate Portrait of the Loyal Institutions* (London).
Elliott, Marianne (1982): *Partners in Revolution: The United Irishmen and France* (New Haven).
—— (1985): *Watchmen in Zion: The Protestant Concept of Liberty* (Derry, Field Day pamphlet).
—— (1989): *Wolfe Tone: Prophet of Irish Independence* (New Haven and London).
Ellis, John S. (1998): 'Reconciling the Celt: British National Identity, Empire, and the 1911 Investiture of the Prince of Wales' *Journal of British Studies*, 37, 4.
Ellis, Steven G. (1985): *Tudor Ireland: Crown, Community and the Conflict of Cultures, 1470–1603* (London).
—— (1986): 'Nationalist Historiography and the English and Gaelic Worlds in the late Middle Ages', *Irish Historical Studies*, XXV, 97. Reprinted in Brady (ed.), 1994.
—— (1991): 'Representations of the Past in Ireland: Whose Past and Whose Present?', *IHS*, XXVII, 108.
—— (1996a): 'Writing Irish History: Revisionism, Colonialism, and the British Isles', *Irish Review*, 19.
—— (1996b): 'The Tudors and the Origins of the Modern Irish States: A Standing Army' in Bartlett and Jeffery (eds).
Ellis, Steven G. and Barber, Sarah (eds, 1995): *Conquest and Union: Fashioning a British State, 1485–1725* (London).
Emenyonu, Ernest (ed., 1989): *Literature and National Consciousness* (Ibadan).
Emmanuel, Arghiri (1972): 'White Settler Colonialism and the Myth of Investment Imperialism', *New Left Review*, 73.
Emmons, David (1989): *The Butte Irish: Class and Ethnicity in an American Mining Town* (Urbana, Ill.).
Engels, Dagmar and Marks, Shula (eds, 1994): *Contesting Colonial Hegemony: State and Society in Africa and India* (London).
Engels, Friedrich (1969): *The Condition of the Working Class in England* (London: orig. pub. 1848).
English, Richard (1994a): *Radicals and the Republic: Socialist Republicanism in the Irish Free State, 1925–1937* (Oxford).
—— (1994b): '"Cultural Traditions" and Political Ambiguity', *Irish Review*, 15.
—— (1996a): '"The Inborn Hate of Things English": Ernie O'Malley and the Irish Revolution 1916–1923', *Past and Present*, 151.
—— (1996b): 'The Same People With Different Relatives? Modern Scholarship, Unionists and the Irish Nation' in English and Walker (eds).
—— (1997): 'Shakespeare and the Identity of Ireland' in Burnett and Wray (eds).
—— (1998): *Ernie O'Malley: IRA Intellectual* (Oxford).
English, Richard and Walker, Graham (eds, 1996): *Unionism in Modern Ireland: New Perspectives on Politics and Culture* (Basingstoke).
Erie, Steven P. (1988): *Rainbow's End: Irish-Americans and the Dilemmas of Urban Machine Politics, 1840–1985* (Berkeley).

Ervine, St John (1915): *Sir Edward Carson and the Ulster Movement* (Dublin and London).

Evans, Estyn E. (1981): *The Personality of Ireland: Habitat, Heritage and History* (Belfast).

Evans, J. Martin (1996): *Milton's Imperial Epic:* Paradise Lost *and the Discourse of Colonialism* (Ithaca, New York and London).

Evans, Richard J. (1997): *In Defence of History* (London).

Evans, Stephen (1998): 'The Conservatives and the Redefinition of Unionism, 1912–21', *Twentieth Century British History*, 9, 1.

Eyler, Audrey S. and Garratt, Robert F. (eds, 1988): *The Uses of the Past: Essays on Irish Culture* (Cranbury, NJ).

Fabian, Johannes (1983): *Time and the Other: How Anthropology Makes its Object* (New York).

Fairweather, Eileen, McDonough, Róisín and McFadyean, Melanie (1984): *Only the Rivers Run Free. Northern Ireland: The Women's War* (London).

Falls, Cyril (1922): *The History of the 36th (Ulster) Division* (Belfast).

Falls Think Tank (1996): *Ourselves Alone? Voices from Belfast's Nationalist Working Class* (Newtownabbey).

Fanning, Ronan (1986/1994): ' "The Great Enchantment": Uses and Abuses of Modern Irish History' in J. Dooge (ed.): *Ireland in the Contemporary World: Essays in Honour of Garret Fitzgerald* (Dublin). Reprinted in Brady 1994.

Fanon, Frantz (1959/1965): *A Dying Colonialism* (orig. pub. Paris 1959; cited from 1965 NY edn).

——(1961/1967): *The Wretched of the Earth* (orig. pub. Paris 1961; cited from 1967 Harmondsworth edn).

——(1964/1970): *Toward the African Revolution* (orig. pub. Paris 1964; cited from 1970 Harmondsworth edn).

Farrell, Alex (1993): 'National Rights or Ethnic Strife?', *Irish Freedom*, 21.

Farrell, Brian (1971): *The Founding of Dail Eireann* (Dublin).

Farrell, Michael (1974): *The Battle for Algeria* (Belfast; People's Democracy pamphlet).

——(1977): 'Northern Ireland—An Anti-Imperialist Struggle', *The Socialist Register 1977*; ed. Ralph Miliband and John Saville.

——(1980): *Northern Ireland: The Orange State* (London, 2nd edn; orig. pub. 1976).

Fay, Marie Therese, Morrissey, Mike, and Smyth, Marie (1997): *Mapping Troubles-Related Deaths in Northern Ireland 1969–1994* (INCORE pamphlet, Londonderry).

Feeley, Pat and O'Riordan, Manus (1984): *The Rise and Fall of Irish Anti-Semitism* (Dublin, Labour History Workshop pamphlet).

Fennell, Desmond (1993): *Heresy: The Battle of Ideas in Modern Ireland* (Belfast).

Ferguson, William (1998): *The Identity of the Scottish Nation: An Historic Quest* (Edinburgh).

Field Day (1985): *Ireland's Field Day* (London: essays orig. pub. as separate pamphlets, Derry 1984).

——(1991): *The Field Day Anthology of Irish Writing*. General Editor Seamus Deane (3 Vols, Derry).

Fieldhouse, D. K. (1961): ' "Imperialism": An Historiographical Revision', *Economic History Review*, xiv, 2.

——(1981): *Colonialism 1870–1945: An Introduction* (London).

——(1982): *The Colonial Empires: A Comparative Survey from the Eighteenth Century* (London).

——(1999): *The West and The Third World: Trade, Colonialism, Dependence and Development* (Oxford).

Fielding, Steven (1993): *Class and Ethnicity: Irish Catholics in England, 1880–1939* (Milton Keynes).

Finlay, Richard J. (1992): 'For or Against?: Scottish Nationalists and the British Empire', *Scottish Historical Review*, 71, 1/2 (191/192).

——(1997): 'The Rise and Fall of Popular Imperialism in Scotland 1850–1950', *Scottish Geographical Magazine*, 113.

Finlayson, Alan (1997a): 'The Problem of "Culture" in Northern Ireland: A Critique of the Cultural Traditions Group', *The Irish Review*, 20.

——(1997b): 'Discourse and Contemporary Loyalist Identity' in Shirlow and McGovern (eds).

——(1998): 'Reconceptualising the Political in Northern Ireland: A Response to Arthur Aughey', *Irish Political Studies*, 13.

Finley, Moses (1976): 'Colonies—An Attempt at a Typology', *Transactions of the Royal Historical Society*, 5th Series, 26.

Finn, Gerry P. T. (1994): 'Sporting Symbols, Sporting Identities: Soccer and Intergroup Conflict in Scotland and Northern Ireland' in Wood (ed.).

Finnegan, Frances (1982): *Poverty and Prejudice: Irish Migrants in York, 1840–75* (Cork).

Fischer, David Hackett (1989): *Albion's Seed: Four British Folkways in America* (New York).

Fisk, Robert (1983): *In Time of War: Ireland, Ulster and the Price of Neutrality, 1939–1945* (London).

Fitzgerald, Garret (1991): 'The British and the Irish in the Context of Europe' in Bernard Crick (ed.): *National Identities* (Oxford).

Fitzpatrick, Brian (1988): *Seventeenth Century Ireland: The War of Religions* (Dublin).

Fitzpatrick, David (1977): *Politics and Irish Life 1913–1921: Provincial Experience of War and Revolution* (Dublin).

——(1978): 'The Geography of Irish Nationalism 1910–1921', *Past and Present*, 78.

——(1989): 'A Peculiar Tramping People: The Irish in Britain 1801–1870' in W. E. Vaughan (ed.): *A New History of Ireland*, Vol. V: *Ireland Under the Union, I, 1801–1870* (Oxford).

——(1994): *Oceans of Consolation: Personal Accounts of Irish Migration to Australia* (Ithaca, New York).

——(1996): 'Militarism in Ireland, 1900–1922' in Bartlett and Jeffery (eds).

——(1999): 'Ireland and the Empire' in Andrew Porter (ed.): *Oxford History of the British Empire*, vol. III: *The Nineteenth Century* (Oxford).

——(ed., 1990): *Revolution? Ireland 1917–1923* (Dublin).

Fitzpatrick, Rory (1989): *God's Frontiersmen: The Scots–Irish Epic* (London).

Fitzsimmons, Paul A. (1993): *Independence for Northern Ireland: Why and How* (Washington, DC).

Flanagan, Thomas (1979): *The Year of the French* (London).

Fogarty, Anne (1995): ' "This Inconstant Sea-Nimph": History and the Limitations of Knowledge in John Davies' Writings about Ireland' in Foley *et al.* (eds).

Foley, Timothy P., Pilkington, Lionel, Ryder, Sean and Tilley, Elizabeth (eds, 1995): *Gender and Colonialism* (Galway).

Follis, Bryan A. (1995): *A State Under Siege: The Establishment of Northern Ireland* (Oxford).

Foot, Paul (1989): *Ireland: Why Britain Must Get Out* (London, Counterblast pamphlet No. 2).

Foot, Rosemary (1979): 'The European Community's Voting Behaviour at the United Nations General Assembly', *Journal of Common Market Studies*, 17.

Foster, John Wilson (1988): 'Culture and Colonisation: View from the North', *The Irish Review*, No. 5.

——(1991): *Colonial Consequences: Essays in Irish Literature and Culture* (Dublin).

——(ed., 1995): *The Idea of the Union: Statements and Critiques in Support of the Union of Great Britain and Northern Ireland* (Vancouver, BC).

Foster, R. F. (1988): *Modern Ireland 1600–1972* (London).

——(1993a): *Paddy and Mr. Punch: Connections in English and Irish History* (London).

——(1993b): 'Anglo-Irish Relations and Northern Ireland: Historical Perspectives' in Keogh and Haltzel (eds).

——(1997): *W. B. Yeats. A Life*, Vol. 1: *The Apprentice Mage* (Oxford).

Frame, Robin (1995): 'Overlordship and Reaction, *c.*1200–*c.*1450' in Grant and Stringer (eds).

——(1996): 'The Defence of the English Lordship 1250–1450' in Bartlett and Jeffery (eds).

Frank, Andre Gunder (1969): *Capitalism and Underdevelopment in Latin America* (New York: rev. edn—orig. pub. 1967).

——(1972): *Lumpenbourgeoisie, Lumpendevelopment* (New York).

Fraser, T. G. (1984): *Partition in Ireland, India and Palestine: Theory and Practise* (London).

——(1996): 'Ireland and India' in Jeffery (ed.).

Friedlander, Saul (ed., 1992): *Probing the Limits of Representation: Nazism and the 'Final Solution'* (Cambridge, Mass.).

Friel, Brian (1981): *Translations* (London).

Fulton, John (1991): *The Tragedy of Belief: Division, Politics, and Religion in Ireland* (Oxford).

——(1995): 'Ethnicity and State Form in the Division of Ireland', *New Community*, 21, 3.

Furlong, Nicholas (1998): *Fr. John Murphy of Boolavogue, 1753–1798* (2nd edn, Dublin: orig. pub. 1991).

Furomoto, Toshi, Hughes, George, Chizuko, Inoue, McElwain, James, McMillan, Peter and Sano, Tetsuro (eds, 1996): *International Aspects of Irish Literature*, Irish Literary Studies, 44 (Gerrards Cross).

Gahan, Daniel (1995): *The People's Rising: Wexford 1798* (Dublin).

——(1996): 'The Scullabogue Massacre 1798', *History Ireland*, 4, 3.

Gailey, Andrew (1987): *Ireland and the Death of Kindness: The Experience of Constructive Unionism, 1890–1905* (Cork).

Gallagher, Frank (1957): *The Indivisible Island: The History of the Partition of Ireland* (London).

Gallagher, Michael (1985): *Political Parties in the Republic of Ireland* (Dublin).

——(1990): 'Do Ulster Unionists Have a Right to Self-determination?', *Irish Political Studies*, 5.

——(1995): 'How Many Nations Are There in Ireland?', *Ethnic and Racial Studies*, 18, 4.

Gallagher, Thomas (1982): *Paddy's Lament: Ireland 1846–1847. Prelude to Hatred* (New York).

Gallagher, Tom (1985): 'Protestant Extremism in Urban Scotland 1930–1939', *Scottish Historical Review*, LXIV, 2.

——(1987a): *Edinburgh Divided: John Cormack and No-Popery in the 1930s* (Edinburgh).

——(1987b): *Glasgow: The Uneasy Peace: Religious Tension in Modern Scotland* (Manchester).

Galliher, John F. and DeGregory, Jerry L. (1985): *Violence in Northern Ireland: Understanding Protestant Perspectives* (Dublin).

Garvin, Tom (1978): 'The Destiny of the Soldiers: Tradition and Modernity in the Politics of De Valera's Ireland', *Political Studies*, 26, 3.

Garvin, Tom (1981): *The Evolution of Irish Nationalist Politics* (Dublin).

—— (1987): *Nationalist Revolutionaries in Ireland 1858–1928* (Oxford).

—— (1991): 'The Rising and Irish Democracy' in Dhonnchadha and Dorgan (eds).

—— (1993a): 'Unenthusiastic Democrats: The Emergence of Irish Democracy' in Hill and Marsh (eds).

—— (1993b): 'Ethnic Markers, Modern Nationalisms, and the Nightmare of History' in Peter Kruger (ed.): *Ethnicity and Nationalism* (Marburg).

—— (1996): *1922: The Birth of Irish Democracy* (Dublin).

Gearty, Conor (1992): 'History à la Carte', *Irish Reporter*, No. 7.

Gellner, Ernest (1994): *Encounters with Nationalism* (Oxford).

Gibbon, Peter (1975): *The Origins of Ulster Unionism* (Manchester).

Gibbons, Luke (1988a): 'Coming Out of Hibernation? The Myth of Modernity in Irish Culture' in Kearney (ed.): *Across the Frontiers*. Reprinted in Gibbons 1996.

—— (1988b): 'Romanticism, Realism, and Irish Cinema' in Rockett, Kevin, Gibbons, Luke and Hill, John (1988): *Cinema and Ireland* (London).

—— (1991): 'Race Against Time: Racial Discourse and Irish History', *Oxford Literary Review*, 13. Reprinted in his 1996.

—— (1992): 'Identity Without a Centre: Allegory, History and Irish Nationalism', *Cultural Studies*, vi, 3. Reprinted in his 1996.

—— (1994): 'Dialogue Without the Other? A Reply to Francis Mulhern', *Radical Philosophy*, 67.

—— (1996): *Transformations in Irish Culture* (Cork).

—— (1997): 'Edmund Burke on our Present Discontents', *History Ireland*, 5, 4 (Winter).

—— (1998): 'Alternative Enlightenments: The United Irishmen, Cultural Diversity and the Republic of Letters' in Cullen (ed.).

—— (1998/9): 'Ireland and the Colonization of Theory', *Interventions*, 1, 1.

Giliomee, Hermann and Gagiano, Jannie (eds, 1990): *The Elusive Search for Peace: South Africa, Israel, Northern Ireland* (Cape Town).

Gilley, Sheridan (1978): 'English Attitudes to the Irish in England, 1780–1900' in Colin Holmes (ed.): *Immigrants and Minorities in British Society* (London).

Gilley, Sheridan and Swift, Roger (eds, 1985): *The Irish in the Victorian City* (Beckenham, Kent).

Gillingham, John (1992): 'The Beginnings of English Imperialism', *Journal of Historical Sociology*, 5, 4.

—— (1995): 'Foundations of a Disunited Kingdom' in Grant and Stringer (eds).

Girvin, Brian (1997): 'Political Culture, Political Independence and Economic Success in Ireland', *Irish Political Studies*, 12.

Glassie, Henry (1982): *Passing the Time in Ballymenone: Culture and History of an Ulster Community* (Philadelphia).

Goldring, Maurice (1990): 'The Northern Ireland Conflict and the French Left' in Darby *et al.* (eds).

—— (1993): *Pleasant the Scholar's Life: Irish Intellectuals and the Construction of the Nation State* (London).

—— (1994): 'The Irish in Contemporary Europe', *Irish Studies Review*, 6.

Goldstrom, J. M. (1981): 'Irish Agriculture and the Great Famine' in Goldstrom and Clarkson, L. A. (eds): *Irish Population, Economy and Society* (Oxford).

Gopal, Sarvepalli (1975): *Jawaharlal Nehru: A Biography*, Vol. 1, *1889–1947* (London).

Gough, Hugh and Dickson, David (eds, 1990): *Ireland and the French Revolution* (Dublin).

Gowan, Ogle Robert (1996): *Murder Without Sin: The Rebellion of 1798* (Belfast; edited extracts from *Orangeism: Its Origin and History*, orig. pub. Toronto 1859. Ed. J. R. Whitten for Grand Orange Lodge of Ireland, Education Committee).

Graham, Brian (1997a): 'Ulster: a representation of place yet to be imagined' in Shirlow and McGovern (eds).

——(1997b): 'Ireland and Irishness: Place, Culture and Identity' in Graham (ed.).

——(ed., 1997): *In Search of Ireland: A Cultural Geography* (London).

Graham, Colin (1994): '"Liminal Spaces": Post-Colonial Theories and Irish Culture', *Irish Review*, 16.

——(1996a): 'History, Gender and the Colonial Moment: *Castle Rackrent*' *Irish Studies Review*, 14.

——(1996b): 'Post-Colonial Theory and Kiberd's *Ireland*', *Irish Review*, 19.

Grant, Alexander and Stringer, Keith J. (eds, 1995): *Uniting the Kingdom? The Making of British History* (London).

Gray, Peter (1993): '*Punch* and the Great Famine', *History Ireland*, 1, 2.

——(1994): 'Potatoes and Providence: British Government Responses to the Great Famine', *Bullan*, 1, 1.

——(1998): *Famine, Land and Politics* (Dublin).

Gray, Sam (1997): 'The Right to March is the Right to Exist', *Ulster Review*, 22.

Greater London Council (1986): *Terence MacSwiney Memorial Lectures* (London).

Greaves, C. Desmond (1961): *The Life and Times of James Connolly* (London).

——(1971): *Liam Mellows and the Irish Revolution* (London).

——(1991): *1916 as History: The Myth of the Blood Sacrifice* (Dublin).

Green, Alice Stopford (1909): *The Making of Ireland and Its Undoing* (2nd edn, London).

Green, Arthur (1988): 'Unionist Horizons', *Irish Review*, 4.

Green, E. R. R. (ed., 1969): *Essays in Scotch-Irish History* (London).

Greene, Jack P. and Pole, J. R. (eds, 1984): *Colonial British America* (Baltimore).

Greenfeld, Liah (1992): *Nationalism: Five Roads to Modernity* (Cambridge, Mass.).

Grene, Nicholas (1996): 'Shaw, Egypt and the Empire' in Massoud (ed.).

Gudgin, Graham (1995): 'The Economics of the Union' in John Wilson Foster (ed.).

Guelke, Adrian (1988): *Northern Ireland: The International Perspective* (Dublin).

——(1994): *Promoting Peace in Deeply Divided Societies* (Frank Wright Commemorative Lecture; Queen's University Belfast Dept. of Politics Occasional Paper No. 6).

Guelke, Adrian (ed., 1994): *New Perspectives on the Northern Ireland Conflict* (Aldershot).

Guillevic (1974): *Selected Poems* (Harmondsworth; trans. Teo Savory).

Gupta, Partha Sarathi (1975): *Imperialism and the British Labour Movement, 1914–1964* (London).

Habermas, Juergen (1989): *The New Conservatism: Cultural Criticism and the Historians' Debate* (Cambridge, Mass.).

——(1990): *Moral Consciousness and Communicative Action* (Cambridge).

——(1993): *Justification and Application: Remarks on Discourse Ethics* (Cambridge, Mass.).

Hackett, Claire (1995): 'Self-determination: The Republican Feminist Agenda', *Feminist Review*, 50.

Hadfield, Andrew (1997): *Edmund Spenser's Irish Experience: Wilde Fruit and Salvage Soil* (Oxford).

Hadfield, Andrew and McVeagh, John (eds, 1994): *Strangers to That Land: British Perceptions of Ireland from the Reformation to the Famine* (Gerrards Cross).

Hainsworth, Paul (ed., 1998): *Divided Society: Minorities and Racism in Northern Ireland* (London).

Hall, Michael (1986): *Ulster: The Hidden History* (Belfast).

——(1993): *Ulster's Shared Heritage* (Newtownabbey, Island pamphlet No. 6).

——(1994a): *The Cruthin Controversy* (Newtownabbey; Island pamphlet No. 7).

——(1994b): *Ulster's European Heritage* (Newtownabbey, Island pamphlet No. 8).

——(ed., 1995): *Beyond the Fife and Drum: Report of a Conference Held on Belfast's Shankill Road, October 1994* (Newtownabbey, Island pamphlet No. 11).

Hall, Michael and Hamilton, Gary (1989): *Cuchulainn, Champion of Ulster* (Newtownabbey).

Halliday, Fred (1997/8): 'Irish Nationalisms in Perspective', 2nd Torkel Opsahl Memorial Lecture, Belfast, 10 December 1997; mimeo, Democratic Dialogue, May 1998.

Hamer, Mary (1989): 'Putting Ireland on the Map', *Textual Practice*, 3, 2.

Hanafin, Patrick (1997): 'Defying the Female: the Irish constitutional text as phallocentric manifesto', *Textual Practice*, 11, 2.

Hannaford, Ivan (1996): *Race: The History of an Idea in the West* (London).

Hannum, Hurst (1990): *Autonomy, Sovereignty, and Self-Determination* (Philadelphia).

Harbinson, John (1973): *The Ulster Unionist Party, 1882–1973: Its Development and Organisation* (Belfast).

Harkness, David (1969): *The Restless Dominion: The Irish Free State and the British Commonwealth of Nations, 1921–31* (London).

——(1970): 'Mr. De Valera's Dominion: Irish Relations with Britain and the Commonwealth, 1932–1938', *Jnl. of Commonwealth Political Studies* viii, 3.

——(1999): 'Ireland' in Robin W. Winks (ed.): *Oxford History of the British Empire. vol. V: Historiography* (Oxford).

Harlow, Barbara (1995): 'Gender and Colonialism in an Age Called "Postcolonial"' in Foley *et al.* (eds).

Harrington, John P. and Mitchell, Elizabeth J. (eds, 1999): *Politics and Performance in Contemporary Northern Ireland* (Amherst, MS).

Harris, Mary (1993): 'The Catholic Church, Minority Rights, and the Founding of the Northern Ireland State' in Keogh and Haltzel (eds).

Harris, Nigel (1990): *National Liberation* (London).

Harris, Rosemary (1972): *Prejudice and Tolerance in Ulster: A Study of Neighbours and "Strangers" in a Border Community* (Manchester).

Hart, Peter (1990): 'Youth Culture and the Cork IRA' in Fitzpatrick (ed.).

——(1996): 'The Protestant Experience of Revolution in Southern Ireland' in English and Walker (eds).

——(1997): 'The Geography of Revolution in Ireland 1917–1923', *Past and Present*, 155.

——(1998): *The IRA and Its Enemies: Violence and Community in Cork, 1916–1923* (Oxford).

Harvie, Christopher (1976): 'Ideology and Home Rule: James Bryce, A. V. Dicey and Ireland, 1880–1887', *English Historical Review*, xci.

Hashem, Evine (1996): 'The Re-enactment of Colonialism in James Joyce's *Portrait of the Artist as a Young Man*' in Massoud (ed.).

Hastings, Adrian (1997): *The Construction of Nationhood: Ethnicity, Religion and Nationalism* (Cambridge).

Hawkins, Richard (1991): 'The "Irish Model" and the Empire: A Case for Reassessment' in David Anderson and David Killingray (eds): *Policing the Empire: Government, Authority and Control* (Manchester).

Hayden, Mary and Moonan, George (1921): *A Short History of the Irish People: From the Earliest times to 1920* (Dublin).

Hayden, Tom (ed., 1997): *Irish Hunger: Personal Reflections on the Legacy of the Famine* (Boulder and Dublin).

Hayes-McCoy, G. A. (ed., 1964): *The Irish at War* (Cork).

——(1969): *Irish Battles: A Military History of Ireland* (Belfast: cited from 1990 reprint).

Hazelkorn, Ellen and Patterson, Henry (1994): 'The New Politics of the Irish Republic', *New Left Review*, 207.

——(1995): 'Reply' (to Porter and O'Hearn 1995), *New Left Review*, 212.

Heaney, Seamus (1975): *North* (London).

——(1988): *The Government of the Tongue* (London).

——(1994): 'Frontiers of Writing', *Bullan*, 1, 1.

——(1995): *The Redress of Poetry: Oxford Lectures* (London).

Heath, Anthony F., Breen, Richard, and Whelan, Christopher T. (eds. 1999): *Ireland North and South: Perspectives from Social Science* (Oxford).

Hechter, Michael (1975): *Internal Colonialism: The Celtic Fringe in British National Development, 1536–1966* (London).

Hempton, David (1996): *Religion and Political Culture in Britain and Ireland: From the Glorious Revolution to the Decline of Empire* (Cambridge).

Hempton, David and Hill, Myrtle (1992): *Evangelical Protestantism and Ulster Society 1740–1890* (London).

Hennessey, Thomas (1993): 'Ulster Unionist Territorial and National Identities 1886–1893: Province, Island, Kingdom and Empire', *Irish Political Studies*, 8.

——(1996): 'Ulster Unionism and Loyalty to the Crown of the United Kingdom, 1912–74' in English and Walker (eds).

Hennessey, Tom and Wilson, Robin (1997): *With All Due Respect: Pluralism and Parity of Esteem* (Belfast; Democratic Dialogue Report No. 7).

Henry, Robert Mitchell (1920): *The Evolution of Sinn Fein* (Dublin: reprinted Port Washington, New York, 1970).

Hepburn, A. C. (1996): *A Past Apart: Studies in the History of Catholic Belfast 1850–1950* (Belfast).

Hepburn, A. C. and Cattaruzza, Marina (1996): 'Minorities and Economic Development on the Ethnic Frontier: Belfast and Trieste, 1850–1920' in Hepburn 1996.

Herr, Cheryl (1991): *For the Land They Loved: Irish Political Melodramas 1890–1925* (Syracuse).

Heslinga, M. W. (1979): *The Irish Border as a Cultural Divide* (Assen).

Hewitt, Christopher (1991): 'The Roots of Violence: Catholic grievances and Irish nationalism during the Civil Rights period' in Barton and Roche (eds).

Hewitt, John (1991): *The Collected Poems* (Belfast; ed. Frank Ormsby).

Hickman, Mary and Walter, Bronwen (1995): 'Deconstructing Whiteness: Irish Women in Britain', *Feminist Review*, 50.

Hill, Christopher (1977): *Milton and the English Revolution* (London).

——(1984): *The Experience of Defeat: Milton and Some Contemporaries* (London).

Hill, Jacqueline (1984): 'National Festivals, The State and "Protestant ascendancy" in Ireland 1790–1829', *Irish Historical Studies*, XXIV, 93.

Hill, Jacqueline and Ó Grada, Cormac (eds, 1993): *The Visitation of God?* (Dublin).

Hill, J. Michael (1993): 'The Origins of the Scottish Plantations in Ulster to 1625: A Reinterpretation', *Journal of British Studies*, 32, 1.

Hill, Myrtle, Turner, Brian and Dawson, Kenneth (eds, 1998): *1798. Rebellion in County Down* (Newtownards, Co. Down).

Hill, Ronald J. and Marsh, Michael (eds, 1993): *Modern Irish Democracy: Essays in Honour of Basil Chubb* (Dublin).

Hill, Tracey (1993): 'Humanism and Homicide: Spenser's "A View of the Present State of Ireland"', *Irish Studies Review*, 4.

Hillyard, Paddy (1993): *Suspect Community: People's Experience of the Prevention of Terrorism Acts in Britain* (London).

Hirst, Derek (1994): 'The English Republic and the Meaning of Britain', *Journal of Modern History*, 66, 3.

Hobsbawm, E. J. (1973): 'Lenin and the Labour Aristocracy' in his *Revolutionaries* (London).

——(1994): *Age of Extremes: The Short Twentieth Century, 1914–1991* (London).

——(1997): *On History* (London).

Hobson, J. A. (1902): *Imperialism, A Study* (London: cited from 1938 3rd edn).

Hofheinz, Thomas C. (1995): *Joyce and the Invention of Irish History:* Finnegan's Wake *in Context* (Cambridge).

Hofmeyr, Isabel (1987): 'Building a Nation from Words: Afrikaans Language, Literature and Ethnic Identity, 1902–1924' in Shula Marks and Stanley Trapido (eds): *The Politics of Race, Class and Nationalism in Twentieth Century South Africa* (London).

Hogan, Edmund (1990): *The Irish Missionary Movement: A Historical Survey, 1830–1980* (Dublin).

Holland, Jack (1989): *The American Connection: US Guns, Money and Influence in Northern Ireland* (Swords, Co. Dublin).

Holland, Jack and McDonald, Henry (1994): *INLA: Deadly Divisions* (Dublin).

Holmes, Colin (1988): *John Bull's Island: Immigration and British Society, 1871–1971* (London).

Holmes, Janice and Urquhart, Diana (eds, 1994): *Coming Into the Light: The Work, Politics and Religion of Women in Ulster 1840–1950* (Belfast).

Holmes, Michael and Denis (eds, 1997): *Ireland and India: Connections, Comparisons, Contrasts* (Dublin).

Holmes, Michael, Rees, Nicholas, and Whelan, Bernadette (1993): *The Poor Relation: Irish Foreign Policy and the Third World* (Dublin).

Holt, Thomas C. (1992): *The Problem of Freedom: Race, Labour and Politics in Jamaica and Britain, 1832–1938* (Baltimore).

Hopkinson, Michael (1988): *Green Against Green: The Irish Civil War* (Dublin).

Hoppen, K. T. (1984): *Elections, Politics and Society in Ireland 1832–1885* (Oxford).

——(1989): *Ireland Since 1800: Conflict and Conformity* (London).

Horn, James (1998): 'British Diaspora: Emigration from Britain, 1680–1815' in P. J. Marshall (ed.).

Horsman, Reginald (1981): *Race and Manifest Destiny: The Origins of American Racial Anglo-Saxonism* (Cambridge, Mass.).

Howe, Stephen (1993): *Anticolonialism in British Politics: The Left and the End of Empire 1918–1964* (Oxford).

——(1998a): *Afrocentrism: Mythical Pasts and Imagined Homes* (London).

——(1998b): 'David Fieldhouse and "Imperialism": Some Historiographical Revisions' in Peter Burroughs and A. J. Stockwell (eds): *Managing the Business of Empire* (London).

——(1999a): 'Speaking of '98: History, Politics and Memory in the Bicentenary of the 1798 United Irish Uprising', *History Workshop Journal*, 47.

——(2000a): 'The Politics of Historical "Revisionism": Comparing Ireland and Israel/ Palestine', *Past and Present* (forthcoming).

——(2000b): Edward W. Said: *The Politics of Criticism and the Criticism of Politics* (forthcoming).

——(2000c): *Decolonisations* (forthcoming).

Howell, David (1986): *A Lost Left: Three Studies in Socialism and Nationalism* (Manchester).

Howes, Marjorie (1996): *Yeats's Nations: Gender, Class and Irishness* (Cambridge).

Hughes, Eamonn (ed., 1991): *Culture and Politics in Northern Ireland, 1960–1990* (Milton Keynes).

Humana, Charles (ed., 1992): *World Human Rights Guide* (3rd edn, Oxford).

Hume, David (1754/1970): *The History of Great Britain: The Reigns of James I and Charles I* (orig. pub. 1754; cited from 1970 Harmondsworth edn).

Hume, David (1996): *The Ulster Unionist Party 1972–92: A Political Movement in an Era of Conflict and Change* (Belfast).

Hurwitz, Leon (1976): 'The EEC and Decolonization: The Voting Behaviour of the Nine in the UN General Assembly', *Political Studies*, 24.

Hussey, Gemma (1995): *Ireland Today: Anatomy of a Changing State* (2nd edn, London).

Hutchinson, John (1987): *The Dynamics of Cultural Nationalism: The Gaelic Revival and the Creation of the Irish Nation State* (London).

——(1996): 'Irish Nationalism' in Boyce and O'Day (eds).

Huttenback, Robert A. (1976): *Racism and Empire: White Settlers and Colored Immigrants in the British Self-Governing Colonies 1830–1910* (Ithaca, NY).

Hutton, Sean and Stewart, Paul (eds, 1991): *Ireland's Histories: Aspects of State, Society and Ideology* (London).

Hyam, Ronald (1993): *Britain's Imperial Century, 1815–1914: A Study of Empire and Expansion* (2nd edn, London).

Hyndman, Marilyn (1996): *Further Afield: Journeys from a Protestant Past* (Belfast).

Ignatiev, Noel (1995): *How the Irish Became White* (New York).

Ikonne, Chidi, Oko, Emelia, and Onwudinjo, Peter (eds, 1991): *African Literature and African Historical Experience* (Ibadan).

Ingram, (Rev.) Brett (1989): *Covenant and Challenge: Reflections on Ulster's Identity* (Lurgan).

Innes, C. L. (1990): *The Devil's Own Mirror: The Irishman and the African in Modern Literature* (Washington, DC).

——(1993): *Woman and Nation in Irish Literature and Society, 1880–1935* (Hemel Hempstead).

——(1994): 'Virgin Territories and Motherlands: Colonial and Nationalist Representations of Africa and Ireland', *Feminist Review*, 47.

Irish Freedom Movement (1983): *An Anti-Imperialist's Guide to the Irish War* (London).

Jackson, Alvin (1989): *The Ulster Party: Irish Unionists in the House of Commons, 1884–1911* (Oxford).

——(1992): 'Unionist Myths 1912–1985', *Past and Present*, 136.

——(1994): 'Unionist History' in Brady (ed.): orig. pub. in *The Irish Review*, Autumn 1989 and Spring 1990.

Jackson, Alvin (1995): *Colonel Edward Saunderson: Land and Loyalty in Victorian Ireland* (Oxford).

—— (1996a): 'Irish Unionism' in Boyce and O'Day (revised version of Jackson 1994).

—— (1996b): 'Irish Unionists and the Empire, 1880–1920: Classes and Masses' in Jeffery (ed.).

Jackson, J. A. (1963): *The Irish in Britain* (London).

Jackson, T. A. (1946): *Ireland Her Own* (London).

Jalland, Patricia (1980): *The Liberals and Ireland: The Ulster Question in British Politics to 1914* (Brighton).

Jameson, Fredric (1988): *Modernism and Imperialism* (Derry; Field Day pamphlet).

JanMohamed, Abdul R. and Lloyd, David (1990): 'Introduction: Minority Discourse— What Is to Be Done?' in ibidem (eds): *The Nature and Context of Minority Discourse* (New York).

Jarman, Neil (1997): *Material Conflicts: Parades and Visual Displays in Northern Ireland* (Oxford and New York).

Jarman, Neil and Bryan, Dominic (1996): *Parade and Protest: A Discussion of Parading Disputes in Northern Ireland* (Coleraine).

—— (1998): *From Riots to Rights: Nationalist Parades in the North of Ireland* (Coleraine).

Jeffery, Keith (1996a): 'Introduction' in idem (ed.).

—— (1996b): 'The Irish Military Tradition and the British Empire' in idem (ed.).

—— (ed., 1996): '*An Irish Empire'? Aspects of Ireland and the British Empire* (Manchester).

Johnson, David S. and Kennedy, Liam (1991): 'Nationalist Historiography and the Decline of the Irish Economy' in Hutton and Stewart (eds).

Johnson, R. W. (1985): *The Politics of Recession* (London).

Jones, Ann Rosalind and Stallybrass, Peter (1992): 'Dismantling Irena: The Sexualizing of Ireland in Early Modern England' in Parker *et al.* (eds).

Jones, Edwin (1998): *The English Nation: The Great Myth* (Thrupp, Gloucestershire).

Jones, Maldwyn A. (1991): 'The Scotch-Irish in British America' in Bailyn and Morgan (eds).

'Jordan, Bob' (pseud.) (1996): 'If This is New Unionism, I Want My Old Sash Back', *Fortnight*, October.

Jordan, Donald (1998): 'The Irish National League and the "Unwritten Law": Rural Protest and Nation-Building in Ireland 1882–1890', *Past and Present*, 158.

Jorstad, Jonas (1990): 'Nations Once Again: Ireland's Civil War in European Context' in Fitzpatrick (ed.).

Joyce, Joe and Murtagh, Peter (1983): *The Boss: Charles J. Haughey in Government* (Swords, Co. Dublin).

Judd, Denis (1996): *Empire: The British Imperial Experience from 1765 to the Present* (London).

Kaviraj, Sudipta (1993): 'The Imaginary Institution of India' in Partha Chatterjee and Gyanendra Pandey (eds): *Subaltern Studies VII* (Delhi).

Kearney, Hugh (1989): *The British Isles: A History of Four Nations* (Cambridge).

—— (1991): 'The Irish and their History', *History Workshop Journal*, 31.

—— (1997): 'Contested Ideas of Nationhood', *The Irish Review*, 20.

Kearney, Richard (1984): *Myth and Motherland* (Derry, Field Day pamphlet: also in Field Day 1985).

—— (ed., 1985): *The Irish Mind* (Dublin).

—— (1988): *Transitions: Narratives in Modern Irish Culture* (Dublin).

—— (1997): *Postnationalist Ireland: Politics, Culture, Philosophy* (London).

—— (ed., 1990): *Across the Frontiers: Ireland in the 1990s* (Dublin).

Kee, Robert (1993): *The Laurel and the Ivy: The Story of Charles Stewart Parnell and Irish Nationalism* (London).

Kelleher, Margaret (1997): *The Feminization of Famine* (Cork).

Kelley, Kevin (1982): *The Longest War: Northern Ireland and the IRA* (Dingle, Westport and London).

Kelly, James (1992): *Prelude to Union: Anglo-Irish Politics in the 1780s* (Cork).

Kendle, John (1989): *Ireland and the Federal Solution: The Debate over the United Kingdom Constitution, 1870–1921* (Kingston and Montreal).

——(1997): *Federal Britain: A History* (London).

Kennedy, Dane (1987): *Islands of White: Settler Society and Culture in Kenya and Southern Rhodesia, 1890–1939* (Durham, NC).

Kennedy, Dennis (1988): *The Widening Gulf: Northern Attitudes to the Independent Irish State, 1919–1949* (Belfast).

Kennedy, Kieran A., Giblin, Thomas and McHugh, Deirdre (1988): *The Economic Development of Ireland in the Twentieth Century* (London).

Kennedy, Liam (1989): *The Modern Industrialisation of Ireland, 1940–88* (Dublin).

——(1993): 'Modern Ireland: Post-Colonial Society or Post-Colonial Pretensions?', *Irish Review*, 13 (reprinted in his 1996).

——(1996): *Colonialism, Religion and Nationalism in Ireland* (Belfast).

Kennedy, Liam and Johnson, David S. (1996): 'The Union of Ireland and Britain, 1801–1921' in Boyce and O'Day (eds) (reprinted in Kennedy 1996).

Keogh, Daire (1993): *The French Disease: The Catholic Church and Radicalism in Ireland 1790–1800* (Dublin).

Keogh, Daire and Furlong, Nicholas (eds, 1996): *The Mighty Wave: The 1798 Rebellion in Wexford* (Dublin).

Keogh, Dermot and Haltzel, Michael H. (eds, 1993): *Northern Ireland and the Politics of Reconciliation* (Cambridge).

Kerr, Adrian (comp. 1996): *Perceptions: Cultures in Conflict* (Derry).

Kiberd, Declan (1984): 'Remembering the Irish Future', *The Crane Bag*, 8, 1.

——(1985): 'Anglo-Irish Attitudes' in Ireland's Field Day (reprinted also in Field Day 1991:III).

——(1988): 'The War Against the Past' in Eyler and Garratt (eds).

——(1991a): 'Autumn of the Patriarch', *The Sunday Business Post*, 5 January.

——(1991b): 'The Elephant of Revolutionary Forgetfulness' in Dhonnchadha and Dorgan (eds).

——(1994): 'Post-Colonial Ireland—"Being Different"' in Ó Ceallaigh (ed.).

——(1995): *Inventing Ireland: The Literature of the Modern Nation* (London).

Kiernan, Cieran (ed., 1986): *Australia and Ireland, 1788–1986* (Dublin).

Kiernan, Victor (1993): 'The British Isles: Celt and Saxon' in Mikulas Teich and Roy Porter (eds): *The National Question in Europe in Historical Context* (Cambridge).

Killen, John (ed., 1995): *The Famine Decade: Contemporary Accounts 1841–1851* (Belfast).

Kinealy, Christine (1994): *This Great Calamity: The Irish Famine 1845–52* (Dublin).

Kinealy, Christine and Parkhill, Trevor (eds, 1997): *The Famine in Ulster* (Belfast).

Kinsela, Anne (1996): '1798 Claimed for Catholics: Father Kavanagh, Fenians, and the Centenary Celebrations' in Keogh and Furlong (eds).

Kissane, Bill (1995): 'The Not-so-Amazing Case of Irish Democracy', *Irish Political Studies*, 10.

Knapp, James F. (1991): 'Irish Primitivism and Imperial Discourse: Lady Gregory's Peasantry' in Jonathan Arac and Harriet Ritvo (eds): *Macropolitics of Nineteenth Century Literature: Nationalism, Exoticism, Imperialism* (Philadelphia).

Knobel, Dale T. (1986): *Paddy and the Republic: Ethnicity and Nationality in Antebellum America* (Middletown, Conn.).

Kockel, Ullrich (ed., 1995): *Landscape, Heritage and Identity: Case Studies in Irish Ethnography* (Liverpool).

Koebner, Richard, and Schmidt, Helmut Dan (1964): *Imperialism: The Story and Significance of a Political Word, 1840–1960* (Cambridge).

Kosok, Heinz (1996): 'Charles Robert Maturin and Colonialism' in Massoud (ed.).

Kuper, Leo (1981): *Genocide: Its Political Use in the Twentieth Century* (Harmondsworth).

Laffan, Brigid (1988): *Ireland and South Africa: Irish Government Policy in the 1980s* (Dublin).

Laffan, Michael (1983): *The Partition of Ireland, 1911–1925* (Dundalk).

——(1985): '"Labour Must Wait": Ireland's Conservative Revolution' in Corish (ed.).

Lamar, Howard and Thompson, Leonard (eds, 1981): *The Frontier in History: North America and Southern Africa Compared* (New Haven and London).

Lane, Christopher (1995): *The Ruling Passion: British Colonial Allegory and the Paradox of Homosexual Desire* (Durham, NC).

Larrain, Jorge (1989): *Theories of Development* (Cambridge).

Lebow, R. N. (1976): *White Britain and Black Ireland: The Influence of Stereotypes on Colonial Policy* (Philadelphia).

Lee, J. J. (1989): *Ireland 1912–1985: Politics and Society* (Oxford).

——(1993): 'Dynamics of Social and Political Change in the Irish Republic' in Keogh and Haltzel (eds).

Leerssen, Joep T. (1986): 'On the Edge of Europe: Ireland in Search of Oriental Roots, 1650–1850', *Comparative Criticism*, 8.

——(1988): *Mere Irish and Fior-Gael: Studies in the Idea of Irish Nationality, its Development and Literary Expression Prior to the Nineteenth Century* (Amsterdam).

——(1996): *Remembrance and Imagination: Patterns in the Historical and Literary Representation of Ireland in the Nineteenth Century* (Cork).

Lees, L. H. (1978): *Exiles of Erin: Irish Migrants in Victorian London* (Manchester).

Legassick, Martin (1980): 'The Frontier Tradition in South African Historiography' in Shula Marks and Anthony Atmore (eds): *Economy and Society in Pre-Industrial South Africa* (London).

Leighton, C. D. A. (1994): *Catholicism in a Protestant Kingdom: A Study of the Irish Ancien Regime* (Dublin).

Lenin, V. I. (1917): *Imperialism, the Highest Stage of Capitalism* (Moscow: cited from 1975 Peking edn).

——(1971): *Critical Remarks on the National Question* (Moscow).

Lennon, Colm (1994): *Sixteenth-Century Ireland: The Incomplete Conquest* (Dublin).

Lennon, Mary, McAdam, Marie and O'Brien, Joanne (1988): *Across the Water: Irish Women's Lives in Britain* (London).

Leonard, Jane (1990): 'Getting Them at Last: The IRA and Ex-Servicemen' in Fitpatrick (ed.).

——(1996): 'The Twinge of Memory: Armistice Day and Remembrance Sunday in Dublin since 1919' in English and Walker (eds).

Lewis, Martin W. and Wigen, Karen E. (1997): *The Myth of Continents: A Critique of Metageography* (Berkeley, CA).

Lijphart, Arend (1975): 'The Northern Ireland Problem: Cases, Theories and Solutions', *British Journal of Political Science*, 5, 3.

——(1977): *Democracy in Plural Societies* (New Haven, CT).

Linder, Seth (1995): 'Sinn Fein's Sisterhood', *The Independent on Sunday*, 19 February.

Livingstone, Ken (1989): *Livingstone's Labour: A Programme for the Nineties* (London).

Lloyd, A. L. (1978): 'On an Unpublished Irish Ballad' in Maurice Cornforth (ed.): *Rebels and their Causes* (London).

Lloyd, David (1987): *Nationalism and Minor Literature: James Clarence Mangan and the Emergence of Irish Cultural Nationalism* (Berkeley).

——(1989): 'Writing in the Shit: Beckett, Nationalism and the Colonial Subject', *Modern Fiction Studies*, 35, 1.

——(1991): 'Race under Representation', *Oxford Literary Review*, 13, 1–2.

——(1993): *Anomalous States: Irish Writing and the Post-Colonial Moment* (Dublin).

——(1995): 'Nationalisms Against the State: Towards a Critique of the Anti-Nationalist Prejudice' in Foley *et al.* (eds).

——(1996): 'Outside History: Irish New Histories and the "Subalternity Effect"' in Shahid Amin and Dipesh Chakrabarty (eds): *Subaltern Studies*, IX (Delhi).

——(1997): Review of Eagleton: *Heathcliff and the Great Hunger*, *Bullan* 3, 1.

Lloyd, David and Thomas, Paul (1998): *Culture and the State* (New York).

Loftus, Belinda (1990): *Mirrors: William III and Mother Ireland* (Dundrum, Co. Down).

Longley, Edna (1986): *Poetry in the Wars* (Newcastle upon Tyne).

——(1991): 'The Rising, the Somme and Irish Memory' in Dhonnchadha and Dorgan (eds).

——(1992): 'Writing, Revisionism and Grass-seed: Literary Mythologies in Ireland' in Lundy and Mac Poilin (eds).

——(1994): *The Living Stream: Literature and Revisionism in Ireland* (Newcastle upon Tyne).

——(ed., 1991): *Culture in Ireland—Division or Diversity?* (Belfast).

Loughlin, James (1986): *Gladstone, Home Rule, and the Ulster Question* (Dublin).

——(1995): *Ulster Unionism and British National Identity since 1885* (London).

——(1999): '"Imagining Ulster": The North of Ireland and British National Identity, 1880–1921' in S. J. Connolly (ed.).

Lowry, Donal (1996a): 'Ulster Resistance and Loyalist Rebellion in the Empire' in Jeffery (ed.).

——(1996b): 'The Alliance that Dare not Speak its Name: Afrikaner and Irish Nationalists and the British Empire-Commonwealth, ca. 1920–1949' Institute of Commonwealth Studies seminar paper, London, 14 November.

Lubenow, William C. (1988): *Parliamentary Politics and the Home Rule Crisis: The British House of Commons in 1886* (Oxford).

Luddy, Maria (1995): *Women in Ireland, 1800–1918: A Documentary History* (Cork).

Lundy, Jean and Mac Poilin, Aodan (eds, 1992): *Styles of Belonging: The Cultural Identities of Ulster* (Belfast).

Lustick, Ian (1985): *State-Building Failure in British Ireland and French Algeria* (Berkeley).

——(1993): *Unsettled States, Disputed Lands: Britain and Ireland, France and Algeria, Israel and the West Bank-Gaza* (Ithaca, New York).

Lynn, Brendan (1997): *Holding the Ground: The Nationalist Party in Northern Ireland, 1945–1972* (Aldershot and Brookfield, VT).

Lyons, F. S. L. (1973): *Ireland since the Famine* (London: 2nd edn).

——(1979): *Culture and Anarchy in Ireland 1890–1939* (Oxford).

Lyons, Laura (1995): 'Towards a Representation of Insurgency: Margaretta D'Arcy's Feminist Tour of Duty' in Foley *et al.* (eds).

Lysaght, D. R. O'Connor (1970): *The Republic of Ireland* (Cork).

——(1980): 'British Imperialism in Ireland' in Morgan and Purdie (eds).

McAleese, Dermot (1986): 'Political Independence, Economic Growth and the Role of Economic Policy' in Drudy (ed.).

Mac Atasney, Gerard (1997): *'This Dreadful Visitation': The Famine in Lurgan/Portadown* (Belfast).

McAuley, James W. (1991): 'Cuchullain and an RPG-7: The Ideology and Politics of the Ulster Defence Association' in Hughes (ed.).

——(1994): *The Politics of Identity: A Loyalist Community in Belfast* (Aldershot).

McBride, Ian (1996): 'Ulster and the British Problem' in English and Walker (eds).

——(1997): *The Siege of Derry in Ulster Protestant Mythology* (Dublin).

McBride, Ian (1998): *Scripture Politics: Ulster Presbyterian Radicalism in the Late Eighteenth Century* (Oxford).

McCaffrey, Lawrence J. (1979): *Ireland: From Colony to Nation-state* (Englewood Cliffs, NJ).

McCall, Cathal (1999): *Identity in Northern Ireland* (Basingstoke).

MacCana, Proinsas (1980): 'Women in Irish Mythology', *The Crane Bag*, 4, 1.

McCann, Eamonn (1980): *War and an Irish Town* (London: 2nd edn).

McCartney, Donal (1994): 'History Revisions—Good and Bad' in Ó Ceallaigh (ed.).

McCarthy, John P. (1993): *Dissent from Irish America* (Lanham, MD.).

McCarthy, Michael J. F. (1904): *Rome in Ireland* (London).

McClelland, Aiken (1990): *William Johnston of Ballykilbeg* (Lurgan).

McClintock, Anne (1992): '"The Angel of Progress": Pitfalls of the Term "Postcolonialism"', *Social Text*, 31/32.

——(1995): *Imperial Leather: Race, Gender and Sexuality in the Colonial Contest* (London).

McCormack, W. J. (1986): *The Battle of the Books: Two Decades of Irish Cultural Debate* (Mullingar, Co. Westmeath).

McCoy, Gerard (1994): '"Patriots, Protestants and Papists": Religion and the Ascendancy, 1714–60', *Bullan*, 1, 1.

McCracken, J. L. (1986): 'Protestant Ascendancy and the Rise of Colonial Nationalism' in T. W. Moody and W. E. Vaughan (eds): *A New History of Ireland, Vol. IV: Eighteenth-Century Ireland, 1691–1800* (Oxford).

McCready, Richard B. (1998): 'Irish Catholicism and Nationalism in Scotland: The Dundee Experience, 1865–1922', *Irish Studies Review*, 6, 3.

Mac Cuarta, Brian (1993): *Ulster 1641: Aspects of the Rising* (Belfast).

McCurtain, Margaret (1980): 'Towards an Appraisal of the Religious Image of Women', *The Crane Bag*, 4, 1.

MacDiarmid, Hugh (1978): *Complete Poems 1920–1976* (London, 2 vols).

MacDonagh, Oliver (1962): 'The Anti-Imperialism of Free Trade', *Economic History Review*, xiv, 3.

——(1983): *States of Mind* (London).

——(1989): *The Emancipist. Daniel O'Connell 1830–1847* (London).

MacDonald, Michael (1986): *Children of Wrath: Political Violence in Northern Ireland* (Cambridge).

McDonald, Peter (1992): 'The Fate of "Identity": John Hewitt, W. R. Rodgers and Louis MacNeice', *Irish Review*, 12.

McDougall, Hugh A. (1982): *Racial Myth in English History: Trojans, Teutons, and Anglo-Saxons* (Hanover, NJ).

McDougall, Sean (1996): 'The Projection of Northern Ireland to Great Britain and Abroad, 1921–39' in Catterall and McDougall (eds).

McDowell, R. B. (1979): *Ireland in the Age of Imperialism and Revolution 1760–1801* (Oxford).

Mac Eoin, Uinseann (1980): *Survivors* (Dublin).

MacFarland, E. W. (1990): *Protestants First: Orangeism in Nineteenth-century Scotland* (Edinburgh).

McFarlane, Graham (n.d.): 'Dimensions of Protestantism: The Working of Protestant Identity in a Northern Irish Village' in Chris Curtin and Thomas M. Wilson (eds): *Ireland from Below: Social Change and Local Communities* (Galway).

McGarry, John (1998): 'Political Settlements in Northern Ireland and South Africa', *Political Studies*, xlvi, 4.

McGarry, John and O'Leary, Brendan (1995): *Explaining Northern Ireland: Broken Images* (Oxford).

McIntyre, Anthony (1995): 'Modern Irish Republicanism: The Product of British State Strategies', *Irish Political Studies*, 10.

MacKenzie, John (1993): 'On Scotland and the Empire', *International History Review*, 15.

——(1995): *Orientalism: History, Theory and the Arts* (Manchester).

——(1998): 'Empire and National Identity: The Case of Scotland', *Transactions of the Royal Historical Society*, 6th Series, VIII (Cambridge).

MacKey, James P. (ed., 1994): *The Cultures of Europe: The Irish Contribution* (Belfast).

Mac Laughlin, Jim (1995): *Travellers and Ireland: Whose Country, Whose History?* (Cork).

McLaughlin, Raymond (1987): *Inside an English Jail* (Dublin).

McLennan, Gregor (1981): *Marxism and the Methodologies of History* (London).

McLoughlin, Thomas (1999): *Contesting Ireland: Irish Voices against England in the Eighteenth Century* (Dublin).

McMahon, Deirdre (1984): *Republicans and Imperialists: Anglo-Irish Relations in the 1930s* (New Haven).

——(1999): 'Ireland and the Empire-Commonwealth, 1900–1948' in Judith M. Brown and Wm. Roger Louis (eds.): *Oxford History of the British Empire. vol. IV: The Twentieth Century* (Oxford).

Macmillan, Gretchen M. (1993): *State, Society and Authority in Ireland: The Foundations of the Modern Irish State* (Dublin).

McNamara, John (1977): 'The Irish Language and Nationalism', *The Crane Bag*, 1, 2.

McNamara, Kevin, Stott, Roger and O'Brien, Bill (1993): *Oranges or Lemons? Should Labour Organise in Northern Ireland?* (pamphlet pub. by Kevin McNamara, London).

McNamee, Peter (ed., 1992): *Traditional Music: Whose Music?* (Belfast).

MacSiomoin, Tomas (1994): 'The Colonised Mind—Irish Language and Society' in Ó Ceallaigh (ed.).

McVeigh, Robbie (1992): 'The Specificity of Irish Racism', *Race and Class*, 33, 4.

——(1995): 'The Last Conquest of Ireland? British Academics in Irish Universities', *Race and Class*, 37, 1.

——((n. d. but) 1996): *The Racialization of Irishness* (Belfast, Centre for Research and Documentation pamphlet).

——(1998a): 'The British/Irish "Peace Process" and the Colonial Legacy' in Anderson and Goodman (eds).

——(1998b): 'Is Sectarianism Racism? Theorising the Racism/Sectarianism Interface' in Miller (ed.).

Magennis, Eoin F. (1998): 'A "Presbyterian Insurrection"? Reconsidering the Hearts of Oak Disturbances of July 1763', *Irish Historical Studies*, 31, 122.

Maguire, W[illiam] A. (comp. and ed., 1998): *Up In Arms: The 1798 Rebellion in Ireland* (Belfast).

Maier, Charles S. (1988): *The Unmasterable Past: History, Holocaust and German National Identity* (Cambridge, Mass.).

Malchow, H. L. (1993): 'Frankenstein's Monster and Images of Race in 19th-Century Britain', *Past and Present*, 139.

——(1996): *Gothic Images of Race in Nineteenth-Century Britain* (Stanford, CA).

Maley, Willy (1994): 'Rebels and Redshanks: Milton and the British Problem', *Irish Studies Review*, 6.

——(1997): *Salvaging Spenser: Colonialism, Culture and Identity* (Basingstoke).

Malik, Kenan (1996): *The Meaning of Race: Race, History and Culture in Western Society* (London).

Mallory, J. P. and McNeill, T. E. (1991): *The Archaeology of Ulster: From Colonization to Plantation* (Belfast).

Mann, Michael (1995): 'Sources of Variation in Working-Class Movements in Twentieth-Century Europe', *New Left Review*, 212.

Manning, Maurice (1972): *Irish Political Parties: An Introduction* (Dublin).

Mansergh, Nicholas (1991): *The Unresolved Question: The Anglo-Irish Settlement and its Undoing* (New Haven and London).

Margalit, Avishai and Raz, Joseph (1990): 'National Self-determination', *Journal of Philosophy*, lxxxvii, 9.

Marshall, P. J. (1995): 'A Nation Defined by Empire, 1755–1776' in Grant and Stringer (eds).

——(ed., 1996): *The Cambridge Illustrated History of the British Empire* (Cambridge).

——(ed., 1998): *The Oxford History of the British Empire*, Vol. 2: *The Eighteenth Century* (Oxford).

Marshall, Tristan (1998): '*The Tempest* and the British Imperium in 1611', *Historical Journal*, 41, 2.

Marshall, William S. (1996): *'The Billy Boys': A Concise History of Orangeism in Scotland* (Edinburgh).

Martin, John (1982): 'The Conflict in Northern Ireland: Marxist Interpretations', *Capital and Class*, 18.

Marx, Karl and Engels, Friedrich (1971): *On Ireland* (Moscow).

Massoud, Mary (ed., 1996): *Literary Inter-Relations: Ireland, Egypt, and the Far East*. Irish Literary Studies 47 (Gerrards Cross).

Matthews, Steven (1997): *Irish Poetry: Politics, History, Negotiation. The Evolving Debate, 1969 to the Present* (Basingstoke).

Maume, Patrick (1993): *'Life that is Exile': Daniel Corkery and the Search for Irish Ireland* (Belfast).

——(1995): 'The Ancient Constitution: Arthur Griffith and his Intellectual Legacy to Sinn Fein', *Irish Political Studies*, 10.

——(1996): 'Ulstermen of Letters: The Unionism of Frank Frankfort Moore, Shan Bullock and St. John Ervine' in English and Walker (eds).

——(1998): 'Nationalism and Partition: the Political Thought of Arthur Clery', *Irish Historical Studies*, 31, 122.

Mayer, Arno J. (1981): *The Persistence of the Old Regime: Europe to the Great War* (London).

Meaney, Geraldine (1991): *Sex and Nation: Women in Irish Culture and Politics* (Dublin).

Melman, Billie (1991): 'Claiming the Nation's Past: The Invention of an Anglo-Saxon Tradition', *Journal of Contemporary History*, 26.

——(1992): *Women's Orients: English Women in the Middle East, 1718–1918* (London).

Miles, Robert (1993): *Racism after 'Race Relations'* (London).

Miller, David (1994): *Don't Mention the War: Northern Ireland, Propaganda, and the Media* (London).

——(1998): 'Colonialism and Academic Representations of the Troubles' in Miller (ed.).

——(ed., 1998): *Rethinking Northern Ireland: Culture, Ideology and Colonialism* (Harlow).

Miller, David W. (1978): *Queen's Rebels: Ulster Loyalism in Historical Perspective* (Dublin).

——(1983): 'The Armagh Troubles, 1784–95' in Clark and Donnelly (eds).

——(ed., 1990): *Peep O'Day Boys and Defenders: Selected Documents on the County Armagh Disturbances 1784–96* (Belfast).

Miller, Kerby A. (1985): *Emigrants and Exiles: Ireland and the Irish Exodus to North America* (Oxford).

Millett, Kate (1994): *The Politics of Cruelty: An Essay on the Literature of Political Imprisonment* (London).

Milotte, Mike (1984): *Communism in Modern Ireland* (Dublin).

Minnerup, Gunter (1979): 'James Connolly and the Partition of Ireland' in Eric Cahm and Vladimir Claude Fisera (eds): *Socialism and Nationalism*, Vol. II (Nottingham).

Mitchell, Arthur (1995): *Revolutionary Government in Ireland: Dail Eireann 1919–22* (Dublin).

Mitchell, B. R. (1978): *European Historical Statistics 1750–1970* (London).

Moane, Geraldine (1994): 'Psychological Analysis of Colonialism in an Irish Context', *Irish Journal of Psychology*, xv, 2–3.

Moffat, Chris (ed., 1998): *Fin de Siecle: Arts and Crafts and the Celtic Revival in Ireland* (*Fortnight*; Supplement to No. 372).

Mokyr, Joel (1983): *Why Ireland Starved: A Quantitative and Analytical History of the Irish Economy 1800–1850* (London).

Mommsen, Wolfgang and Osterhammel, Jurgen (eds, 1986): *Imperialism and After: Continuities and Discontinuities* (London).

Moody, T. W. (1978/1994): 'Irish History and Irish Mythology'; orig. pub. in *Hermathena*, 124, 1978; reprinted in and cited from Brady (ed.).

——(1981): *Davitt and Irish Revolution 1846–82* (Oxford).

Moon, Parker Thomas (1926): *Imperialism and World Politics* (New York).

Moore, Jonathan (1988): 'Historical Revisionism and the Irish in Britain', *Linenhall Review*, Autumn.

Moore-Gilbert, Bart J. (1997): *Postcolonial Theory: Contexts, Practices, Politics* (London).

Moran, Sean Farrell (1994): *Patrick Pearse and the Politics of Redemption: The Mind of the Easter Rising, 1916* (Washington, DC).

Morash, Christopher (1995): *Writing the Irish Famine* (Oxford).

——(1997): 'Sinking Down into the Dark: The Famine in Stage', *Bullan*, 3, 1.

Morash, Christopher and Hayes, Richard (eds, 1996): *'Fearful Realities': New Perspectives on the Famine* (Dublin).

Morgan, Austen (1980): 'Socialism in Ireland—Red, Green and Orange' in Morgan and Purdie (eds).

——(1988): *James Connolly: A Political Biography* (Manchester).

——(1991): *Labour and Partition: The Belfast Working Class 1905–23* (London).

Morgan, Austen and Purdie, Bob (eds, 1980): *Ireland: Divided Nation, Divided Class* (London).

Morgan, Hiram (1993a): *Tyrone's Rebellion: The Outbreak of the Nine Years' War in Tudor Ireland* (Dublin).

——(1993b): 'Empire-Building: An Uncomfortable Irish Heritage', *The Linen Hall Review* 10, 2.

Morgan, H. J. (1993): 'Deceptions of Demons', *Fortnight*, September.

Morgan, Philip D. (1991): 'British Encounters with Africans and African-Americans, circa 1600–1780' in Bailyn and Morgan (eds).

Morrill, John (1995): 'Three Kingdoms and One Commonwealth? The Enigma of Mid-seventeenth-century Britain and Ireland' in Grant and Stringer (eds).

Morris, Benny (1990): *1948 And After: Israel and the Palestinians* (Oxford).

Morris, James (1968, 1973, 1978): *The Pax Britannica Trilogy: Pax Britannica; Heaven's Command; Farewell the Trumpets* (London).

Morrow, Duncan (1997): 'Suffering for Righteousness' Sake? Fundamentalist Protestantism and Ulster Politics' in Shirlow and McGovern (eds).

Moxon-Browne, Edward (1983): *Nation, Class and Creed in Northern Ireland* (Aldershot).

Muldoon, Paul (1986): *Selected Poems 1968–1983* (London).

Mulhern, Francis (1993): 'A Nation, Yet Again. The Field Day Anthology', *Radical Philosophy*, 65. Reprinted in Mulhern 1998.

——(1995): 'Postcolonial Melancholy: A Reply to Luke Gibbons', *Radical Philosophy*, 72. Reprinted in Mulhern 1998.

——(1998): *The Present Lasts a Long Time: Essays in Cultural Politics* (Cork).

Munck, Ronnie (1992): 'The New Marxist Revisionism in Ireland', *Capital and Class*, 46.

——(1993): *The Irish Economy: Results and Prospects* (London).

Munger, Frank (1975): *The Legitimacy of Opposition: The Change of Government in Ireland in 1932* (Beverly Hills, CA).

Murphy, Brian P. (1991): *Patrick Pearse and the Lost Republican Ideal* (Dublin).

——(1994): 'Past Events and Present Politics—Roy Foster's *Modern Ireland*' in Ó Ceallaigh (ed.).

Murphy, John A. (1975): *Ireland in the Twentieth Century* (Dublin).

——(1991): 'Ireland: Identity and Relationships' in Bernard Crick (ed.): *National Identities* (Oxford).

Murphy, Richard (1989): *New Selected Poems* (London).

Murray, Raymond (1990): *The SAS in Ireland* (Cork).

Nairn, Tom (1981): *The Break-Up of Britain: Crisis and Neo-Nationalism* (London).

——(1997): *Faces of Nationalism: Janus Revisited* (London).

Nandy, Ashis (1983): *The Intimate Enemy: Loss and Recovery of Self Under Colonialism* (Delhi).

Nash, Catherine (1993): 'Remapping and Renaming: New Cartographies of Identity, Gender and Landscape in Ireland', *Feminist Review*, 44.

——(1997): 'Embodied Irishness: gender, sexuality and Irish identity' in Graham (ed.).

——(1998): 'Visionary Geographies: Designs for Developing Ireland', *History Workshop Journal*, 45.

Nash, R. C. (1985): 'Irish Atlantic Trade in the Seventeenth and Eighteenth Centuries', *William and Mary Quarterly*, 3rd series, xliii.

Neal, Frank (1988): *Sectarian Violence: The Liverpool Experience, 1819–1914. An Aspect of Anglo-Irish History* (Manchester).

Neary, Joyce (1987): 'Republican Plot' (review of The Prison Letters of Countess Markievicz), *Chartist*, No. 116.

Neary, Peter (1984): 'The Failure of Economic Nationalism', *The Crane Bag*, 8, 1.

Neeson, Eoin (1989): *The Civil War 1922–23* (Swords, Co. Dublin: 2nd edn).

Nehru, Jawaharlal (1955): *An Autobiography* (London).

Nelson, Sarah (1984): *Ulster's Uncertain Defenders* (Belfast).

New Left Review (1969): 'Discussion on the Strategy of People's Democracy', *New Left Review*, 55.

Newman, Gerald (1987): *The Rise of English Nationalism: A Cultural History, 1720–1830* (London).

Niranjana, Tejaswini (1992): *Siting Translation: History, Post-structuralism, and the Colonial Context* (Berkeley).

Nolan, Emer (1995): *James Joyce and Nationalism* (London).

Noonan, Kathleen M. (1998): '"The Cruel Pressure of an Enraged, Barbarous People": Irish and English Identity in Seventeenth-Century Policy and Propaganda', *Historical Journal*, 41, 1.

Norton, Philip (1996): 'Conservative Politics and the Abolition of Stormont' in Catterall and McDougall (eds).

Norval, Aletta J. (1996): *Deconstructing Apartheid Discourse* (London).

Novick, Peter (1988): *That Noble Dream: The 'Objectivity Question' and the American Historical Profession* (Cambridge).

O'Brien, Brendan (1995): *The Long War: The IRA and Sinn Fein From Armed Struggle to Peace Talks* (2nd edn, Dublin).

O'Brien, Conor Cruise (1962): *To Katanga and Back* (London).

—— (1965): *Writers and Politics* (New York).

—— (1974): *States of Ireland* (London: pbk edn, orig. pub. 1972).

—— (1978): *Herod: Reflections on Political Violence* (London).

—— (1985): 'Why Israel Can't Take "Bold Steps" for Peace', *Atlantic Monthly*, October.

—— (1986): *The Siege: The Saga of Israel and Zionism* (London).

—— (1988a): *Passion and Cunning and Other Essays* (London).

—— (1988b): *GodLand: Reflections on Religion and Nationalism* (Cambridge, Mass.).

—— (1994): *Ancestral Voices: Religion and Nationalism in Ireland* (Dublin).

—— (1998): *Memoir. My Life and Themes* (Dublin and London).

O'Brien, George (1921): *The Economic History of Ireland from the Union to the Famine* (London).

O'Brien, Gerard (1987): *Anglo-Irish Politics in the Age of Grattan and Pitt* (Dublin).

O'Brien, Jack (1993): *The Unionjacking of Ireland* (Cork).

O'Broin, Eoin (1996): 'The Trouble with Liberals', *Fortnight*, November.

Ó Buachalla, Breandán (1992): 'Irish Jacobite Poetry', *Irish Review*, 12.

—— (1995): 'Irish Jacobitism and Irish Nationalism: the Literary Evidence' in Michael O'Dea and Kevin Whelan (eds): *Nations and Nationalisms: France, Britain, Ireland and the Eighteenth-Century Context* (Oxford).

Ó Ceallaigh, Daltun (1991): *Labour, Nationalism and Irish Freedom* (Dublin).

—— (1994): 'Reconsiderations' in Ó Ceallaigh (ed.).

—— (ed., 1994): *Reconsiderations of Irish History and Culture* (Dublin).

O Connor, Fionnuala (1993): *In Search of a State: Catholics in Northern Ireland* (Belfast).

Ó Crualaoich, Gearóid (1991): 'Responding to the Rising' in Dhonnchadha and Dorgan (eds).

O'Day, Alan (1994): *The English Face of Irish Nationalism* (Aldershot, 2nd edn; orig. pub. 1977).

O'Day, Alan (1996): 'Revising the Diaspora' in Boyce and O'Day (eds).

Ó Dochartaigh, Niall (1995): '"Sure, It's Hard to Keep up with the Splits Here": Irish-American Responses to the Outbreak of Conflict in Northern Ireland 1968–1974', *Irish Political Studies*, 10.

O'Doherty, Malachi (1998): *The Trouble with Guns: Republican Strategy and the Provisional IRA* (Belfast).

O'Donnell, E. E. (1977): *Northern Irish Stereotypes* (Dublin).

O'Donnell, Ruan (1998): *The Rebellion in Wicklow 1798* (Dublin).

O'Dowd, Liam (1990): 'New Introduction' to Albert Memmi: *The Colonizer and the Colonized* (London).

——(1991): 'Intellectuals and Political Culture: A Unionist-Nationalist Comparison' in Eamonn Hughes (ed.).

——(1994): *Whither the Irish Border? Sovereignty, Democracy and Economic Integration in Ireland* (Belfast, Centre for Research and Documentation pamphlet).

O'Dowd, Liam (1998): '"New Unionism", British Nationalism and the Prospects for a Negotiated Settlement in Northern Ireland' in Miller (ed.).

O'Dowd, Liam, Rolston, Bill and Tomlinson, Mike (eds, 1980): *Northern Ireland—Between Civil Rights and Civil War* (London).

O'Dowd, Mary and Wicher, Sabine (eds, 1995): *Chattel, Servant or Citizen: Women's Status in Church, State and Society* (Belfast: *Historical Studies*, XIX).

Ó Drisceoil, Proinsias (ed., 1993): *Culture in Ireland. Regions: Identity and Power* (Belfast).

O'Farrell, Padraic (ed., 1998): *The '98 Reader: An Anthology of Song, Prose and Poetry* (Dublin).

O'Farrell, Patrick (1971): *Ireland's English Question: Anglo-Irish Relations 1534–1970* (London).

——(1987): *The Irish in Australia* (Kensington, NSW).

——(1990): *Vanished Kingdoms: Irish in Australia and New Zealand* (Kensington, NSW).

Ó Gráda, Cormac (1989): *The Great Irish Famine* (London).

——(1994): *Ireland: A New Economic History, 1780–1939* (Oxford).

——(1996): 'Making Irish Famine History in 1995', *History Workshop Journal*, 42.

O'Halloran, Claire (1987): *Partition and the Limits of Irish Nationalism* (Dublin).

O'Halpin, Eunan (1999): *Defending Ireland: The Irish State and its Enemies since 1922* (Oxford).

O'Hearn, Denis (1989): 'The Irish Case of Dependency: An Exception to the Exceptions?', *American Sociological Review*, 54, 4.

——(1998a): *Inside the Celtic Tiger: Reality and Illusion in the Irish Economy* (London).

——(1998b): 'The Two Irish Economies: Dependencies Compared' in Miller (ed.).

Ohlmeyer, Jane H. (1996): 'The Wars of Religion, 1603–1660' in Bartlett and Jeffery (eds).

——(1998): '"Civilizing of Those Rude Partes": Colonization within Britain and Ireland, 1580s–1640s' in Canny (ed., 1998).

O'Leary, Brendan (1999): 'The Nature of the Anglo-Irish Agreement' (9th John Whyte Memorial Lecture), *New Left Review*, 233.

O'Leary, Brendan and McGarry, John (1993): *The Politics of Antagonism: Understanding Northern Ireland* (London).

O'Leary, Cornelius (1993): 'Northern Ireland, 1921–72: Misshapen Constitutional Development and Scholarly Silence' in Hill and Marsh (eds).

Olinder, Britta (1996): 'Hewitt's Region in Post-Colonial Perspective' in Furomoto *et al.* (eds).

Ollerenshaw, Philip (1996): 'Businessmen in Northern Ireland and the Imperial Connection, 1886–1939' in Jeffery (ed.).

O'Mahony, Patrick and Delanty, Gerard (1998): *Rethinking Irish History: Nationalism, Identity and Ideology* (Basingstoke).

O'Malley, Eoin (1981): 'The Decline of Irish Industry in the Nineteenth Century', *Economic and Social Review*, 13.

——(1989): *Unequal Competition: The Problem of Late Development and Irish Industry* (London).

O'Malley, Ernie (1936): *On Another Man's Wound* (Dublin: cited from 1979 edn).

——(1982): *Raids and Rallies* (Dublin).

O'Malley, Padraig (1983): *The Uncivil Wars: Ireland Today* (Boston).

——(1990): *Biting at the Grave: The Irish Hunger Strikes and the Politics of Despair* (Belfast).

O'Meara, Dan (1983): *Volkskapitalisme: Class, Capital and Ideology in the Development of Afrikaner Nationalism 1934–1948* (Cambridge).

O'Neill, Shane (1994): 'Pluralist Justice and its Limits: The Case of Northern Ireland', *Political Studies*, xlii.

The Orange Standard (various issues, 1975–95).

O Riordan, Michelle (1990): *The Gaelic Mind and the Collapse of the Gaelic World* (Cork).

O Snodaigh, Padraig (1991): *Two Godfathers of Revisionism: 1916 in the Revisionist Canon* (Dublin).

Osterhammel, Jurgen (1997): *Colonialism: A Theoretical Overview* (Princeton and Kingston).

O'Suilleabhain, Micheal (1965): *Where Mountainy Men Have Sown* (Tralee).

O'Toole, Fintan (1994): *Black Hole, Green Card: The Disappearance of Ireland* (Dublin).

——(1995): *Meanwhile Back at the Ranch: The Politics of Irish Beef* (London).

Ó Tuama, Seán and Kinsella, Thomas (eds, 1981): *An Duanaire 1600–1900: Poems of the Dispossessed* (Dublin).

O Tuathaigh, M. A. G. (1972): *Ireland Before the Famine, 1798–1848* (Dublin).

——(1994): 'Irish Historical Revisionism: State of the Art or Ideological Project?' in Brady (ed.).

Pagden, Anthony (1995): *Lords of All the World: Ideologies of Empire in Spain, Britain and France c.1500–c.1800* (New Haven and London).

——(1998): 'The Struggle for Legitimacy and the Image of Empire in the Atlantic to *c.*1700' in Canny (ed.).

Pakenham, Thomas (1969): *The Year of Liberty* (London).

Paor, Liam de (1970, 1971): *Divided Ulster* (Harmondsworth, 1st and 2nd edns).

——(1986): *The Peoples of Ireland: From Prehistory to Modern Times* (London).

——(1990): *Unfinished Business. Ireland Today and Tomorrow* (London).

Parker, Andrew *et al.* (eds, 1992): *Nationalisms and Sexualities* (New York).

Parker, Patricia (1987): 'Rhetorics of Property' in her *Literary Fat Ladies: Rhetoric, Gender, Property* (New York).

Parker, Tony (1993): *May the Lord in His Mercy be Kind to Belfast* (London).

Parkinson, Alan F. (1998): *Ulster Loyalism and the British Media* (Dublin).

Parry, Benita (1987): 'Problems in Current Theories of Colonial Discourse', *Oxford Literary Review*, 9.

Patterson, Henry (1980): *Class Conflict and Sectarianism: The Protestant Working Class and the Belfast Labour Movement 1868–1920* (Belfast).

Patterson, Henry (1989): *The Politics of Illusion. Republicanism and Socialism in Modern Ireland* (London).

—— (1997): *The Politics of Illusion: A Political History of the IRA* (London: rev. edn of 1989).

—— (1999): 'Sean Lemass and the Ulster Question, 1959–65', *Journal of Contemporary History*, 34, 1.

Patterson, Iain D. (1993): 'The Activities of Irish Republican Physical Force Organisation in Scotland, 1919–21', *The Scottish Historical Review*, 72, 1 (193).

Paulin, Tom (1984): *Ireland and the English Crisis* (Newcastle).

—— (1998): *The Daystar of Liberty: Hazlitt's Radical Style* (London).

Perceval-Maxwell, M[ichael] (1991): 'Ireland and the Monarchy in the Early Stuart Multiple Kingdom', *Historical Journal*, 34.

—— (1994): *The Outbreak of the Irish Rebellion of 1641* (Montreal and London).

Pettit, Philip (1997): *Republicanism: A Theory of Freedom and Government* (Oxford).

Philpin, Charles (ed., 1987): *Nationalism and Popular Protest in Ireland* (Cambridge).

Phoenix, Eamonn (1994): *Northern Nationalism: Nationalist Politics, Partition and the Catholic Minority in Northern Ireland, 1890–1940* (Belfast).

Pocock, J. G. A. (1975): 'British History: A Plea for a New Subject', *Journal of Modern History*, 47, 4.

—— (1982): 'The Limits and Divisions of British History: In Search of the Unknown Subject', *American Historical Review*, 87, 2.

—— (1995): 'Conclusion: Contingency, Identity, Sovereignty' in Grant and Stringer (eds).

Pollack, Andy (ed., 1993): *A Citizens' Inquiry: The Opsahl Report on Northern Ireland* (Belfast).

Poole, Michael (1990): 'The Geographical Location of Political Violence in Northern Ireland' in Darby *et al.* (eds).

—— (1997): 'In Search of Ethnicity in Ireland' in Graham (ed.).

Porter, Bernard (1968): *Critics of Empire* (London).

—— (1984): *The Lion's Share: A Short History of British Imperialism 1850–1983* (2nd edn, London).

Porter, Norman (1996): *Rethinking Unionism: An Alternative Vision for Northern Ireland* (Belfast).

—— (ed., 1998): *The Republican Ideal: Current Perspectives* (Belfast).

Porter, Sam and O'Hearn, Denis (1995): 'New Left Podsnappery: The British Left and Ireland', *New Left Review*, 212.

Prager, Jeffrey (1986): *Building Democracy in Ireland: Political Order and Cultural Integration in a Newly Independent Nation* (Cambridge).

Probert, Belinda (1978): *Beyond Orange and Green: The Political Economy of the Northern Ireland Crisis* (London).

Provisional IRA (n.d. but 1973): *Freedom Struggle* (no place of publication given; probably Dublin).

Purdie, Bob (1972): *Ireland Unfree* (London).

—— (1990): *Politics in the Streets: The Origins of the Civil Rights Movement in Northern Ireland* (Belfast).

—— (1994): 'An Ulster Labourist in Liberal Scotland: William Walker and the Leith Burghs Election of 1910' in Wood (ed.).

—— (1995): 'Riotous Customs: The Breaking Up of Socialist Meetings in Belfast, 1893–1896', *Saothar*, 20.

—— (1998): 'Irish Revisionism and Labour History: The Case of William Walker', Lecture to Ulster Association for Irish Historical Studies, Belfast, 16 April.

Quinn, D. B. (1940): *The Voyages and Colonising Enterprises of Sir Humphrey Gilbert* (London).

Quinn, James (1998): 'The United Irishmen and Social Reform', *Irish Studies Review*, 31, 122.

Rajan, Rajeswari Sunder (1993): *Real and Imagined Women: Gender, Culture and Post-colonialism* (London).

Ram, Uri (1993): 'The Colonization Perspective in Israeli Sociology: Internal and External Comparisons', *Journal of Historical Sociology*, 6, 3.

Ramirez-Faria, Carlos (1991): *The Origins of Economic Inequality Between Nations* (London).

Ranger, T. O. (1965): 'Strafford in Ireland: A Re-interpretation' in T. H. Aston (ed.): *Crisis in Europe 1550–1660* (London).

Reed, David (1984): *Ireland, the Key to the British Revolution* (London).

Regan, Colm and Sinclair, Scott (eds, 1986): *Half the Lies are True: Britain/Ireland—a Microcosm of International Misunderstanding* (Birmingham/Dublin).

Regan, Stephen (1992): 'Ireland's Field Day', *History Workshop Journal*, 33.

——(1995): 'W. B. Yeats and Irish Cultural Politics in the 1890s' in Scott McCracken and Sally Ledger (eds): *Cultural Politics at the Fin de Siecle* (Cambridge).

Republican Sinn Fein (1996): *Eire Nua—A New Ireland* (Dublin; downloaded from RSF Website).

Richards, Shaun (1991a): 'Polemics on the Irish Past: The "Return to the Source" in Irish Literary Revivals', *History Workshop Journal*, 31.

——(1991b): 'Field Day's Fifth Province: Avenue or Impasse?' in Hughes, Eamonn (ed.): *Culture and Politics in Northern Ireland, 1960–1990* (Milton Keynes).

Robb, John (1992): 'A Divided Community: The Effect of Cultural Divisions' in Lundy and Mac Poilin (eds).

Robbins, Bruce (1992): 'Colonial Discourse: A Paradigm and Its Discontents', *Victorian Studies*, 35, 2.

Roberts, Hugh (1986): *Northern Ireland and the Algerian Analogy: A Suitable Case for Gaullism?* (Belfast).

Robertson, John (ed., 1995): *A Union for Empire: Political Thought and the British Union of 1707* (Cambridge).

Robinson, Philip (1984): *The Plantation of Ulster: British Settlement in an Irish Landscape, 1600–1670* (Dublin).

Robinson, Ronald and Gallagher, John, with Denny, Alice (1961): *Africa and the Victorians: the Official Mind of Imperialism* (London).

Roche, Patrick (1994): 'Northern Ireland and Irish Nationalism—A Unionist Perspective', *Irish Review*, 15.

Roche, Patrick and Birnie, Esmond (1995): *An Economics Lesson for Irish Nationalists and Republicans* (Belfast).

——(1996): 'Irish Nationalism—Politics of the Absurd', *Ulster Review*, 20.

Rockett, Kevin, Gibbons, Luke and Hill, John (1988): *Cinema and Ireland* (London).

Rodgers, W. R. (1947): *The Ulstermen and their Country* (London).

Roediger, David R. (1991): *The Wages of Whiteness* (London).

——(1993): 'Race and the Working-Class Past in the United States: Multiple Identities and the Future of Labor History' *International Review of Social History*, 38, Supplement.

Rokkan, Stein (1980): 'Territories, Centre, and Peripheries: toward a geoethnic-geoeconomic-geopolitical model of differentiation within western Europe' in Jean Gottmann (ed.): *Centre and Periphery: Spatial Variations in Politics* (London).

Rokkan, Stein and Urwin, Derek (1983): *Economy, Territory, Identity: Politics of Western European Peripheries* (London).

Rolston, Bill (1980): 'The Limits of Trade Unionism' in O'Dowd *et al.* (eds).

—— (1992a): *Drawing Support: Murals in the North of Ireland* (Belfast).

—— (1992b): 'More, Not Less, Dialogue', *The Irish Reporter*, No. 7.

—— (1993): 'The Training Ground: Ireland, Conquest and Decolonisation', *Race and Class*, 34, 4.

—— (1998a): 'Culture As Battlefield: Political Identity and the State in the North of Ireland', *Race and Class*, 39, 4.

—— (1998b): 'What's Wrong with Multiculturalism? Liberalism and the Irish Conflict' in Miller (ed.).

—— (1999): 'Music and Politics in Ireland: The Case of Loyalism' in Harrington and Mitchel (eds).

Rolston, Bill and Miller, David (eds, 1996): *War and Words: The Northern Ireland Media Reader* (Belfast).

Rose, Richard (1971): *Governing Without Consensus: An Irish Perspective* (London).

Ross, Bianca (1998): *Britannia und Hibernia: Nationale und Kulturelle Identitäten im Irland des 17 Jahrhunderts* (Heidelberg).

Roulston, Carmel (1991): '"Accentuating the Social Aspect": Social Republicanism and the Communist Party of Ireland', *Irish Political Studies*, 6.

Rowthorn, Bob and Wayne, Naomi (1988): *Northern Ireland: The Political Economy of Conflict* (Cambridge).

Ruane, Joseph (1992): 'Colonialism and the Interpretation of Irish Historical Development' in Silverman and Gulliver (eds).

Ruane, Joseph and Todd, Jennifer (1991): '"Why Can't You Get Along with each Other?" Culture, Structure and the Northern Ireland Conflict' in Hughes (ed.).

—— (1996): *The Dynamics of Conflict in Northern Ireland: Power, Conflict and Emancipation* (Cambridge).

Rumpf, Erhard and Hepburn, A. C. (1977): *Nationalism and Socialism in Twentieth Century Ireland* (Liverpool).

Russell, Conrad (1991): *The Fall of the British Monarchies, 1637–1642* (Oxford).

—— (1995): 'Composite Monarchies in Early Modern Europe: The British and Irish Example' in Grant and Stringer (eds).

Ryan, Louise (1995): 'Traditions and double Standards: The Irish Suffragists' Critique of Nationalism', *Women's History Review*, 4.

—— (1997): 'A Question of Loyalty: War, Nation and Feminism in Early Twentieth-Century Ireland', *Women's Studies International Forum*, 20.

Ryan, Mark (1994): *War and Peace in Ireland: Britain and the IRA in the New World Order* (London).

Ryan, Meda (1982): *The Tom Barry Story* (Cork and Dublin).

Ryder, Chris (1989): *The RUC: A Force Under Fire* (London).

Ryder, Sean (1995): 'Gender and the Discourse of "Young Ireland" Cultural Nationalism' in Foley *et al.* (eds).

Said, Edward W. (1978): *Orientalism* (London).

—— (1988): *Yeats and Decolonization* (Field Day pamphlet, Derry).

—— (1993): *Culture and Imperialism* (London).

Sales, Rosemary (1997): 'Gender and Protestantism in Northern Ireland' in Shirlow and McGovern (eds).

Salmon, Trevor C. (1989): *Unneutral Ireland: An Ambivalent and Unique Security Policy* (Oxford).

Samuel, Raphael (ed., 1989): *Patriotism: The Making and Unmaking of British National Identity* (London, 3 vols).

——(1998): *Island Stories: Theatres of Memory*, Vol. II (London).

Scally, Robert James (1995): *The End of Hidden Ireland: Rebellion, Famine, and Emigration* (New York and Oxford).

Schmitt, David E. (1994): 'Resolving Conflict in Bicommunal Political Systems' in Guelke (ed.).

Schneider, Klaus-Gunnar (1998): 'Irishness and Postcoloniality in Glenn Patterson's *Burning Your Own*', *Irish Studies Review*, 6, 1.

Schulze, Kirsten E. (1997): 'The Northern Ireland Political Process: A Viable Approach to Conflict Resolution?', *Irish Political Studies*, 12.

Schutz, Barry and Scott, Douglas (1974): *Natives and Settlers: A Comparative Analysis of the Politics of Opposition and Mobilisation in Northern Ireland and Rhodesia* (Denver, Col.).

See, Katherine O'Sullivan (1986): *First World Nationalisms: Class and Ethnic Politics in Northern Ireland and Quebec* (Chicago).

Seeley, J. R. (1883): *The Expansion of England* (London).

Sekyi-Otu, Ato (1996): *Fanon's Dialectic of Experience* (Cambridge, Mass.).

Shankill Think Tank (1995): *A New Beginning* (Newtownabbey, Island Pamphlet No. 13).

Sharabi, Hisham (1988): *Neopatriarchy: A Theory of Distorted Change in Arab Society* (New York and Oxford).

Shaw, Francis (1972): 'The Canon of Irish History: A Challenge', *Studies*, lxi.

Shearman, Hugh (1946): *Northern Ireland: Its History, Resources and People* (Belfast, HMSO).

Sheehan, Aideen (1990): 'Cumann na Mban: Policies and Activities' in Fitzpatrick (ed.).

Sheehy, Jeanne (1980): *The Rediscovery of Ireland's Past: The Celtic Revival 1830–1930* (London).

Shirlow, Peter (1997): 'Class, Materialism and the Fracturing of Traditional Alignments' in Graham (ed.).

Shirlow, Peter and McGovern, Mark (eds, 1997): *Who Are 'The People'? Unionism, Protestantism and Loyalism in Northern Ireland* (London).

Shlaim, Avi (1988): *Collusion Across the Jordan: King Abdullah, the Zionist Movement, and the Partition of Palestine* (Oxford).

Sibbett, R. M. (1997): *The Sunshine Patriots: The 1798 Rebellion in Antrim and Down* (Belfast; edited extracts from *Orangeism in Ireland and Throughout the Empire*, orig. pub. Belfast 1914).

Silverman, Marilyn and Gulliver, P. H. (eds, 1992): *Approaching the Past: Historical Anthropology through Irish Case Studies* (New York).

Simmons, Clare A. (1990): *Reversing the Conquest: History and Myth in Nineteenth Century British Literature* (New Brunswick, NJ).

Sinha, Mrinalini (1995): *Colonial Masculinity: The 'Manly Englishman' and the 'Effeminate Bengali' in the Late Nineteenth Century* (Manchester).

Sinn Fein (1994): *The Economics of a United Ireland* (Dublin).

Sluka, Jeffrey A. (1992): 'The Politics of Painting' in Carolyn Nordstrom and JoAnn Martin (eds): *The Paths to Domination, Resistance and Terror* (Berkeley, CA).

——(1996): 'The Writing's On the Wall: Peace Process Images, Symbols and Murals in Northern Ireland', *Critique of Anthropology*, 16, 4.

Smith, Anthony D. (1986): *The Ethnic Origins of Nations* (Oxford).

Smith, David J. and Chambers, Gerald (1991): *Inequality in Northern Ireland* (Oxford).

Smith, Howard (1996): 'BBC Current Affairs Coverage of the 1981 Hunger Strike' in Catterall and McDougall (eds).

Smith, M. L. R. (1995): *Fighting for Ireland? The Military Strategy of the Irish Republican Movement* (London).

Smyth, Clifford (1986): 'The DUP as a Politico-Religious Organisation', *Irish Political Studies*, 1.

Smyth, Gerry (1998): *Decolonisation and Criticism: The Construction of Irish Literature* (London).

Smyth, Jim (1992): *The Men of No Property: Irish Radicals and Popular Politics in the Late Eighteenth Century* (Basingstoke).

—— (1995): 'The Men of No Popery: The Origins of the Orange Order', *History Ireland*, 3, 3.

Smyth, William J. (1997): 'A Plurality of Irelands: regions, societies and mentalities' in Graham (ed.).

Smythe, Colin (1996): 'The Gregorys and Egypt, 1855–56, 1881–82' in Massoud (ed.).

Sokal, Alan and Bricmont, Jean (1998): *Intellectual Impostures* (London).

Steiner, George (1971): *In Bluebeard's Castle* (London).

Stevenson, Jonathan (1996): *'We Wrecked the Place': Contemplating an End to the Northern Irish Troubles* (New York).

Stewart, A. T. Q. (1977): *The Narrow Ground: Patterns of Ulster History* (London).

—— (1993): *A Deeper Silence: The Hidden Origins of the United Irishmen* (London).

—— (1995): *The Summer Soldiers: The 1798 Rebellion in Antrim and Down* (Belfast).

Stewart, Bruce (1998): 'Inside Nationalism: A Meditation upon *Inventing Ireland*', *Irish Studies Review*, 6, 1.

Stewart, Paul (1991): 'The Jerry-Builders: Bew, Gibbon and Patterson—the Protestant Working Class and the Northern Ireland State' in Hutton and Stewart (eds).

Stoler, Ann Laura (1995): *Race and the Education of Desire: Foucault's* History of Sexuality *and the Colonial Order of Things* (Durham, NC).

Stone, John (ed., 1979): 'Internal Colonialism': *Ethnic and Racial Studies*, special issue, 2, 3.

Strauss, Eric (1951): *Irish Nationalism and British Democracy* (London).

Sugden, John and Bairner, Alan (1993): *Sport, Sectarianism and Society in a Divided Ireland* (Leicester).

Sullivan, A. M. and Sullivan, T. D. (eds, 1890/1968): *Speeches from the Dock* (orig. pub. 1890; cited from 1968 Dublin edn).

Tamir, Yael (1993): *Liberal Nationalism* (Princeton, NJ).

Tangen Page, Michael von (1996): 'The Inter-relationship of the Press and Politicians during the 1981 Hunger Strike at the Maze Prison' in Catterall and McDougall (eds).

Taylor, Patrick (1989): *The Narrative of Liberation: Perspectives on Afro-Caribbean Literature, Popular Culture and Politics* (Ithaca, NY).

Taylor, Peter (1999): *Loyalists* (London).

Taylor, Rupert (1994): 'A Consociational Path to Peace in Northern Ireland and South Africa?' in Guelke (ed.).

Taylor, Timothy D. (1998): 'Living in a Postcolonial World: Class and Soul in *The Commitments*', *Irish Studies Review*, 6, 3.

Thomas, Nicholas (1994): *Colonialism's Culture: Anthropology, Travel and Government* (Oxford).

Thompson, E. P. (1975): *Whigs and Hunters: The Origin of the Black Act* (Harmondsworth).

Thornton, A. P. (1965): *Doctrines of Imperialism* (New York).

Tierney, Michael (1919): *Education in a Free Ireland* (Dublin).

Tifft, Stephen (1992): 'The Parricidal Phantasm: Irish Nationalism and the *Playboy* Riots' in Parker *et al.*

Tillyard, Stella (1997): *Citizen Lord: Edward Fitzgerald, 1763–1798* (London).

Todd, Jennifer (1987): 'Two Traditions in Unionist Political Culture', *Irish Political Studies*, 2.

——(1990): 'Northern Irish Nationalist Political Culture', *Irish Political Studies*, 5.

——(1995): 'Beyond the Community Conflict: Historic Compromise or Emancipatory Process?', *Irish Political Studies*, 10.

Toibin, Colm (1996): 'Playboys of the GPO', *London Review of Books*, 18 April.

——(1998): 'Erasures', *London Review of Books*, 30 July.

Tomlinson, John (1991): *Cultural Imperialism* (London).

Tomlinson, Mike (1994): *25 Years On: The Costs of War and the Dividends of Peace* (Belfast; West Belfast Economic Forum pamphlet).

——(1995): 'Can Britain Leave Ireland? The Political Economy of War and Peace', *Race and Class*, 37, 1.

Toolis, Kevin (1995): *Rebel Hearts: Journeys within the IRA's Soul* (London).

Townshend, Charles (1975): *The British Campaign in Ireland 1919–1921* (Oxford).

——(1983): *Political Violence in Ireland: Government and Resistance since 1848* (Oxford).

——(1998): 'The Meaning of Irish Freedom: Constitutionalism in the Free State', *Transactions of the Royal Historical Society*, 6th Series, VIII (Cambridge).

Trainor, Luke (1994): *British Imperialism and Australian Nationalism: Manipulation, Conflict and Compromise in the Late Nineteenth Century* (Cambridge).

Treadwell, Victor (1998): *Buckingham and Ireland 1616–1628: A Study in Anglo-Irish Politics* (Dublin).

Tully, James (1993): *An Approach to Political Philosophy: Locke in Contexts* (Cambridge).

Turner, John (1995): 'Letting Go: The Conservative Party and the End of the Union with Ireland' in Grant and Stringer (eds).

Ulster Society (1986): *Ulster: An Ethnic Nation?* (Lurgan).

Valente, Joseph (1995): *James Joyce and the Problem of Justice: Negotiating Sexual and Colonial Difference* (Cambridge).

Vandervort, Bruce (1998): *Wars of Imperial Conquest in Africa 1830–1914* (London).

Van Duin, Pieter (1994): 'Ethnicity, Race and Labour, 1830s–1930s: Some Irish and International Perspectives', *Saothar*, 19.

Vaughan, W. E. (ed., 1989): *A New History of Ireland*, Vol. V, *Ireland Under the Union, Part 1, 1801–1870* (Oxford).

Vaughan, W. E. and Fitzpatrick, A. J. (eds, 1973): *Irish Historical Statistics, Population, 1821–1971* (Dublin).

Wade, Wyn Craig (1987): *The Fiery Cross: The Ku Klux Klan in America* (New York).

Walker, Brian (1989): *Ulster Politics: The Formative Years 1868–86* (Belfast).

——(1990): 'Ireland's Historical Position—"Colonial" or "European"?', *The Irish Review*, 9.

——(1992): '1641, 1689, 1690 And All That: The Unionist Sense of History', *Irish Review*, 12.

——(1996): *Dancing to History's Tune: History, Myth and Politics in Ireland* (Belfast).

Walker, Graham (1985): *The Politics of Frustration: Harry Midgley and the Failure of Labour in Northern Ireland* (Manchester).

Walker, Graham (1992a): 'Old History: Protestant Ulster in Lee's Ireland', *Irish Review*, 12.

—— (1992b): ' "The Irish Dr. Goebbels": Frank Gallagher and Irish Republican Propaganda', *Journal of Contemporary History*, xxvii.

—— (1992c): 'The Orange Order in Scotland Between the Wars', *International Review of Social History*, 37, 2.

—— (1994): 'Empire, Religion and Nationality in Scotland and Ulster before the First World War' in Wood (ed.).

—— (1995): *Intimate Strangers: Political and Cultural Interaction between Scotland and Ulster in Modern Times* (Edinburgh).

Wall, Maureen (1989): *Catholic Ireland in the Eighteenth Century* (ed. G. O'Brien, Dublin).

Waller, Philip J. (1981): *Democracy and Sectarianism: A Political and Social History of Liverpool 1868–1939* (Liverpool).

Wallis, Roy, Bruce, Steve and Taylor, David (1986): *'No Surrender!': Paisleyism and the Politics of Ethnic Identity in Northern Ireland* (Belfast, Queen's University Dept. of Social Studies pamphlet).

Walter, Bronwen (1986): 'Ethnicity and Irish Residential Segregation', *Transactions of the Institute of British Geography*, 11, 2.

Walzer, Michael (1983): *Spheres of Justice: A Defence of Pluralism and Equality* (Oxford).

Wannan, Bill (ed., 1965): *The Wearing of the Green: The Lore, Literature, Legend and Balladry of the Irish in Australia* (London).

Ward, Alan J. (1994): *The Irish Constitutional Tradition: Responsible Government and Modern Ireland, 1782–1992* (Dublin).

Ward, Margaret (1983): *Unmanageable Revolutionaries: Women and Irish Nationalism* (London).

—— (1998): 'National Liberation Movements and the Question of Women's Liberation: The Irish Experience' in Clare Midgley (ed.): *Gender and Imperialism* (Manchester).

Warren, Bill (1980): *Imperialism, Pioneer of Capitalism* (London).

Waters, Hazel (1995): 'The Great Famine and the Rise of Anti-Irish Racism', *Race and Class*, 37, 1.

Waters, John (1991): *Jiving at the Crossroads* (Belfast).

—— (1995a): *Every Day Like Sunday?* (Dublin).

—— (1995b): *Race of Angels: Ireland and the Genesis of U2* (Belfast).

Watson, Daphne G. (1991): 'The Cross of St. George: The Burden of Contemporary Irish Literature' in Robert Giddings (ed.): *Literature and Imperialism* (London).

Weitzer, Ronald (1990): *Transforming Settler States: Communal Conflict and Internal Security in Northern Ireland and Zimbabwe* (Berkeley).

—— (1995): *Policing Under Fire: Ethnic Conflict and Police-Community Relations in Northern Ireland* (Albany, NY).

Wessels, J. A. (1996): 'Irish Nationalism and the Anglo-Irish: Historical and Literary Parallels to Afrikanerdom' in Massoud (ed.).

West, Francis James (1999): 'The Colonial History of the Norman Conquest?', *History*, 84, 274.

Whelan, Christopher T. (ed., 1994): *Values and Social Change in Ireland* (Dublin).

Whelan, Kevin (1991): 'Come All You Staunch Revisionists: Towards a Post-Revisionist Agenda for Irish History', *The Irish Reporter*, 2.

—— (1993): 'The Bases of Regionalism' in O Drisceoil (ed.).

—— (1996a): *The Tree of Liberty: Radicalism, Catholicism and the Construction of Irish Identity 1760–1830* (Cork).

——(1996b): 'Reinterpreting the 1798 Rebellion in County Wexford' in Keogh and Furlong (eds).

——(1998): *Fellowship of Freedom: The United Irishmen and 1798* (Cork).

White, Hayden (1983): *Tropics of Discourse: Essays in Cultural Criticism* (Baltimore).

——(1987): *The Content of the Form: Narrative Discourse and Historical Representation* (Baltimore).

Whitelam, Keith W. (1996): *The Invention of Ancient Israel: The Silencing of Palestinian History* (London).

Whyte, John (1974): 'Ireland: Politics without Social Bases' in Richard Rose (ed.): *Electoral Behaviour: A Comparative Handbook* (New York).

——(1990): *Interpreting Northern Ireland* (Oxford).

Williams, Emyr Wyn (1988): *National Identity in the British Isles* (Pontyclun; Plaid Cymru National Left Paper No. 8).

Williams, Gwyn A. (1985): *When Was Wales? A History of the Welsh* (Harmondsworth).

Wills, Clair (1991): 'Language Politics, Narrative, Political Violence', *Oxford Literary Review*, 13, 1–2.

——(1993): *Improprieties: Politics and Sexuality in Northern Irish Poetry* (Oxford).

Wilson, Andrew J. (1995): *Irish America and the Ulster Conflict: 1968–1995* (Belfast).

Wilson, David (1998): *United Irishmen, United States: Immigrant Radicals in the Early Republic* (Dublin).

Wilson, Robin (1985): 'Imperialism in Crisis: the "Irish Dimension" in Mary Langan and Bill Schwarz (eds): *Crises in the British State 1880–1930* (London).

Wilson, Tom (1989): *Ulster: Conflict and Consent* (Oxford).

Wood, Ian S. (ed., 1994): *Scotland and Ulster* (Edinburgh).

Woodham-Smith, Cecil (1962): *The Great Hunger. Ireland 1845–9* (London).

Woods, Oona (1995): *Seeing is Believing? Murals in Derry* (Derry).

Wormald, Jenny (1992): 'The Creation of Britain: Multiple Kingdoms or Core and Colonies', *Transactions of the Royal Historical Society*, 6th series, 2.

Wright, Frank (1972): 'Protestant Ideology and Politics in Ulster' *European Journal of Sociology*, 14.

——(1981): 'Case Study III: The Ulster Spectrum' in David Carlton and Carlo Schaerf (eds): *Contemporary Terror: Studies in Sub-State Violence* (London).

——(1987): *Northern Ireland: A Comparative Analysis* (Dublin).

——(1994): 'Asymmetry in Cross-Communal Meetings' in Guelke (ed.).

——(1996): *Two Lands on One Soil: Ulster Politics Before Home Rule* (Dublin).

Wyatt, Petronella (1995): 'Why it is Time for the British to Stop Feeling Guilty', *Sunday Telegraph*, 5 February.

Yamasaki, Hiroyuki (1996): 'Yeats and Orientalism' in Furomoto *et al.* (eds).

Young, James D. (1993): 'A Very English Socialism and the Celtic Fringe 1880–1991', *History Workshop Journal*, 35.

Young, Robert (1990): *White Mythologies: Writing History and the West* (London).

INDEX

Adams, Gerry 48, 60, 64, 83, 88, 90–1, 140, 160–1, 164, 174, 217, 264 n. 34, 266 n. 15, 267 n. 4, 269 n. 19, 278 n. 10
Adams, Hazard 115
Adamson, Ian 97–8, 116, 276 n. 31, 278 n. 11
Aden 67, 170
Africa: colonialism in 2, 11, 13, 15, 23, 26, 28, 47, 59, 67, 68, 79, 89, 139, 200, 201, 204, 231, 246 n. 2, 248 n. 2; Irish Republic's relations with 156; nationalism in 39, 48, 89, 155, 163, 233, 234; postcolonial 106, 124, 148–9, 151, 162, 165, 233
African-Americans: Irish attitudes to 47, 50
African National Congress (ANC) 54, 60, 253 n. 26
Afrikaners 46, 57, 221–2, 227
Ahern, Bertie 88
Aiken, Frank 155, 157
Akenson, Donald Harman 55–6, 89, 221–2, 252 n. 13
'al-Afghani' (Jamal ad-Din) 62
Albanians 233
Alcock, Anthony 194
Alexander, Archbishop William 104
Algeria: French rule in compared with Ireland 71, 123, 125, 170, 173, 200, 203, 220, 222–3, 224, 226, 233, 267 nn. 4, 6, 274 n. 17, 275 n. 25
Algiers 220
Allen, Jim 183
Allen, Kieran 146
Allen, Theodore 38, 49
Althusserianism 182
American Civil War 45, 103
Americas: English/British colonies in 2, 11, 13, 14, 21–2, 23–5, 29, 32, 34, 201, 229, 246 n. 4; Irish migration to 33, 51, 56, 251 nn. 9, 10, 12, 252 n. 13; Irish role in 22, 55–6, 252 n. 22; nationalism in 35, 37, 248 n. 29
Amin, Samir 75, 148, 149
Ancient Order of Hibernians 99
Anderson, Benedict 86, 89, 263 n. 29
Andrews, J. H. 6, 261 n. 7
Andrews, Niall 92
Anglo-Boer War (1899–1902), impact in Ireland 46, 56–8
Anglo-Irish Agreement (1985) 71, 100, 171, 198, 238, 272 n. 5
'Anglo-Irish' political identity 33, 34, 55, 137–8, 171
Anglo-Irish Treaty (1921) 58, 64, 152, 153, 171–2, 250 n. 1
Angola 169

Anti-Apartheid Movement, Irish 158
Appeals, Act of (1533) 19
Arab nationalism 89, 256 n. 7
Arab–Israeli conflict 85, 222, 223, 277 n. 10; Conor Cruise O'Brien on 217
archipelago model for British–Irish history 14–15, 30–1, 79, 143, 145, 240–2, 245 n. 5, 250 n. 42, 258 n. 25
Arden, John 151
Aretxaga, Begona 190
Argentina 156
Armenian genocide 237
Armitage, David 23–4, 260 n. 2
Arnold, Bruce 92
Arnold, Matthew 40, 81
Arrighi, Giovanni 75
Arthur, Chester 273 n. 13
Arts and Crafts Movement 40
Aughey, Arthur 201, 205, 242, 264 n. 36, 274 nn. 19, 20, 21
Aughrim, battle of (1691) 30, 31, 98, 247 n. 21
Aunger, Edmund 218
Australia 11, 12, 25, 45, 65, 66, 68, 165, 204, 208, 231, 261 n. 11; Irish in 33, 51, 251 n. 12

Bacon, Francis 27, 223
Baldwin, Stanley 195
Ballagh, Robert 201
Bangladesh 228
Bangor, monastery at 97
banners, historical images on 99, 207
Banville, John 124
Bardon, Jonathan 101–2, 271 n. 3
Barnard, T. C. 3–4, 29, 32, 33, 203
Barr, Glen 188
Barry, Kevin 133
Barry, Tom 57, 231
Bartlett, Robert 15
Bartlett, Thomas 23, 35, 157
Basque country 170, 218
Beckett, Samuel 124, 236
Behan, Brendan 124
Beirut 219, 220
Belfast 25, 37, 98, 104, 105, 157, 179, 180, 181, 183, 187, 188, 189, 190, 196, 197, 208, 219–20, 237, 259 n. 36, 270 n. 28; violence in 39, 145, 215, 250 n. 41, 255 n. 5
Bell, Desmond 238
Belloc, Hillaire 46
Bengal Tenancy Act (1885) 66
Benjamin, Walter 94